The Politics of High-Tech Growth
Developmental Network States in the Global Economy

The 1990s saw a surprising economic boom in the Republic of Ireland's "Celtic Tiger" economy, driven by high-tech foreign investment. This book argues that beneath the Irish trade and foreign investment boom lies a much more interesting story of regional innovation promoted by an alliance between the state and local technical communities. This alliance was governed through a decentralized set of state institutions, drawing on "global" and "local" economic and political resources. This "Developmental Network State" has had a significant impact on the growth of Ireland's high-tech cluster and is central to the emergence of an international network of "global high-tech regions" from Silicon Valley to Ireland, Taiwan, and Israel. The book provides a detailed study of the rise of the software industry in Ireland and of the state institutions and political conditions that promoted it. It shows how new "network-state" policies and institutions have been central to high-tech regions elsewhere. Ultimately, the analysis points to an emerging political choice between neoliberal policies that attack these social and political institutions and social democratic policies that sustain the social embedding of the global information economy.

Seán Ó Riain is Professor of Sociology, National University of Ireland, Maynooth.

Structural Analysis in the Social Sciences

Mark Granovetter, editor

Other Books in the Series:

The Politics of High-Tech Growth

Developmental Network States in the Global Economy

Seán Ó Riain

National University of Ireland, Maynooth

CAMBRIDGE UNIVERSITY PRESS

PUBLISHED BY THE PRESS SYNDICATE OF THE UNIVERSITY OF CAMBRIDGE
The Pitt Building, Trumpington Street, Cambridge, United Kingdom

CAMBRIDGE UNIVERSITY PRESS
The Edinburgh Building, Cambridge CB2 2RU, UK
40 West 20th Street, New York, NY 10011-4211, USA
477 Williamstown Road, Port Melbourne, VIC 3207, Australia
Ruiz de Alarcón 13, 28014 Madrid, Spain
Dock House, The Waterfront, Cape Town 8001, South Africa

http://www.cambridge.org

First published 2004

Printed in the United States of America

Typeface Times Roman 10/12 pt.   *System* LᴬTᴇX 2$_\varepsilon$ [TB]

A catalog record for this book is available from the British Library.

Library of Congress Cataloging-in-Publication Data
Ó Riain, S. (Seán)
Developmental network states: the politics of the global informational
economy / Seán Ó Riain.
p.   cm. – (Structural analysis in the social sciences)
Includes bibliographical references and index.
ISBN 0-521-83073-7
1. Information technology – Economic aspects – Ireland.
2. Economic development – Social aspects – Ireland.
3. Industrial policy – Social aspect – Ireland.   4. Technological innovations –
Government policy – Ireland   5. Computer software industry – Ireland.
I. Title: Global information economy.   II. Title.   III. Series.
HC260.5.Z91556   2004
338.9417′06 – dc21   2003053299

ISBN 0 521 83073 7 hardback

CONTENTS

CONTENTS

LIST OF TABLES

LIST OF FIGURES

ABBREVIATIONS

ABT	An Bord Tráchtála
BDCC	Buyer-Driven Commodity Chain
BIRD	Bi-National Industrial R&D
CBT	Computer-Based Training
CS	Computer Science
CSE	Center for Software Engineering
CSO	Central Statistics Office
DBS	Developmental Bureaucratic State
DCU	Dublin City University
DNS	Developmental Network State
EC	Electronic Commerce
EDB	Economic Development Board
EDP	Enterprise Development Program
EEC	European Economic Community
EI	Enterprise Ireland
ELI	Export Led Industrialization
EPTR	Export Profit Tax Relief
EPZ	Export-Processing Zone
ERSO	Electronics Research and Service Organization
ESRI	Economic and Social Research Institute
EU	European Union
FÁS	Forás Áiseanna Saothair (labor-market services agency)
FDI	Foreign Direct Investment
GDP	Gross Domestic Product
HEA	Higher Education Authority
HSIP	Hsinschu Science-Based Industrial Park (Taiwan)
IBEC	Irish Business and Employers Confederation
IC	Irish Computer
ICSA	Irish Computer Services Association (currently ISA)

ICSTI	Irish Council for Science, Technology, and Innovation
ICT	Information and Communication Technologies
IDA	Industrial Development Authority
IEP	Irish Pounds (unit of currency)
IMF	International Monetary Fund
ISA	Irish Software Association (formerly ICSA)
ISI	Import Substitution Industrialization
IT	Information Technology
ITRI	Industrial Technology Research Institute (Taiwan)
LRC	Localization Resources Center
LSM	Labor Settlement Movement (Israel)
MAC	(National) Microelectronics Application Center
MNE	Multinational Enterprise
MTI	Multimedia Technologies Ireland
NBST	National Board for Science and Technology
NESC	National Economic and Social Council
NESF	National Economic and Social Forum
NIHE	National Institutes for Higher Education
NMRC	National Microelectronics Research Center
NSC	National Software Center
NSD	National Software Directorate
OCS	Office of the Chief Scientist (Israel)
ODM	Original Design Manufacturing
OECD	Organization for Economic Cooperation and Development
OEM	Original Equipment Manufacturing
OTP	Office of Technology Policy (Israel)
PAT	Program in Advanced Technologies
RTC	Regional Technical College
PAP	People's Action Party (Malaysia)
PDCC	Producer-Driven Commodity Chain
PRC	People's Republic of China
R&D	Research and Development
SLIG	Software Localization Interest Group
SME	Small/Medium Sized Enterprise
SSISI	Statistical and Social Inquiry Society of Ireland
STAG	Science and Technology Advisory Group
STIAC	Science, Technology, and Innovation Advisory Council
TDCC	Technology-Driven Commodity Chain
TFP	Total Factor Productivity
TNC	Transnational Corporation
UCD	University College Dublin
UL	University of Limerick
VEC	Vocational Education Committee
WAIPA	World Association of Investment Promotion Agencies

PREFACE

In 1992, I took the path followed by many young Irish people at that time and emigrated to the United States. In my case, I left Dublin for Berkeley, California, to get a Ph.D. in sociology and, within a year or two, I found myself beginning to study the Irish software industry from 6,000 miles away in Silicon Valley. Over the next ten years or so, I followed the social ties within the industry – at first through the transnational ties that connected Silicon Valley and Ireland, then within a software development team in a Silicon Valley company in Dublin, and on through interviews in corporate and state offices, as well as with software developers themselves.

Ultimately, this project took me far from where I had expected to travel in the course of my sociological journey. I had begun my research as an investigation into the underdevelopment of the Irish economy and the accompanying mass unemployment and emigration of the 1980s. My initial research, however, revealed a more complex picture with glimmers of industrial revival – an impression confirmed by my early visits to Irish software firms. To my surprise, I found myself walking through the cubicles of youthful software developers as I met the managers that I was interviewing, and I discovered a world of vibrant social spaces and commercial entities that turned my project on its head. The ethnographic moment of those interviews challenged what I felt I knew about the inevitability of industrial underdevelopment in Ireland and defined the puzzle for my research: how to reconcile the development that I observed around me, which soon became central to the "Celtic Tiger" boom, with the empirical reality and sociological theorization of overpowering global forces. This book is an attempt to grapple with the ambiguities of this situation and to provide a way to think through its dilemmas and possibilities.

However, if this research took me to unexpected sociological destinations, it also took me to social destinations more familiar than I had expected. I had expected to face the ethical and political dilemmas of "studying down" – a male, middle-class researcher eliciting stories of exclusion in the kitchens of the high-unemployment regions around Dublin. Instead, I found myself sitting in comfortable offices and the bars of affluent Dublin, getting to know a world parallel to that in which I had grown up – a world dominated by middle-class men.

By the time I carried out my research in Ireland, I had made many of the connections and followed many of the transnational career paths that were such a big part of my coworkers' experience. My own life in the social sciences had mirrored the experiences of many of those I met in my research – educated on different sides of the same college campuses; working at home and abroad on emerging meanings and logics; one foot in the local culture, the other in the global economy. Software had seemed like a distant world, only for ethnography to reveal the many aspects already familiar to me from life in the Irish knowledge-worker diaspora.

To my surprise, I was "studying up" and even "across" in socially familiar and politically uncertain territories. The dilemmas of this research were challenging – trying to maintain political heterodoxy without breaching the assumed trust that comes with social similarity; respecting the abilities and insights of participants in the high-technology world of the Celtic Tiger, while maintaining an analytical distance from the assumptions of that world; and attempting to fashion an argument that might bridge the worlds of high technology and progressive political change. This social separation also made me less comfortable in the worlds of sociology and progressive politics because there have been few clear-cut political projects to which I could connect the findings of my research. This book is an attempt – written from a place of social familiarity and sociological ambiguity – to make some of those connections among the global information economy, its social conditions and consequences, and the political choices and possibilities contained within them.

Individual projects are always profoundly shaped by their barely hidden foundation of institutional and, more importantly, social supports – both the research in this book and the trajectory of the project itself have confirmed this for me. Financial support for this research was provided by the Graduate Division, University of California, Berkeley; the Department of Sociology, University of California, Berkeley; the John L. Simpson Fellowship of the Institute for International Studies, University of California, Berkeley; the Economic and Social Research Institute (ESRI), Dublin; Forfás and Forbairt, Dublin; the Joint Committee on Western Europe of the American Council of Learned Societies and the Social Science Research Council, with funds provided by the Ford and Mellon Foundations; the Academic Senate, University of California, Davis; Institute for Governmental Affairs, University of California, Davis; and the Institute for Labor and Employment, University of California.

I received helpful comments at presentations of parts of this research at the ESRI, Dublin; Conference on "Ireland, Europe, and the Global Information Society," Dublin; the Center for Western European Studies, University of California, Berkeley; the Center for Work, Technology, and Organizing, Stanford University; Braverman Memorial Conference on the Labor Process, SUNY-Binghamton; the Sloan Foundation Globalization Workshop for Junior Scholars, Duke University;

and Departments of Sociology at Queens College, City University of New York; Indiana University, Bloomington; University of California, Davis; Stanford University; University of California, Berkeley; Northwestern University; and the University of Arizona.

Invaluable research assistance was provided by Brooke Bennett, Matt Keller, Niall Moran, Dina Biscotti, and Julie Collins. Alia Winters has been a wonderfully patient and supportive editor. I received detailed and very constructive comments from two referees, Lars Mjoset and Neil Fligstein. And I give special thanks to Mark Granovetter, who believed in this book when it was a very raw dissertation – Mark's calm encouragement and wry sense of humor have helped me to keep going over the past few years.

The ESRI provided invaluable support to me during the past ten years, above and beyond the call of duty. Special thanks go to Damian Hannan, Kieran Kennedy, Brendan Whelan, and Chris Whelan. A special word of appreciation goes to John Sterne, without his dedicated and insightful journalism during the past twenty-five years, a great deal of the analysis in this study would not have been possible. He has been extremely generous with time, encouragement, comments, and access to back issues.

Vicki Smith, Fred Block, Patrick Carroll, Ryken Grattet, Laura Grindstaff, Diane Wolf, and Ming Cheng Lo were the best colleagues and friends that I could have hoped for at University of California, Davis, where I had many wonderful colleagues. Damian Hannan showed me the passion of the sociological imagination in action. Rory O'Donnell's intellectual openness and political imagination have been a continual inspiration. Steve Lopez has been a stimulating colleague and a wonderful friend. Thanks also to Duncan Temple Lang for long hours of technical education, encouragement, and emigrant friendship. Seán Ó Foghlú has been a personally supportive and intellectually challenging friend. Peter Evans provided incisive comments and great encouragement along the way. Anno Saxenian has been a great guide through the world of high-technology regions and a supportive mentor and encouraging friend. Michael Burawoy's contribution to this book has been immense – as a dedicated, insightful, and provocative dissertation advisor and friend and by creating a remarkable intellectual community of critical sociologists at Berkeley and beyond. I cannot thank these friends enough.

Many thanks to the several friends and colleagues who provided valuable information, advice, and encouragement through the long process that led to this book: Kilmacud Crokes Junior Hurling Champions (1992), Brian Nolan, Tim Callan, Alan Barrett, Maura Rohan, Breda McCabe, Tony Fahey, James Williams, Claire Collins, Philip O'Connell, Bernice Clancy, Maeve O'Reilly, Annette Moran, Gerard Garbutt, Séamus Gallen, Marcus Breathnach, Rhona Dempsey, Dermot O'Doherty, Proinsias Breathnach, James Wickham, Peter Murray, Kathleen Schwartzmann, Ted Egan, Balaji Parthasarathy, Gerald Autler, Matt Zook, Joe Blum, Teresa Gowan, Lynne Haney, Sheba George, Millie Thayer, Zsuzsa Gille, Maren Klawiter, Amy Schalet, Jim Skalla, Hilary Tovey, Eddie Hyland, Denis O'Hearn, Andrew Schrank, Neil Brenner, Nicole Biggart, David Kyle, John Hall,

John Walton, Michael Peter Smith, Frank Hirtz, Mike Hout, Hugh King, JoAnn King, Debbie Burns, Bob Burns, Art O'Connor, and the Starry Plough soccer team.

Thanks for everything to my family in Dublin, especially for letting me come and go around the world without guilt or dispute. Thanks to Eimer, Gearóid, and Ciarán for being great brothers and sister. All my love and thanks to my parents, Seán and Brighdín, who always tried to give us a broad-minded view on life, a curiosity about the world, and a sense of justice – values that I hope run throughout this book. I dedicate this book to you both. Thanks also for invaluable indexing and proofreading!

Aidan and Aisling – thanks for regularly interrupting the work on this book and sorry for the time it has cost you. Finally, all my love and thanks to my fantastic wife, Rebecca King. You have been great – the demands of listening to job talks over and over look easy now compared to raising children and writing books . . . it would hardly have been possible without you, but it certainly wouldn't have been nearly as much fun.

PART I

DEVELOPMENT IN THE GLOBAL INFORMATION ECONOMY

NETWORKS OF DEVELOPMENT
Globalization, High Technology, and the Celtic Tiger

UNCERTAINTIES OF GLOBALIZATION

The end of the twentieth century has brought with it troubling and uncertain times. The market triumphalism of the 1990s seemed to offer new certainties to replace those of the earlier period of the "Golden Age" of postwar Western capitalism and global "development." If the victory of global capitalist "market society" brought the depressing project of global exploitation, it also offered the prospect of new movements of resistance and antiglobalization. New political certainties were emerging – clear dividing lines that would be the basis of new struggles for and against corporate globalization. Globalization from above met globalization from below in dramatic struggles in the streets, each offering a different moral and political vision of the global capitalist order.

But as these grand political struggles are fought out at Seattle, Davos, and around the world, they are also fought out daily in the more mundane, everyday political economies of the new era. "Global markets" rely on a wide variety of institutional and social supports and are increasingly dominated by the central position of the leading transnational corporations. These corporations, powerful as they are, are themselves rooted in their intersection with workplaces, households, business networks, state strategies, regional industrial cultures, global cities, and elsewhere. Globalization is a grounded process, which is contested at the micro and meso levels, as well as at the macro level of transnational capital and the social movements that have emerged in such exciting fashion to challenge it (Burawoy et al., 2000).

Far from being bypassed in this process, states are experimenting with organizational and strategic changes nationally and internationally to respond to a networked economy and polity. The governance of the economy has been transformed, and states are scrambling to learn the lessons of the new environment. Economic life and political governance have been rescaled as the national level has become destabilized, from both above by globalization and below by the increasing salience of regional economies. In this situation, the "glocal" state aims to promote capital accumulation by linking the local to the global, thereby creating a location ideal for accumulation within a global set of connections (Brenner, 1998, 1999). The organizational structure and strategy of these glocal states are only now beginning to be explored. The state that connects a wide range of local networks to a diverse set of global actors and networks must itself be more decentralized and flexible than states that presided over a centrally negotiated national development coalition (Ó Riain, 2000).

Understanding these grubby scrambles to promote and shape capitalist development and the new political struggles for the rewards of that development is critical not only to developing new "models of development" but also to understanding the possibilities for transformation within the contemporary world system. Ultimately, the "winners" in the struggle for sociopolitical transformation will be those who can connect a moral and ideological victory in the grand struggle over globalization with a myriad of institutional victories in the more mundane world of developmental strategies and coalitions.

This book examines just such a set of capitalist development strategies, investigating the promises and dilemmas of high-tech industrial development in the Republic of Ireland. Once a poster child for the ills of globalization, hollowed out by foreign investment and "brain drain," in the 1990s the "Celtic Tiger" appeared to be a shining star of neoliberal orthodoxy. When we look beneath the neoliberal veneer, however, we find a much richer story of state–society alliances, state involvement in industrial development, and the emergence of new organizational and institutional capacities that both adjust to neoliberalism and seek to protect themselves from it.

From within a neoliberal order, a new form of state developmentalism emerged in Ireland, as it did elsewhere around the world in this period. A network of "global regions" – dense clusters of technological practice and learning linked by transnational corporate, scientific, and occupational ties – is at the heart of the emerging information economy. In a world of increased corporate power and growing exploitation of labor and nature, the global regions of the informational economy are the critical points where the most dynamic elements of the capitalist economy come to ground and might be turned to developmental and social purposes. Although it is transformed to deal with the new circumstances, the national state still plays a critical role in shaping markets by mediating those connections between the local and the global and by influencing how local-specific assets are mobilized within the range of opportunities available in the global economy.

Castells (1997) argues that the state is increasingly moving toward a position as a "Network State," embedded in a variety of levels and types of governance institution. Ansell's research on regional development in Europe suggests that "the 'Network State' can operate as a liaison or broker in creating networks and empowering non-state actors, especially when state actors occupy a central role in these networks" (Ansell, 2000, p. 35). Network centrality is critical to this new state – isolation from the local or the global renders it ineffective. A Developmental

Network State (DNS) attempts to nurture localized Post-Fordist[*] networks of production and innovation within global investment flows by shaping the character of the various local connections to global technology and business networks. This is made possible by the multiple embeddedness of state agencies in professional-led networks of innovation and in international capital, as well as by the state's networked organizational structure. However, these multiple state–society alliances lead to uneven internationalization of society and growing inequality, generating political tensions with which the fragmented state structure cannot deal effectively. A crucial contested terrain of the global political economy will be these networked developmental strategies and the class compromises, state and social institutions, and patterns of solidarity and inequality that emerge around them.

Through a detailed examination of the growth of an information technology-based global region in Ireland, the significance of the DNS in promoting that growth, and the patterns of class and state politics associated with those changes, this book explores the possibilities and dilemmas of the real world of global informational capitalism in the early years of the twenty-first century. Drawing on six years of research and using ethnographic, historical, interview, and survey analysis, this book explains how "network development" has come to be the central institutional form of capitalist development in a global network of high-tech regions around the world, centered around "core" regions such as Silicon Valley. It provides a detailed exploration of the workings of the DNS in the Republic of Ireland – deeply integrated in this network of high-tech regions and one of the fastest growing economies in the world in the 1990s. Finally, I undertake a comparative analysis of how the "network" developmental states of Taiwan, Israel, and Ireland shape growth in ways that are significantly different from the "bureaucratic" developmental states that prevail in South Korea and Japan.

THE REAL WORLD OF THE GLOBAL INFORMATION ECONOMY

To explore these concrete tactics and strategies of development in a neoliberal era, we must tread the rough ground of the real world of the global economy, looking for ethnographic purchase on the slippery world of global flows and networks. The global information economy is an ideal location for such exploration because it is the paradigm of the new global capitalism – fast, virtual, and deeply integrated in global markets.

Since the 1980s, information and communication technologies (ICT) have accounted for growing shares of world trade, investment, and consumption. In the 1990s, trade in ICT goods grew at almost double the rate of total trade, which itself almost doubled over that period. Intrafirm trade through foreign investment grew rapidly and technological standards and learning became increasingly globally

---

[*] 'Fordism' refers to an economy based primarily on mass production, mass consumption and bureaucratic organizational structures. 'Post-Fordism' refers more loosely to a contemporary era of more fragmented and differentiated production and consumption with less centralized, 'networked' organizations.

integrated (OECD, 2002). If the 1990s was the era of the "globalization project" (McMichael, 1996), then ICT was the "project team leader." Furthermore, ICT was central to the "New American Economy" (Gilpin, 2002, p. 4). ICT sectors accounted for a large part of U.S. growth; the application of new ICTs improved productivity throughout the economy; and the freewheeling, market-led image of Silicon Valley became the symbol of the triumph of Anglo-American capitalism on the global stage.

But if the image of software programmers linked together through virtual digital networks in a global market for knowledge is a powerful icon of the contemporary information economy, it is also largely a mirage. For wherever we find such programmers, we find them embedded in a dense web of institutional supports – from the technical communities of their peers, through the tight networks of business and technology, to the broader institutional supports of education, research and development (R&D) systems, and state industrial-promotion agencies. The specific ways in which these institutions are connected and rewards allocated across them have varied historically and comparatively, but development of the ICT industries has always been a socially and politically embedded process. The ICT boom is neither the market panacea that its boosters claim nor the speculative "flash in the pan" that its critics observed in 2002. It is the basis of a new "techno-economic paradigm," a new constellation of technological and organizational innovations that provide the basis for new processes of capital accumulation and technological development (Freeman and Louca, 2002). What precise form this takes remains to be seen, but it will be a crucial issue in the development of global capitalism for the next half-century and beyond.

The emergence of the computer industry was itself deeply tied to the state in advanced capitalist countries, particularly to military funding for technology research. In the United States, this took the form of "military developmentalism" in which private firms were heavily subsidized by public research funds and military markets were critical to the growth of firms such as IBM and regions such as Silicon Valley. The U.S. state was central to the founding of the basic building blocks of ICT today – the academic discipline of computer science, the programming labor force, and the leading firms and regions of the private sector (see Chapter 4).

In the 1960s and 1970s, U.S. ICT industries faced their greatest challenges, posed by the East Asian "developmental bureaucratic states." Driven forward by an alliance between a cohesive state bureaucracy (with strong informal internal ties based on school affiliations) and the large firms and business groups (*keiretsu*), a form of "alliance capitalism" emerged in countries such as Japan and Korea, which proved to be remarkably successful in international competition (Gerlach, 1992). Building on a set of economic institutions that had emerged since the late nineteenth century (Dore, 1973), the Japanese state stimulated domestic demand for Japanese computers, promoted public and private R&D, and provided a variety of investment incentives for domestic firms – challenging U.S. supremacy in electronics by the 1980s.

In the 1990s, however, the developmental state seemed to have had its day in the sun. The Japanese and Korean states appeared too inflexible to cope with rapidly

changing informational industries and decentralized Post-Fordist industrial structures. Korean and Japanese firms ran into increasing difficulties throughout the
1990s in rapidly changing high-technology markets. The developmental states
also appeared too weak to manage the increasingly internationalized economies
over which they presided, as evidenced in the financial crisis of 1997 and 1998.
The emergence of flexible regional economies and dispersed transnational networks of technology and finance appeared to have simultaneously undermined the
developmental state from below and from above.

However, even as these forces have challenged the developmental bureaucratic
states, state and social actors around the world have experimented – under intense
pressure – with new forms of developmental strategy that might be effective in a
neoliberal international order. Regions around the world have built network developmental strategies, often by connecting to regions such as Silicon Valley. Israel,
India, Taiwan, Singapore, and Ireland are particularly interesting cases of regional
development, given that each is a surprising "success story." Each economy has
undergone liberalization, to the point where they are "open" to the global economy, and each has pursued foreign investment through financial incentives and
investment in a technical labor force. But each has also seen the emergence within
its borders of regional agglomerations where technical innovation and economic
growth have been concentrated – in many cases, transforming the urban spaces
where they emerge. Furthermore, these agglomerations are characterized by relatively decentralized industrial systems, supported by dense social networks of
technical professionals and entrepreneurs. In many of these successful economies,
a DNS has emerged that promotes local learning within global networks through
a decentralized but accountable set of state institutions that maintains close ties to
local technical communities and international capital. The institutional structures
and political alliances underpinning the role of the state in promoting economic
development have also been transformed, and new local and national economic
developmental strategies of network development have emerged from within the
dynamics of the global information economy. Through their connections to U.S.
ICT, these regions also played an important role in the U.S. dominance of high
technology in the 1990s.

If the United States has been reinstated at the center of the system, other countries
have been able to move up the hierarchy of the international division of labor over
the course of this historical shift from bureaucratic to network development in information technology (IT). This is borne out in a study of indicators of "technology-
based competitiveness" in thirty-three countries between 1993 and 1999 (Porter
et al., 2000). During the 1990s, the United States pulled away from Japan to
be the clear global leader in high-tech, whereas the leading "Asian Tigers" –
Singapore, South Korea, and Taiwan – are now comparable in their technological
strength to the relatively stable Western European economies. The "Asian Cubs" –
Malaysia, China, Thailand, Indonesia, the Philippines, and India – are growing
in high-tech competitiveness, but much more unevenly. The emergence of China
in the 1990s is striking. Ireland and Israel were only added to the index in 1999,
but are technologically strong and comparable in many ways to the Asian Tigers.

Whereas the Latin American countries are slipping backward the Eastern European economies are emerging as likely future locations of high-tech production. The United States is pulling away as East Asia and the newly emergent DNSs such as Ireland and Israel narrow the gap with the rest of the core. Meanwhile, the distance to those falling behind and being excluded grows rapidly.

A set of countries has emerged in the 1990s, therefore, that has pursued such network developmental strategies for mobility in the hierarchy of the international economy, and network development has emerged as an international "social structure of accumulation" (Gordon et al., 1982) in the ICT industry. Built on various prior forms of development, it operates through global networks, linking together socially and institutionally "dense" regions. New state–society alliances have emerged on this terrain of development and, through their various successes and failures, have reshaped the global networks themselves. Not surprisingly, the character of the world system has been changed as this new social structure of accumulation – operating through network institutional forms and across spatial scales – has remade relations of power in the global economy – creating opportunities for inclusion for some, raising the stakes of exclusion and, in its most surprising consequences, reshaping the "Asian miracle" to reconstitute the United States as an economic power at the center of a global network of high-technology regions. Network development is, however, a profoundly unstable social structure of accumulation, based as it is on volatile capital markets and generating high levels of income inequality and highly polarized patterns of economic demand.

In most cases, these changes have led to greater exploitation of labor and the environment and to exclusion from the fruits of development, but other regions have been able to build a viable developmental strategy based on the deepening of local learning and innovation within global networks. The multiple state–society alliances of the DNS lead to uneven development and internationalization of society and growing inequality, generating political tensions with which the fragmented state structure cannot deal effectively. Nonetheless, if state developmental strategies can play this significant role in an era characterized by hostility to state intervention, DNSs are likely to prosper further if international institutions to regulate markets and to facilitate local and national social regulation of economic life are strengthened. As will be seen throughout this book, effective developmental strategies in the era of the neoliberal globalization project require not state retreat, but rather extensive state shaping of the political economy.

THE CELTIC TIGER

The experience of the Celtic Tiger economy of the Republic of Ireland is a fascinating case where we might excavate this terrain, seeking out both a model of developmental strategy and the dilemmas of that model and what it can tell us about the broader political economy. Deeply integrated in global investment and trade flows since the 1960s, Ireland had been a tragic example of the ills of globalization – the "sick man" of Europe beset by branch plants and brain drain, as well as rampant clientelism. What better example for the errant patients of the neoliberal world economy than a miraculous deathbed recovery? In the 1990s, Ireland cut taxes, attracted huge amounts of foreign investment, and underwent an economic boom that leapfrogged it toward the top of the European income league. There is much more here, however, than a simple story of neoliberal globalization. The industrial heart of the Celtic Tiger was its connection to the global information economy and the growth and boom in the ICT industries in the 1980s and 1990s, respectively. Foreign investment remained central to Irish industry, but indigenous industry – supported by the state – also became increasingly sophisticated and internationally competitive. Furthermore, public-sector employment expanded significantly, local demand was critical to growth, and all of this was managed through an increasingly dense network of institutions of "social partnership" extending across almost all spheres of the political economy and integrating local actors, state agencies, and European Union programs.

The ebb and flow of the fortunes of the Irish economy and society pose an intriguing set of dilemmas. If Ireland has ruthlessly integrated itself into global flows since the 1960s, do the ebbs and flows of capital and labor explain the cycles in the national economy? Critics and supporters of capitalist development in Ireland seem to agree that, under current conditions, the only development option is to simply "connect" to the global economy and train your labor force toward this purpose. A persistence with export-orientation, free trade, and foreign investment is argued to be the key to Irish development in the 1990s. Economists see only the power of global market forces at work, with free trade and foreign investment producing growth (Sachs, 1998; Barry, 2000) – although the same formula had yielded only economic failure before the 1990s. Critics of the economists often mirror their arguments: the Celtic Tiger is the outgrowth of international capital flows (O'Hearn, 1998, 2001) or the activities of a market-conforming "competition state" (Kirby, 2002). The critics, however, are in a bind. With no positive account of the causes of change in the Celtic Tiger, they are pushed toward agreeing with the economists that market-led solutions are the only available political choices. Their response is to critique the character of the change itself: the industrial base is weak, the state remains corrupt, and inequality is rising. Although the critique of the cheerleading for the Celtic Tiger is welcome, the overall thrust of the argument fails to recognize the character of change that has occurred in Ireland.

If steady economic growth, increasing productivity and R&D, growth in indigenous industry, elimination of mass unemployment, reversal of mass emigration, increased female labor-force participation, and a renewed sense of cultural vitality are taken seriously, then it is clear that there has been significant transformation. This transformation is all the more remarkable given the context from which it emerged in the 1980s – dependency on international capital was equaled only by the extent of local corruption and clientelism (extending, as we now know, to the leading sectors of beef, property, and banking). How could parts of the Irish population turn global–local connections to their advantage in the 1990s where they had been so hopelessly debilitating in the 1980s?

The explanation can be found in the institutional transformation of the Irish state and the emergence of new state–society alliances. These transformations include the creation of institutions of social partnership, increasing connections to the various administrative bodies of the European Union (EU), and the diversification and strengthening of industrial development agencies (O'Donnell, 2000; Ó Riain, 2000a; Ó Riain and O'Connell, 2000).

The most widely recognized institutional change in the Irish political economy has been the "social partnership" between business, unions, and government. These series of agreements – initially on wages, but increasingly on a wider range of issues – were based on the trade-off of modest wage increases for tax cuts, stabilizing the public finances and macroeconomy in the 1980s, and laying the foundation for growth in the 1990s. This is as far as most accounts of institutional change go – this is "market-conforming" competitive corporatism. But social partnership has gone beyond the specific wage deals to become the institutional mechanism of public governance through almost all spheres of Irish public life (O'Donnell, 2000). The emergence of these new public institutions has not reformed the corrupt political system but has essentially emerged alongside it as a much more effective and accountable mode of governance, even as corruption continues within the established political institutions.

Furthermore, this macroeconomic stabilization was accompanied by changes in state action in promoting industrial development – in addition to attracting foreign investment, state agencies now provided finance; promoted improved research and management; and fostered the growth of a network of centers, associations, and other supporting institutions for business. In the process, a remarkable turnaround was effected in the fortunes of indigenous industry – ranging from the widely publicized software success stories to the relatively mundane improvement of tourist facilities. Taken together, there has been a widespread upgrading and deepening of the organizational capacities of Irish society, supported by state agencies. These institutions have often, in turn, been financed by EU programs – indeed, the availability of EU funding fostered institutional innovation by allowing new institutions to avoid the worst of head-to-head competition for resources with established interests within the national political system.

Ireland is a case, then, that is fraught with contradictions: the classic contradictions of state developmentalism in a neoliberal global order. Caught up in these contradictions, developmentalist projects in Ireland have grappled with the dilemmas of semiperipheral industrialization within liberal politics. With liberal democratic institutions, high rates of foreign investment, and free trade, Ireland may be less an exception than a vision of the future under neoliberal capitalism. The state proved to be central to the process of semiperipheral industrial upgrading, as an alliance of state technology and industrial agencies with a rising technical, professional class became the foundation of a glocal system of innovation. However, this industrial development occurred in a tense relationship with the institutions of social partnership, because these "knowledge-economy" sectors expanded faster than the sectors where the union movement was strongest and were able to push hardest their claims for pay increases. By the end of the 1990s, tensions between production and public-sector workers and the rising technical professionals were creating great difficulties in renegotiating social partnership deals. A rich network of institutions had developed alongside a party political system that remained mired in a dubious mix of neoliberalism and populism.

By 2001 and 2002, the tensions between this populist neoliberalism of the party political system and the developmentalism of state–society alliances and social-partnership institutions left the Celtic Tiger balanced between cannibalizing itself and building upon its own successes. As the global information economy went into a rapid downturn, the Irish high-tech sector suffered and growth rates in Ireland declined to around 3 percent per annum. Orthodox economic analyses blamed declining wage competitiveness and rising public spending, whereas others found the underlying weaknesses of the Irish economy coming home to roost once the foreign investment boom was over. However, the story is more complex – state developmentalism exposes the contradictions in capitalist development between the sociopolitical creation of markets and the cannibalization by markets of the very institutions that support them (Polanyi, 1944). The developmentalist and social-partnership institutions that had developed through the 1990s now faced major challenges from the still dominant political practices and ideologies of the party political system – a neoliberal obsession with competitiveness pursued through clientelist networks. Public spending cutbacks began to weaken labor supply, increase social exclusion, and undermine the institutions that had become increasingly effective in supporting R&D and innovation. The lack of political support for the developmentalist project and the obsession with a narrow conception of competitiveness also had important geopolitical ramifications. Despite overwhelming public opposition to the Bush administration's 2003 war in Iraq, the Irish government stealthily offered a variety of supports to the U.S. military during the course of the war. By the time of the war in Iraq, Ireland stood at a crucial point of political choice and struggle over future directions: a clear official ideology of liberal competitiveness and a loose affiliation of complex interests supporting different parts of the developmentalist and social-rights projects. In the absence of a cohesive political coalition and an organizing ideology that could contest the neoliberal competitiveness discourse, the Celtic Tiger faced enormous political and institutional challenges in the early years of the twenty-first century.

If we do not understand the institutions of the Celtic Tiger, we are in danger of missing both the real causes of the "miracle" of the 1990s, the sources of its limitations and, indeed, its unrealized potential. Profound reforms in the "globalization project" (McMichael, 1996) remain necessary – if the institutions of the Celtic Tiger could generate the results they did in the face of domestic neoliberal populism and an international order hostile to state and social shaping of economic life, what might they achieve given a more supportive political order? The neoliberal discourse has become the organizing framework for both supporters and critics of the Celtic Tiger: if political coalitions and strategies are to be built that can realize the potential for expanding the developmentalist and social rights projects within the Celtic Tiger – and, indeed, the global information economy – an alternative set of concepts and perspectives is necessary. This book is intended to be a modest effort in that direction.

STRUCTURE OF THE BOOK

The book draws on extensive documentary, survey, interview, ethnographic, and comparative research[1] to explore the emergence of network development and DNSs in the global economy. It examines the process through which network development became the dominant mode of development within the international computer industry and how bureaucratic and network forms of state developmentalism emerged in different success stories of international IT – focusing particularly on South Korea, Taiwan, Singapore, and Israel. The Irish case, however, is the focus of the most in-depth study, in which the evolution of the Celtic Tiger economy, the surprising success of the Irish software industry, and the institutional and political conditions of the Irish DNS are explained.

The next chapter develops the theoretical concepts and perspective used in the book. It argues that *development* has not been rendered irrelevant by capitalist globalization but rather has been transformed. The chapter explores the economic, institutional, and political dimensions of developmental network and bureaucratic states and points out the particular dilemmas raised in the pursuit of autocentric development in an era of Global Post-Fordism.

Concluding Part One, Chapter 3 analyzes the case of the Celtic Tiger, the booming economy of the Republic of Ireland in the 1990s. It documents the remarkable turnaround in Irish fortunes in the 1990s, even as the policy of pursuing foreign investment remained relatively consistent. Increasing investment, rising productivity, increased R&D spending, professionalization of the labor force, and the growth of Irish-owned firms were all distinctive features of the 1990s economy – resulting in rapid economic growth, net immigration, and almost full employment. These changes can be explained not through the logic of foreign capital flows nor by local cultural transformation but by the emergence of a "Developmental Network State" that could link these local and global forces together to build a coherent developmental strategy around foreign investment.

The four chapters in Part Two explore the dynamics of industrial upgrading, state intervention, and rising inequality in the emerging Irish software industry. Chapter 4 outlines the factors that explain the ability of the Irish state to attract extremely high levels of foreign investment in software and investigates the extent to which this investment has been locally embedded. Chapter 5 documents how state agencies shaped the indigenous software industry by prompting investment, rewarding firms that produced technology-based products for export, and "making winners" by providing support for R&D, marketing, and management development. Chapter 6 explores the ongoing integration of local software firms into global networks through alliances, acquisitions, and stock listings. The state continues to play an important role in ensuring that local firms benefit from

---

1 For details of research methods and statistical analysis, see Appendix A.

international networks of innovation rather than become trapped in international labor contracting relations. The state also underwrites an "associational infrastructure" of innovation centers, industry associations, university–industry links, and so on, which help to mesh local and global innovation networks. However, the success of the state in promoting this internationalization itself poses a problem as the firms become increasingly independent of state or social control. Finally, Chapter 7 investigates the rise of a technical, professional class in software, their often international careers, the politics of the glocal workplaces they inhabit, and their place in the increasingly intense politics of inequality in Ireland.

Part Three of the book analyzes the institutional and political conditions and dilemmas of the DNS. Chapter 8 outlines the institutional conditions of the DNS through a close analysis of the institutions of the Irish state. The DNS is characterized by multiple embedded autonomies – connecting to local and international technical communities and international capital, as well as to domestic capital. The perils of being "captured" by these social groups would seem all the more pressing, therefore; however, autonomy is secured through a constant series of evaluations, assessments, and other forms of external accountability. Finally, the state system as a whole is integrated in a loosely coupled bureaucratic structure, rather than the tightly coupled, more centralized structure of the Korean state.

Taken together, these institutional structures support a state that is oriented toward adaptation and learning, as well as strategy and planning. National economic development is not abandoned as the motivating ideology of the DNS, but is recast as the management of local and global connections in order to create national competitiveness. Once again, we find a state that has not abandoned the cause of national development, but rather pursues that goal through strategies and structures that are developed for a world that is both more globalized and more localized.

How did these institutional structures emerge? Chapter 9 examines the creation of these institutions in Ireland through an analysis of two major crises in the Irish political economy. The resolution of the first socioeconomic crisis in the 1950s led to the emphasis on foreign investment, whereas the socioeconomic crisis of the 1980s ultimately led to the formation of the DNS. In each case, a socioeconomic crisis delegitimated the existing set of economic and industrial policies – at least enough to create new political spaces in which alternative models could emerge. The models that were institutionalized after each crisis were supported by an alliance between a rising social group and a section of the state organization and were facilitated by a particular set of institutions within the global political economy. After the 1950s, the newly formed Industrial Development Authority (IDA) filled a policy vacuum (left by the weakness of domestic capital) with its agenda of attracting foreign investment and was able to draw on Ireland's participation in the Marshall Plan as a source of resources and legitimacy. After the 1980s, previously marginal state agencies focused on science and technology were able to build an alliance with a rising technical, professional class to support an agenda of greater indigenous innovation. In this case, the availability of legitimate international institutions such as the Organization for Economic Cooperation and Development (OECD) and the EU that were promoting an agenda of science, technology, and innovation provided invaluable support to this "domestic" coalition.

Chapter 10 compares successful developmental states, distinguishing them along a continuum from network to bureaucratic. Most state-centered analyses present Taiwan, Korea, and Singapore as essentially similar cases of state-led development. Analysts who focus on business organization emphasize the differences among these political economies – noting Taiwan's networks of small firms, Korea's centralized *chaebol* business groups, and Singapore's heavy reliance on foreign investment. Understanding Taiwan as a DNS and Korea as a Developmental Bureaucratic State (DBS) allows us to understand how different forms of developmental statism shape different industrial structures and trajectories. They also help to explain why Taiwan has fared better in the era of economic globalization by adapting to the process of network development. Singapore is analyzed as an intermediate case that, although possessing a centralized state, has pursued significant elements of the network developmental strategy due to its long-time reliance on foreign investment.

Taiwan and Israel are presented as cases of DNS – in some ways more effective versions of the model than the Irish case. Both Taiwan and Israel have states that intervene in important ways in the economy, but not by directly influencing the key decisions of leading firms. Instead, they foster a range of firms in key sectors and shape the types of firms that they become – providing support for exporting, research, innovation, and so on. Each state has done so within the context of increasing international integration – through subcontracting networks in Taiwan and migrant communities in Israel. Furthermore, each state has operated through a range of decentralized industry associations, state-sponsored venture-capital funds, migrant networks and associations, and a variety of other decentralized mechanisms of influence. In short, they are classic DNS cases and are among the fastest growing industrial economies of the 1990s.

Finally, Chapter 11 explores the broader theoretical and political implications of the analysis. State developmentalism casts the political struggle between neoliberal and social-rights regimes in ever starker terms. Where the social institutions of innovation in the global economy are being cannibalized by financial speculations, a similar tension exists in the Celtic Tiger, where neoliberal populism threatens to undermine the public investment and social dialogue that underpinned the Irish economic transformation. I suggest how certain strands in network development might be refashioned to create a more egalitarian developmental model: building on an increased emphasis on external accountability to democratize development, taking advantage of changing definitions of professionalism to socialize knowledge networks, and addressing widespread fears of individualized labor-market insecurity by collectively distributing the risks of flexibility. Developmental states can become the basis for reinvented social-rights regimes on local, national, and global scales – but whether they are thus transformed or simply become vehicles for mobilizing populations to be competitive depends on the strength and creativity of forces mobilizing for social rights. The DNS is, however, a crucial terrain where these struggles will be contested.

2

STATE DEVELOPMENTALISMS AND CAPITALIST GLOBALIZATIONS

The language of globalization evokes images of celebration and despair, domination and resistance, and totalizing forces overwhelming local variations. Where observers find important variations within the global economic order, they typically forego the language of global capitalism to focus on institutional variations in political economies and "varieties of capitalism" (Fligstein, 2001; Hall and Soskice, 2002). What language might we develop that takes capitalism seriously as a "structured totality" (Burawoy, 1985) but that sees that totality as itself constituted by multiple overlapping institutional complexes? Such a language could provide both the analytical "bite" necessary to explain contemporary processes of globalization and their effects while also allowing us to identify important political spaces of contestation and structuration of global capitalism.

This chapter undertakes that task. The first sections briefly outline a theoretical perspective on capitalism and the state that, with Marx, sees capitalism as a system of exploitation, accumulation, and uneven development but, with Polanyi, sees those relations as always and everywhere socially and politically embedded. Capitalism is a "structured totality" but one that is shaped by multiple and intersecting political logics, not by a "logic of the capitalist system." Furthermore, states and other institutions of governance do not simply "regulate" a system with its own logic but rather constantly structure and restructure capitalist social relations, even as they are constrained by them. Emphasizing the political creation of capitalism means that developmental states are central to the project of global capitalism; the next section outlines the characteristic dilemmas of semiperipheral capitalist development. However, forms of state developmentalism vary enormously across time and space in their developmental strategies and tactics, institutional and geopolitical foundations, social consequences, and the ensuing political possibilities. The remainder of the chapter explores those variations in developmental states, concentrating on an important conceptual distinction between two clusters of cases of contemporary state developmentalism: the DBSs of East Asia and the DNSs of the "global regions" emerging in Ireland, Israel, Taiwan, and elsewhere.

GOVERNING CAPITALIST GLOBALIZATIONS

Mirroring the grand political struggles over globalization, academic analyses have often celebrated or deplored the rise of global capitalism. But whereas their evaluations of capitalist globalization are very different, neoclassical economics and orthodox Marxism share a similar underlying view of capitalism: Although supporting institutions may be necessary to secure the foundations of capitalism, capitalism operates according to its own systemic logic, overwhelming all institutional and political forms that do not conform to that logic (Block, 2001). A growing institutionalist literature does pay attention to the varieties of ways in which capitalist economies are organized, even in the face of globalization (Boyer and Hollingsworth, 1997; Fligstein, 2001; Hall and Soskice, 2002). However, most of this literature fails to take the power of capitalist social organization seriously enough (Burawoy et al., 2000), posing capitalism as a context – a set of property and exchange relationships that can accommodate multiple institutional forms. Both Marxist and institutionalist analyses offer compelling critiques of capitalist globalization – exposing the domination and exploitation at the heart of capitalist social relations and the social embeddedness and institutional variability of capitalist organization, respectively. But while each strand of analysis effectively debunks neoclassical views of capitalism as inherently progressive and apolitical, we await an effective synthesis of Marxist and institutionalist critiques that can provide the basis of a coherent alternative view of the global economy. This chapter does not provide such a synthesis but rather develops some theoretical arguments along those lines that enable us to look more closely at the persistent variety of capitalist developmentalisms, even in an era of globalization.

Capitalist globalizations: multiple, political, interlocking

The "new economic sociology" has largely posited the object of its analysis as social relations within markets, taking on neoclassical economics by problematizing its assumptions of an asocial market (Granovetter, 1985). *Capitalism*, as a category of analysis, has been largely ignored and even the market has been accepted too easily as an unanalyzed context of those analyses (Krippner, 2001). The starting point of the analysis in this book, therefore, is that capitalism is indeed a structured totality, which is as much about class, exploitation, capital accumulation, and social reproduction as it is about markets and private property (Burawoy, 1985).

However, in "bringing capitalism back in," we should resist the temptation to posit a totalizing logic of global capitalism that renders local institutional forms irrelevant (Burawoy, 2001). Capitalism is an historical form of social organization that is always politically embedded and in the making (Polanyi, 1944) and cannot simply be regulated but rather is created, maintained, undermined, and restructured. States play a critical role in constructing markets by guaranteeing their rules of operation but also by creating new market actors and shaping their strategies (Block, 1994; Fligstein, 2001). However, they must balance this activity with the need to maintain support from the society that they claim to represent, placing the state at the heart of the process of managing the tensions between market and society. Society, too, is caught between supporting state efforts to promote growth and living standards through the market while simultaneously turning to the state for protection against the market (Polanyi, 1944). Marxist theorists suggested in the 1970s that these tensions were insurmountable (Habermas, 1976; Offe, 1984). However, the tensions have been reconciled historically in a variety of institutionalized national and international models of capitalism, underpinned by different state–society alliances (Block, 1987; Evans et al., 1985; Ó Riain, 2000b; Scharpf, 1999).

Ultimately, then, there are capitalisms, shaped by multiple political logics (Block, 1987). But these are not the "comparative capitalisms" of much of economic sociology in which differing – typically national – institutional frameworks compete with each other within increasingly global marketplaces. Instead, the building blocks of global capitalism are a variety of "social structures of accumulation" (Gordon et al., 1982): a particular set of social arrangements that sustain capitalist growth in a specific time and place. In Block's interpretation of the concept (which departs significantly from the more deterministic conceptualization by Gordon et al.).

"The 'social structure of accumulation' comprises particular configurations of urban growth, particular types of financial and governmental mechanisms for structuring demand, and specific ways of organizing the relations between workers and employers . . . . As long as we remember that there is not one unique social structure of accumulation at a given moment, but multiple possibilities, then this conceptualization reinforces the Polanyian idea that one cannot simply separate out economic development from the political–economic context that makes it possible." (Block, 1987, p. 177)

The global information economy has emerged around a model of network development as a social structure of accumulation in its own right, not as an institutional complex competing with other institutional forms in global markets. The social structures of network development shape global markets just as global markets shape the system of network development. Network development also exists alongside other social structures of accumulation, each based on its own distinctive intersection of sectoral connections and local, national, and global institutions. Global capitalism, then, is not built of a unitary single logic but rather of a variety of social structures of accumulation with multiple points of intersection. This in turn makes it both easier than skeptics suggest to find spaces for politics within global capitalism and more difficult to build antisystemic movements because the "system" itself consists of multiple overlapping, shifting, and often contradictory interests and projects.

Governing in an era of global capitalisms

The recent crisis of the Asian developmental states challenged a major alternative to neoliberal globalization. Some authors have argued that those changes have diminished the role of the state, weakening it to the point where it is essentially bypassed by the formation of a global system and transnational social structure

(Mittelman, 1997; Robinson, 1998; Sklair 1991). Others rightly argue that the intensification of global processes has made the role of the state more important because an effective state becomes critical to promoting competitiveness within a global economy. However, this increased state role is limited to promoting economic competition and accumulation – even as the state becomes an increasingly critical enterprise association, its role as a civil association diminishes (Cerny, 1995). Cerny argues that all states are now faced with the imperatives of global competition, causing a convergence around the model of the "competition state." Jessop (2002) provides a more specific analysis of the policy form this takes as he argues that capitalist states are pushed to replace "Keynesian welfare" as a form of regulation with "Schumpeterian workfare." Certainly, this resonates with aspects of the experience of recent years as states – both within and across national boundaries – compete to offer the greatest incentives and concessions to attract mobile investment, create a variety of institutions to support entrepreneurship, and often roll back welfare entitlements.

However, the concepts of competition state and Schumpeterian workfare state extend important observations about the specific features of many contemporary capitalist states into too general an argument regarding a new mode of capitalist regulation. The notion of competition or Schumpeterian workfare states does not capture the empirical complexity of uneven development in contemporary capitalism and unnecessarily narrows our understanding of the institutions underpinning economic growth. More importantly, the notion of a competition state fails to recognize the internally contradictory nature of "market liberalism" itself. Far from being smoothly integrated with market competitiveness, the institutions supporting capitalist development need to be protected from excessive marketization of the institutions of the economy, particularly the growing financialization of its firms and institutions (Lundvall et al., 2002). Finally, these concepts obscure the existence of a political space for struggles within and through existing institutions over how development could and should be structured. To simply describe the institutions supporting capitalist development as oriented toward competitiveness ignores the many political possibilities that the institutions of economic development present for future transformation. Such institutions can either be undermined by neoliberal strategies or be part of the economic basis of a move toward social democracy. The social democratic states that are rightly taken as paradigmatic of welfarist Keynesianism were also competition, Schumpeterian, and workfare (in the broad sense of being dependent on high rates of employment) states. Indeed, the Schumpeterian concept of the national system of innovation, in its broad form as the social embedding of innovation activity, was developed as a way to understand the economy that underpinned Scandinavian social democracy (Lundvall et al., 2002; Mjoset, 1992). Rather than reducing the complexities of institutions and politics in capitalist development under globalization to competition, we need to provide a better understanding of the effects and possibilities of institutions – such as those underpinning national systems of innovation – and other critical institutional realms such as industrial relations, social partnership, and the welfare state. The state still matters because (to use Cerny's terms) (Cerny, 1995) it is *both* a civic association – an arena for advancing legitimate political claims – *and* an enterprise association, promoting economic development.

We can expect states to consistently play a role in shaping economic action because the state can provide a vision that can move the economy beyond damaging equilibria sustained by uncertainty and fragmentation, coordinate economic actors to exploit economic externalities, build the institutions necessary for this purpose, and mediate the conflict created in the process (Chang, 1999; Vartiainen, 1999). But we must also locate particular forms of state action in "time and place" and, more specifically, within particular social conditions, political institutions, and discourses and patterns of international hegemony. The developmental state is likely to emerge in different guises under varying *sociopolitical conditions* at different times and places. The emergence of the Northern European social democracies, the temporary success of Brazil in building "dependent development," the "East Asian miracle," and the emergence of fast-growing economies such as Israel, Ireland, and even Taiwan in the 1990s can all plausibly be seen as examples of different types of developmental states. This, therefore, suggests a reorienting of our perspective on developmental states toward an understanding of the social, political, and world-historical conditions under which particular forms of "the" developmental state emerge and change.

In addition to this analysis of external conditions of particular forms of statehood, we need concepts that can provide insight into particular forms of *state structure* and the variety of ways in which state and society become fused and shape one another historically. Evans's (1995) analysis of the importance of Weberian bureaucracy is an important step in the revival within state theory of a tradition of organizational sociology, which itself began with Weber but has advanced well beyond him. At the very least, the issues of the boundaries between public and private, centralization and decentralization, and multiple "patterns of bureaucracy" within developmental states cry out for sustained organizational analysis (Perrow, 1986).

Finally, each incarnation of state developmentalism will have a particular *spatial form* (Brenner, 1998, 1999). World systems and world-cultural analyses posit a secular trend toward a movement of the scale of social action "up" towards global markets and global political institutions. Castells (1997), however, argued that globalization produces a pooling of economic sovereignty between institutions and across levels of governance, reconfiguring the state's relation to the local and the global.

This "networked polity" consists of the "intermeshing of overlapping [policy] networks operating simultaneously in multiple functional areas and at multiple geographical scales." (Ansell, 2000, p. 35)

Ansell pointed to the possibilities that this presents for local interests to empower themselves by bypassing the national state and appealing to the transnational bodies. Sassen (1997, 1998), on the other hand, pointed to the privatization of transnational economic governance with a rapid growth in bodies such as private commercial arbitrators that compete with public corporate regulation. Once again, globalization is seen as an uncertain process: presenting opportunities for those excluded from national power structures, even while freeing capital from public regulation.

The glocal state aims to promote capital accumulation by linking the local to the global and creating a location ideal for accumulation within a global set of connections (Brenner, 1998, 1999). The organizational structure and strategy of the glocal states are only now beginning to be explored. Increasingly constituted as a glocal network, the state relies less on its claim to legitimate encompassing authority (although this claim can never be neglected or "stateness" is forfeited) than on its organizational capacities. The organizational capacities can be mobilized through a wide range of organization structures and strategies; there is no reason why a state must be bureaucratic rather than networked, for example.

States play critical roles in capitalist economic development by providing certain universal elements of vision, coordination, and conflict management – often, though not always, solving problems for capitalists that they cannot solve themselves. However, important differences arise in how these universal elements become institutionalized in certain organizational cultures and structures and spatialized in specific ways, under particular domestic political and world-historical conditions. The perspective outlined herein insists that if the state is embedded in capitalist social relations, capitalist social relations are themselves politically embedded. Every moment of state regulation in capitalist social relations presents possibilities of both domination and transformation. Developmental statism is particularly critical politically and analytically because such regimes walk a thin line between neoliberalism (due to their development of increasingly capitalist social relations) and the expansion of social rights (due to the role of the state in social reproduction and the creation of new social actors alongside capital). State developmentalism creates not only new economic contested terrains but also new political arenas of struggle within the state itself.

The next section examines how these dynamics play out in the typical dilemmas of semiperipheral development: forging a collective strategy for development despite inequalities and hierarchy in the international economy, building institutions to pursue that strategy, and fostering self-reproducing autocentric development through shaping the relationship between the developmentalist coalition and the national and world-system structures within which it is embedded. These dilemmas then serve as the basis for the dimensions along which we can distinguish between cases of bureaucratic and network-state developmentalism.

SEMIPERIPHERAL DEVELOPMENT AFTER THE "DEVELOPMENT PROJECT"

Capitalist development is the exception, not the rule. Indeed, as the capitalist world system has expanded and deepened, inequality and peripheralization have increased (Amsden, 2001; Freeman, 2002; Senghaas, 1985). As Senghaas stated,

"In view of the development history of the past 250 to 500 years . . . it would seem more sensible to regard peripheralization as the norm and successful development as the exception." (1985, p.16)

In the "Third World," income per capita ~~almost~~ barely doubled between 1750 and 1977, whereas it increased sixty times over in "developed countries" (Freeman, 2002, p.192). Even in the era of development after World War II, Amsden identified only twelve economies as "the rest" that came to challenge "the West" industrially – a much larger number fell farther behind as the "remainder" (Amsden, 2001).

The task of capitalist development becomes ever more difficult as the technological sophistication and commercial power of the core countries expand. Competition from the leading economies undermines local industry and weakens institutions and motivations in less-developed countries (Senghaas, 1985, p.15). Dependency theorists have argued that connecting to the core economies through foreign investment will generate short-term growth spurts but will not contribute to long-term development of the local economy for various reasons: the low levels of linkages between Transnational Corporations (TNCs) and the local economy, the repatriation of capital and decapitalization of the local economy, and the disarticulation of the local economy between an advanced foreign-dominated sector and a backward indigenous sector (Dixon and Boswell, 1996a,b; O'Hearn, 1989, 1998).

Nonetheless, some economies have been able to move up the hierarchy of the international division of labor and increase national income levels. For the purposes of this book, this will be our primary definition of *development*. Although the discussion relates this analysis of capital accumulation and growth to broader social inequalities and patterns of social development, these issues are kept separate analytically in order to analyze how economic and social outcomes relate to one another and are politically shaped. Capital accumulation has been a necessary but hardly sufficient condition for social progress in capitalist economies. The emergence of global regions as a critical location for the organization of capital accumulation – and the role of particular forms of state action in shaping them – offers a new terrain for development struggles, not necessarily a panacea for global ills.

The experience of semiperipheral economies is a critically important location for examining the shifting terrain of the global economy, with its constraints and possibilities. Although the definition of *semiperipheral* is notoriously controversial, it typically refers to national economies that have relatively high levels of dependency on core economies but that are involved in unequal relations with dependent *peripheral* economies. There are numerous difficulties with such a definition, particularly with the organization of the world economy into "national" economies. In a world where national economies are composed of transnational production networks, a national economy may be composed of various core, semiperipheral, and peripheral locations in different production networks. Semiperipheral economies become, then, those national economies that have managed to stake out intermediate positions in a variety of transnational production networks.

We can look for possible strategies for development; not a ready-made model to replace that of the postwar "Development Project" but rather a set of mechanisms that provide insight into what entails putting together a "developmental coalition" under contemporary conditions. Because societies are reluctant to wait for system change before pursuing improved social welfare, this is a crucial issue. In semiperipheral economies, there also are significant insights into the character of the changing capitalist world system itself, for it is often at the boundaries where inclusion and exclusion are contested that the tensions at the heart of any social system are made most lucid. Finally, and for much the same reason, it is in the social groups and social struggles in such semiperipheral economies where new forces for systemic change and the most creative strategic and institutional innovations are likely to be found.

Ireland is best seen as a high-income semiperipheral economy; in fact, despite its relatively high per-capita income and liberal democratic institutions, its economy has a highly dependent, even peripheral character (Peillon, 1994; Van Rossem, 1997). Attempts to manage the economy through the mechanisms available to other higher income countries have foundered historically on the underdevelopment of indigenous business, mass emigration, and remarkably high levels of imports and exports. Many commentators have remarked on the need for a stronger indigenous industrial base, even as they struggled to develop strategies for doing so within a liberal democratic political regime. But if Ireland is an unusual case, it will be all the more interesting for that. What development has occurred in Ireland has been built from deep within global financial, trade, and migration flows. The Irish combination of clientelism, formal democracy, and external investment and trade is found ever more frequently around the globe. Although Irish state institutions are well developed and stable, recent development has occurred within a negotiated, liberal democratic system unlike the more authoritarian regimes typical of the early and middle stages of industrialization in "the rest" (Amsden, 2001). There is some promise, then, in the Irish case, although this book should not be read as offering the Celtic Tiger experience as a model of development to be followed in its entirety. Rather, the Celtic Tiger is analyzed for the lessons that can be learned for semiperipheral developmental strategies, institution-building, and social and political transformation from within a globalizing capitalist world economy. The remainder of this section considers three major types of dilemmas for such semiperipheral development.

Collective developmental strategies

Capitalist development in the face of the obstacles presented by an exploitative global economy depends on collectively coordinated strategies for the transformation of interests (Evans, 1995; Hirschman, 1958) through learning (Gerschenkron, 1962; Sabel, 1994) in the face of unequal competition (Senghaas, 1985). Late industrializing economies face significant barriers to entry into existing markets and industries as they attempt to compete with political economies with greater financial, organizational, and institutional resources (O'Malley, 1989). Even in new industries such as ICTs, entry barriers are daunting. Ernst and O'Connor (1992, p. 24) summarize the results of their comprehensive investigation into the experience of late industrializing economies in the electronics industry in the 1980s:

"Technological change and changes in demand continuously create new products and markets and thus new entry possibilities. Yet, it would be misleading to claim that oligopolistic control has been weakened decisively. Entry barriers have declined for a number of product groups and segments. Simultaneously, however, they have increased in particular for those stages of the 'value chain' which today are of crucial importance for competitive success."

In such a situation, late industrializing economies feel compelled to participate in industries such as electronics but are unlikely to leave their fate in such emerging industries to market forces. Indeed, the most successful late industrializers relied heavily on state intervention in their attempts to industrialize (Amsden, 2001; Evans, 1995; Woo-Cumings, 1999).

Developmental states achieve their goals in the contemporary era not by taking on the tasks of development but rather by shaping the capabilities of society and the market to do so. Researchers have moved from an emphasis on an authoritarian directive style of state intervention to an understanding of how the state pokes and prods domestic firms to compete in the global economy and to constantly upgrade their organizational and technical capabilities to that end. The state assists in the birth and growth of domestic, national firms through its roles as "midwife" of new firms and sectors and by tending to the "husbandry" of those growing industries (Evans, 1995).

However, the tasks of a "conspiracy for development" (Hirschman, 1958) go much deeper. Emerging firms not only need resources but also must often be prodded to reconceptualize their own commercial interests. In a situation with significant barriers to entry, the clearest self-interest of those social actors with resources will often lie in exploiting "easy," local opportunities – using those resources to capture local markets, sustain patronage, or pursue "low-value-added" niches in the global economy. The pursuit of private interests through the market will just as easily lead to underdevelopment as to development. The shaping of private interests becomes a critical part of the development project (Evans, 1995, 1997). As much recent research has shown, the interest and capacity to pursue technological entrepreneurship and development are profoundly shaped by the many and varied institutions of the "system of innovation" within which market actors are embedded (Lundvall et al., 2002; Nelson, 1993; Perez, 2002).

Institutions of developmentalism

Onerous as these strategic demands may be, the development poses further challenges. To build such collective strategies of development, the institutions that make the economic strategy possible must also come into existence. Developmental states are still the most likely candidate for boosting an economy beyond the narrow logic of private investment, thereby improving its position in the international division of labor. The state cannot achieve these ends in isolation but, in fact, depends on its relation to society for its success. In particular, developmental states are characterized by what Evans calls *embedded autonomy*. Such states are embedded in local capital through the close social ties between state bureaucrats and domestic business owners and managers. However, effective developmental state apparatuses retain their autonomy due to the presence of a classic Weberian bureaucracy, based on meritocratic recruitment and promotion and norms of objective, procedural rationality. Whereas embeddedness allows the state to gather information and mobilize resources, autonomy (safeguarded by bureaucracy) guarantees that national developmental goals remain central to state action (Evans, 1995; Evans and Rauch, 1999; Schneider, 1997).

Developmental states avoid the potentially disastrous predatory relationship between the state and the market or society (Evans, 1995). In such cases, individuals and agencies within the state treat their state power as a resource to be used to plunder resources generated by the market or within society. However, developmental states are typically exclusionary: although an educated labor force organized for learning is critical, labor is typically excluded from the key institutions of the developmental state (Amsden, 1989; Deyo, 1989).

Structures of autocentric development

Industrialization and building institutions of innovation to support it are only the beginning of a project of *autocentric development* that can generate self-reproducing dynamics and an ever broader developmental effect. The dynamic of industrial change interacts with three other major factors: the tensions around the reproduction of the sociopolitical coalition supporting development; the "feedback loop" between the social structural effects of industrial change and industrialization; and, finally, the reaction of other actors in the world system to the opportunities and challenges that "successful development" poses to them. When industrial development is embedded within and reproduces those surrounding social structures in such a way that they contribute to a constant deepening of industrial and innovative capabilities, the result is a process of autocentric development.

I have argued that any successful strategy of industrial change will be embedded in a broader set of developmental institutions and this, in turn, will be underpinned by a political coalition. However, this coalition and the institutions that it supports will be affected by the success of industrial change: the balance of power will shift within the coalition itself (Evans, 1995; Herring, 1999). The interests of certain parties in the coalition will change as they come to rely less on state support, for example, and as they forge new relationships with actors outside the developmental coalition (Evans, 1995). Such a fracturing of developmental coalitions is evident in the dismantling of its own successful state developmental institutions by South Korea in the early 1990s and in the growing conflicts over neocorporatist arrangements in Ireland after a decade of steady growth.

Industrial change is also unlikely to sustain itself for long without self-reinforcing dynamics in the broader social structures within which it is embedded, which Senghaas (1985) refers to as *autocentric development*. This concept will be investigated in more detail, but it implies that industrial change is accompanied by a broader set of transformations: the development of productive forces in all important spheres and sectors; the growing capacity for independent self-control and autonomous political, social, and cultural development; and the broad development of skills and learning capacity (Senghaas, 1985, p. 227). In particular, domestic demand becomes a crucial element in facilitating development, as domestic production and consumption facilitate autocentric development and selective and strategic engagement with external actors (Figure 2.1). As Mjoset (1992) points out, Senghaas's approach is consistent with the model of National Fordist accumulation that characterized the postwar Golden Age in the advanced capitalist countries. It is critical, however, to be able to use the concept of autocentric development outside of the context of the National Fordist historical compromise; therefore, this chapter and the next advance an account of how the basic dynamics of autocentric development might be reconceptualized for an era of global Post-Fordist accumulation.

Finally, the dynamics of industrial change in local or national economies intersect with the dynamics of the world system. The emergence of significant new locations of capital accumulation and new economic actors will pose threats and opportunities to powerful actors in the world system. The emergence of strong indigenous industry in a new location is likely to attract foreign investment, posing the peril of ongoing dependence as well as the opportunity of new resources and networks (Harrison, 1994). Existing actors will defend their perceived interests: Ernst and O'Connor (1992, p. 45) pointed to the widespread entry-deterrence

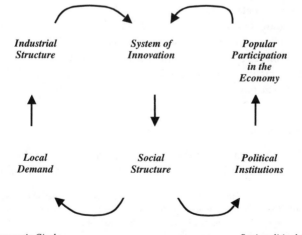

Industrial Structure	System of Innovation	Popular Participation in the Economy
Local Demand	Social Structure	Political Institutions

Socioeconomic Circle   *Sociopolitical Circle*

Figure 2.1. Stylized Version of Senghaas/Mjoset Model of Autocentric Development

strategies used by lead firms and countries in electronics in the 1980s in the face of the challenge from newly industrializing countries. Ultimately, they concluded,

"In the final analysis, latecomers can only succeed if they can postpone as long as possible any frontal conflict with the industry leader(s)."

Finding niches where they can avoid these confrontations will be much easier for smaller countries such as Ireland, but their impact on the overall shape of the world system will be much less than, for example, the emergence of China as a major world economic power. The global region typically brings together a variety of such niches within global networks – in a context of dense institutional and associational supports – as a strategy for managing such world-system pressures. Managing the effects of a global region accumulation strategy on developmental coalitions is a final challenge for contemporary developmental strategies.

DEVELOPMENTAL BUREAUCRATIC AND NETWORK STATES

A set of economies emerged that has grown rapidly throughout the 1990s and whose experience gives us reason to rethink some of the most critical dimensions of the accepted analysis of the developmental state (which has been based primarily on the Asian Tigers). This section develops a detailed conceptual analysis of DNSs, typified by economies such as those of Ireland and Israel, and of DBSs, typified by Japan and South Korea. Each represents a different organizational structure and spatialization of the state and is inserted differently into the world economy. This in itself does not represent a reformulation of the "theory of the developmental state." The DBS–DNS distinction developed herein allows for the identification of different clusters of cases of developmental states and, for the most part, treats literature on the DBS as a valuable contribution to understanding those particular kinds of developmental states.

In the remainder of this chapter, the DBS–DNS distinction is developed through an analysis of the contemporary challenges faced by DBS regimes along each dimension outlined previously: development strategy, institutions, and autocentric development structures. The typical form taken by the DBS and DNS is contrasted along each dimension.[1]

Developmental strategies: the challenge of the global region

The most influential studies of the role of the state in development have analyzed the success of the Asian Tiger economies such as Japan and South Korea. Through

---

1   In previous writings (Ó Riain, 2000a, 2000c), I have characterized the DNS as a flexible developmental state. The DNS terminology is preferable for two reasons: (1) the term *flexible* was open to too many interpretations, particularly because it has been central to a number of bitter debates in critical political economy and is a favorite battle cry of neoliberals; and (2) there is a greater symmetry to the terms *network* and *bureaucratic* because both refer to structural features of organizations rather than properties of those structures.

policies such as the selective and strategic use of protectionism, the provision of industrial subsidies and programs tied to performance, and the creation of close ties between financial capital, industrial capital, and the state, economies such as Japan, South Korea, and Taiwan were able to industrialize rapidly based on improved productivity in manufacturing and "industrialization by learning" (Amsden, 1989).

In DBS regimes, state intervention in the economy focused on the creation of new domestic capabilities that could then be brought to bear in global markets. The global economy was held at bay for strategic periods and was constructed as a context in which states and national capitals can compete. However, under the globalization project, transnational firms, networks and flows of money, information, and resources have deeply penetrated the most successful localities and nations – the global is no longer a context for developmental strategies but rather a constitutive element of them.

However, we also see tendencies toward the localization of production and innovation. Certain regions have been able to develop a sustainable economic base from close cooperation and intense local learning based on relations of trust built up through repeated face-to-face interactions (Castells and Hall, 1994; Piore and Sabel, 1984; Porter, 1990; Saxenian, 1994; Storper, 1992, 1997). Although the output of "informational goods" (e.g., software packages, books and magazines, videos) are highly portable around the world, the conditions of effective innovation and design of such "information-intensive" goods (i.e., their inputs) are fundamentally territorial.

The literature on territorial economies provides several reasons why regional production systems are fundamental elements of globalization. Significant cost economies result from the agglomeration of firms and industries in a specific region as traded and untraded interdependencies develop between employers, workers, and regional institutions (Saxenian, 1994; Storper and Walker, 1989).

"In very general terms, territorial complexes not only lower tangible costs of transport and communication, but ease information-sharing, allow pooling of labor and fixed capital, stabilize physical and social relations, help people identify with each other (and against outside competitors), and generate distinct cultural practices over time." (Storper and Walker, 1989, p. 139)

Localities, therefore, can develop significant sources of competitive advantage and cost economies based precisely on the fact that they are "local." There are three main sources of "regional advantage": the availability of a pool of skilled labor, the creation of a subsupply infrastructure organized largely through "traded dependencies" between local firms, and the creation of "technological spillovers" within an "innovative milieu" based on "relational assets" shared by local actors[2]

2 Storper (1997) distinguishes between dependencies between firms that are "traded" (i.e., consciously included in the cost–benefit calculus of market exchanges) and those that are "untraded" and may be "relational assets" to a firm or region. The relational assets consist of resources that are generated through the social relationships between economic actors, which are part of the fabric of local economic life and are not included in the market-exchange calculus. Similar concepts underlie

(Storper, 1997). Each dimension represents a deepening of local advantage because local cultures of innovation are more difficult to re-create elsewhere than subsupply infrastructure, which is, in turn, more difficult to create than a skilled labor pool. Too often, global and local perspectives have been considered contradictory when they represent two sides of the same coin; that is, the emergence of a 'flexible' global capitalism that is organized through a lucky few highly concentrated regions. These global regions are central nodes for the organization of capital accumulation in globalizing capitalism – functioning as locations for the production of learning, control, and competition (Brenner, 1998; Dicken et al., 1994; Ó Riain, 1997; Sassen, 1990). On the other hand, although local relations are crucial to generating the knowledge for effective production and innovation, gaining access to production technologies and opportunities as well as to technical standards and communities will require integration into "global commodity chains" (Gereffi, 1994) and international technology alliances dominated by large firms (Ernst and O'Connor, 1992; Harrison, 1994).

There is, therefore, a functional interdependence between processes of localization and globalization, what Brenner calls "glocalization" (Brenner, 1998). Furthermore, this interdependence is a dynamic relationship as successive rounds of internationalization and localization restructure industries in specific places. New locations emerge to challenge existing territorial concentrations, new rounds of investment are embedded in the local economy, new organizational ties may disrupt or reinforce existing networks, and so on. Internationalization and localization exist in an historical as well as a functional relationship to one another (Ó Riain, 1997).

The relationship between global and local is political. Political coalitions to promote specific development strategies, and state actions in particular, shape how local and global networks articulate with one another. State action becomes a central factor shaping local capacities but also in shaping how those local capacities are realized within global technology, production, and marketing networks. The developmental state therefore, is increasingly cast in a role mediating between the global and the local, connecting them and shaping the nature of their relationship. The state also may be involved in creating the very actors that it hopes will participate in those global–local connections and the development project more generally.

These patterns support the findings of an extensive body of research that has now shown the importance of "systems of innovation" for supporting technological innovation. The systems of innovation, at least as articulated by the European version of the school, go well beyond simple policies to promote the commercialization of scientific research (Lundvall et al., 2002). Innovation and learning are profoundly interactive processes – occurring in communities of scientists, technologists, and users – and shaped by much broader economic, social, and cultural structures (Lundvall et al., 2002; Nelson, 1993; Perez, 2002). Although these systems

Krugman's recent work in geographical economics, although he is reluctant to analyze relational assets, avoiding the major development issues in the interests of mathematical rigor (Krugman, 1992; Martin and Sunley, 1996).

of innovation have typically been conceived of as "national" and analysis has focused on advanced capitalist countries, more recent research has extended the paradigm. Freeman (2002) shows that the rising economies in modern world history – that is, Britain, the United States, and the newly industrializing countries – were able to blend subnational and continental elements with their national institutions to forge effective systems of innovation. New research has also shown the importance of national innovation systems in shaping the development trajectories of newly industrializing countries (Freeman, 2002; Hobday, 1995; Kim and Nelson, 2000; Lundvall et al., 2002). The integration of local, national, and global structures of innovation into a system that can support effective participation in the new techno-economic paradigm of ICT is, therefore, central to network development. Central to this project is a DNS that is the most likely candidate to take on a lead role in implementing the integration of institutions across multiple scales of organization and governance. How this integration occurs, where the lines of inclusion and exclusion are drawn, and the form of power relations within these networks will shape the patterns of stratification and inequality that emerge in such patterns of development.

In DNS regimes, the institutional framework of the region – its associations, educational institutions, support industries, and state agencies and policies – play an ongoing role in shaping the high-tech region. States are particularly crucial in contexts where high-tech regions are built from a relatively low position in the international division of labor. Indeed, state policies and practices have been important in shaping high-tech growth in India, Israel, and Ireland. By educating labor, defining industries through incentives, building connections to emigrant professionals, sponsoring or supporting industry and other associations, priming venture-capital funds, and working directly with firms to develop their capacities and build their ties to other firms, states have been central to the emergence of regional innovation. Whether or not they thought of it in those terms, state officials have – in certain times and places – reshaped the "relational assets" that are so important to regional dynamism. Where it has been more difficult to develop such regionally based assets or to build indigenous innovation around them, such as in India, it is partly due to the lack of an active state role in pushing firms to innovate, strengthening local institutions and users, and ensuring a flow of capital into the industry. India has had the greatest difficulty in moving up the technology chains of the global production system. Trapped for a long time in long-distance labor contracting, India's high-tech regions are increasingly becoming "remote development centers" with close organizational connections to the United States in particular.

Although the state has been active in those countries in promoting high technology, it has done so in ways that are often quite different from the developmental states of Japan and Korea. The Irish and Israeli states in particular are more likely to stimulate venture-capital investment, create a range of innovation centers, provide R&D funding, and foster international networks than to try and directly influence firms' business decisions (Autler, 1999; Ó Riain, 2000a). Although the DBS also promoted the creation of economic actors, it focused on hierarchical business groups as "national champions" instead of the transnationally integrated local networks promoted by the DNS.

Institutions: developmentalism and the network state

These multiple connections to the local and global suggest that the social and institutional foundations of the DNS are quite different from those of the DBS. State–society relations in DBS regimes are channeled primarily through ties between key state bureaucrats and domestic entrepreneurs and executives. The state, however, may be embedded in numerous other social groups and shaped by its multiple "embedded autonomies." The DNS is based on a multiple embeddedness in local and foreign capital and local – particularly professional – networks of innovation.

The organizational structure of the DNS consists of a range of embedded autonomies of the state, linking the organizational cultures and capacities of specific state agencies to particular social groups. State agencies have significant internal flexibility in dealings with their constituencies. The state structure is also characterized by a high degree of flexibility in the relationship between the units of the state apparatus, partially diffusing the significant conflict that remains. Rather than a cohesive and relatively insulated national state apparatus, the DNS consists of a state apparatus that is deeply embedded in a "network polity," forging sociopolitical alliances out of constantly shifting local, national, and global components (Ansell, 2000).

Furthermore, coherent state bureaucracies are not the only organizational structures that may promote embedded autonomy. Embedded autonomy in the DNS is not guaranteed by a coherent bureaucracy but rather by the flexibility of the state structure. Whereas the DBS has a "tightly coupled" organizational structure, the DNS is built around a "loosely coupled" organizational model (Orton and Weick, 1990; Perrow, 1986, Chap. 4). The decentralization of state agencies enables them to become deeply embedded in their clients and constituencies, despite the fact that they are often dealing with a wide range of individuals and organizations across widely dispersed networks. However, the agencies also retain a certain autonomy because they are held accountable by the setting of performance requirements, constant informal monitoring by their social constituencies, and formal evaluations (typically carried out by external consultants, often published, with relatively easy availability). The internal accountability of Weberian bureaucracy is supplemented by the external accountability of particular units to performance criteria.

Figure 2.2 illustrates the primary institutional dilemmas for those who might build a developmental state, illustrated along two dimensions of organization-building. The first is the balance between embeddedness and autonomy; the second refers to the extent to which developmental states, even when characterized by

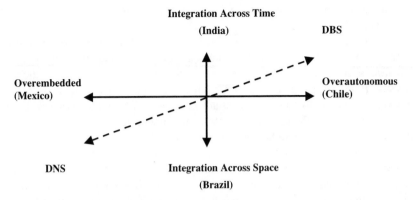

Figure 2.2. Dilemmas of Institution-Building in Developmental States

embedded autonomy, can maintain that institutional integration – both over time in the face of economic and political change and over space in the face of national fragmentation and conflict.

Turning to the dilemmas of embeddedness and autonomy, a balance of embedded autonomy is not easy to construct – most polities are overembedded and racked by clientelism, arbitrary personalism, and even corruption. State-building exercises, however, can often veer in the other direction, toward an overautonomous state that may be able to develop cohesive policies and even implement them in the public sector, but which cannot mobilize the private sector to support those developmental projects.

Overembeddedness is endemic to Latin American states such as Brazil and Mexico, where an appointive bureaucracy generates a political capitalism in which success and failure depend as much on effective political action as effective production; this in turn is reinforced by the need to be involved in politics to be effective in business (Ross-Schneider, 1999, p. 296). Such a description bears more than a passing resemblance to the contemporary U.S. polity.

Despite the emphasis among state theorists on state autonomy, overautonomy can also be a problem – with perhaps the classic examples being the state socialist economies of Eastern Europe. Chile is a particularly chilling case of overautonomy. After the U.S.–backed overthrow of Allende in 1973, a military dictatorship under Pinochet crushed opposition and implemented a radical neoliberal program. The neoclassical economist "Chicago boys" were put in charge of the economy in 1975 and were highly insulated from business – and even from the technocracy (Silva, 1997). Unable to convince business to cooperate, their program generally failed to produce investment and a short boom collapsed in crisis in 1982 – a crisis made worse by the rigidity of Chilean institutions at the time (Silva, 1997). It is only since the turn toward greater embeddedness (under pragmatic neoliberalism in the 1980s and democratization in the 1990s) that industrial development has occurred, based on a more networked policy regime, state developmentalism within a context of neoliberalism, and associational cooperation and learning (Perez-Aleman, 2000; Sherman, 1996; Silva, 1997).

The second dimension of Figure 2.2 refers to the ability of developmental states to integrate institutionally over time and space. Brazilian state developmentalism has flourished at times, despite the overembeddedness of elements of the state (Evans, 1995; Ross-Schneider, 1999). There are "pockets of bureaucracy" that have contributed to the success of certain subsectors of Brazilian industry (Evans, 1995; Schmitz and Hewitt, 1992). Cassiolato, Hewitt, and Schmitz (1992) argue that since the 1982–83 debt crisis, Brazil has not had an industrial policy and never replaced the dismantled market reserve. This leads to policy conflicts such as between the free-trade zone for consumer electronics at Manaus, where inputs could be imported duty-free, and the attempts to grow a domestic semiconductor industry that would have needed to sell primarily to those same firms at Manaus. They argue that by the 1980s, a platform had been built up from which new sectoral strategies could be pursued in the 1990s, but that the overall national institutional capacity to do this was being undermined by liberalization. There are sectors that prove successful, such as financial automation (Cassiolato, 1992; Evans, 1995); however, the overall context is one in which the state is embroiled in crisis management, has no overall strategic approach to industrial policy, and is politically vulnerable (Cassiolato, Hewitt, and Schmitz, 1992).

Parthasarathy (2000) argues that India faces a quite different problem: a lurching between embeddedness and autonomy and a failure to integrate the developmental state across time. This is seen most clearly in India's shifting relationship to liberalization. The Indian state grew in power through the 1970s, even bargaining effectively with a number of TNCs (Grieco, 1984; Heeks, 1996). An initial liberalization in 1984 loosened import controls but was incoherent and resulted in a backlash from business sitting between a relatively incoherent set of export promotion measures and varying levels of import controls. Rajiv Gandhi's temporary state autonomy in 1984, based on his mother's assassination, along with growing foreign influence and the interests of the industry itself combined to push liberalization. However, in the late 1980s, industrial development was shifted off the agenda by political considerations and the push from within the state for liberalization was weakened (Heeks, 1996, p. 329). The year 1990 brought renewed liberalization and export promotion by the state, lifting import controls as foreign firms pushed for import liberalization,

"using their willingness to assist exports from India as a lever to allow more exports to India of their own products" (Heeks, 1996, p. 332)

More important were the demands of the International Monetary Fund (IMF), which India couldn't resist due to its indebtedness and need for IMF money. Eventually, in the 1990s, a coalition of industrialists, foreign firms, foreign agencies, and bureaucrats formed behind liberalization. However, a cohesive set of institutions that might support effective industrial development within a neoliberal context was still only in its infancy (Parthasarathy, 2000).

Finally, Figure 2.2 suggests that the characteristic problems of the DNS and DBS are different: the DNS faces the dilemmas of becoming overembedded or fragmented, whereas the DBS faces dilemmas of overautonomy or rapid changes in orientation based on who can capture the powerful state apparatus. The flexibility and loose coupling of DNS institutions creates characteristic problems of organizational cohesion and political control, with the possibility of loose networks fragmenting into sectional coalitions or personal favors. An effective DNS depends on a strong element of centralized coordination for the overall integration of its decentralized networks. The cohesiveness of DBS institutions presents a vary different set of problems because the institutions may become insulated and isolated while also vulnerable to sharp changes of direction if captured by one section of the political economy. The DBS also depends on a surrounding network of institutions and ties to support its own ability to pursue a coherent policy.

Therefore, the institutional demands of developmental statism are daunting. The political demands of state-building may ultimately be as problematic for developmental coalitions as the very constraints of the global economy that demand the building of such impressive institutions. The neoliberal project of creating rules for global markets extends the reach of capitalism but simultaneously undermines the institutional conditions that secure the development of capitalist social relations. Essential as effective developmentalist institutions are to capitalism, they emerge only occasionally and with great difficulty.

Autocentric Development: from National Fordism to Global Post-Fordism

Contrary to neoclassical emphases on international competitiveness, industrial change cannot become the basis of a virtuous development circle without some self-reinforcing dynamics within the broader social structures within which it is embedded. Senghaas (1985) argued that "autocentric development" occurs when industrial change is accompanied by a broader set of transformations – the development of productive forces in all important spheres and sectors; the growing capacity for independent self-control and autonomous political, social, and cultural development; and the broad development of skills and learning capacity (Senghaas, 1985, p. 227).

The concept of autocentric development is a crucial one and exposes the limits of the neoclassical emphasis on competitiveness as the condition of development. However, Senghaas's concept is limited by its application to a particular era of capitalist organization: an era of National Fordism (Mjoset, 1992), underpinned on the one hand by an international regime of "embedded liberalism" – which sustained national economies – and a social structure based on mass production, mass consumption, and, ultimately, underpinned by the patriarchal family. Each of these conditions has been eroded, posing the question of what autocentric development might look like in an era of Global Post-Fordism.

McMichael (1996) argued that the postwar era was dominated by a concept of international economic development that emphasized many of the features of Senghaas's autocentric development: the creation of a dynamic of autonomous national development based on a broad range of sectors and a coherent national economy. This development project was also consistent with an international order of embedded liberalism, institutionalized internationally after World War II and underpinning stable national economies (Ruggie, 1982). These economies were tied together through a negotiated regime of multilateral trade but buffered from the full effects of the international markets by institutions limiting trade and capital flows. A diversity of national models of state–market interaction co-existed uneasily within these institutions, even as international markets gradually expanded in scope. Although embedded liberalism only extended to the industrialized capitalist countries, its institutions also shaped the relationships between those countries and peripheral states and created the conditions in the core for the development project.

The compromises of embedded liberalism and the development project have been challenged by the growing hegemony of the globalization project (McMichael, 1996). World trade has expanded rapidly as a proportion of world income since at least the 1970s. More significant since the 1980s the value of world trade has been surpassed by the value of internal transnational corporate transactions as transnational industrial capital has become increasingly globalized (Held et al., 1999; Ruggie, 1995). Both are dwarfed by the enormous volume of international financial transactions, affecting both governments' ability to control their own fiscal and monetary policy and making much more significant the market for corporate governance.

Furthermore, the intensified patterns of globalization are accompanied by major transformations in social structure particularly around gender relations and family structures, and in social organization, particularly the decentralization of bureaucratic organizations and the application of the new ITs. Social structural change was critical to Senghaas's concept of autocentric development because the emergence of a class structure based on mass production and mass consumption provided a homogeneous class basis for a national economy. Furthermore, the unpaid labor of women in the patriarchal family underpinned this relatively egalitarian labor-market structure of Fordism – gender inequality masked by relative class equality.

In recent decades, the conditions underpinning this social structure of Fordism have been eroded. Occupational change has transformed the class structure, with a rapidly declining manufacturing working class being replaced by a highly polarized expansion of both well-paid professional jobs and poorly paid service occupations. Just as significant as the impact of globalization has been the emergence of a Post-Fordist production and consumption system, deeply fragmenting the class structure (Castells, 1997) and the structure of demand (Piore and Sabel, 1984). The paid labor force has been increasingly feminized, transforming the worlds of both production and social reproduction. The gender inequality hidden in the family under Fordism has been brought firmly into the market under Post-Fordism. Furthermore, the multiplier effects of industrial development and expanding employment under these conditions result not only in growing mass consumption but also in highly exploitative markets for personal services. Consequently, within- and between-country inequality has increased rapidly (Korzeniewicz and Moran, 1997).

The multiplier effects of Post-Fordist accumulation are neither contained within national borders nor egalitarian as those of National Fordism were. Although there are still autocentric processes of intersectoral learning, market expansion, and political coalition-building under Post-Fordist development, these processes operate glocally and often have highly unequal local effects. Unable to "free-ride" on the structural advantages provided by relatively bounded national societies and economies, national political actors face persistent dilemmas of fragmentation and inequality. Unions everywhere have struggled to develop new models of organizing and organization to tackle these pressures, and their difficulties in doing so have been a major reason for increasing income inequality (Lopez, 2003). States, too, have scrambled to develop new strategies, as the fragmentation of national societies and economies has made politics more rather than less crucial to the construction of egalitarian development. States are now faced with politicized issues of social and system integration that were once embedded in the established relations of national societies.

In the classic DBSs of South Korea and Japan, the state's power to influence increasingly powerful and internationalized firms declined as these firms turned more frequently to international financial speculation and accumulation. The *chaebol* and *keiretsu* had become disembedded from the national developmental coalition, using the very financial resources built up by that regime to disembed themselves from it (Chibber, 2002; Gao, 2001; Wade and Veneroso, 1998). The balance of class and state forces that had enabled the paradigmatic developmental bureaucratic state to emerge in the 1960s in South Korea and had sustained the rapid growth in the following three decades was now being undermined by the clash between its own institutions and the opportunities for disembedding offered to large corporations by the increasingly globalized and speculative world economy. South Korea remained one of the fastest growing economies in the world at the end of the 1990s, even after the disasters of 1997–98, but a deep ambiguity shrouded the developmental statism that had once presented a sure façade to the world economy (Chibber, 2002).

Network-state structures have emerged in response to this fragmentation of social relations (Castells and Carnoy, 2002). Network states may be better able to diffuse tensions between partly conflicting agendas within the state itself – their task is not to disorganize resistance (already accomplished by the fragmentation of social relations) but rather to coordinate collective action (Castells and Carnoy, 2002).

Does the DNS, therefore, present a solution to the dilemmas of developmental states in an era of globalization, the third dimension of the theory of the developmental state? There are no such easy answers because the DNS is itself threatened by its own limitations. The DNS's organizational strength is its ability to connect networked and fragmented labor to networks of international capital. This internationalization of capital does not necessarily undermine local accumulation, however, as territorialized innovation and production networks form a glocal circuit of autocentric development. However, this process does result in an uneven and unequal internationalization of society because some sections of labor connect to the global directly whereas others are left largely servicing those groups' local needs (Sassen, 1990). Spiraling national and international inequality, even as local accumulation proceeds apace, becomes the dilemma of the DNS developmental model. This in turn creates political dilemmas for the DNS because the flexibility that enables the state to connect local and global in various ways becomes a liability. The flip side of this flexibility is the fragmentation of the state, making it all the more difficult for the state to sustain a national developmental coalition around those uneven and unequal local–global connections.

CONCLUSION

Many contemporary authors draw on the insights of Karl Polanyi to develop their critiques of globalization. Heterodox economists such as Stiglitz draw on Polanyi's notion of the social embeddedness of market action to point to the necessity of building a dense social and institutional foundation for effective markets, whereas critical analysts use Polanyi's notion of a collective mobilization based on the self-protection of society as a source of hope for effective resistance to the same project of building market society. Polanyi can be read in various ways with different political consequences; however, drawing on both strands of Polanyi's theory of the relationship between society and market offers the possibility of a dynamic analysis of the political embeddedness of capitalist social organization (Block, 2002; Burawoy, 2002; Silver and Arrighi, 2002). For if capitalist markets are always and everywhere embedded in broader social and political structures, markets and society remain in a profound tension with one another (Block, 2002). Polanyi's "double movement" of marketization (based on social relationships) and social protection is a terrain of political struggle in global capitalism, not necessarily a single moment of titanic struggle and "great transformation."

Developmental states occupy a particularly strategic position in this politics of the global economy. They are typically central to the most dynamic centers of capital accumulation, innovation, and employment growth. Economically crucial, they are also politically pivotal. Their resolute dedication to capitalist development makes developmental state regimes vulnerable to transformation into neoliberal regimes. However, their extensive state involvement in organizing social relationships and social reproduction creates institutions that can be used in the service of building a "social rights" state (see Block, 1994; and Ó Riain, 2000a, for this terminology). Indeed, both the neoliberal regimes of the United States and the social-rights states of Northern Europe rest on extensive historical periods of state developmentalism.

The approach outlined herein bears many similarities to the "strategic–relational" approach of Jessop (2002) and much recent thinking on the capitalist state has explored the specific forms of "relative autonomy" of the state – as it was conceived in neo-Marxist thought – and its "embedded autonomy," – as conceived in neo-Weberian analyses. The key differences among analyses such as those of Jessop and Evans (1995) rest less on their conceptualization of state structures and strategy than on the degree to which they conceive of the state as subordinate to capitalist logic or able to shape that logic to a significant extent. In this chapter, I have argued for a concept of capitalism as a powerful structuring force but one that is itself politically embedded. Therefore, as widespread as state developmentalism is in the history of capitalism, it has taken different forms under varying domestic and international conditions. It becomes analytically and politically critical, therefore, to understand the specific form of different developmental state regimes.

Table 2.1 summarizes the differences between DBSs and DNSs along each of the three dimensions identified as critical to state developmentalism. First, in DBS regimes, states manage dependency by intervening to create new domestic capabilities to be brought to bear in global markets, by the DNS mediates local and global connections and plays a key role in fostering "better" connections to the global. Although the DBS promoted hierarchical business groups as "national champions," the DNS fosters transnationally integrated local networks.

Secondly, the multiple connections to local and global suggest that the social and institutional foundations of the DNS are quite different from those of the DBS. DBS regimes are characterized by close ties between key state bureaucrats and domestic entrepreneurs and executives, but the DNS is multiply embedded in local and foreign capital and local – particularly professional – networks of

Table 2.1. Developmental Bureaucratic and Network States

	Developmental Bureaucratic State (DBS)	Developmental Network State (DNS)
Collective Development Strategies	Building National Champions by Managing Dependency • Strategic Use of Protectionism • Industrial Subsidies • Domestic Banking System	Building Global Regions by Mediating Global Connections • Building Local Networks Around Global Capital • Taking Local Innovation Networks Global
Institutions of Embedded Autonomy	Coherence of State Bureaucracy • Embedded • Internal Accountability • Tightly Coupled	Flexibility of State Structure • Multiply Embedded • External Accountability • Loosely Coupled
Dilemmas of Global Post-Fordist Development	Internationalization of Capital and Politics of National Control Rigidity of State Bureaucracy	Internationalization of Society and Politics of Inequality Fragmentation of State

innovation. To avoid capture and clientelism, developmental state agencies must retain a measure of autonomy. In DBS regimes, this is secured through a tightly coupled, cohesive Weberian bureaucracy. DNS regimes may be no less bureaucratic but their multiple embeddednesses are monitored through a loosely coupled state structure subject to external evaluations.

Finally, each regime faces particular challenges of Global Post-Fordism. Whereas the national developmental coalition of DBS regimes is fragmented by the integration of capital into international networks of finance and production, this is the starting point of the DNS. Giving up national control, the DNS hopes to substitute local embeddedness in the global region. Ultimately, however, it will face an increasingly contentious politics of national inequality because unequal integration into the globalization project undermines solidaristic national social contracts. The remainder of this book explores the dilemmas of DNS regimes in the Republic of Ireland and elsewhere in the global information economy.

3

EXPLAINING THE CELTIC TIGER

THE ROCKY ROAD: THE VICIOUS CIRCLE
OF UNDERDEVELOPMENT

Contemporary globalization appears to have found Ireland well before it found the rest of the globe. From the late 1950s forward, Ireland pursued an uninterrupted strategy of increasing integration into the global economy – actively pursuing foreign investment and becoming one of the most open economies in the world. Ireland is perhaps not so much a special case as a harbinger of other economies' experience of economic developmental strategy in a world where national restrictions on foreign investment and trade are increasingly difficult to sustain.

Upon (partial) independence from Britain in 1922, the largely agricultural Irish Free State (as it was then known) embarked on a strategy of free trade and fiscal conservatism. The Irish transition to independence was remarkable for the stability of the new state, with the losing party in the Civil War of 1922–23 entering parliament in 1927 and government in 1932. Indeed, this broadly populist party, Fianna Fáil, would dominate Irish politics until the present day, where it remains a major force. Emphasis was administratively placed on continuity with the old bureaucratic system inherited from Britain, with most of the personnel and procedures remaining the same (Breen et al., 1990).

When Fianna Fáil came to power in 1932, its economic ideology of national self-sufficiency dovetailed with international trends toward increasing protection. Through the 1930s, Ireland fought an economic war with Britain over agricultural exports and built up some of the most extensive tariffs and quotas on imports anywhere in the world (Girvin, 1989). Inside this hothouse, Irish-owned industry grew rapidly. Furthermore, the state became deeply involved in the Irish economy, managing protection and setting up a range of semi-state monopolies in areas such as electricity and air travel. Nonetheless, the Irish economy remained heavily dependent on agriculture: in 1960, 37 percent of the labor force worked in agriculture and exports were dominated by live animals and meat, sent primarily to Britain. The colonial administrative legacy of a cohesive bureaucracy was left to preside over an equally colonial economic structure of unequal exchange in agricultural trade.

Mjoset (1992) provides a nuanced account of the vicious circles that underpin this failure of socioeconomic development. At the heart of this failure is a weak national system of innovation, generating social marginalization and hastening emigration and population decline. Ultimately, the weakness of the system of innovation was itself reinforced by the structure of agriculture in which the combination of prosperity from the cattle trade and the persistence of a small-farm–based agrarian social structure combined to block the kinds of agriculture–industry linkages that had been the basis of development elsewhere in Europe (Mjoset, 1992; Senghaas, 1985). This was reinforced by Ireland's postcolonial dependency on a declining imperial power, so that Ireland became a free rider on Britain's decline (Mjoset, 1992, p. 9; Kennedy, 1992). Unusual among Northern European nations, Ireland failed to develop a National Fordism that could generate development through mass production and consumption.

The 1950s brought on a severe economic crisis with mass unemployment and emigration; from this crisis emerged a new policy focusing on attracting foreign investment. Economic and industrial policy in Ireland shifted dramatically between the mid-1950s and the early 1960s, at least partly in response to an economic and social crisis of disastrous proportions in the 1950s and the failure of fifteen years of sporadic efforts to cajole and coerce the sluggish Irish firms that had prospered under economic protectionism. After 1958, protectionist measures were eased for foreign investors and removed entirely in 1964. Full integration into the international economy has been the central plank of Irish economic policy since this period and protectionist measures were almost completely dismantled by the 1970s. The state became the key actor in attracting foreign direct investment, and creating a 'world-class' location for mobile investment became a motivating policy goal for the following forty years. State agencies were placed at center stage in industrial policy by efforts to continually upgrade the factors of production. The IDA, the state agency charged with attracting foreign investment, took on the role of "hunter and gatherer" of foreign direct investment (FDI) and became unusually powerful within the national state system. When most national economies were still attempting to negotiate with and control foreign capital, the Irish state turned to a relatively unconditional pursuit of such investors – creating the first free-trade zone in the world (at Shannon) and providing generous tax incentives and grants, a transnational-friendly environment, a young and cooperative labor force, and, in the 1980s, a world-class telecommunications system.

The transformations went further. Irish political and economic institutions were radically reshaped through the 1970s, primarily in pursuit of foreign investment. The structure of state finances has been transformed to greatly reduce taxes on capital and profits in an effort to attract foreign investment, leaving the state heavily reliant on revenues from personal income taxes. The percentage of government revenues from taxes on capital and corporations declined from 2.3 percent of Gross Domestic Product (GDP) in 1965 to 1.2 percent in 1985, whereas the taxation burden on personal income increased enormously from 4.3 percent of GDP in 1965 to

11.4 percent in 1985 (OECD, 1997). The educational system has been transformed, primarily through the creation of a third-level sector that is oriented heavily toward business and technology. Major investments were made in upgrading the telecommunications system in the early 1980s and the attempts to create Ireland as a "location" have redefined the nature of the nation and its territory.

Throughout the 1960s, foreign investment grew rapidly, with foreign firms accounting for 2.3 percent of gross output in 1960 but 15.9 percent in 1973 (O'Malley, 1989, p. 102). The inflow of foreign investment in the 1960s and 1970s fueled a period of rapid economic growth and, with it, the growing legitimacy and power within the state of the IDA. Throughout the 1970s, the focus on attracting FDI was consolidated with the institutionalization of the IDA's role as the leading strategic force in industrial policy. Indeed, the pursuit of foreign investment transformed the structure of the state itself as the IDA became a powerful agency that was semi-autonomous from the civil service after 1969.

Mjoset (1992) argued that the persistent weakness of the national system of innovation meant that the Irish economy was unable to take advantage of the opportunities for economic growth, technology diffusion, and social structural change provided by its growing connections to the hegemonic U.S. economy. Ireland's attempts to "import" industrial development were undermined by the well-known problems of the lack of linkages between foreign and domestic firms, the low level of technical sophistication of TNC operations, and the poor capacity of the existing industrial base and system of innovation to capitalize on what resources were available through the TNCs. A weak national system of innovation was once more caught up in a vicious circle – increasingly reliant on foreign investment that could only provide a narrow and unstable basis for industrial development (Figure 3.1).

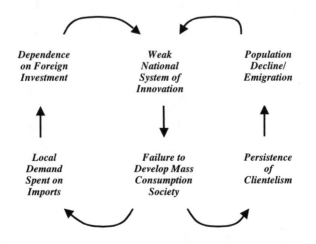

Socioeconomic Circle   *Sociopolitical Circle*

Figure 3.1. The Vicious Circle of Fordist Underdevelopment

Furthermore, the vicious circles of weak national innovation and industrial underdevelopment were reinforced by a sociopolitical vicious circle. Two "catch-all" parties dominated the political system, while clientelism, populism, and rural fundamentalism dominated political relationships. Meanwhile, the remarkable waves of emigration at crucial periods of economic difficulty and social discontent operated as a "safety valve," releasing pressure for change in the political system (Mjoset, 1992, p. 7). As long as a weak national system of innovation continued to produce conditions favorable to mass emigration, it seemed unlikely that the political pressure necessary to transform that system would emerge. The technoeconomic and sociopolitical vicious circles interacted to produce a deeply depressing prospect for Irish society in the 1980s (Table 3.1).

In the 1980s the full implications of the industrial policy compromises of the 1950s became clear. The existing industrial development regime, reliant on importing a notoriously fickle foreign investment with little connection to the local economy, was simply not up to the task of generating employment for a burgeoning population – in fact, employment was falling most disastrously just as the largest demographic bulge pushed into the labor market in the 1980s. As the international economy grew sluggishly in the early 1980s, foreign investment slowed – particularly from Britain where Thatcherism was decimating Britain's manufacturing base. Irish catch-all politics combined disastrously with the easy availability of

Table 3.1. Key Indicators of Turnaround in the Irish Economy, 1970–2002

	1970–79	1980–89	1990–93	1994–97	1998–2000	2001–2002
Average Annual Percentage Change						
GDP	4.900	3.170	4.4	7.700	10.0	6.6
Exports	7.500	8.350	9.3	12.650	18.3	5.8
Consumer Prices	14.000	9.530	2.75	2.170[1]	3.2	4.7
Employment	—	−0.430	1.45	3.700	6.6	3.3
Household	0.367	0.352	0.362	—	—	—
Disposable Income	(1973)	(1987)	(1994–5)			
Inequality*	—	—	0.377	0.373	—	—
(Gini Index)			(1994)	(1997)		
Unemployment	—	15.870[2]	14.78	13.150[3]	5.7	4.1
(Average Rate)						
Net Migration PA	+1,038[4]	−5,342[5]	−4,475	+4,100	+10,300	+14,300
(Total Numbers)						

[1] 1994–96
[2] 1976–89
[3] 1994–95
[4] 1971–81
[5] 1981–90

Sources: Gray, 1998; NESC, 1991; CSO, 1997.
Note: Top line of income statistics derived from Household Budget Survey; bottom line from ESRI Living in Ireland survey.

international loans in the 1970s and 1980s (Stallings, 1992) to create an explosion in public spending and ballooning national debt. Ireland's industrial and trade structure ensured that most of the multiplier effects of this spending were exerted outside the national economy. The Irish economy's second social and economic crisis in thirty years was created in the bust of the 1980s by the vicious circle of interactions between developmental and distributive roles of the state. Irish economy and society lurched once again into a crisis of such proportions that it became difficult to see which roads might possibly lead out of the morass. Ireland had become a nightmarish specter of the doom promised to over-enthusiastic globalizing economies – a "black hole" for international capital flows while its population hankered after the "green cards" that would get them into the United States (O'Toole, 1994).

EXPLAINING AWAY THE CELTIC TIGER: MARKET-CENTERED PERSPECTIVES

However, this depressing prospect poses a genuine puzzle when viewed from the vantage point of ten years of rapid economic and employment growth, reversal of mass migration, rapidly growing female labor-force participation, and industrial upgrading – combined with rising income inequality since the 1980s (Table 3.1 lists indicators of changes in Irish economic fortunes).

Clientelism is still pervasive within Irish politics, no new electoral coalition has emerged to mobilize popular support for a developmentalist agenda, and the headlong pursuit of foreign investment and integration into the global economy have proceeded unabated. Despite these constant features of Irish economic and political life since the 1960s, however, the country's economic and social fortunes have waxed and waned dramatically. De la Fuente and Vives's (1998) statistical analysis predicting Irish growth rates based on the experience of the OECD countries found that between 1970 and 1985, Ireland lagged significantly behind the expectations of the model in terms of growth (see also Barry, 2000). However, between 1985 and 1995, Ireland jumped ahead of the model's expectations. This exceptional recent performance would be emphasized if the boom of 1997–2000 was considered – although a recent downturn in economic fortunes would, of course, paint a more negative picture.

Most explanations of this improvement in industrial fortunes focus on processes of marketization – for both orthodox economists and their critics, institutions have been made to serve the market and organize the population into conformity with market forces. For orthodox economists, the turnaround since 1987 is explained by the ongoing commitment to foreign investment and free trade. Barry (2000) emphasizes how a combination of shifting external circumstances and domestic policies facilitated "convergence" with economies in the EU and OECD. Externally, a boom in FDI occurred at the same time that the Single European Market project was being implemented, creating an enormous opportunity for Ireland. Domestic policy and institutional changes facilitated the free operation of the market.

According to this perspective, protectionist policies, agricultural supports, low levels of education, prominent state–sector monopolies, and pluralist industrial relations inhibited Irish benefits from the market between 1950 and 1988. Free trade, declining agriculture, rising levels of education, state deregulation, and "responsible" central wage bargaining enabled markets to operate more smoothly in the 1990s, bringing with them growth.

The premise of that strategy – the ability to attract U.S. FDI – held true during the 1990s as U.S. foreign investment in Europe rose dramatically in the late 1980s in preparation for the Single European Market, and Ireland's share of U.S. FDI increased rapidly from the early 1990s (Barry, 1999). The story of the Celtic Tiger was still seen as one of connecting to foreign investment; it simply needed more time and market-conforming policies to unfold. Krugman explains the emergence of the Celtic Tiger in the following terms:

"Thanks in part to luck, in part to policies ... Ireland got a head start over other European locations in attracting what became a surge of inward FDI; the early investments both generated a cascade through informational effects and, eventually, created external economies that further reinforced Ireland's advantages." (Krugman, 1998, p. 51; see also Barry, 2000)

The similarities in the explanation provided by a more critical analyst, O'Hearn, are striking, as he explains Irish industrial growth in the following terms:

"American corporations made major moves to increase their presence in the European market; they tended to agglomerate their new projects to take advantage of the flexibility this allowed; and Ireland was fortunate enough to receive a major share of American-owned electronics projects in Europe because they agglomerated around other major firms such as Intel." (O'Hearn, 1998, p. 153)

Although inspired by dependency theory, O'Hearn's explanation of Irish growth shares with the orthodox economists the view that the dynamic of industrial growth is driven by foreign investment, facilitated by a neoliberal state getting the conditions "right" (O'Hearn, 1998, 2001). For both, the institutions of the EU act to secure international markets whereas social partnership acts to discipline and co-opt Irish workers and communities under the neoliberal project.

O'Hearn differs from the economists in his evaluation of this strategy. Irish dependence on FDI as the basis of economic development makes the growth strategy fundamentally flawed because such growth without development of local capabilities and the embedding of higher value activities in the local economy can only deliver a bubble economy – doomed to burst once FDI flows dry up. Foreign investment will generate short-term growth spurts but will not contribute to the long-term development of the local economy for several reasons: the low levels of linkages between TNCs and the local economy, the repatriation of capital and decapitalization of the local economy, and the disarticulation of the local economy between an advanced, foreign-dominated sector and a backward indigenous sector. Where inequality is seen by economists as determined by the "fair wage" that skilled workers can demand in a global labor market, O'Hearn argues that the neoliberal strategy adopted by the Irish state leaves less-skilled workers in particular with few social protections, falling farther behind the rest of Irish society.

However, growth accounting analyses (O'Leary, 2000; Harmon et al., 1999) show that the contribution of capital to growth in Ireland has been relatively low and much less than in the Asian Tigers. These analyses show that, unlike the Asian Tiger economies, high rates of investment do not play a critical role in Irish growth. Ireland has certainly benefited from an increasing supply of educated labor, with this supply coming in more or less equal parts from natural population increase, increased female labor-force participation, rising immigration (particularly return migration), and higher educational levels (Fitzgerald, 2000, p. 53). Growth in Ireland depended heavily on the contribution of labor and on a steadily increasing unexplained "productivity" of these flows of capital and labor. The Irish success story is not one driven by a logic of capital investment but rather an increasing contribution of the labor force and a rising productivity.[1]

VIRTUOUS CIRCLES AND POST-FORDIST DEVELOPMENT

In the 1990s, Ireland experienced a partial transformation of the dynamics that had underpinned the vicious circles of the 1980s and reproduced underdevelopment (Table 3.2). At the heart of this change and the emergence of a new set of economic and political virtuous circles is a process of industrial upgrading. Exports and output grew rapidly but, more importantly, so did employment, professional employment, and R&D spending. A system of innovation emerged that supported relatively broad industrial upgrading and a particularly dynamic high-technology sector – among both foreign and indigenous firms. The weaknesses of dependence on foreign investment were not eliminated; however, whereas in the 1980s Ireland had underperformed with foreign investment, in the 1990s it outperformed based on a system of innovation that created new dynamics of indigenous upgrading, only partly based on foreign investment flows.

This industrial upgrading was at the heart of improved economic growth rates from the late 1980s forward. However, it was only when these changes were reinforced by broader socioeconomic changes that economic growth – particularly employment growth – experienced the rapid expansion that saw Ireland leapfrog to the top of the EU in terms of income per capita and increase the numbers at work by almost 70 percent from 1987 to 2001. A series of "social-partnership" agreements

---

1 It is also important to recognize that these "growth-accounting" exercises assume that growth is an effect of increased supply of capital and labor, when it is just as plausible that the supply of capital and labor responds to growth, or the realistic expectation of growth. This is particularly true in countries with high levels of capital flows and migration, such as Ireland. Return migration accelerated rapidly after growth had been initiated and investment actually dropped steadily until 1994, when investment responded to growth and began to increase. It is likely, therefore, that such growth-accounting exercises systematically overstate the importance of simple supply of capital and labor and underestimate the contribution of deepening within the economy (see Rodrik, 1997, for a discussion of "capital deepening" in the Asian Tigers and a critique of Krugman, 1994).

Table 3.2. Institutional Change in the Irish Political Economy, 1960–2000

Period	Developmental State	Distributive State
1960–1973	I. Move to Attracting FDI II. Integration into International Economy	I. Welfare State Expansion
1973–1987	III. Consolidation of FDI Policy IV. Consideration of Supplementary Strategies in Face of Industrial Contraction	II. Welfare State Consolidation III. Rapid Expenditure Growth
1987–2000	V. Increased Focus on Indigenous Industry and "Deepening" VI. Definition of Key Sectors and Activities	IV. Structural Adjustment with Social Partnership

Source: Ó Riain and O'Connell, 2000, p. 335.

since 1987 traded wage restraint on the part of employees and unions for tax cuts by government, providing wage competitiveness for firms that would presumably deliver employment. The importance of wage competiveness has arguably been overstated by commentators relative to the significance of improvements in the national system of innovation, which supported the most dynamic high-technology sectors particularly effectively. However, social partnership was crucial to stabilizing the public finances and macroeconomic circumstances. Employment increased steadily in export-oriented manufacturing and services, as well as in public-sector social services such as health and education. Together, these ultimately provided a huge boost to local demand, creating an employment boom in personal services, producer services, and construction. Employment grew rapidly and, although professional employment grew most rapidly, the overall occupational structure became more polarized with the expansion of personal service and retail jobs at the lower end of the post-industrial hierarchy (Breathnach, 2002).

For a time at least, the socioeconomic virtuous circles were further reinforced by sociopolitical dynamics. The national system of innovation mobilized new constituencies into the dynamic high-tech sectors, drawing on a young, university-educated labor force. Generally, however, a growing pluralism in the definition of Irishness combined with improved economic performance to broaden the range of lifestyles available to the Irish population. Emigration was reversed and female labor-force participation grew. In the 1990s, wage increases ran ahead of inflation and tax decreases, and growing labor-force participation led to rapid rises in incomes for most workers. Union workers continued to support social partnership even as the new class of technical professionals was able to claim much higher wage raises from its non-union employers and as low-wage service work became increasingly widespread. Underpinning growth in the 1990s, the Irish formula of "solidarity without equality" came under its stiffest political tests after 2001 as the middle classes of the public sector in particular grew disenchanted with wage restraint in what was now a context of rapid inflation and rising house prices (Ó Riain and O'Connell, 2000).

Table 3.2 shows the institutional developments and trends within the Irish political economy across three critical periods: the period of growth from 1960 to 1973, the period of crisis and contraction from 1973 to 1987, and the period of recovery and boom from 1987 to 2000. The table indicates the emergence of the dominant features of the Irish economy in the 1960s. A developmental strategy based on economic openness and attracting FDI has been dominant since that period as have the populist, catch-all politics that underpinned the welfare state expansion of that era.

The 1970s saw the consolidation of each strategy as they became institutionalized within the state through the emergence of the IDA as the center of industrial policymaking and the increasing significance of organized political interests in pushing for state spending. This pressure from organized interests operated primarily through a decentralized British-style model of industrial relations and macroeconomic management – although there were some initial experiments with corporatist arrangements. The crisis of the 1980s presented challenges to those institutions but did not necessarily destroy them. Instead, a certain amount of political space emerged for the consideration of alternative and supplementary roles for the state in the economy.

Into those spaces a number of new institutions emerged. Chief among them were, as we have seen, the increasingly significant set of industrial development agencies focused on indigenous industry and on business and technological upgrading, and the social-partnership institutions put in place in 1987 that took on the macroeconomic and fiscal problems of the state without dismantling existing social protections.

The Irish growth experience of the 1990s was characterized by the intersection of three major dynamics: industrial upgrading supported by a national system of innovation, reinforced by a broader set of socioeconomic changes generating local demand for technology goods and a variety of services, underpinned by an increasingly tenuous political compromise of solidarity without equality. The Irish economy may not have shaken off the fundamental features that make it particularly open to the vicissitudes of the global economy; nonetheless, Ireland has managed in the past ten years to stake out a more rewarding form of participation within that economy. However, the commitment to social welfare, which had grown during the initial period of growth and even during the crisis years of the 1980s, has been diminished; welfare effort has decreased even as national wealth has increased. The remainder of this chapter investigates each element of the virtuous circle of the 1990s, while considering the accompanying dilemmas of autocentric development in a Global Post-Fordist economy.

INDUSTRIAL UPGRADING

The Irish economy experienced an upgrading of investment, R&D, skills, and productivity throughout the 1990s.[2] Although concentrated in certain sectors and particularly strong among the transnational firms, these trends apply quite broadly across most sectors and nationalities of ownership of firms (Ó Riain, 2003). Investment flows shifted toward "intangible" investments as R&D spending increased by 142 percent between 1991 and 1999.[3] Manufacturing employment expanded by 26.5 percent over the same period and saw a significant degree of "upskilling," at least as measured by occupational category. Administrative and technical workers (not including clerical workers) grew by 50.4 percent across manufacturing, almost double the rate of general employment growth in the sector.[4]

This picture of relatively widespread industrial upgrading is consistent with national trends in R&D spending and personnel. Gross domestic expenditure on R&D was 0.6 percent of GDP in 1981, 0.9 percent in 1990, 1.28 percent in 1997, and 1.21 percent in 1999 (failing to keep up with the surge in growth in the late 1990s) – although still well below the EU average of 1.8 percent and the OECD average of 2.2 percent. Consistent with the labor-intensive character of the Irish transformation, Ireland does significantly better in terms of researchers per ten thousand labor force: increasing from seventeen in 1981 to thirty-two in 1989 to fifty-seven in 1995, passing the EU average of forty-nine and the OECD average of fifty-five. Among OECD countries, Ireland and South Korea show the fastest rates of increase in R&D spending in the 1990s – after respectable average annual growth rates of 6.0 percent in the 1980s, Irish R&D spending increased by an average of 16.7 percent between 1991 and 1995 and by 12.0 percent between 1995 and 1997. The average rate of increase in the EU from 1995 to 1997 was 1.9 percent. Ireland shows by far the fastest rate of increase of researchers, with increases of 7.4 percent from 1981 to 1985 and 9.9 percent from 1985 to 1989 (above the OECD average of 4.4 percent). In the 1990s, when OECD growth slowed dramatically, the Irish researcher labor force took off, increasing an average of 10.5 percent per annum from 1991 to 1993 and 15.2 percent from 1993 to 1996 (OECD, 2000).

There is also evidence of a significant transformation of activities within firms, particularly regarding the spread of inter-firm networking and team-based work within organizations. A 1996–97 survey of a representative sample of enterprises in Ireland, carried out by the Graduate School of Business at University College Dublin (UCD), gathered data on a wide range of workplace practices and modes of workplace governance. Roche and Geary (2001) found that, although there has been rapid recent change within Irish workplaces, Ireland is not "ahead of"

2   For a more detailed account of industrial upgrading, see Ó Riain, 2003.
3   Unfortunately, there is no information on other intangible investments in marketing and related business activities, which also seem likely to have expanded and which are increasingly critical sources internationally of industrial competitiveness in technology-based sectors (Ernst and O'Connor, 1992).
4   These figures are based on Census of Industrial Production data provided by the Central Statistics Office (CSO).

other industrialized countries nor can the incidence of teamwork be used to explain its growth performance of the past ten years. However, the survey results show a significant shift toward teamwork within firms in Ireland (Geary, 1999; Roche and Geary, 2001). Employee involvement is most developed in the area of quality improvement within teams, less so in the organization of work activities themselves, and least of all in the control of team and organizational boundaries (Geary, 1999, p. 877). Teamwork is most firmly established in firms in financial services or high-tech sectors and where product customization is a critical competitive aspect of the firm's business. Perhaps surprisingly, teamwork has spread most widely among Irish-owned firms. Results regarding the diffusion of teamwork, therefore, support a view similar to that in the industrial statistics – a significant upgrading of organizational capacities across a range of sectors, with the most intensive upgrading concentrated in high-tech and internationally traded services sectors.

The overall figures mask a more complex sectoral picture because a high-tech sector and foreign investment have grown alongside more traditional sectors. Tables 3.3 and 3.4 provide data on the important sectoral trends among foreign and indigenous firms. High-tech foreign investment grew particularly rapidly, especially in terms of output. However, the entrepôt character of much of FDI in Ireland, combined with transfer pricing and other factors, means that output figures are notoriously unreliable as a measure of genuine industrial transformation (Honohan et al. 1998; O'Hearn, 1998; Stewart, 1989). Although there are significant entrepôt characteristics to foreign firms in Ireland, there is also evidence of significant industrial upgrading across a wide range of sectors. There is growth almost completely across the board in investment, R&D, employment, professionalization, and productivity. Perhaps the central contradiction of Irish industrial development that has fostered the controversies of recent years is that entrepôt activity and industrial upgrading have occurred within the same sectors and even within the same firms.

These data shed light on three key issues in the Irish industrial transformation: whether a sophisticated indigenous industrial base has developed, whether foreign-owned firms have become more sophisticated in the technological opportunities they offer their employees, and what relationship exists between foreign investment and indigenous-firm growth.

Dwarfed by the expansion of U.S. investment, the turnaround in Irish industry has only recently gained the attention it deserves, particularly because the employment impact of reversing the catastrophic decline of the 1980s may have been more significant than the boom in foreign investment (O'Malley, 1998). From 1991 to 1999, Irish manufacturing industry saw significant rises in investment, R&D, employment, professionalization, and productivity in almost all sectors (Ó Riain, 2003). Most striking, however, is the emergence of a cluster of sectors in the "knowledge economy." These are sectors that are fundamentally based on the processing of information or where, for the most part, indigenous firms spend a greater proportion of their revenues on R&D than the OECD averages for

Table 3.3. Irish-Owned Industry, 1991–1999

Sector	Output 1999 (£ million)	Employment 1999	% Total Employment Change 1991–99	% Professional Employment Change 1991–99	% R&D Change 1991–99	R&D as percent of Output (OECD Averages)	R&D per Employee (£)	R&D per Professional Employee (£)
1. "Knowledge Economy" (high growth, R&D intensity above OECD average)								
Software[1]	N/A	16,504	258%	N/A	841%	N/A	5,521	N/A
Other Internationally Traded Services[1]	N/A			N/A	59%	N/A		N/A
Electronics and Electrical Equipment	222.8	4,437	84.7%	90.6%	570.8	6.3 (5.6)	5,593	29,401
Instruments	31.9	719	245.5%	199.1%	1,030.5	5.9 (7.0)	4,343	15,480
2. Manufacturing/Subsupply								
(a) R&D intensity low but similar to OECD average								
Rubber and Plastic	219.3	3,720	68.1	121.7	218.8	1.3 (1.2)	1,045	8,243
Metals, Metal Products	490.6	9,039	28.7	28.2	79.8	0.7 (0.7)	480	3,957
Machinery and Equipment	236.7	5,302	46.8	60.8	276.7	2.2 (2.1)	1,557	11,496

(b) R&D intensity low and below OECD average

Paper, Print, and Publishing (Including Recorded Media)	776.9	13,297	23.5	37.9	170.5	0.2 (0.4)	153	931
Pharmaceuticals and Chemicals	455.4	3,305	35.4	18.4	51.7	1.1 (11.5/3.2*)	1,548	7,761
Nonmetallic Minerals	461.1	8,194	7.5	26.0	50.2	0.4 (0.8)	437	3,234
3. "Traditional" Industries								
Food/Drink/Tobacco	5,436.3	31,790	8.9	90.6	44.6	0.3 (0.3)	609	4,968
Clothing/Textiles/Leather	359.7	11,944	−35.0%	83.4	−19.8	0.8 (0.3)	365	3,537
Wood, Furniture	174.0	3,718	20.0	14.9	1034.7	0.9 (0.2)	741	7,820

[1] Export-oriented firms only.

Sources: R&D data from Forfás, 1999, and special tabulations; employment data for software and international services from Forfás, 2000; all other data from special CSO tabulations of Census of Industrial Production data.

Table 3.4. Foreign-Owned Industry, 1991–1999

Sector	Output (£ million)	Employment 1999	% Total Employment Change 1991–99	% Professional Employment Change 1991–99	% R&D Change 1991–99	R&D as percent of Output (OECD Averages)	R&D per Employee (£)	R&D per Professional Employee (£)
1. "Knowledge Economy" (high growth, R&D intensity above OECD average)								
Software[1]	N/A	33,973	404 percent	N/A	681 percent	N/A	1,794	N/A
Other Internationally Traded Services[1]	N/A			N/A	914 percent	N/A		N/A
Electronics and Electrical Equipment	2,967.6	18,706	111.7	137.3	281.6	1.3 (5.6)	5,130	25,808
Instruments	625.6	8,550	65.1	124.9	315.6	1.2 (7.0)	1,406	7,957
2. Manufacturing/Subsupply								
(a) R&D intensity low but similar to OECD average								
Rubber and Plastic	295.9	4,359	−2.1	13.4	352.8	0.7 (1.2)	664	7,810
Metals, Metal Products	378.1	3,634	4.8	12.4	48.0	0.3 (0.7)	393	4,133
Machinery and Equipment	494.8	6,998	−5.5	8.1	93.3	0.8 (2.1)	857	7,288

(b) R&D intensity low and below OECD average

Paper, Print, and Publishing (Including Recorded Media)	867.6	3,336	126.6	116.4	−34.3	0.01(0.4)	52	222
Pharmaceuticals and Chemicals	2,229.8	11,343	62.8	77.3	164.8	0.5 (11.5/3.2*)	4,168	16,050
Nonmetallic Minerals	120.9	1,848	−16.5		256.7	0.9 (0.8)	1,071	9,137
3. *"Traditional" Industries*								
Food/Drink/Tobacco	2,370.6	12,683	−0.8	1.2	196.1	0.3 (0.3)	1,083	6,991
Clothing/Textiles/Leather	595.7	15,539	−47.9	−33.2	−19.7	0.1 (0.3)	58	695
Wood, Furniture	56.0	480	127.9	232.3	7,775	0.7 (0.2)	1,079	11,469

[1]Export-oriented firms only.

Sources: R&D data from Forfás, 1999, and special tabulations; employment data for software and international services from Forfás, 2000; all other data from special CSO tabulations of Census of Industrial Production data.

its sector (Forfás, 1999).[5] As well as being the most knowledge-intensive sectors, these are the fastest growing in terms of employment, output, and R&D spending.

We can use these insights into the indigenous sector to cast some light on the foreign-owned sector, where it is extremely difficult to assess the sophistication of firms' activities, given the distortion of output figures by entrepôt activities. However, Table 3.3 gives us an estimate of employees' access to technology and research in the more sophisticated indigenous sectors, operating at or above international standards, which is important because these firms are not affected by the statistical problems that affect data on foreign-owned firms. The best measure of this access to technological learning is the R&D spending per employee, which is between £4,343 and £5,521 for the leading indigenous sectors.

R&D is a tiny proportion of output in almost every sector among foreign-owned firms. Clearly, the revenues generated in Ireland by foreign firms are not being reinvested in developing local capabilities; Ireland has failed to capture the rewards of these enormous revenues (many of which, of course, are based on transfer pricing and entrepôt activities). However, R&D spending per employee – a measure of employee access to R&D rather than a firm's R&D investment effort – presented a more complex picture. Irish industry remained a better bet in most sectors in providing employees with access to R&D funds. The gap was particularly striking in software and instruments in which a high-tech image was associated with decidedly low-tech R&D levels among foreign firms. On the other hand, foreign firms' R&D spending in electronics and electrical equipment was similar to indigenous firms (which spend over the OECD average). Workers in foreign-owned chemicals and pharmaceuticals plants had similarly high levels of R&D funding available to them, although these levels were probably significantly lower than international R&D levels in the industry. The data suggest, therefore, that the activities of foreign firms became more sophisticated, even as they continued to operate as management points for entrepôt activities.

Comparing R&D spending per employee in Irish and foreign firms also shows that there is much to be explained in terms of the relationship between foreign and indigenous firms. There are sectors in which R&D spending per employee in both foreign and indigenous firms grew to relatively high levels (e.g., electronics, wood/furniture) – supporting some form of linkages argument. However, in sectors such as software and instruments, indigenous firms are much more sophisticated than foreign firms, with much higher levels of R&D spending per employee and more rapid growth in R&D. Finally, the relatively high levels of R&D spending per employee in foreign chemical and pharmaceutical firms have not generated employment or R&D growth among indigenous firms. Foreign investment generates both negative "competition effects," in which TNCs draw resources away from indigenous firms, and positive "linkage effects," in which TNCs generate new

---

5   Generally, care must be taken with such comparisons across OECD countries because the surveys that form the basis of the figures are often not strictly comparable. However, the patterns are clear enough that we can identify basic patterns within Irish industry.

opportunities and resources for indigenous firms. It becomes critical to investigate the intervening social relationships and state institutions that shape how these competition and linkage effects concretely shape the development of indigenous sectors.

As we have seen, a political space emerged in the crisis of the 1980s for new institutional projects and state–society alliances. A little-recognized but highly significant alliance among science and technology-oriented state agencies, technical professionals, and university constituencies emerged that supported the deepening of technical capabilities and collective learning across the Irish economy. This process was underpinned by the state because state agencies – through their participation in this alliance – defined general priorities, provided finance and institutional supports, and legitimated this agenda. The state agencies played a central role in upgrading industry and deepening Ireland's production and innovation capabilities in the 1990s, and were rewarded with a greater legitimation of their own position within the state system. The emergence of this alliance – embedded in both the global and the local and mobilizing resources from each – is the decisive feature that explains the transformation in Irish technological and organizational capabilities in the 1990s.

Elements of the state had already played a central part in transforming the educational system – an institutional transformation that was now paying off in terms of a plentiful supply of skilled labor. Furthermore, a reserve of emigrant professionals waited for opportunities to return, doing so in large numbers since the mid-1990s. During the 1980s, the state began to pursue a wider range of industrial developmental strategies. New sectors had been added to the list of target sectors – most important of which were software and financial services. By defining the character of industrial strategies, implementing company development through grant aid, and creating an associational infrastructure for innovation, the state was able to contribute handsomely in the 1990s to the development of indigenous industry and to the upgrading of the national system of innovation more generally (Ó Riain, 2000c).

There is significant *a priori* evidence that state supports have made a difference. Agriculture remains perhaps the primary "cluster" within the Irish economy (O'Malley and Van Egeraat, 2000) and agricultural upgrading has been underpinned by the emergence of significant basic and industrial research capabilities within the universities. Stagnant since the 1960s, Irish tourism enjoyed the highest rates of growth in the OECD since 1986 and saw a significant upgrading in its "product," as well as enjoying greater international demand (Barrett, 1997). Barrett provides data that suggest that public subsidy accounts for approximately 30 percent of the rapidly increasing investment in tourism, whereas the private sector accounts for around 22 percent. Although he comments on the rent-seeking opportunities generated, it seems much more likely that state support enabled the rapid expansion by providing valuable funds for "kick-starting" small- and medium-sized tourism-oriented commercial operations, as well as improving infrastructure.

In manufacturing, O'Malley et al. (1992) found that in the 1980s

"Both new and already existing grant-assisted industries have made a substantial positive contribution to employment, and that existing grant-assisted industry has had a substantially better employment record than corresponding non-assisted firms." (1992, p. 89)

Furthermore, they found that grant-assisted firms' employment performance improved significantly faster than non–grant-assisted firms and that this could not be explained by a one-time boost given by the grant funding. They concluded that their analysis

"suggests that the grants were not only awarded more selectively by means of refraining from aiding weaker firms, but that they were also awarded to the stronger firms with good growth prospects in a manner or in a context which raised the average performance of such firms in succeeding cohorts of grant recipients . . . it is clear in the circumstances that job creation in relation to state expenditure must have improved considerably since 1984." (O'Malley et al., 1992, pp. 97–8)

There is strong evidence, then, that shifting state strategies had a substantial impact on firm performance. Those strategies, embedded in the social relations and practices of this "indigenous innovation" alliance, have contributed handsomely to making the connections between the TNC economy and local upgrading.[6] In the absence of this alliance and its institutions and practices, it is difficult to see how the Irish economy would have broken out of its vicious cycle of a "hollowing out" of local capacity by footloose capital and mass emigration. Acting to support and mobilize social relationships within the market, the state formed an alliance with a technical–professional class that provided a supportive constituency for state agencies, such as Forbairt and Enterprise Ireland (EI). The upgrading occurred as some of the elements of a national system of innovation were still being developed – significant research and investment funding emerged only *after* growth and industrial learning were well under way (see Hobday, 1994 and 1995 for a similar point regarding industrial upgrading in the East Asian Tigers). State-supported, socially embedded relationships of technological and organizational learning are critical to not only generating economic growth but also to creating the coalitions that can build political support for the new economic relationships and institutions.

SOFTWARE: THE LEADING SECTOR OF THE CELTIC TIGER

The software industry has been the leading edge of indigenous industrial upgrading in the Celtic Tiger, whereas foreign firms have expanded employment in what are often lower still parts of the industry. The institutions of the national system of

6   One reason why an indigenous chemicals and pharmaceuticals industry has not emerged in a fashion similar to the IT cluster is that the particular mode of Irish state intervention, unlike Israel, is not based on mobilizing large amounts of capital for science-based firms but rather on distributing relatively small amounts of capital linked to employment (Breznitz, 2002a). This model has been used effectively by software firms but is unsuitable for the long lead R&D times in activities such as the development of new drugs (see Oakey, 1995, on the variable barriers to growth among software, electronics, and biotechnology firms).

Table 3.5. Number of Companies, Employment, and Revenues of Foreign and Irish Ownership in the Irish Software Industry, 1987–1997

	Foreign-Owned			Irish-Owned		
Year	Firms	Employment	Revenue ($ m.)	Firms	Employment	Revenue ($ m.)
	(% Growth in Previous Two Years)					
1987	25	600	NA	140	1,230	65
1991	74	3,992	2,465	291	3,801	234
1993	81	4,448	2,739	336	4,495	368
	(9%)	(11%)	(11%)	(15%)	(18%)	(57%)
1995	93	6,011	4,125	390	5,773	610
	(15%)	(35%)	(51%)	(16%)	(28%)	(66%)
1997	108	9,100	6,214	571	9,200	834
	(16%)	(51%)	(51%)	(46%)	(59%)	(37%)

Source: National Software Directorate, 1995, 1997; Córas Tráchtála, 1987.

innovation were most effective in promoting the software industry because state supports for employment and innovation were well suited to an industry that is both labor- and knowledge-intensive. Software is not, however, merely one sector among others but rather is increasingly the central activity of the knowledge economy. Software accounts for an increasing proportion of the costs of all ICT development (Ernst and O'Connor, 1992; Mowery, 1996), and the boundaries between the software industry and other industries such as computers, telecommunications, and business services are increasingly blurred.

The Irish software industry grew rapidly throughout the 1990s (Table 3.5) with this growth intensifying in the late 1990s: indigenous firms' exports increased by 92 percent and sales by 112 percent between 1997 and 2000 (Breznitz, 2002a). The industry is divided relatively equally in employment terms between foreign- and Irish-owned firms; the revenues (and exports) of the former are much higher than those of the latter. However, the revenue figures for the foreign-owned sector are inflated due to the presence of high-visibility packaged software firms such as Microsoft, Claris, and Symantec, which carried out significant disk duplication, packaging, and software-localization[7] work in Ireland, mainly for the European market. These companies generate huge sales from their Irish operations, but relatively little value is added in the Irish operation because most of the core software development takes place at the U.S. headquarters. Nonetheless, Ireland

7 "Localization" of software refers to the process of customizing existing software packages for specific national and linguistic markets. The main activity is the translation of the text, but it may also involve changing date formats, letter formats, and other culture-specific aspects of the software. In U.S. software companies, the work of designing the software program so that it can be customized in this way is called "internationalization" and is generally carried out in the United States. The work of actually customizing the program for specific markets is called "localization." This work is relatively uncomplicated, and should not be confused with the socioeconomic processes of the "localization" or "territorialization" of production and innovation discussed in Chapter 1.

is a particularly important node in U.S. software companies' global operations. In the 1990s, U.S. software companies, the leading firms in the industry, were particularly eager to expand their global operations. Exports of software from the United States grew from $1,328,000 in 1990 to $3,030,000 in 1994. Meanwhile, U.S. overseas affiliates in computer services have grown rapidly, increasing from 97 in 1982 to 398 in 1993; employment in those affiliates expanded by approximately 68,000 (OECD, 1997, p. 83). The exports of foreign-owned software firms in Ireland in 1993 came to $2,774,000, with U.S. firms accounting for approximately 60 percent of those firms and well over two thirds of the export revenues. Exports from the Irish export platform were a highly significant part of the overall exports of the U.S. software industry: total software exports from the United States came to $2,526,000 that year (OECD, 1997, p. 58). Although the figures are not strictly comparable, a conservative estimate would suggest that – even in the early 1990s – the exports of U.S. software firms from Ireland came to at least half of their exports from the U.S. and may be as high as three fourths of the U.S. figure. Those proportions would be even higher if only exports into Europe were considered.

As we have seen, however, foreign firms invest sparingly in R&D and have significant entrepôt characteristics. Indigenous industry is much more research-intensive and historically has consisted of numerous small firms, many of which engage in product development for export markets. In the late 1990s, growth was even more rapid and a number of leading firms emerged. A comprehensive survey of indigenous software firms carrying out software product development found that by 2001 there were at least 250 such companies, more than half of which were set up after 1999 and more than 70 percent since 1996 (HotOrigin, 2001). Turnover among those firms grew at 30 to 40 percent PA in recent years. Seven Irish companies were publicly quoted in 2001 – Smartforce (ex-CBT), Iona Technologies, Baltimore Technologies, Trintech, Riverdeep, Parthus, and Datalex – and they accounted for five thousand of the sector's eleven thousand employees and for half of the sector's revenues, with a combined annual turnover of 500 million Irish pounds (IEP). HotOrigin claimed that another thirty to forty companies were on the brink of reaching this level of success. When a number of the larger companies ran into difficulties in 2001 and 2002, the network of small- and medium-sized companies beneath them became once more the motor of industry growth because firm and region exist in a dynamic relationship – and because private companies proved somewhat better able to ride out the difficulties of the industry downturn. Nonetheless, industry employment declined significantly in 2002–3.

The Irish indigenous industry is similar in magnitude to other emerging software industries such as in India and Israel (Table 3.6). Care should be taken in using these figures to compare the three industries because there are a number of differences in how the figures were calculated. The Irish industry's export orientation is similar to that of the Indian industry, although the Indian industry's exports consisted primarily of offshore development and international labor-contracting during this period (Parthasarathy, 2000). The Irish industry is similar to the Israeli and, indeed, the U.S. industries in its greater focus on software products and avoidance of

who are the entrepreneurs? what resources have they used?

Table 3.6. Sales and Exports in the Indigenous* Software Industry in India,
Ireland, and Israel, 1993–1997

	Sales ($ Million)			Exports ($ Million)			Exports as % of Total Sales		
Year	India	Ireland	Israel	India	Ireland	Israel	India	Ireland	Israel
1993	388	368	700	225	190	175	58%	52%	25%
1994	554	—	790	330	—	220	60%	—	28%
1995	823	610	—	485	357	—	59%	59%	—
1997		834			577			69%	

data updated (handwritten note)

Sources: NASSCOM, 1996; National Software Directorate, 1993, 1995, 1997; Israeli Association of Software Houses, 1995; Ó Riain, 1997.
Note: Figures may not be strictly comparable because survey coverage and methodologies are different.
* Figures for India include TNCs; figures for Ireland and Israel do not.

large-scale labor-contracting. However, it is less sophisticated than either of those industries, with a lower level of productivity (i.e., sales per employee) than either the Israeli or the U.S. industry (Breznitz, 2002a).[8] Nonetheless, the proportion of firms engaging in product development is similar to the U.S. industry, and many of them are highly export-oriented and technology-based (Ó Riain, 1999). McIver Consulting (1998) characterizes the industry as one based on "competitive product creation" and argues that

"The indigenous sector is in advance of most service-oriented software sectors [internationally] in terms of its capability to produce innovative products that are relevant to market requirements. At the same time, it is behind the main centers in the United States, and also Israel and perhaps Australia, in terms of innovative capability." (1998, p. 74)

These innovative capacities have arguably improved in the years since this assessment.

Software is unusually significant within high technology in Ireland – both the United States and Israel have much more diverse ICT sectors. However, the industry knits together an interesting set of relationships among a variety of sectors in Ireland. Generally, software capabilities have become increasingly important in ICT industries – even in sectors that are ostensibly focused on "hardware." The indigenous-software industry's major subsectors include communications software (with ties to the telecommunications manufacturing sector), banking and finance software (with ties to financial services), and systems software (with ties to the computing sector). This suggests that something of a high-tech cluster exists, consisting of overlapping and interconnected sectors and underpinned by growing

8 Breznitz (2002a) argues persuasively that this is because Irish firms support product development with services, promoted by an industrial regime that makes less capital available than in Israel, and that this in turn is shaped by the Irish state's focus on adding employment rather than the Israeli state's emphasis on improving technological capacity.

competencies in software design and production that are being applied across sectors (see Ó Riain 1999, for more on the software industry, narrowly defined).[9] In examining the growth of software in Ireland, therefore, we investigate the emergence of a critically important set of capabilities within the economy, as well as an industrial sector in its own right. It is for this reason that Chapters 4 through 7 take a closer look at the software industry as a particularly significant source of insight into the economic development model of the DNS.

AUTOCENTRIC DEVELOPMENT WITHIN GLOBAL POST-FORDISM

Ireland has experienced significant industrial upgrading alongside a boom in employment, even as entrepôt activities persist and even flourish. However, Ireland is also a particularly clear case in which the conditions of National Fordist autocentric development (Mjoset, 1992; Senghaas, 1985) have been undermined by globalization and postindustrialism. Global Post-Fordism is the new terrain where experiments with new development strategies and their social and political consequences are contested.

Under National Fordist autocentric development, industrial upgrading was embedded in national "feedback loops" in which the growth of the middle class and expanding domestic markets promoted growth and intersectoral learning and generated broad sociopolitical support. The fiscal 'pump-priming' of Keynes and the innovation dynamics of Schumpeter could be combined to generate a dynamic "national economy," within a broader world order of "embedded liberalism." Globalization has undermined the cohesion of national societies, economies, and polities so that many of the economic and political feedback loops can no longer be relied on to be a major motor of growth. Ireland is a striking example: profoundly globalized by free trade, foreign investment, migration, tourism, and other transnational social relationships, the Irish economy has also shifted markedly toward a postindustrial sectoral and employment structure (Table 3.7).

The Irish labor force has undergone a structural shift since the 1970s with a marked trend toward a post-industrial workforce. In the 1990s, even as agricultural employment continued its steady decline, manufacturing grew 3.6 percent PA, social services grew 4.4 percent PA, and market services grew 5.7 percent PA. The transformation looks more dramatic when we focus on key sectors such as insurance, finance, and business services (incorporating producer services and software) and health and education – the only sectors to record steady employment growth in every period in the table. Taken together with the improved overall employment creation performance of the 1990s, Ireland has undergone a rapid shift toward a Post-Fordist economy and a postindustrial workforce – driven in large part by high-tech manufacturing, producer services, and social services. The boom of the 1990s only solidified an existing trend toward a post-industrial economy.

This has, in turn, resulted in rapid occupational change: the most rapidly expanding categories between 1981 and 1995 include catering, personal services, sales

9   For a more detailed discussion of sectoral differences, see Ó Riain, 2003.

Table 3.7. Sectoral Employment Growth, 1961–2000

	Annual Percentage Change in Employment				
	1961–73	1973–79	1979–87	1987–93	1993–2000
Agriculture	−3.3	−2.4	−3.7	−2.1	−2.3
Industry	2.3	1.4	−2.4	0.6	6.0
Manufacturing	2.0	1.2	−1.7	1.3	3.6
Building	3.4	2.3	−4.3	0.0	12.7
Utilities and Mining	1.6	0.7	−2.2	−4.4	1.4
Market Services	0.6	1.7	1.1	2.3	5.7
Wholesale and Retail	0.5	1.2	0.7	2.0	3.4
Transport, Communication	1.4	1.1	−0.5	0.7	5.4
Insurance, Finance, and Business	3.8	6.5	2.9	2.7	6.5
Other (Personal) Services	−0.4	1.8	2.1	3.5	8.0
Social Services	2.8	4.5	2.0	0.9	4.4
Public Administration	2.6	4.1	0.0	−0.7	2.7
Health and Education	3.0	4.8	3.0	1.5	5.0
Total Employment	0.2	1.2	−0.6	0.9	4.7

Source: NESC, 2002

workers, and security workers, which added fifty-nine thousand employees to their numbers during those years (i.e., an increase of 35.5 percent). However, by 1995, there were also ninety-four thousand more managers, professionals, and associate professionals, an increase of 44 percent. Meanwhile, more classically Fordist occupations such as clerks, typists, operatives, transport workers, and skilled and craft workers added only seven thousand extra jobs, and farmers and laborers decreased by sixty-eight thousand, or 27.3 percent (Tansey, 1998, p. 41). In short, occupational change has simultaneously upgraded and polarized the labor force, similar to trends in the United States, Canada, and the United Kingdom over the past twenty years (Castells, 1997, pp. 208–31).

Industrial development in Ireland has been embedded within social structural conditions of Global Post-Fordism rather than National Fordism. Industrial upgrading has contributed to occupational upgrading but also to a more polarized occupational structure, even while reversing mass unemployment and emigration. This social structure has generated a set of socioeconomic feedback loops that operate across global regions rather than within the national territory (Figure 3.2). Unable to take advantage of national social relationships, development strategy relies ever more heavily on the everyday political construction of autocentric developmental conditions. However, the sociopolitical circumstances for securing such conditions become ever more difficult as social partnership institutions find it more challenging to bind together an increasingly polarized society in a national development alliance.

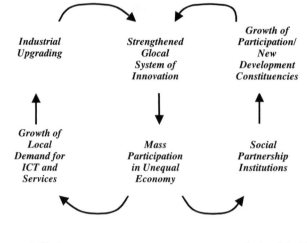

Figure 3.2. The Virtuous Circle of Post-Fordist Development

The socioeconomic virtuous circle of global post-fordism

Industrial development is embedded within a broader set of socioeconomic relationships, and it is the relationship between the industrial base and the broader
institutionalized patterns of economic activity that can create vicious or virtuous
developmental circles. In the 1980s, a Keynesian attempt to boost demand interacted with a weak industrial base to produce a boom in the consumption of
imports and a financial crisis. In the 1990s, Keynesian demand management was
forsaken in favor of emphasis on international competitiveness. The sectors that
have grown and been increasingly successful in international markets are locally
and globally connected and their business dynamics similarly operate across the
local and the global. ICT exports have increased rapidly and the local ICT market has also grown enormously, although reliable statistics are difficult to find.
Data on manufacturing-industry acquisition of computer hardware and software
show that ICT goods are primarily purchased by firms in the high-tech sectors
of communications, chemicals, printing (e.g., software manuals), computers, and
medical equipment (Central Statistics Office, 2002). Although a major part of the
local ICT market is sales between ICT companies, computing technologies have
spread among the general population. In mid-1998, 18.6 percent of all households
owned a home computer and 26.8 percent of them were connected to the Internet;
eighteen months later, 32.4 percent of households had a computer with 63 percent
of them connected to the Internet (Central Statistics Office, 2001). It seems likely
that these patterns of ICT use reflect the digital divide emerging in other countries.
User–producer relationships, both with individuals and organizations, are crucial
to learning in systems of innovation (Lundvall et al., 2002) and these relations
operate both globally and locally in the Irish ICT industry.

However, national employment growth has been generated around this glocal business dynamic. Manufacturing accounted for only 18.6 percent of total Irish employment in 2001 and for 14.5 percent of the growth in employment between 1987 and 2001. The employment growth that has been the most impressive feature of the Irish economy in the past ten years is based not only on transformations in internationally competitive industry but also on expanding national social-service employment and expanding local demand for business, retail, construction, and personal services. If export competitiveness has driven some of this growth, it has gone hand in hand with public-sector expansion of social-service employment. Together, these twin drivers of economic development generated huge local demand from 1994 to 2001, resulting in rapid increases in employment in personal services and construction. Foreign investment and export competitiveness in internationally traded sectors interacted with such unfashionable factors as public-sector employment in creating patterns of local demand that generate further employment increases.

There is a deep tension, however, within this national-growth model as the glocally connected elite of the knowledge economy begin to pull away from others in the economy – particularly the personal-service workers who often work for low wages and under appalling conditions. Inequality has risen rapidly within the Irish economy, including both the increasing share of national income going to capital rather than labor (O'Hearn, 1998, p. 125) and the most rapid rise in wage inequality within the OECD in the 1990s (Barrett, Callan, and Nolan, 1999).

Ironically, it has been as Global Post-Fordism has flourished that national corporatist arrangements have been most widely developed in Ireland. Neocorporatist wage agreements encouraged wage restraint, particularly among unionized workers, and kept inflation low in order to improve the competitiveness of industry in Ireland. In return, workers received a succession of cuts in personal income taxes so that net wages rose rapidly for many people. However, the public finances were steadily undermined by the eroding revenue base, an erosion that could be ignored during the high growth rates of the late 1990s but that became a major political issue in 2001–02 with the slowing of the economy. We must be careful how we interpret the significance of the wage–tax trade-off to the Irish economy. Foreign investment obtained much higher rewards from tax breaks, particularly in the context of the massive entrepôt activities discussed previously, than from Ireland's relatively low wages within Europe. Furthermore, high income inequality means that Ireland is least competitive in precisely those high-tech sectors that rely most heavily on professional labor and that have been expanding most rapidly – often paying employees well above the wage-agreement pay increases. Wages have remained too low in many services sectors. Where wage restraint has been most important is in the least sophisticated sectors of Irish industry and in managing the public-sector pay bill to assist in reducing public debt. Different sets of choices were possible and could have ameliorated rising inequality. Because national social structures no longer embed autocentric development processes, the political construction of national social inclusion in the development project becomes even more crucial. However, the conditions for such political strategy become more complex.

The sociopolitical virtuous circle of global post-fordism

These socioeconomic changes have occurred within a shifting sociopolitical context, which has involved an increased emphasis on competitiveness but also the emergence of a dense set of local and national institutions of social partnership. Clearly, there are elements of "competitive corporatism" (O'Hearn, 2001; Streeck, 1999) and of the "competition state" (Cerny, 1995; Kirby, 2002). However, these formulations capture only one dimension of the changing political context. Interacting with the marketization of social life has been the fragmentation since the 1980s of a hegemonic national culture and the emergence of a diversity of new institutional forms in both state and civil society. It is in these political spaces that we find the institutional underpinnings of the new capacities of the Irish social economy.

The 1980s saw the disintegration of the cultural hegemony of a long-established vision of the nation that tied nationalism to Catholicism, agriculture, and social conservatism (Fitzgerald and Girvin, 2000). Although nationalism persists as a dominant cultural value, it now exists in a form that is compatible with a much wider range of sociopolitical projects and economic development strategies. It became increasingly difficult to hold together this hegemonic version of Irishness in the face of the diversity of the Irish population (i.e., ever younger, more internationalized, better educated, and less Catholic) and the increasing problems of the Catholic Church and other hegemonic institutions to maintain the organizational conditions of their own reproduction (i.e., declining vocations, scandals, and declining legitimacy taking their toll) (O'Donnell, 2000).

State strategies created two social classes that now mobilized to try and reverse the disastrous situation of the 1980s. State investment in education had created a burgeoning professional class, many of whom emigrated but enough of whom stayed behind to form a new industrial development coalition with dissident elements from the IDA and other more marginal state agencies. The hegemony of the FDI strategy and the IDA within the national policy regime was shaken by the events of the early and mid-1980s. This space allowed an alliance among marginalized state agencies, technical professionals, and university constituencies to emerge. This coalition became the basis of indigenous upgrading and deepening in the 1990s. A second group of unionized workers, many in the public sector, was mobilized through the union movement to enter the social-partnership agreements and protect employment levels in the face of hard economic times. These two coalitions between different classes of employees, employers, and sections of the state existed throughout the 1980s in an arm's-length but complementary relationship. The modified industrial policy finally created the growth that could create a sustainable dynamic of development. Meanwhile, the social-partnership agreements restored the macroeconomic and fiscal stability necessary for industrial success. Whereas the terms of this accord between the state and the social partners ensured that basic levels of protection were guaranteed to those excluded from national economic recovery, the equality agenda characteristic of more traditional forms of corporatism was marginalized.

Each of the two major developmental and distributional coalitions in Ireland have held the other's ambitions in check, assisted by the structure of the Irish state. The neoliberal impulses of the rising class of internationalized professionals are at least partly held in check by the continuing ability of the unions to safeguard the basic social rights guaranteed (at a low level) by the universalistic elements of the Irish welfare state and by the middle class's own self-interest in maintaining the subsidies provided by the pay-related welfare state. The social-partnership agreements ensured that integration into the global economy has not decimated social rights. However, the agreements have also presided over a period of rising inequality and weakening welfare effort. This is at least partly due to the increasing lack of voice of unions and other social actors in shaping the lead sectors of the economy. The new classes of technical professionals and self-employed small businesses largely fall outside the institutions of social partnership and have become the basis of spiraling inequality in market incomes in Ireland. In the early years of the new century, these tensions around inequality and competing conceptions of worth and value are coming to the fore in Irish political debate, particularly around the future of social partnership (Ó Riain and O'Connell, 2000).

If virtuous circles emerged in the 1990s that sustained a genuine deepening of the capacities of economy and society, they did not deliver the egalitarianism that Senghaas's vision of autocentric development had promised. Rising income inequality was tempered by increased female labor-force participation from households lower in the income distribution. The national cohesion that Senghaas saw as central to autocentric development was present politically throughout the social-partnership approach but not socially in the face of rising inequality.

However, this should not lead us to dismiss the significance of the Irish case. We cannot ignore the importance for students of development of a case where socioeconomic disaster was followed rapidly by massive increases in employment and return migration – fueled by industrial upgrading, public-sector expansion, and rising local demand and underpinned by dramatic institutional change. The Irish case points up the challenges of autocentric development in an economy that is increasingly glocal rather than national, postindustrial in structure, and Post-Fordist in organization, and offers an opportunity to assess the potential and dilemmas of that development terrain. These contradictions were most evident in the economic downturn of 2001–03, when the tensions between the neoliberal, developmental, and social-rights projects of the Celtic Tiger became more evident. These tensions are discussed in detail in Chapter 11. Chapters 4 through 7 turn to a detailed examination of the glocal software industry and its relationship to a national but networked polity. Chapters 8 and 9 examine the national institutions and politics of industrial development in such a DNS.

PART II

SOFTWARE AND THE CELTIC TIGER

4

"LOCATION NATION": REMAKING SOCIETY FOR FOREIGN INVESTMENT

BULLETS, BYTES, AND BUREAUCRATS

If, as Mao famously claimed, power comes from the barrel of a gun, then so too did the computer. Where states are found, warmaking cannot be far behind. However, it was only with the "industrialization of war" from the 1840s forward that technological advances and state militarization became intimately linked (Arrighi, 1999; McNeil, 1982). World War II led to what some call the first modern computer, developed through the work of Alan Turing in British code-breaking activities. The war played a critical role in the development of the computer industry as "the degree to which scientists and engineers were mobilized in support of the Allied war effort and the scale of their activities were unprecedented." (Flamm, 1987, p. 6).

After the war, support for high-tech research continued; U.S. government support for the emerging computer industry was massive, with the government accounting for the majority of R & D funding and being the primary market during the critical years when the industry was developing after World War II (Flamm, 1987; Langlois and Mowery, 1996). The contribution of the military to the computer industry in the United States was marked by the combination of a massive centralized military side of the state with an economic ideology that theoretically favored the "free market." The result was a form of military developmentalism with a dominant role for government in both funding development and purchasing the products of that development, but in which technology development remained largely in private firms that held the proprietary rights to the technology (Gordon, 2001, p. 19). The firms involved in this early period of the industry (extending to a greater or lesser extent across thirty years) were in essence quasi-public institutions, more dependent on state decision-making than market principles. Nonetheless, they were market actors and garnered significant advantages from this dual position. Although it is difficult to quantify, the extent and duration of the U.S. government subsidy of what are now its leading industries is perhaps unmatched in the recent history of industrial policy worldwide. This also was combined at critical junctures with a strong policy emphasis on antitrust regulation, including major cases involving Bell Labs in the 1950s, IBM in the 1960s and 1970s, and Microsoft in the 1990s. Such a state role, although ostensibly market-conforming, can potentially redefine the key actors within a market and shape their strategic actions (Campbell and Lindberg, 1990). Arguably, these actions helped diffuse semiconductor, computer, and possibly software technology.

Although the military provided the initial impetus for much of European participation in high technology, the scale of the resources committed to military spending generally, and technology specifically, was not comparable to the resources expended within the United States (Dedrick and Kraemer, 1998; Flamm, 1987; Hendry, 1989, p. 48). Furthermore, the U.S. state was more developmental in its practice than the European states, which were often more explicitly developmental in their ideology (Loriaux, 1999). In the United States, the state – particularly through the military – mobilized society to participate in the market, whereas in Europe, the state incorporated society into itself on a greater scale through the institutions of the "national champion." It was the state, not private capital, that put ICT industries in place and provided the basis for the future globalization of both high-tech investment and the academic discipline of computer science.

U.S. high-technology dominance formed the context for development strategies around the world and simultaneously set the stage for the future development of the U.S. industry itself. As Gordon argued,

"Technical dominance and expansive markets subject to minimal foreign competition provided a high rate of potentially marketable innovations in conjunction with a favorable structure for economic risk-taking and technical experimentation." (Gordon, 2001, p. 15)

The high profits that the leading firms and regions such as Silicon Valley enjoyed were the basis of continuing rounds of innovation in the United States itself and created an industrial base unconstrained by government policy, which soon began to look overseas for lower-cost locations.

High-tech foreign investment increased rapidly from the 1960s. Numerous countries pursued a direct connection to the leading high-technology industries by attempting to lure U.S. companies as direct investors in their rapidly spreading export-processing zones (EPZ), industrial parks, and free-trade zones that combined infrastructure with special regulatory regimes, which suspended many of the rights that workers had gained throughout the nation. Those efforts attracted many willing investors:

"The first EPZ appeared at Shannon, Ireland, in 1958; India established the first Third World EPZ in 1965; and by the mid-1980s, roughly 1.8 million workers were employed in a total of 173 EPZs around the world." (McMichael, 1996, p. 92)

Global flows and stocks of FDI and the volume of global trade increased much more rapidly than world GDP in the late 1960s and the 1970s, before recession and protectionism in the 1980s reined in this particular outburst of globalizing activity (Held et al., 1999, p. 242). In keeping with this broader trend, American and Japanese electronics firms began to move production "offshore" in the 1960s – first to Korea, Taiwan, Hong Kong, and Singapore, then, beginning in the mid-1980s, throughout Southeast Asia (Henderson, 1989).

Whereas Japanese firms, in expanding their foreign operations, were motivated by an interest in servicing Asian markets and by the attraction of low-wage labor that would facilitate their push into the large and lucrative American market, the strategy of American firms was largely a defensive antidote to stiff Japanese competition. The advent of open systems created enormous opportunities for firms to divide up the various segments of the industry and its labor processes, going well beyond the separation of assembly and design that was the initial impetus behind the drive toward a "new international division of labor" in semiconductors in the 1970s (Henderson, 1989; Dedrick and Kraemer, 1998). It was in this context that the Irish state began to pursue U.S. high-tech foreign investment in earnest in the 1970s, marked in particular by the arrival of Digital in Galway in 1971. When the Irish state entered the free market for mobile electronics investment, it was free-riding on an earlier period of U.S. military developmentalism. In searching for FDI, moreover, the Irish state transformed the national territory, population, and – ultimately – itself.

Reshaping the national territory: trade, incentives, communications

An array of financial incentives was offered for foreign investors and exporters in Ireland since the 1950s. Many of the policies were originally tested in the free-trade zone around Shannon Airport in the west of Ireland (i.e., the first such free-trade zone in the world, established in 1958) but were gradually extended to the rest of the country (Share, 1992; Sklair, 1988). Since 1964, "There has been no restriction on foreign ownership or control . . . and no restriction on the repatriation of profits." (O'Malley, 1989, p. 74). In 1958, Export Profits Tax Relief (EPTR) was provided on 100 percent of increase in profits from exports and, therefore, to all the export profits of new firms. Although originally intended to last for ten years, the period of tax relief was extended to fifteen years in 1960; the policy itself, originally intended to terminate in 1979–80, was extended to 1989–90. The Irish government came under pressure from the European Economic Community (EEC) regarding this discrimination in favor of exports, and the state introduced a new policy in 1978 providing a 10 percent corporation tax for all manufacturing from 1981 to 2000 inclusive. This was extended to firms in the internationally traded services sector (including software and data processing) in 1981 and guaranteed until 2010 the same year. However, all firms that qualified for EPTR before 1981 received full tax remission until 1990. These incentives, along with a package of grants available to new investors, meant that Ireland provided the most competitive location within the EU by the early 1970s when it joined the EEC (O'Malley, 1989, p. 76).

The physical territory itself was also remade, particularly when the telecommunications system was upgraded in the early 1980s. The overhauling of the telecommunications system was prompted less by developmental concerns than by public outrage at the poor level of service in the ordinary telephone service. The waiting list for telephones had grown from 10,600 in 1958 to approximately 34,000 in 1973, and almost doubled within five years to 63,000 in 1978 – despite a deliberate discouraging of demand for telephones (Hall, 1993, p. 58). The state committed to investing 1,000 million pounds in the telecommunications system and "the engineering branch of the then Department of Posts and Telegraphs bravely, at the time, opted for digital technology for the future development of the network" (Euristix, 1991, p. 2.2). For part of the 1980s, Ireland actually led Europe in some aspects of the technological sophistication of its telecommunications infrastructure (Euristix, 1991; Forfás, 1994; Hall, 1993) and the system was almost completely digitized by the mid-1990s.

Specifically, there was a bias within telecommunications pricing in favor of businesses dealing with international markets and against local business and residential callers. In 1994, broad comparisons showed that Ireland's cost competitiveness was ahead of the European average for national data services and some data service to the United States; ahead of the European average for telephone calls of a typical multinational company with a high level of international calls; but behind the European average for the telephone calls of a typical indigenous company, with a high level of domestic calls; (Forfás, 1994, p. 6). Cheaper international calls were subsidized by increases in local calling rates. Trinity College Dublin was also one of the early "backbone" sites for European access to the Internet, bringing free access relatively early to some within the Irish industry.

The state was also deeply involved in the distribution of global connectedness across the national territory through its efforts to shape internal patterns of the location of TNCs. Throughout the 1970s and into the 1980s, an explicit policy of industrial decentralization and rural industrialization was pursued with some success as manufacturing employment grew much more rapidly outside Dublin. A major tool in this project was the direct provision of land and advance factories built by the IDA. The extent of state restructuring of the economy to create an attractive location is evident from the fact that by 1983, the IDA had been associated with nearly one third of the factory units developed in Dublin since 1960 and was the largest owner of industrial space in the city. Furthermore, the second and third largest owners of Dublin industrial space were a bank and an insurance company that were both owned by the state (MacLaran, 1993, p. 159). This even extends to the IDA becoming a significant property owner and acting unofficially to facilitate the TNCs. One TNC vice president in Silicon Valley pointed to a photograph of the Irish facility of his company in an industrial park on the outskirts of Dublin: "We will need to expand soon and you see that piece of empty land behind our place. We haven't bought it yet but the IDA is holding it for us in case we do need to expand there." Many of the software localization TNCs are located in industrial estates and office parks around Dublin, such as the South Dublin Office Park in Leopardstown designed specifically to mimic the suburban landscaped office parks of the United States (*Irish Computer*, April 1985).

Regional policy waned in the crisis years of the 1980s, and the 1990s saw the concentration of employment growth around Dublin. Housing costs and commuting times increased precipitously as the wealth created in the economy – but distributed highly unequally – poured into urban consumption. The irony is that, faced with these dilemmas of social and corporate reproduction in Dublin, a "spatial" regional policy has made a comeback. After turning away for fifteen years from the issue of the distribution of employment within the country, the IDA end-of-year statement for 1999 reported:

"The unevenness of job creation across the country is a cause of great concern. It requires radical action and a timely response on infrastructure issues. There are too many regions at a disadvantage from uncompetitive infrastructure and lack of business support services to be able to attract the required level of new and modern business investment. Dublin is surging ahead because of the strong attractions it can offer international businesses. Similar growth is not yet happening elsewhere but IDA is committed to playing its part in a concerted national effort to achieve balanced regional growth." (IDA Ireland, 2000)

The project of attracting foreign investment resulted, therefore, not in the depoliticization of space and territory but rather in the hyperpoliticization of the national territory as the territory itself became an object of political (specifically state) action. Reshaping the nation into location through incentives, telecommunications, and regional and land-use policy has been a major strategy in the pursuit of mobile investment – a strategy that has drawn the state ever more deeply into the management of space (Brenner, 1998). This hyperpoliticization of the national territory was ironically consolidated with the full economic integration of the EU throughout the 1990s – from the Single European Market in 1992 to the introduction of the Euro currency and the passing of the Nice Treaty (at the second attempt) in 2002. Its privileged location as a low-tax, English-speaking territory within the EU was crucial to the foreign investment boom of the 1990s.

Reshaping the national population: the expansion of education

Tax incentives and market access, however, do not provide all the conditions for a "successful" location for foreign investment. A skilled labor force became more critical throughout the 1990s, and the Irish state's greatest efforts were dedicated to the mobilization and restructuring of local society through the creation and shaping of a "suitable" labor force: "the people" were to be molded into a suitably attractive labor force. The most critical factor of production for a learning industry is educated labor; the Irish educational system expanded rapidly from the 1960s forward with public expenditure on education growing from just over 3 percent of GNP in 1961–62 to 6.3 percent in 1973–74 (Breen et al., 1990, p. 123). Free post-primary school education and free school transport were introduced in 1967. The reforms that would most directly affect the IT sector would be at third level, however. The absolute numbers in third-level education more than tripled between 1963–64 and 1984–85, largely because of increased participation rates rather than due to increasing population (Breen et al., 1990, p. 129).

Although the state was the agent of change, state ties to international forces such as the World Bank and OECD were also significant. The catalyst for the change in the educational system was the 1965 OECD report, *Investment in Education*, which drew on the increasingly influential human-capital theory of education to argue that "manpower" training would be essential to a growing economy like Ireland's. Vocational education was seen as particularly important by both the OECD analysts and the Minister of Education of the time (Breen et al., 1990, p. 127). The state financed but did not control primary and academic post-primary education in Ireland because the power of the Catholic Church within the educational system and its ownership of school buildings and facilities gave it extensive control over primary and academic secondary education (Breen et al., 1990, p. 125).

The major thrust of educational expansion after the *Investment in Education* report was toward the expansion of vocational and technical education at the post-primary and tertiary levels. Furthermore,

"The growing utilitarianism in policy has been achieved by a progressive process of state intervention." (Clancy, 1989, p. 129)

Ignoring alternative proposals, the government pursued a strategy of educational change based on building up new institutions alongside the existing "academically oriented" institutions rather than taking on those institutions directly:

"The principal strategy chosen to effect this policy reorientation was to establish new colleges which were directly controlled by the Department of Education." (Clancy, 1989, p. 123)

This state-led reorientation of the educational system was reinforced over time by the increasing influence of the new colleges; specifically, the newly founded National Institutes of Higher Education (NIHE), whose success put pressure on the existing universities to change their orientation to technical and scientific education and to links between industry and academia (Osborne, 1996, p. 47; Share, 1992). The universities responded early to those pressures, as shown in their generally positive responses to an invitation for proposals for new courses in engineering and computer science in 1979 (O'Donnell, 1981). In general, then,

"It could be argued that in Ireland over the past two decades the provision of higher education has been supply-led rather than demand-led. The huge growth in the non-university short-cycle sector reflects more the decisions of government than the nature of client demand." (Clancy, 1989, p. 129)

Indeed, the goal of policy was to create demand by increasing supply.

The state was also willing to use its new-found capacity to influence labor supply more directly. In particular, the expansion of engineering and computer-science education undertaken in the late 1970s was accomplished through increased state funding earmarked specifically for those disciplines – including 1.725 million pounds of extra funding put aside in 1979. By 1980,

"Some form of computer-related courses had commenced or was due to be available at almost all tertiary level institutions." (Drew, 1994, p. 58)

The Computer Industry Joint Education Committee on skills needs in the computer industry had reported that Ireland was facing a significant shortfall in computer skills in the years ahead and a flurry of policy activity resulted in extra funding for places in computer science. In 1978, there were thirty graduates of computer-science degrees (Drew, 1994, p. 60); between 1984 and 1995, the number of degrees awarded in computer science increased 177 percent from 140 to 389 and in electrical and electronic engineering they increased 56 percent from 254 to 396 (HEA, various years). Although Ireland was behind most developing countries in its provision of engineers and systems analysts and programmers in 1980 (O'Donnell, 1981), it moved up the ladder relatively rapidly. Between 1991 and 1994, Ireland was among the leading four or five OECD countries in percentage of university-level graduates in science-related fields in the labor force and toward the middle of the OECD distribution in percentage of graduates in mathematics, computer science, engineering, and overall university graduation rate among the relevant age cohort (OECD, 1992, 1993, 1996). The Irish population had been dramatically reshaped during a thirty-year period.

Reshaping the national state: the "IDA way"

Putting in place a set of policies to attract foreign investment was one thing, getting the companies to locate in Ireland was quite another. Ireland was one of the first countries to actively pursue mobile foreign investment using the full resources of the state, working particularly through the IDA, which became one of the "star" foreign-investment–attraction agencies internationally.[1] Investment-promotion agencies have become a fully institutionalized element of the world polity (Boli and Thomas, 1998; Meyer and Rowan, 1997) with their own international association founded in 1995. A UN survey revealed that half of the 106 investment-promotion agencies surveyed had been founded in the 1990s, and many of them in the latter part of the decade. The IDA was one of the first such agencies – founded in 1949, focusing on attracting foreign investment in the early 1960s, and becoming a semiautonomous agency in 1969.

The IDA became a highly effective organization in promoting a specific set of global connections: attracting foreign investment, primarily from the United States, to Ireland. Its method consisted largely of approaching small but promising companies through its international offices, building a relationship with them at that stage, and then perhaps enticing them to locate in Ireland three to four years later when they are looking for a base in Europe. Some of the jewels in the IDA crown, such as Intel and Hewlett Packard, took significantly longer to persuade.

---

1   One of the early Presidents of the World Association of Investment Promotion Agencies (WAIPA) after its founding in 1995 was Paid McMenamin, a longtime IDA official.

"The primary objective of WAIPA ... is to exchange experiences in investment promotion and to provide a range of related training and advisory services to its members." (UNCTAD, 2000)

IDA executives often spoke of themselves in terms of a "marketing" organization, driven by "sales" targets. As one ex-IDA executive interviewed stated:

"The IDA is very target driven – they identify a sector, then their aim is X number of jobs from X number of projects. They establish contacts with companies as they are emerging, then they catch them later. For example, the IDA was talking to Intel for years before they came. That's how they got Microsoft and Lotus too."

IDA strategy has always been to identify key emerging sectors and to pursue firms within those sectors. In some cases, this involved "making the globalization pitch" to the companies before the companies had seriously considered investing overseas:

"We were selling the distance–independence concept to companies – they hadn't thought of it, we were putting it to them." (IDA executive)

Another IDA executive argued (regarding the successful attempts to attract pharmaceutical companies):

"What the IDA did was to get the information to the decision-makers in the pharmaceutical companies. We pioneered a new technique – we approached them. The companies were flabbergasted, no one else was doing that, we pioneered that. The early IDA top executives, they wanted a marketing perspective in the IDA. Michael Killeen [the first IDA chief executive] brought in Brendan Swan, who had no civil-service background and had been in the United States. Swan brought a marketing focus – we have to go out and get them, not wait for them to come to us. It was like going out to preach the Gospel, it was a tough job."

As one IDA project officer who has worked internationally put it,

"All this talk about strategy is bolox. I get annoyed at people who come up with these strategies and analyses with 20/20 hindsight. What the IDA did was put people where the companies were, we did this early on. We are quick on our feet and will move to where the companies are. The people build up contacts, they work hard, they have good communication skills. What we are doing is a selling job. The IDA sets out to identify fast-growing companies with a potential market in Europe. Then we approach them, show them what they could get from Europe, and tell them what they can get from Ireland. Then we just work on them. We have contacts at very high levels within the large companies."

Sectors are "picked" not through a magical crystal ball of superior state rationality but rather through international information-gathering and attempting to follow international trends as closely as possible. One IDA executive's account of the decisions in the early 1970s to pursue electronics and pharmaceuticals investment is revealing regarding the IDA's perspective on its own activities:

"You can't finger a person who made the decision but it was the start of a process within the IDA where we would look at our advantages – tax and skills – and our main disadvantages – location and distance. Then we looked for product areas that fit this. Pharmaceuticals fit it because it's profitable (tax) and research and development–based (skills). Electronics is not as clear-cut, but it was very high growth. We were low cost, English-speaking, had available property, and in some cases, the tax was important."

This deeply pragmatic approach to "planning" has characterized the IDA throughout its history – and indeed, for the most part, it thinks of itself as a marketing organization rather than a planning organization.

Shifts in sectoral focus reflect this. The IDA was relatively early to focus its efforts on "international services," adding to the existing emphasis on manufacturing. Drawing on reports by international consultants and their own information from investment-promotion activities, as early as 1975 an international services program was founded that extended some of the promotional efforts and incentives aimed at manufacturing to service industries – with a particular focus on engineering consulting and software (*IDA News*, May 1975). This was only five to ten years after the emergence of an independent software industry in the United States (Mowery, 1996; Steinmuller, 1996). In fact, the early emphasis seems to have been on engineering consulting with almost ten times as many jobs approved by the IDA for grant aid than in software firms between 1975 and 1978 (*IDA News*, September 1978). However, many of those jobs never materialized and by 1981 – when a ministerial order created eleven "designated" internationally traded service sectors for assistance – the two sectors made eligible for the new 10 percent tax were software and data processing. A 1984 report by the consultancy firm of Arthur D. Little confirmed the central importance of software (Coe, 1997).

The state, therefore, sent an early signal to foreign investors, but also indirectly to indigenous business, that software was a sector that would receive state support for the foreseeable future. By 1990, and even more clearly by 1996, software dominated the international services program of the industrial-development agencies, with only data processing and international financial services also showing significant (although much lower) employment (Department of Enterprise and Employment, 1997, p. 7). The increasing emphasis on international services was shown in the increase in interest in services in the three industrial plans published by the IDA in the 1970s. The first plan (1973–77) focused on regional development issues and made no mention of international services; the second plan (1977–80) had a sectoral focus and briefly mentioned services (including software); and the third plan (1978–82) had a full section on services, although the emphasis was still on engineering consultancy (IDA, 1972, 1976, 1977).

Within each sector, the IDA focuses its attention on attempting to attract "flagship" projects that can then be used to "sell" the country as a location to other firms within the industry. Pfizer has played this role in pharmaceuticals; in electronics, Digital, in an earlier period, and Microsoft and Intel have served a similar purpose.

"We do go for a name and then use it as a flagship – it's the most powerful draw. That is still at the heart of our marketing and selling. We always use that in our first call – firms are always fascinated to learn about their competitors,"

said one top IDA executive. Once the company has located in Ireland, the IDA remains the most relevant part of the state bureaucracy for it, despite the occasional visit by a government minister to the company's facility (organized by the IDA). If a company has a problem with any aspect of infrastructure or state policy, it will turn almost immediately to the IDA, which works diligently to insulate the TNCs from the vagaries of the system as a whole.

This ongoing relationship between the IDA and its "client" companies is critical to future-investment attraction efforts because visits to existing companies, where senior management is usually Irish, form a central part of attempts to lure future investors. The IDA becomes deeply locked into the interests of its client companies. As one more skeptical observer, who works primarily with indigenous technology firms, put it:

"The IDA mission was foreign investment, indigenous development was tacked on, it was that way from the beginning. The IDA is great on foreign investment. It has a system which is superficial but effective – you get out there, talk to as many companies as possible, get some over to visit, wine and dine them, take them everywhere you can in the country, give the tax breaks, and so on. This has not even a remote relationship to the painful, fraught process of growing indigenous firms."

Within the IDA, the goal of economic development is often expressed in terms of a focus on marketing the nation as a location. For the IDA, national developmentalism and location marketing are often seen as the same thing, as illustrated in this quote from a senior IDA official:

"We see ourselves as a business, we are looking for new markets, new products, and so on. We never saw ourselves as grant processors, we're an economic development agency."

The official rejects a view of the IDA as simply administrators of grants to foreign investors and identifies its marketing work as central to its economic-development work. Such an approach has clearly been highly effective in attracting foreign investment – the limits of this organizational culture and ideology of economic development in fostering indigenous development are examined in later chapters.

TECHNOLOGY-DRIVEN COMMODITY CHAINS

The efforts of the Irish state to create an infrastructure and provide incentives for knowledge-based industry bore fruit in the large number of TNCs that located software operations in Ireland. Irish subsidiaries remained relatively low, however, in the hierarchy of software industry "global commodity chains" (Gereffi, 1994). Gereffi argued that in producer-driven commodity chains (PDCCs), a large integrated industrial enterprise (typically a TNC) controls the commodity chain through its control of the critical elements of the manufacturing process. In buyer-driven commodity chains (BDCCs), "large retailers, brand-name merchandisers, and trading companies play the pivotal role in setting up decentralized production networks in a variety of exporting countries." (Gereffi, 1994, p. 221). PDCCs are most common in capital-intensive industries such as automobiles, whereas BDCCs are most common in labor-intensive industries such as apparel. But this distinction, important as it is, neglects the particular characteristics of production networks where control over technological design, standards, and trajectories is the central element of business power (see UNCTAD, 2002, for analyses of the

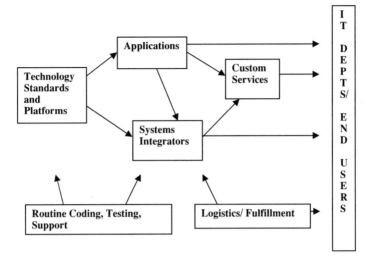

Figure 4.1. Technology-Driven Commodity Chains

Intel and Ericsson technology-driven commodity chains [TDCC]). To analyze the global information economy, we must extend Gereffi's concept of global commodity chains to incorporate new modes of business organization and to rethink commodity chains as dynamic, politically contested forms of organization.

Figure 4.1 illustrates the basic structure of a TDCC, most common in industries that are research-intensive. At the heart of TDCCs are the technology standards and platforms upon which other products are built and with which they interact. Next most important are firms that provide applications sold as standardized products in which the potential of securing a major part of the value added in the commodity chain is relatively high. System integrators do the work of pulling together systems for customers and integrating a variety of technologies to presumably meet a user's needs. Finally, a large variety of custom-service providers tailor systems and even write new code but on a much smaller scale. This segment and the work of coding, testing, and support throughout the system are the most visible but the least significant parts of TDCCs.

Where economies of scale and production efficiencies are central to PDCCs and control of marketing and distribution to BDCCs, it is control over technical standards that is critical to power in TDCCs (Mowery, 1996, p. 10).

"Standards setters have the opportunity to lock-in customers around their product and will lock customers in for future generations as well." (Dedrick and Kraemer, 1998, p. 259)

"Lock-in" is reinforced by users who must invest substantial time and money in learning how to use the technologies and by applications developers who tailor their products to be compatible with certain operating systems or applications. It is further reinforced because the success of a particular platform increases the potential markets for applications developers. Taken together, these characteristics mean that many ICT markets are characterized by increasing returns to the standards setters, often the first movers who are able to set the terms of the deals made throughout the commodity chain. Important network externalities emerge

"in which an individual's decision to adopt a given design is influenced positively by the number of other adopters"

and, typically, these

"network externalities have less to do with physical interconnection than with the ability of a dominant design to create a 'bandwagon effect' among the independent software developers. . . ." (Khazam and Mowery, 1996, p. 86)

Furthermore, as Ernst and O'Connor argue in their analysis of the global electronics industry in the late 1980s,

"while production-related economies of scale continue to matter, the epicenter of competition has shifted to R&D and other forms of intangible investment and to the coordination of increasingly complex corporate networks . . . our research shows that competitive success increasingly depends on the capacity to reduce the huge coordination costs of network transactions. . . ." (1992, p. 24)

The importance of network externalities in TDCCs was cemented by the shift from proprietary systems – typically self-contained systems operating to a standalone company standard – to open systems, which were in principle compatible with a wide variety of other hardware and software components (Egan, 1997; Steinmuller, 1996). This created the basis for an independent software industry that rapidly became a critical part of the computer industry: although hardware costs in computers were five times that of software in 1970, by 1990 they were equal (Ernst and O'Connor, 1992). The industry structure itself, therefore, moved toward the increasing importance of building alliances and creating technical communities around particular technologies, in the process locking in users and technology developers (Egan, 1997; Khazam and Mowery, 1996).

Power in TDCCs resides, therefore, in *what* is getting made and in mobilizing networks of support for those products rather than in *how* that product is produced – emphasizing the place of intellectual-property holders in the system. The power of expert labor, however, will also be enhanced as firms offer inducements to "scarce" technical professionals to help them be first to define new standards or new types of products and markets. The central class compromise in TDCCs is, therefore, between a class of technical professionals and the technology firms that cluster around particular technologies. The dominant hand in this bargain is held by the firms that have the intellectual-property rights to the critical standards-defining technologies. But even those firms are left somewhat insecure because intellectual property rights are notoriously vulnerable to informal information-sharing and collaborative learning in technical communities. Indeed, they must be vulnerable to such collective learning if they are to persist as the standard and develop a loyal user base. Technical communities and global technology networks interact to produce the uneven geography of the global information economy. Network externalities in technology development mean that simply emulating dominant models of growth in those industries or mobilizing massive resources is not enough. Competing effectively in those industries requires that both firms and technical communities, although locally embedded, must have close ties to global technology networks of innovation and learning. There remain, however, multiple nodes within those commodity chains in which subordinate firms can be integrated, often with dramatically varying developmental results. Where did the software TNCs in Ireland fit into the TDCCs?

MOVING UP AND DIGGING IN? FOREIGN-OWNED SOFTWARE FIRMS IN IRELAND

Foreign software firms in Ireland can be divided into two main categories: firms focusing on the manufacturing, distribution, and localization of mass-market software packages; and firms providing systems integration and software services or with dedicated software-development centers. Each sector has a distinctly different profile and makes a different contribution to industrial development. Each has also undergone a succession of rounds of globalization and localization (Ó Riain, 1997).

Software localization and the growth of local suppliers

Table 4.1 outlines the major companies involved in the manufacturing, distribution, and localization of mass-market software packages throughout the 1990s. Although many of the most prominent software publishers have extensive facilities in Ireland, their operations rarely include significant elements of software development – instead focusing on disk duplication, packaging, fulfillment, localization, and porting.[2]

Although they are the least sophisticated foreign-owned software firms, local management has been able to gradually add significantly to their operations in Ireland, starting out with disk-duplication operations – typically between 1985 and 1988 for the longest established – and gradually moving into documentation and localization (1988–89) (Irish Computer, July 1991, p. 32). Although a few companies, such as Lotus, Oracle, and Visio, have flirted with product modification and development, most have not been able to move significantly beyond localization.

---

2 "Localization" of software refers to the process of customizing existing software packages for specific national and linguistic markets. The main activity is the translation of the text but it may also involve changing date formats, letter formats, and other culture-specific aspects of the software. In U.S. software companies, the work of designing the software program so that it can be customized in this way is called "internationalization" and is generally carried out in the United States. The work of actually customizing the program for specific markets is called "localization." This work of localization is relatively uncomplicated and should not be confused with the socioeconomic processes of the localization or territorialization of production and innovation discussed previously. "Porting" is the process of making software compatible with new technological platforms and operating systems, and involves more genuine software development.

Table 4.1. Software Localization and Fulfillment, 1992–2001

Company Name	Country of Origin	Location in Ireland	Employment 1992	1996	2001	Turnover (£,m) 1992	1996	2001
Software Publishers								
Microsoft	U.S.	Dublin	300	875	1,592	60(e)	924(e)	3,534(e)
Oracle	U.S.	Dublin			800			1,400
Lotus	U.S.	Dublin	250	400	664	65(e)	130(e)	425(e)
Creative Labs	Singapore	Dublin		240	525		269(e)	399.5
Symantec	U.S.	Dublin		199	503		64	224
Sun Microsystems	U.S.	Dublin			250			65.1
Novell	U.S.	Dublin		70	92		310	400
Corel	Canada/U.S.	Dublin			16			150.8
Claris	U.S.	Dublin	65	125	0	15	50(e)	0
Borland	U.S.	Dublin	86	90	0	57.2	45	0
Quarterdeck	U.S.	Dublin		50	0		7	0
Printing and Fulfillment Companies								
BG Turnkey/Banta	Ireland/U.S.	Cork	100	150	650	5(e)	6.5(e)	150
Dakota Group	Ireland	Dublin		322	290		19	23.5(e)
Saturn Fulfillment	Canada	Dublin			270			25.8
Microprint	Ireland	Dublin	90	130	100	5.6	9	12.5(e)
Stream International	U.S.	Dublin	350	700		18(e)	37.2	
Mount Salus Press	Ireland	Dublin	120	127	*	9	14.35	*
Printech	Ireland	Dublin	324			19.27		
Localization Companies								
Berlitz	U.S.	Dublin		220	420		13(e)	21(e)
Lionbridge	U.S.	Dublin			160			14
SDL Intl.	U.S.	Bray			150			25
Havas Interactive	France	Dublin			100			47
JLS	U.S.	Dublin			80			14(e)

* Taken over by Adare Printing Group, which in 2001 had turnover of £213 million and employed 1,599 people in a broad range of businesses.
(e) estimate.
Sources: "Top 1,000 Companies," *Business and Finance*, 1992, 1996, 2001.
Note: Only companies included in the "Top 1,000" are included in this table. Where data are not present, companies may still be operating but have not reached the turnover threshold for the "Top 1,000." This threshold was £1.5m in 1992, £3m in 1996, and £9.8m in 2001. Some companies' revenues include sources other than software and care should be taken in interpreting these figures. The company name given is that used in 2001, although every effort has been made to assure a consistent series across the *Business and Finance* listings.

Many managers in software-localization operations said that getting TNCs to locate product development in Ireland, or anywhere outside the United States, is "a constant struggle."

"It's keeping an eye on the crown jewels, they won't let them go. They are afraid of losing control, that's a big issue for them,"

said one Dublin engineer with extensive experience in a TNC. Another manager in a U.S. TNC said that although headquarters might worry initially about the technical ability in Ireland, over time it becomes an issue of control:

"I don't think it's a skill thing, it's a control thing. It's a distance thing too, they can't see what's going on." (Ó Riain, 1997)

A U.S.–born manager in a third TNC that does significant "porting" in Dublin had experienced similar problems in getting development work moved out of the United States.

"They like to keep control of development. And then communication problems are a big issue when you can't just walk down the hall to talk to someone and you have to deal with the time differences. . . . There are some U.S.–centric attitudes in the company. Some people in the United States don't even know we're here, it's such a big organization. . . . Our group had an idea for collaborating with a leading Irish company on some quite sophisticated development but HQ in California was very reluctant. They also had another strategy which affected their decision not to go ahead with that."

A vice president of a prominent Silicon Valley company with an operation in Ireland argued, "we are too [San Francisco] Bay Area–centric. But software development is global. . . . The fundamental problem is trying to get the local Bay Area software community within the company to give Ireland a clear mission and charter." Although some more development work may move to the firms' Irish subsidiaries, the impulse toward centralized control and the continuing difficulties (social rather than technical) of transnational communication mean that this process is often slow and limited.

The impact on indigenous software is minimal, with few examples of spin-offs or management mobility from foreign firms into indigenous software-development companies. However, those companies have been the basis of a sub-supplier base in turnkey services and software-manual printing (Jacobson and O'Sullivan, 1994, 1997). The printing industry had a pre-installed base in Ireland and was helped by the fact that the TNCs never printed their own manuals in-house. The Irish-born managers of those TNCs reputedly told the local printing firms, "We have the business for reprinted software manuals, it's there for you if you can get it." Those companies invested heavily in new technology and the industry grew from $9 million to $135 million in five years from the late 1980s, based almost totally on the demand of the foreign software firms (IDA, n.d.; Jacobson and O'Sullivan, 1994). TNCs were also beginning to rely increasingly on outsourcing as a strategy during the 1980s to take advantage of external economies of scale and the potential for shifting costs onto suppliers. This trend intensified over the period; for example,

Lotus and Microsoft, which set up in the mid-1980s, did nearly all of their own work in-house, whereas Oracle (set up in 1990) and Novell (1995) outsourced practically all their work and simply managed those relationships from their Dublin operations.

There were further opportunities for turnkey services companies such as BG Turnkey, which was set up by an ex-Apple employee across the road from Apple in Cork. Those companies tended to start with basic operations and expanded to full turnkey operations, in which they would take responsibility for a whole segment of the production process. As more TNCs invested in Ireland, the supplier base grew, with turnkey services growing from zero to $150 million in five years from the late 1980s (IDA, n.d.). In the localization area, a number of Irish-owned translation bureaus emerged that offered full translation services to TNCs doing localization in Ireland. Typically, the founders of those firms had worked for TNCs doing localization work. The state played a key role in supporting the growth of those subsupplier industries, specifically by providing finance and advice to the entrepreneurs in the newly minted sectors and by coordinating relations among Irish-born managers of TNCs and the emerging firms. Printing firms, for example, received significant funding from the IDA for the expensive new web-print technologies required for software-manual printing (Jacobson and O'Sullivan, 1994).

Whereas the major market for these services – the software publishers – was almost entirely foreign-owned, many of the early companies established in those sectors were Irish-owned. As Ireland became established as the center for software localization in Ireland, it attracted many of the major international firms in the software documentation and localization industry. Major firms such as Berlitz and Stream International located in Ireland by acquiring established Irish companies. By the late 1990s the localization industry was dominated by foreign-owned firms, shifting the ownership of the industry even as Ireland became more clearly established as the territorialized center of software localization in Europe. The Dublin region had become a global region for software fulfillment and localization, albeit one dominated by foreign firms.

Upgrading software services and development

Nonetheless, localization remains relatively low in the TDCC hierarchy. Systems integration and software development offered an avenue to more rewarding niches in the global information economy. Table 4.2 gives basic data on the leading foreign-owned firms carrying out such operations in the 1990s. Working on systems integration or custom software-development projects has the potential to provide a number of skills that are useful to development work more generally. Most basic is the chance to get some experience working on particular platforms or languages; for example, IBM provides experience on AS400 and other IBM platforms, ICL focuses on Unix, Amdahl uses a variety of object-oriented approaches, and so on. Such skills mean that employees of those companies are potential candidates for moving into key development roles in other companies.

Table 4.2. Foreign-Owned Companies with Software Development Operations, 1992–2001

Company Name	Country of Origin	Location in Ireland	Employment			Turnover (£,m)		
			1992	1996	2001	1992	1996	2001
IBM**	U.S.	Dublin	402	500	4,200	66.7	66.9	156
LM Ericsson**	Sweden	Athlone	662	1,010	1,900	52.7	86.14	260
Apple**	U.S.	Cork	950	1,500	1,050	525	706.51	600(e)
Siemens	Germany	Dublin	165	151	688	50	48	170
Compaq/ Digital**	U.S.	Galway	850(e)	400	535	500(e)	270(e)	330
Motorola	U.S.	Cork		122	460		7.64	32
EDS	U.S.	Dublin			330			24.8
Bull CARA	France	Dublin			300			73.4
Silicon & Software Systems	Netherlands	Dublin	89	155	300	4.5	8.1	30
Alcatel**	France	Bandon, Co. Cork	115	108	199	12.5(e)	24	43
AMT/ Sybex**	U.K.	Dublin			175			33.5
Amdahl	U.S./Japan	Dublin	590	167	100	307**	115**	30(e)
Critical Path	U.S.	Dublin			100			11(e)
Cambridge Technology Partners	U.S.	Dublin			80			10
Memorex Telex**	U.S.	Dublin	60	51	68	9	8	19
Avid Technology**	U.S.	Dublin			65			127
Trinity Technology	U.K.	Dublin			60			24
Eicon Networks**	U.K.	Dublin			50			63

Sources: "Top 1,000 Companies," *Business and Finance,* 1992, 1996, 2001.
(e) estimate.
Note: Only companies included in the "Top 1,000" are included in this table. Where data are not present, companies may still be operating but have not reached the turnover threshold for the "Top 1,000." This threshold was £1.5m in 1992, £3m in 1996, and £9.8m in 2001. The company name given is that used in 2001, although every effort has been made to assure a consistent series across the *Business and Finance* listings.
** These companies' revenues include significant sources other than software and care should be taken in interpreting these figures.

Furthermore, depending on the company, there may be an opportunity for developing project management skills – an area that the major firm EDS, for example, claims is a competency of its remote software engineering center (Coe, 1997; *IT's Monday*, January 12, 1998).

The firms in this sector generally located in Ireland to gain access to labor that was in short supply in their own country (e.g., EDS, Cambridge Technology) or were able to build up systems-integration businesses around an earlier sales (e.g., IBM) or hardware-manufacturing (e.g., Amdahl) operation. It is noticeable that these firms are concentrated in the computer systems and communications areas and are more diverse in their national backgrounds. They have either built up these operations by strategically adding to an existing hardware operation (e.g., Ericsson, Siemens Nixdorf, Lucent) or entered Ireland primarily through social networks and ties that went beyond simply negotiating with the IDA. Siemens Nixdorf and S3 (a Phillips subsidiary that carried out sophisticated development work) had built up a connection to Ireland through the heavy hiring of Irish graduates in the mid-1980s (*Irish Computer*, November 1986) and – in the case of S3 – through the presence in the Netherlands of an Irish engineering lecturer who is the current managing director of S3. Critical Path took over ISOCOR, whose headquarters was in Los Angeles but which maintained most of its development team in Dublin, where it was put together by one of the founders who had worked in Dublin with an earlier telecommunications software company called Retix. Motorola bought another company in the United States that happened to have an operation in Cork; the local management was able to grow the facility and develop a reputation for excellent quality standards.

Many of the Irish subsidiaries have been able to develop more sophisticated operations through corporate "intrapreneurialism." Intrapreneurialism is easier in more diverse parent corporations. Companies such as Microsoft and Lotus concentrate on a relatively small number of strategic software packages: their software development operations are highly concentrated and the opportunities for building up capabilities around complex implementation, systems integration, or sales support are limited. However, there are significantly greater opportunities in companies such as Digital, Amdahl, IBM, Siemens Nixdorf, and Phillips, which sell hardware and software in a variety of "bundles," or in telecommunications companies such as Ericsson or ATT/ Lucent Technologies, which have both hardware and software operations.

Successful intrapreneurs among subsidiary management can maintain their own embedded autonomy within the corporation. Limited though they are by the parent's European strategy (Coe, 1997), subsidiaries usually have some measure of autonomy as long as they follow the broad corporate strategy and maintain "your numbers." The Irish manager of a U.S. TNC that had built up its development functions over the years claimed:

"A high proportion of our parent's sales are in Europe, that leads to development, especially where you are dealing with customer facing technologies."

The regionalization of TNC marketing strategies between North America, Europe, and Asia in recent years (Gereffi, 1994) facilitated the expansion of the Irish operations.

One manager in a European subsidiary of a Silicon Valley company claimed:

"When we're in Europe, we do things our own way. Local knowledge is a big plus – we had a U.S. guy, he was a disaster, it's hard to manage in another culture. You do things your own way on the ground, you follow the corporate strategy but implement things your own way."

Local managers often see themselves as serving a project of national economic development through promoting the Irish operation and agitating for more sophisticated work for the Irish operation.

"There's a feeling that we're all in this to develop the industry in Ireland, so we help each other out by letting people over from the States visit each others' places and so on." (Irish manager, U.S. TNC)

This outlook has been present among Irish managers since the 1970s – emerging from the Irish management of Digital in particular – and was further strengthened by a shift in IDA focus in the 1980s to pressuring and supporting managers in hardware and telecommunications TNCs to upgrade their operations, often by expanding into software (*Irish Computer*, April 1985).

Autonomy is only beneficial insofar as the subsidiary can also maintain the critical connections to leading customers and key executives at headquarters. One manager of a U.S. TNC had previously worked for a number of years at the company's headquarters and had traveled to the United States fourteen times the year before. He commented on the lack of connections another Irish subsidiary had to its parent in the United States:

"They are at risk now. The Irish people should be very close to the guys in the United States, they should be mutually adjusting to one another. I get little surprises all the time; they are getting big surprises because they are not close to those guys."

In many cases, such as Amdahl and Sun Microsystems, the combination of an energetic local manager with close ties to an executive in the United States who is either Irish-born or has Irish ancestry can be of great value to the local subsidiary. In some cases, the close connections are present from an early stage or even from when the company sets up in Ireland. Philips had a close connection to Ireland through its hiring of Irish graduates in the mid-1980s and the role of Dr. Maurice Whelan, who had worked in Phillips in Holland for years before returning to run S3. In some cases, these transnational social networks are in place before the company arrives in Ireland but for most, building the ties becomes a critical component of the subsidiary manager's work.

It would seem, then, that the majority of foreign companies – entering the country almost exclusively through negotiations with the state and largely unable to add development functions to their operation – contribute much in the way of employment but little to the development of a learning industry and region.

However, a significant minority of companies do contribute to the creation of a learning region because they add strategically to their existing operations or can carve out a space within their corporate parent, which allows for an upgrading of the functions within the Irish operation. Although constrained by corporate decisions largely out of their control, the subsidiaries have been able to slowly inch their way farther up the hierarchy of the TDCCs in which they are embedded.

FOREIGN INVESTMENT AND THE SHAPING OF IRISH SOFTWARE

The pursuit of foreign investment has been central to Irish industrial policy and has a major impact on Irish industrial development through tax income, local spending, and direct and indirect employment (Breathnach, 2002). The software industry has been a critical plank of that strategy. Few other countries have reshaped their population, territory, and institutions to attract foreign investment to the degree that has happened in Ireland. Singapore has been equally resolute in making foreign investment the basis of its developmental strategy and has been even more successful in the volume of investment that it has attracted. Singapore also shares with Ireland the dubious honor of being one of the major regional entrepôts in the world economy. However, the two economies have built different indigenous industrial structures around those foreign-investment hubs. The Singaporean state has channeled revenues from industrial development into state enterprises and public funds, using those funds to subsidize social reproduction, as well as building up state enterprises as major firms in infrastructural industries across the region (Huff, 1995a). By contrast, the Irish state has partly privatized such state enterprises and has weakened its commitment to state-supported social reproduction through the welfare state.

The puzzle that the Irish case presents is how an indigenous high-technology industry such as software could emerge in the context of an entrepôt-style foreign-owned sector. This question is more critical given the increasing emphasis on attracting foreign investment by national economies around the world. Other emerging software industries have grown in circumstances much less radically shaped by the demands of foreign investment. India's initial reliance on "body-shopping" and labor-contracting has been lessened by state policy focused on creating development centers in India and boosting India's status as a location for remote software development. Although foreign firms have been important to the Indian software industry, the major development challenge has been to reverse the twin "brain drains" of professional emigration and short-term labor-contracting and to develop local development centers and ICT markets (Parthasarathy, 2000). In Israel, the most successful of all the semiperipheral software regions, the industry has been built on technical communities rooted in U.S.–Israeli ties and the Israeli military as a "public space" for technologists (Breznitz, 2002a, 2002b). Irish indigenous software remains, therefore, not an "ideal model" of industrial development but rather a particularly fascinating one: How was an industrial system molded to meet the needs of foreign investment changed to support the development of an indigenous innovative milieu? This chapter has shown that although the FDI strategy has made a contribution to high-tech industrial development in Ireland, it has clear limits, even with intrapreneurial upgrading. The next chapter examines how a dynamic indigenous industry emerged in such unlikely circumstances.

5

INDIGENOUS INNOVATION AND THE
DEVELOPMENTAL NETWORK STATE

During the crisis of the 1980s, analysts proposed – often in hope rather than conviction – a variety of "models" for tackling the dilemmas of industrial development in the Irish economy. For most economists, and particularly with Thatcherism in full swing in nearby Britain, the solution was a more resolute shift toward a market-driven economy. Economic development was to rely on the positive effects of foreign investment and/or the emergence of local entrepreneurs through the selection mechanisms of the marketplace. As we have seen, we cannot rely on FDI as an explanation of the indigenous-software success story, nor can upgrading be ascribed to entrepreneurship given free rein through the market. The "supply of entrepreneurs" in Ireland in the 1990s was no higher than elsewhere and probably lower, given massive professional emigration; nor can the "selection effects" of the "shake-out" of Irish industry in the 1980s, leaving only the strongest firms standing, explain the Irish miracle. Important segments of the revived indigenous industry are dominated by new firms, and what is most striking is the emergence of new technical–professional entrepreneurs in a complex interaction of market, state, and society where entrepreneurship was profoundly shaped and promoted by a dense network of public and semipublic institutions. The critical difference between the 1980s and the 1990s was a state–society alliance between this technical-professional class and relevant state agencies – in economists' terms, improving the *productivity* of the entrepreneurial base rather than simply increasing its supply.

Other analysts called for a "developmental state" on the Korean model that could sponsor and support a number of "national-champion" firms (O'Malley, 1989). Such a model has been enormously effective in high-tech industries elsewhere around the globe. However, the Irish state, active as it was in the development of indigenous software and in upgrading industry more generally, adopted an approach quite different from that of the classic DBSs. State influence operated less through the shaping of decisions of lead national-champion firms than by shaping the characteristics of a wide variety of firms. Whereas developmental-state theorists emphasize the direct negotiation between firms and state elites over firm-based decisions, neoliberals emphasize transforming the environment so that it conforms to the classical market model. The DNSs of Ireland, Taiwan, and Israel also shape the environment but are less obsessed in practice with market conformity than they claim. Instead, they aim to shape the social and institutional environment of firms by creating networks of associations and shaping industrial cultures of innovation. Furthermore, they influence firm decisions indirectly – primarily by attempting to create specific kinds of firms: those that are oriented toward learning, R&D, and "high-value-added" competition. Sitting ambiguously between market fundamentalism and autonomous statism, the Irish state shaped the growth of the indigenous software industry in profound ways.

FOREIGN FIRMS AND LOCAL TECHNICAL COMMUNITIES

Firebaugh (1992, 1996) argued that although foreign investment produces worse growth effects than domestic investment, FDI does not inhibit growth. However, Dixon and Boswell (1996a, b) found that dependence on foreign investment also appears to inhibit domestic investment through negative externalities associated with dependence, ultimately reducing growth over the long term (see also Kentor, 1998). O'Hearn (1989) argued, similarly, that although foreign investment had a positive (albeit weak) effect on industrial output in Ireland from the 1960s to the 1980s, the associated policy of free trade had a stronger damaging effect on industrial development. This resulted in a net loss to the Irish economy from foreign-investment–led development. In the absence of such externalities, however, policymakers could feel justified in pursuing FDI as a "second-best option" if domestic investment proved difficult to elicit.[1] What then has been the contribution of foreign-owned firms in Ireland to the growth of indigenous software?

Many policymakers hoped that the foreign firms attracted to Ireland would in time spin-off a range of Irish-owned firms. O'Gorman et al. found that one third of the indigenous software entrepreneurs whom they interviewed in 1997 had worked in a TNC directly before starting their own company – in both TNCs in the IT sector and in the IT sections of TNCs in other sectors (1997, p. 35). Another third or so had come directly from indigenous software firms, and the final third had come from indigenous firms in other sectors, most notably software distribution and computer hardware. TNCs provide a significant stimulus to indigenous firms. However, direct spin-offs of software firms from software TNCs are relatively rare: the dynamic of generating new companies is strongest in the indigenous sector, therefore, and especially within the software industry. In recent years, start-ups have emerged primarily from the leading indigenous software firms (HotOrigin, 2001).

1   For a detailed discussion of the indigenous industrial development effects of FDI in the economy as a whole, see Ó Riain, 2003.

Leaving aside the direct sources of start-ups, two thirds of indigenous en-trepreneurs had worked for a TNC in Ireland at some stage of their careers: half had worked abroad in software or a related sector, and half had worked in a sector that was now a customer of their firm (O'Gorman et al., 1997, p. 35; for a similar dynamic in the early 1980s, see Cogan and Onyenadum, 1981; Onyenadum and Tomlin, 1984). Although this international and TNC experience might be expected given the dominance of TNCs in the Irish economy and the mass emigration of the 1980s, it is nonetheless an important factor in the early growth of the industry.

As elsewhere, early software firms in Ireland were involved primarily in provid-ing software services. Cara and System Dynamics, both founded in 1968, offered bureau and software services to domestic industry and mostly stayed in the con-sulting and contracting end of the business. However, another group of firms, such as Kindle, GC McKeown, and Insight, was founded in the 1970s and moved into export markets within specialized product areas. Almost without exception, those companies grew and gained access to international markets by starting out as a programming house for one of the leading computing companies at the time. They developed a software application for a multinational firm that had located in Ireland, piggybacking on that customer to gain access to its sites around Europe and beyond.

Due to the small size of the Irish market, the leading international computer-makers used contractors in Ireland to implement their software development work. Because computer hardware platforms were proprietary and noncompatible at the time, being tied in to one or more of those companies (e.g., ICL, Digital, IBM) was critical to any software company. Furthermore, the multinationals did not import existing computer systems at headquarters into their relatively small Irish operations, creating a market for Irish software companies to develop new systems (McAteer and Donohoe, 1996). One such company was Triple A Software (later MA Systems and currently Kindle Banking Systems), founded in 1978. It received an important contract from the Ansbacher Bank (a U.S. bank) in Dublin to develop a banking software product for an ICL platform, leading to a series of contracts with ICL. This is reflected in today's distribution of Kindle's exports, which are primarily to former colonies of the British Empire where ICL is strongest – despite the fact that ICL is now owned by Fujitsu (a Japanese company) and that Kindle moved away from the ICL platform to the personal computer DOS platform in the mid-1980s. Nonetheless, the combination of a multinational customer and access to software-development opportunities with a leading platform provider was crucial to the early success of Kindle.

Multinational investment and access to multinational technologies, therefore, were important to the early history of the industry – not so much by creating direct spin-offs from computer companies locating in Ireland, as the architects of the FDI model had hoped, but by providing a marketing link to the outside world. However, this simply begs the question of how an industry that emerged initially as a small software contracting component of a foreign-owned sector was transformed into a local dynamic of learning, spin-offs, and growth. The majority of indigenous software companies emerged through technical communities that existed in a tangential relationship to foreign-owned firms, not through direct intrapreneurialism or spin-offs.

Moreover, the specific effects are embedded within a broader set of trade-offs in which foreign firms shape indigenous firms through a mix of negative "competition effects," (where TNCs draw resources away from indigenous firms) and positive "linkage effects," (where TNCs generate new opportunities and resources for indigenous firms). We have seen that some linkages existed in software that contributed to the growth of the indigenous software industry. However, those linkages existed in a broader context, which was shaped by the needs of foreign investment and often created obstacles for the growth of indigenous technology firms. If foreign firms created markets for local firms, they also competed in the local market. If they provided learning opportunities for labor, they also competed for scarce labor, creating significant overqualification in the Irish economy (Hannan, McCabe, and McCoy, 1998), aggravated by TNC employment of graduates for relatively low-skilled tasks (McGovern, 1998; Ó Riain, 1997). Furthermore, state institutions were focused primarily on attracting and supporting foreign investment until the institutional shifts of the 1980s, which obstructed the development of capacities for promoting indigenous learning and growth.

In the mid-1980s, a small software industry had emerged based on ties to foreign firms and fragile local technical communities, but no one would have predicted the success of the industry fifteen years later. Most critically, the state – through its heavy investment in education – had created a skilled labor force that would prove to be the basis of the new software industry. Despite a massive brain drain, a number of those who stayed started their own companies and combined with a trickle of people from the foreign-owned sector and other organizations to form the basis of a fragile set of overlapping technical communities in the 1980s. The industry culture was relatively open in the early years, and something of a technical community, linked to international trends, developed.

"There was a lot of swapping of ideas going on from about the mid-80s on. Anything real that goes on is informal." (developer/entrepreneur, Irish software-development firm)

Such technical communities have been central to the development of high-tech industries elsewhere, helping to explain, for example, why Silicon Valley was better able to adapt to changing technological trajectories than Route 128 in Boston (Saxenian, 1994). They have also been central to semiperipheral industries. Israel's technology sectors were built on the close ties between the United States and Israel since the foundation of the Israeli state, resulting in the emergence of transnational technical communities linking Israel closely to the major actors in the U.S. technology industry (Autler, 1999). As soon as migration to the United States grew after changes in U.S. immigration law in 1965, the Taiwanese state acted quickly to make the most of the rapidly growing ties to U.S. technology centers, incorporating expatriate technologists into policy as well as business circles

(Saxenian, 2002). Many of India's difficulties in sustaining an indigenous system of innovation have been rooted in the "hollowing out" of technical communities by migration and labor-contracting and the difficulty of attracting "non-resident Indians" in the United States back to India. Ireland sits somewhere between these cases of long-established transnational technical communities and the hollowing out of local community; although brain drain emigration has taken a disastrous toll on Irish industry, return migration has been common among professionals since the 1980s. The remainder of this chapter considers how the limited resources offered by foreign-owned firms and the fragile technical communities emerging in the 1980s were built on by a new alliance between the state and local technical communities to become the basis of a thriving indigenous sector.

FROM TECHNICAL COMMUNITY TO DYNAMIC INDUSTRY

Localized social networks and cultural practices exist in many more regions than there are fast-growth or innovative regions. As Evans points out in his review of a number of studies of "state–society synergy":

"Ties among friends and neighbors based on trust and rooted in everyday interactions are essential foundations. Without them there would be nothing to build on. The key point is that such ties seem to be a resource that is at least latently available to most Third World communities. Based on these cases, it seems reasonable to argue that if synergy fails to occur, it is probably not because the relevant neighborhoods and communities were too fissiparous and mistrustful but because some other crucial ingredient was lacking. The most obvious candidate is a competent, engaged set of public institutions." (Evans, 1996, p. 1125)

The state, in fact, played a critical role in "scaling up" the social networks within technical communities into an innovative and growing industry. These efforts were organized largely through the industrial development agencies, including in the 1980s and early 1990s the IDA, Eolas, An Córas Tráchtála, and the National Software Center (NSC), and in the 1990s Forbairt, IDA Ireland, Forfás, An Bord Tráchtála, and the National Software Directorate (NSD). The state was the major provider of funding to the industry until 1996. However, state agencies also used connection to firms, established through this funding role, to both learn from and educate the industry. Agencies helped define the nature of the software industry in Ireland and constantly pressured firms to upgrade their capabilities while directing them to the resources to make this possible. The role of state agencies in the development of Irish software bears out the claims of Ventresca and Lacey (2003) that the state can often play a critical role as an "industry entrepreneur," defining the character of an emerging industry. Furthermore, the central part of the state's role is the shaping of the "social worlds of production" and the "relational assets" within the industry (Storper, 1997) – going well beyond the provision of collective inputs to actually shape the social relationships through which those inputs are mobilized.

Prompting investment and R&D

Woo-Cumings (1990, 1999) points out that finance is the lifeblood of the developmental state – the provision of capital to industry has been crucial in the East Asian developmental states in opening up firms to state influence. The Irish state has provided much smaller amounts of capital to indigenous technology firms than the South Korean state, but the state was nonetheless an important source of capital for firms. Crucially, the application for state grant aid opened up firms to an ongoing relationship with state agencies and those relationships became an important channel of information-gathering for state officials.

The level of state investment during the 1990s compares favorably with the contribution of private venture capital. *IT's Monday's* survey of venture-capital investments in software in 1997 estimated that total venture-capital investments in Irish software companies was approximately 15 million Irish pounds, with 5 million of that accounted for by ICC's (a semi-investment bank) investment in Aldiscon. The ICC fund was partly funded by the EU and supported by the Irish state – one of its executives being a former IDA software executive. In fact, much of the venture capital that became available to the industry was induced into the industry by state actions, even as awareness grew of the money to be made in software companies. Some 66 million Irish pounds of venture capital funds was potentially available under a scheme, using mainly EU money, in which Forbairt would provide half of the money in the venture-capital fund if the private fund would provide the other half. In 1997, two funds made 13 million IEP available through this scheme (*IT's Monday*, February 1997). The state, therefore, was the major provider of capital to the indigenous software industry until 1998. This capital was provided through grants and equity, with the state providing 20 million Irish pounds between 1988 and 1992. The state also induced other capital investors into the software investment market, although Forbairt remained practically the only source of seed capital for small start-up ventures (*IT's Monday*, February 1997). Furthermore, this more direct involvement of the state was significantly more effective in promoting productive investment than previous schemes aimed at providing business expansion funds for start-ups. These schemes, with less state agency oversight, became more politicized and degenerated into subsidies for well-established firms or into a peculiarly effective means of avoiding tax (Stewart, 1992).

The importance of the state in providing financing and in stimulating private investment is indicated in Table 5.1, which provides data on private-equity investments between 1997 and 1999, the period when private, increasingly international investment took off in Ireland. Those investments were concentrated in computer-related sectors, electronics, other manufacturing, and (in 1999) communications. The Irish share of European private-equity investment increased from 0.3 percent in 1995 to 0.8 percent in 1998 and 1.2 percent in 1999.

In 1997, all investment was from domestic sources and one third of that was from the state. A significant portion of the remaining investment was stimulated

Table 5.1. Trends in Private Equity Investment, 1997–1999
(000s of Irish Pounds)

	1997	1998	1999
Total Funds	27,713	163,626	316,232
Total State Funds	10,048	20,775	12,151
	Selected Major Types of Investors		
Government	36.3%	12.7%	3.8%
Private Individuals	13.7%	26.2%	21.7%
Banks	17.1%	3.7%	25.0%
Pension Funds	7.3%	8.2%	26.8%
	Geographic Breakdown of Private Equity Raised		
% Domestic	100%	44.7%	42.8%
% Other European	0%	35.7%	19.6%
% Other Non-European	0%	25.2%	32.0%

Source: European Venture Capital Association, Annual Reports.

by the state through "matching funds" arrangements – perhaps up to an additional 25 percent. In 1998, domestic investment increased but, more important, international investors flooded into the increasingly successful Irish economy. The primary source of funds became private individuals as institutions such as pension funds, banks, and insurance funds lagged behind. In 1999, however, institutional investors finally took the lead in funding. Non-European sources accounted for fully one third of funds in 1999, up from a quarter in 1998.

By 1999, Ireland was well integrated in international institutional investment circles and the state withdrew from its previously dominant role as a source of funds. However, individual and institutional investors have mostly followed rather than led the growth of the high-tech industries in which most of this funding is concentrated. Although those investors began to provide the large amounts of funding required by the most prominent companies, they have done so only when the growth potential of the software industry and other high-tech sectors has been clearly demonstrated. Ironically, the risk-taker in this scenario is the state. Indeed, when private capital became more cautious in 2001–02 the state once again took on a crucial role.

Defining an innovation industry

Although software is clearly a knowledge-intensive industry, some forms of participation, such as product development, offer greater potential returns than others, such as labor-contracting. Software product development offers software companies the chance to occupy a strategic position within technology networks and to provide key platform technologies for other companies, reaping the increasing returns from such a position (Egan, 1997). However, product development is demanding and it is not a given that an individual entrepreneur or investor would see product development as a more sensible investment than labor-contracting. The science and innovation agencies of the Irish state, however, did have a clear interest in promoting the higher return segments of the emerging software industry. In its strategic review of 1993, the NSD identified software products as the major focus of the Irish industry, publicly stating what had been the attitude of the state agencies for some time:

"In general, products are easier to export than services, and tend to be less vulnerable in times of recession . . . . Products are quicker to sell: they are tangible and can be objectively evaluated in terms of functionality, ease of use, documentation etc." (NSD, 1993, p. 3-3)

Furthermore, the NSD identified the need of software-product firms to export early in their development – due to the small size of the Irish domestic market – as a critically important issue for the Irish industry. State agencies focused on encouraging firms with software products for export, being more receptive to such firms in their grant applications and focusing some state supports (especially in marketing) on the problems of product-exporting. This path was also realistic because a majority of Irish firms in the early 1990s were mainly product-oriented (NSD, 1993, p. 3-3). The focus of the IDA on attracting foreign investment rather than on trying to develop international services or labor-subcontracting may have been an advantage. At no stage was there a concerted state effort to promote those forms of integration into the global economy – commercial forms that might have encouraged indigenous firms to retreat from the more challenging product-export path in favor of the easier profits from various versions of "bodyshopping." Without trying to direct the technology or market activities of particular firms, the state supported a development path for the indigenous software industry that was both more sustainable and had better prospects for moving up the value chain.

The state, primarily through EU programs, has also been an important stimulus to R&D spending in the software industry. Software firms were unusually innovative among Irish industry: 33 percent of R&D–performing firms in the industry were found to have a "relatively strong commitment" to technological innovation in 1995, compared to 14 percent in all sectors and 28 percent in the high-technology sector as a whole (Forfás, 1997; see also Tables 3.3 and 3.4). Because the international software industry is R&D–intensive, an international comparison would be more enlightening. Unfortunately, however, such statistics are not available. R&D expenditure has been increasing in the Irish industry, with *all firms in the industry* spending 9.6 percent of their sales revenues on R&D in 1995, compared to 7.1 percent *among R&D performers* in 1993 (Forfás, 1997, 1995). This increase is understated by the inclusion in the 1995 survey of the 24 percent of software firms that showed an absence of any innovation (Forfás, special tabulation).

Drawing on surveys carried out by Forfás, Table 5.2 shows the sources of funding used by indigenous software firms in 1993 and 1995. TNCs financed their R&D almost entirely from company funds (Forfás, special tabulations). A striking aspect of R&D funding is the critical importance of state and EU funding in the earlier

Table 5.2. R&D Funding in Indigenous Software Firms, 1993–1995

Total R&D Spending (millions Irish Pounds)	Source of Funding					
	Own Company	Other Irish Companies	State Grants	Other Irish Sources	European Union	Other Foreign Sources
1993 14.77	58.1%	3.3%	13.4%	3.6%	14.4%	10.5%
1995 17.00	84.7%	4.7%	6.0%	1.9%	2.8%	0.0%

Source: Forfás (1995), special tabulations from Forfás.

period – accounting for almost 30 percent of funding directly and, because many of those funds were provided on a matching funds basis, for perhaps about half of all R&D funding in the indigenous software companies in 1993. Those governmental policies were critical, therefore, in stimulating R&D in the earlier stages of the industry's development.

Under the EU second and third framework programs for R&D, Ireland received the fourth highest amount of funding per capita and the highest amount per R&D employee of any country in the EU (Peterson and Sharp, 1998, p. 144). In the years after 1993, when the key EU ESPRIT program had been restructured, the proportion of funds coming from government was heavily reduced. Absolute spending by firms increased dramatically, however, from 9.9 million to 14.4 million Irish pounds. This increased internal capability of the industry and an increase in sources of private funding within Ireland signaled that state funds had stimulated significant R&D investment from within the industry.

Indeed, the importance of the governmental funds is underestimated by the figures in Table 5.2 because some of the keenest participants in EU projects were university computer-science departments, from which projects leading indigenous companies such as Iona Technologies and Piercom emerged. Furthermore, a range of schemes promoted university research to the industry, although university links were apparently stronger to the TNCs than to the smaller indigenous firms (Clarke, 1995, p. 34). Overall, however, it is clear that even in the area of formal R&D spending, governmental funds provided a stimulus to R&D within the indigenous software sector.

"Making Winners"

Telling firms to "follow the yellow brick road" to the wizard's castle of innovation and product exports was not the same as helping them to actually walk the road itself. The hazards of this particular path are illustrated by the experience of a group of companies that emerged in the 1980s and attempted to penetrate international markets by using their own sales subsidiaries and relying on external venture financing – companies such as Intelligence Ireland in communications software, RTS and COPS in IBM applications, and Software Labs in accounting packages for UNIX. Despite some initial success and good sales, those companies were laid low by the huge financial demands of entering export markets and, ultimately, by severe cash-flow problems.

State agencies intervened to encourage and support the firms that were beginning that difficult path. The Telesis Consultancy report of 1982 had been deeply critical of Irish industrial policy and had advocated a policy of selective support for the more promising indigenous firms rather than a continuing reliance on foreign investment – a policy widely known as "picking winners." Industrial policy shifted through the 1980s toward a greater focus on indigenous industry and a greater selectivity in grant-giving (O'Malley, 1992; O'Malley, Kennedy, and O'Donnell, 1992). State agencies, however, focused not only on picking winners but also on a more generalized strategy of "making winners" out of the many firms with whom they dealt. Whereas state officials saw themselves as producing "enterprise" rather than "development" (Carr, 1995, 1998), they institutionalized programs and developed activities that spurred on the industrial-development process, regardless of how they were conceived by the officials who implemented them.

The first contribution of the state to making winners was financial because private investors contributed little to the growth of the industry. IDA grant payments to Irish-owned software companies rose from less than a quarter of a million pounds in 1983 and 1984 to 2 million in 1986, and to 2.65 million in 1988 (*Irish Computer*, August 1989, p. 5). Grant-aid policy shifted during that period from an emphasis on feasibility study grants (approximately ten thousand pounds over two to three years) given to groups of potential entrepreneurs who presented product plans to an increasing focus on preformed companies who received larger grants (approximately 100 thousand pounds over two to three years) for various purposes. This was in keeping with the more selective grant-giving by the IDA during this period (O'Malley, 1992). Using a broader definition of the software industry (including subsuppliers of disk duplication, assemblers, and so on), Clarke (1995) reports that grants continued to increase during the late 1980s and early 1990s. Total grant payments by state agencies to indigenous software companies increased from 3 million to 3.5 million PA between 1988 and 1990 up to 5.4 million in 1991 and 5.66 million in 1992 (Clarke, 1995, p. 143).

This level of financing of the indigenous software industry, although minimal by international standards, was significant in the context of a severe shortage of other capital sources for the industry. Most of the funding for software companies came out of their own earnings, a severe challenge for product-oriented companies in particular, who face long development and marketing lead times before they earn significant income (Clarke, 1995). During the late 1980s, the IDA gradually took more equity in the companies it was supporting: by 1992, the IDA had investments totaling 2.7 million pounds in forty-eight software companies. By 1997, Forbairt (the successor to the IDA as the support agency for indigenous industry) was reported to have investments in "close to 100" software companies (*IT's Monday*, February 1997).

The Enterprise Development Program (EDP), established in 1978, put together an overall package of assistance for particularly promising firms. The scheme not only provided extra funding to promising companies but also assessed the strengths and weaknesses of young firms, helping them compile the resources necessary to tackle those weaknesses and build a successful firm. The Forbairt executive in charge of the program claimed in 1997 that

"Even more important [than grants] is the provision of one-on-one support and advice in terms of business plan development, business plan assessment, and sourcing of finance . . . . The proportion of these companies which grow to more than fifty employees appears to be about eight times higher than for start-up companies in general and over 70 percent of the companies are exporting." (McCall, 1997, p. 14)

The scheme is focused on highly skilled owner–entrepreneurs whose companies are in leading technical markets with strong export potential. Many electronics companies with strong links to software have gone through the EDP program successfully, including Mentec, Trintech, Eurologic, and MDS Telephone Systems. A number of "pure" software companies were similarly supported through the international service program in Forbairt.

Alongwith this greater selectivity and focus on leading firms, the IDA and, later, Forbairt and Enterprise Ireland, tie funding to various aspects of company development – in particular, marketing and management development. The typical grant package to a software firm in the mid-1990s was 150,000 to 180,000 Irish pounds. About one third of that amount was in the form of equity, 20,000 to 25,000 was for management development (either through recruitment or training), and the rest went to employment grants (NSD executive interview, 1997). Marketing grants accounted for a growing proportion of grant aid to software companies (Clarke, 1995).

State grant-giving practices, therefore, promoted a general company development program including marketing, management development, training, and R&D. The precise form this took was flexible, depending on the company, but the state agencies required that such efforts at company development take place. Some IDA executives were involved in company development in the 1980s before the policy shift had found its way into official policy. One IDA executive who has worked with software companies for some time recalls:

"I got involved in company development, on my own time. We helped restructure the companies that needed it. In the early years, everyone was a techie, nobody knew anything about business and selling. They might not agree of course . . . . We had to get a lot of companies to let go, to admit they needed someone to do the selling, that they needed to have financial controls in place. We had to get them to believe in us. We found certain companies coming back for advice; some of them never came back, of course."

Forbairt's goal by the late 1990s was to provide for each stage of company development – feasibility grants as seed capital for start-ups, employment grants for the early growth phase, and then funding for R&D, training, and management development for the company development phase. State agencies took a self-conscious developmental approach to companies as well as to the industry – even though this approach is often couched in the more neoliberal language of "enterprise" (Carr, 1995, 1998).

State officials also played an important informal role in networking different parties in the industries together, even at the level of individual companies. The small size of the industry made it possible to maintain this firm-level awareness of trends in the industry (Coe, 1997). "Softer" supports were also significant, such as the mentoring scheme in which small companies are put in touch with experienced industry figures who become a "guide, philosopher, and friend" to the company, sometimes ultimately becoming company directors. Whereas twelve software companies availed of this scheme between 1989 and 1992, fifty-three did so between 1993 and 1996. A total of 450 companies in all sectors was part of the mentor network in 1999; an EI survey of a sample of participating companies revealed a high level of satisfaction with the program (Enterprise Ireland, 2000).

A Forbairt executive summarizes the agency's approach as follows:

"The development agencies learned that the lone ranger approach doesn't work. A company needs partners, the mentoring program helped with that. The agencies also played an informal role in introducing people. That's something we would have pushed, the partnerships. The other thing the agencies pushed was the capital issue. Forbairt has been priming venture capital funds.... Our role is not picking winners but 'helping to make winners.' It's too difficult to predict winners to pick them; otherwise, we wouldn't need to be working! A lot of our discussions with companies are not regarding the money but regarding business issues .... There is a lot of company capability development work, we were less proactive than that in the days of COPS [an indigenous company that went bust in 1990]. The agencies have gone from being funding agencies to doing company development."

State agencies worked to build the "relational assets" so critical to industrial development (Storper, 1997).

Assessing the effect of state aid

The question, of course, is whether those strategies had the desired effect. O'Malley et al. (1992) showed that manufacturing firms receiving grant aid had higher levels of employment and faster rates of employment growth between 1984 and 1990. Furthermore, larger firms were more likely to receive grant aid, suggesting that state agencies were able to distinguish the most promising candidates for growth, and even the larger firms that received grant aid subsequently grew more quickly. The implication of their analysis is that the types of claims that state officials make regarding the impact of their aid to firms are usually correct.

Using data from the 1997 software industry survey and grants data provided on a confidential basis by Forfás, this analysis can be extended for a more restricted group of firms: 141 Irish-owned firms that gain 100 percent of their revenues from either software products or services. Although applied to a more restrictive group of firms, this analysis extends that of O'Malley et al. in a number of ways: (1) it investigates the impact of grant aid up to 1997, in particular from 1993 to 1997; (2) it is based on the exact amount of total grant aid received, rather than on a necessarily crude distinction between grant-aided and non-grant-aided firms, and (3) it can investigate the impact of grant aid on outcomes other than employment, including product orientation, export orientation (described in this chapter), and internationalization of interfirm networks and employment (see Chapter 6). In the sample, 42.4 percent of firms had received no grant aid, 33.5 percent less than 100 thousand pounds, 18.7 percent between 100 thousand and 500 thousand pounds 1.6 percent between 500 thousand and 1 million pounds, and 3.4 percent (i.e., six firms) had received more than 1 million pounds. The maximum received among those firms was just over 3.5 million pounds.

Table 5.3 investigates some of the major claims made for the effect of state grant aid. Given that this is cross-sectional data, assumptions must be made regarding the causal order of the variables in the analysis. It is assumed that product orientation is the most immutable element of the firm, rooted as it usually is in the founding characteristics of the firm. It is understood that export orientation is more likely to affect employment, rather than vice versa. Equation (1) in Table 5.4 shows that those firms that receive high levels of grant aid are more likely to produce software products, an effect that is statistically significant. This effect declines somewhat as levels of grant aid increase, probably because many firms develop services that support successful products. Younger firms are more likely

Table 5.3. The Impact of State Grant Aid and Other Factors on Product Orientation, Export Orientation, and Employment among Indigenous Software Firms

	(1) % of Revenues from Products	(2) % of Revenues from Exports	(3) Permanent Employees
Age of Firm	−1.31**	−0.50	0.30
Grant Aid 1980–1996 (in 10,000s)	0.45**	0.15**	0.46*
Grant Aid Squared	−0.002**		
Product Orientation		0.32*	−0.18**
Export Orientation			0.15***
Constant	55.1*	28.8*	11.1*
Adj. R2	0.05	0.13	0.34
N	137	133	132

*p < 0.01
**p < 0.05
***p < 0.10

Table 5.4. A Longitudinal Analysis of the Impact of Grant Aid on Employment among Indigenous Software Firms, 1994–1997

	(1) Grant Aid Received 1994–1996 (All Firms with 1993 Data Available)	(2) Permanent Employees 1997 (All Firms with 1993 Data Available)	(3) Permanent Employees 1997 (Firms with < 10 Employees in 1993)
Age of Firm	−8,695**	−0.82	−0.42
Grant Aid 1994–1996		1.7*	1.0*
(in 10,000s)			
Product Orientation		−0.254***	−0.004
Export Orientation		0.101	0.14
1993 Employment:			
11–30 employees	10,681	11.11	
31–50 employees	300,869*	6.91	
51–100 employees	273,441*	77.2*	
Constant	120,963*	22.43*	10.34*
Adj. R^2	0.15	0.56	0.14
N	62	59	37

*$p < 0.01$
**$p < 0.05$
***$p < 0.10$

to produce products and the overall level of product orientation is high, suggesting that there is a strong and increasing industry-wide orientation toward product development that is augmented by state intervention, if not driven by it. The equation only explains 5 percent of the variation in product orientation. Equation (2) in Table 5.4 investigates the export orientation of software firms. Product orientation strongly increases export orientation, as suggested in Table 5.3. Grant aid has a positive effect on export orientation and 13 percent of export orientation is explained. Overall, then, the goal of state policy – the creation of a product-exporting software industry – is being furthered by state grant aid, which apparently takes the form of the augmentation and reinforcement by the state of development dynamics that are institutionalized within the industry. Younger firms are more likely to export and produce products, suggesting a strengthening of this trend over time.

State aid is effective in the promotion of employment growth, as shown in Equation (3) in Table 5.4. Whereas product-oriented firms employ fewer people, exporting firms and firms that receive more grant aid employ significantly more people. The standardized coefficients (not presented herein) suggest that state aid is marginally more important than export orientation in explaining employment performance. Overall, the analysis also explains significantly more of the variation in employment performance than in product or export orientation. There is strong evidence, therefore, that software firms that receive higher levels of grant aid perform significantly better in terms of product orientation, export orientation, and employment.

It is possible that this is simply a selection effect in which firms that would have done better anyway receive more grant aid, particularly given the increasing selectivity within Irish industrial policy. However, this strains credulity because it implies a degree of foresight on the part of state planners in "picking winners," which is hardly plausible. We can examine this issue more directly using data available from the *1993 Directory of the Software Industry* (NSD, 1993). These data are only available for some of the firms in the sample and only in a limited level of detail (i.e., less than 10, 11 to 30, 31 to 50, and 50 to 100 employees).

Equation (1) in Table 5.4 shows that larger firms receive more grant aid, with firms with more than thirty employees in 1993 receiving an average of approximately 300 thousand pounds more than those with fewer than thirty employees. This suggests that the stronger firms are more likely to receive state support, although younger firms are also likely to receive more support – suggesting that the state is not "propping up" stagnant firms but supporting younger "fast-growth" firms (Hogan and Foley, 1996). As one state official states:

"VCs [venture capitalists] won't back obvious losers, so it's not like you're backing everybody, you start with the at least half-decent ones."

But does this grant aid add to the performance of those firms? Equation (2) in Table 5.4 examines the effect of grant aid between 1994 and 1996 on employment in 1997, controlling for employment levels in 1993. Again, product orientation reduces firms' sizes, and larger firms tend to remain larger. However, the effect of grant aid remains and is indeed strengthened in this analysis of a more clearly defined time frame. Between 1994 and 1996, 100 thousand pounds of grant aid produced on average seventeen more jobs in the firm by 1997. In Equation (2), firms with fewer than ten employees in 1993 are the reference category; however, they are also the majority of firms for which data are available. Equation (3) estimates the effect of grant aid on employment among those firms in 1997. Again, grant aid has a strong and significant effect, although less than in Equation (1) (producing ten extra jobs per 100 thousand pounds). It is striking that even in this global industry, state support is at least as important as orientation to international markets in explaining employment performance.

The statistical evidence regarding the positive effect of grant aid on Irish software firms is supported by the firms' own statements. Clarke (1995, p. 104) found that companies say they were able to grow faster, take more risks, and raise more external finance due to government support. In their interviews with thirty-six indigenous software companies (including most of the larger companies), O'Gorman, O'Malley, and Mooney (1997) found that

"Four-fifths of the respondents said that they had received some form of state financial assistance. Of those who had received such financial assistance, just over half said that this had been important or very important for their company's development, while the remainder said that it had not been particularly important for them. If financial assistance from state agencies had an important or very important positive influence on half or more of assisted companies, it must have made an appreciable contribution to the sector's overall growth."

O'Gorman et al. find that there was less uptake of nonfinancial supports and fewer positive views of their importance, although a minority of companies – especially smaller and medium-sized companies – found them very valuable. This might be expected given that these supports (e.g., management development, business-plan advice, and so on) are aimed at helping start-up companies overcome their inexperience. The state agencies, therefore, have played a crucial role in defining a development path for the Irish industry and in supporting companies traveling that path by financing and "educating" them about the requirements for becoming a successful company.

FIRMS FROM REGIONS: INDIGENOUS SOFTWARE IN THE 1990s

Taking a closer look at the development of the leading indigenous firms provides a more nuanced view of how state developmentalism shaped industry dynamics. Whereas the indigenous-software sector was dominated in the early 1990s by small firms, by 2001 seven indigenous software-product-development companies were publicly listed on NASDAQ: Smartforce (formerly CBT), Iona Technologies, Baltimore Technologies, Trintech, Riverdeep, Parthus, and Datalex. These seven companies accounted for five thousand of the sector's eleven thousand employees and half of the sector's revenues, as well as generating numerous spin-offs (HotOrigin, 2001). Table 5.5 provides employment and revenue information for these and other leading indigenous companies in the 1990s.[2]

The earliest indigenous software firms focused either on services (e.g., GC McKeown and Core) or made a transition to product development based on con-nections with large international customers located in Ireland (e.g., Kindle and Insight). By 2001, however, a new generation of firms, created under different cir-cumstances, was more significant. Those firms were rooted in state investments in education and telecommunications, as well as being able to draw on state resources to help them mobilize a combination of global and local resources.

The state had undertaken large investments in third-level education and telecom-munications to attract foreign investment. However, those investments had the unexpected consequences of contributing to growth of indigenous industry. As the 1980s ended, the computer-science departments in the universities had been firmly established for several years and were beginning to branch out in terms of research. Several schemes were put in place to encourage academics to com-mercialize their research. Since the mid-1980s, firms were emerging in systems software and/or development tools – heavily technology-oriented areas that sell mainly to the software-development community. This subsector came into its own in the early 1990s as the growing computer-science and engineering disciplines

---

2   Riverdeep is not included in the *Business and Finance* listings, presumably because it is based primarily in the United States.

Table 5.5. Leading Indigenous Software Companies, 1992–2001

Company Name	Location in Ireland	Employment			Turnover (£m)		
		1992	1996	2001	1992	1996	2001
Iona Technologies	Dublin			740			82.94
Trintech**	Dublin		55	600		4.9	23.60
Smartforce	Dublin	34	190	500	3.2	13.6	160.50
Baltimore	Dublin			480			29.55
Kindle	Dublin	200	300	465	12.0	23.5	50.73
Datalex	Dublin			450			28.10
Fineos	Dublin			250			10.50
Mentec**	Dublin	170	185	210	15.6	18.6	22.40
MV Technology	Dublin			150			25.00 (e)
GC McKeown	Dublin	120	125		4.6	7.3	
Core Computer Consultants	Cork	50	50		5.7	3.5 (e)	
Insight	Dublin	68			2.3		

Sources: "Top 1,000 Companies," *Business and Finance*, 1992, 1996, 2001.
Note: Only companies included in the "Top 1,000" are included in this table. Where data are not present, companies may still be operating but have not reached the turnover threshold for the "Top 1000." This threshold was £1.5m in 1992, £3m in 1996, and £9.8m in 2001. The company name given is that used in 2001, although every effort has been made to assure a consistent series across the *Business and Finance* listings.
**These companies' revenues include significant sources other than software and care should be taken in interpreting the figures.
(e) estimated

within the universities became increasingly established and innovative, assisted by programs to upgrade research capabilities in the universities.

Trintech was founded in 1987 by two brothers who parlayed a final-year undergraduate research project at Trinity College Dublin into a company that initially developed payment software for offline credit-card transactions. Supported by employment and R&D grant aid from the IDA, Trintech grew; by the late 1990s, it was a leader in its field of payment software, going public in the United States and Germany in 1999. By 1999, EI had spent 909,000 Irish pounds acquiring equity in Trintech – a significant proportion of which was taken well before the external funding that Trintech received in the mid-1990s. Just before its initial public offering in 1999, EI held 7.6 percent of Trintech's shares and had a representative on the company's board. Trintech's path to global success took the road of export success and international alliances, certainly, but was rooted in the educational system and in state support – particularly early in its existence.

Iona Technologies and Baltimore Technologies also emerged from the educational system but with a greater emphasis on sustained research through European programs. Both had drawn heavily on EU programs to support their research efforts: Baltimore as a private company since 1976 and Iona in its existence as a research group at Trinity College in the 1980s before incorporating as a company in 1991. Academics were leading figures in both companies, with faculty members from the departments of math and computer science at Trinity as their first managing directors. Baltimore was transformed from a "research house" on cryptography to a highly successful commercial company focused on Internet security when it was purchased by an Irish investment house in 1997. The state continued to play a role in supporting Baltimore, however, with funding for marketing and R&D.

Iona Technologies was founded by a number of lecturers from the computer-science department at Trinity College Dublin, led by Chris Horn. A group of researchers at Trinity had been active in a variety of European research projects through the ESPRIT program from 1984 to 1989, growing until they had a team of twenty-five by 1988. Those projects focused on what was called "distributed computing", part of the open-systems revolution in computing. The Trinity group got a further boost when the National Board for Science and Technology (NBST) named distributed computing as one of the technologies whose development it wished to support within its software program. In 1989, the Trinity researchers became members of the newly founded Object Management Group, a body based in the United States and dominated by the major computing companies (except Microsoft) that were trying to establish an open-systems standard for sharing "software objects" across different platforms. When this standard was established in 1990, Iona moved quickly to commercialize its research. With equity and other support provided by IDA Ireland, Iona established a significant presence in the United States in 1991, and was able to gain essential external funding from Sun Microsystems. Iona emerged, then, from a technical community rooted in a university, supported by state agencies but also drawing on EU and international technology consortia as resources – the local basis of the firm was forged within the global with state support.

In addition to educational investment, the early 1980s saw the upgrading of the telecommunications system, including a commitment to digitize the system and use the latest communications technology available. This decision was taken with a view to providing infrastructure for participation in the global economy, but limited efforts were also made to build industrial-development criteria into the lucrative contracts for the telecommunications system itself. The NBST (1980) argued that there should be a requirement for the major contractors for the system to locate in Ireland, and Alcatel and Ericsson were required to manufacture their switching hardware in Ireland. Ericsson in particular became a foundation stone of the telecommunications-software sector in Ireland, managing to move successfully into the software side of the business through clever corporate "intrapreneurialism" and also by providing a helping hand to others in the industry. Other multinationals such as ATT (now Lucent) and Motorola played significant roles also, although they were not as heavily involved in the telecommunications-system upgrading. Communications software is one area in the Irish software industry in which TNCs make the strongest contribution.

The indigenous communications-software industry emerged indirectly from this era-Jim Mountjoy, who had completed a Ph.D. in telecommunications engineering, worked for the Department of Posts and Telegraphs and the NBST before becoming managing director of Baltimore Technologies in 1984. In 1990, Mountjoy went on to found a specialized telecommunications software services company called Euristix, which became a leading firm in the indigenous communications-software sector. Another major indigenous firm, Aldiscon, was founded by Jay Murray, owner of the company that had the main contract for laying telephone cables for the new telecommunications system in the early 1980s. Murray founded Aldiscon in 1988 to create software applications for telecommunications systems. Having little technical background himself, he hired the leading technical and management staff from the open market, the majority being Irish people returning from working abroad. Those companies provided the foundation for a growing telecommunications industry. Once again, the focus of the state on upgrading for international investment had resulted in unintended beneficial consequences for indigenous industry.

Smartforce had its origins in the early 1980s when a number of computer-based training, or "courseware," companies were founded. AnCO, the state industrial training board, was active in using courseware – developing courseware products and offering courses that would provide the specific skills needed in the courseware sector. Smartforce, then known as CBT Systems, received consistent state financial support through its checkered early history.

Datalex provides a different example of a 1980s firm. Founded in 1985 by people with a background in the airline industry and in IT, Datalex grew steadily by developing mainframe-based niche applications that could link travel agents and airline computer systems. In 1998, it refocused its business on Internet applications for the travel industry, acquiring ten other companies with backing from a local investment house and from EI (which had taken a half-million IEP in equity by 2000).

Parthus is involved in the design of integrated circuit chips and is the only one of the seven companies to have significant origins in a multinational subsidiary. When Digital laid off eight hundred workers in its Galway computer-hardware operations, the IDA moved quickly to provide support for those laid off and to encourage many of the technical staff to start up their own companies – providing financial and mentoring support as well as a small 'incubator center' where many ex-Digital staff located their start-ups. One of them was Parthus, then known as SSD, founded by a one-time DEC engineer. Much of Parthus's early funding came from the state agencies, including support through equity and grants for capital equipment. Fineos also received substantial state support, with EI holding about 10 percent of its equity in 2001.

By the end of the 1990s, each company had become an important international actor within the industry. Each was involved in a range of international alliances, was listed on one or more international stock exchanges, and had undertaken a variety of acquisitions and/or mergers. Each had a range of international marketing and development offices and many are co-headquartered in the United States and Ireland. However, each company also had its origins in a particular local technical culture that, in many cases, was underwritten by the state. Early computer-based training (CBT) industry initiatives were supported by the IDA, government training agencies, and the export board. Support for research in the universities came primarily through the EU, mediated by a small but supportive group of industrial-development agency officials. Digital's operations in Galway were heavily supported by state grants and incentives. But the state was also vital to the process through which those firms navigated from the local communities to the status of Irish transnational firm. Having taken significant equity in those firms, EI realized 25 million IEP on the sale of shareholdings in 1998 and 50 million IEP in 1999. The majority of this return – which made the state development agencies into a profit-making entity – was realized through investments in Iona, Trintech, and Parthus. Again, we find in the case of the seven leading software companies a state-mediated process of building on embeddedness in local technical communities to create successful transnational firms, which remained embedded in Ireland despite expanding internationally.[3] The next chapter explores in greater detail the simultaneous processes of globalization and localization among indigenous software firms and indeed their recent commercial difficulties.

CONCLUSION

State support, as the visible edge of a broader state–society alliance, has had a significant effect on the development of an indigenous Irish software industry. Whereas neoliberals proposed leaving firms to compete in the market and argue that the state should simply create the conditions for "the market," the Irish state has been successful through a much closer relationship with firms, negating the argument that state ties to firms must inevitably lead to clientelism and rent-seeking. Indeed, the state promoted precisely those business strategies that avoided the "easy" forms of local rent-seeking. Nonetheless, the influence exercised by the DNS is more diffuse than in the DBSs, where state agencies can negotiate key decisions with lead firms who then mobilize the firms within their business groups. The DNS in Ireland deals with a large "portfolio" of firms and aims to promote particular types of activities – R&D, business development, increased employment, and product-exporting – rather than to shape specific decisions or create particular industrial structures. In this respect, it is similar to other DNSs such as Taiwan or Israel, where policy has emphasized promoting higher-end business activities and relationships across a wide range of (often competing) firms.

Significant differences between these countries remain; as Breznitz (2002a) points out, Israeli state policy emphasized the development of national

---

3   This continuing embeddedness in Ireland is secured largely through the dependence of the firms on their "human capital," or the technical communities in which they are embedded – unlike the manufacturing firms of South Korea, for example, which have rapidly shifted production out of Korea using their large capital reserves. I am indebted to Peter Evans for this point.

technological capacity (driven by the national political focus on military power) and state aid has been channeled in much larger amounts toward firms and is more closely tied to R&D activities. By contrast, the motivating goal of Irish industrial policy was employment growth rather than military technological capacity. State aid has been closely tied to employment grants and expansion of the technical labor force. Although Ireland has seen the fastest increase in the scientific and technical labor force in the OECD in the 1990s, the emphasis on employment expansion has encouraged firms to fund product development with service work, resulting in lower levels of productivity per employee (Breznitz, 2002a). Although Ireland and Israel share similar styles of state–firm relationships, those DNS relationships are put to different ends due to their differing development contexts and goals. Nonetheless, DNSs have been critical in glocalizing emerging software industries; it is to the dilemmas of this process in Irish software that the next chapter turns.

6

MAKING GLOBAL AND LOCAL

THE "GLOCALIZATION" OF SOFTWARE FIRMS

In an era of Global Post-Fordism, capital accumulation is increasingly organized through processes of "glocalization" (Brenner, 1998, 1999). By the late 1990s, a number of leading indigenous software firms were quickly becoming a major motor of regional industry growth, spawning a high proportion of the many new software start-ups (HotOrigin, 2001). However, this was not a triumph of the local over the global but rather a deepening of both local and global embeddedness of firms and the industry. This chapter examines the variety of ways in which Irish software firms became integrated into global business networks, labor markets, and finance. This process is also mediated by state agencies and the "indigenous innovation" alliance. "Development" of the Irish software industry has not meant the creation of a local industry protected from the perils of global integration but rather of an industry that has pursued ever deeper but gradually more rewarding global connections, going beyond subsidiaries and subsuppliers to technology- and business-development alliances.

This process of globalization was sustained by a simultaneous process of localization through the development of a dense associational life within Irish high-tech industry. Integration into capital markets promised to transform corporate governance, but the stock-market collapse of 2001–02 left corporate governance in Irish software in an uncertain position, as the pendulum swung away from the large firms back toward regional dynamics of growth. Nonetheless, the software industry has advanced beyond a pool of skilled labor, building subsuppliers around foreign firms (see Chapter 4) and, more strikingly, supporting an "innovative milieu" based largely on technical communities in the indigenous sector (see Chapter 5). Each dimension represents a deepening of local advantage as local cultures of innovation are more difficult to re-create elsewhere than subsupply infrastructure, which is, in turn, more difficult to create than a skilled labor pool (see Chapter 2). Indeed, the major threat to these social foundations of the industry comes not from globalization per se, but from an Anglo-American version of globalization that privileges financial markets for corporate governance over long-term investment.

LOCAL AND GLOBAL NETWORKS IN IRISH SOFTWARE

Firms internationalize not only through market strategies of exporting and hierarchical strategies of expanding overseas offices, but also through building international networks. Many firms are unable or prefer not to maintain the stock of all the skills and capabilities they need within the firm, and must marshall such skills and resources outside the company. These interfirm networks are an increasingly important part of global commodity chains and production networks (Gereffi, 1994; Harrison, 1994), and are particularly critical to small technology-based firms. Table 6.1 outlines the structure of interfirm alliances in the Irish software industry in 1997, including the nature of those alliances (i.e., technology, business, labor-contracting, services-contracting, and political) and the nationality and location of the firms that participate in them (i.e., Irish companies, TNCs in Ireland, and companies outside Ireland). Companies surveyed were asked if they have alliances in any of the following areas with other firms. The precise meaning of *alliances* was left unspecified but implies at the very least an ongoing and recognized relationship, something significantly stronger than would be suggested by *ties* or *links*.

Most companies had some alliance with other firms – only 14.1 percent of Irish firms and 17.2 percent of TNCs had no alliances in the areas mentioned previously. The clearest point to be taken from Table 6.1, however, is the weak networking of TNCs with other firms in the industry, with both other TNCs and Irish firms. Their local networks were primarily centered on contracting-labor from Irish companies to provide them with flexibility in their staffing. Some companies contracted for programming and coding services rather than labor directly. There is also strong evidence of the role of the TNCs in developing the localization, translation, assembly, and logistics subsupply industry given their relatively extensive contracting with both Irish and TNC companies for those services. Of the TNCs, 26 percent were involved in contracting for localization and/or translation, and all of them carried out some localization work in-house as well. An additional 31 percent of TNCs carried out localization in-house and do not contract for any external localization work.

However, apart from these low-end activities, there was little connection between the Irish and TNC sectors: 82 percent of Irish companies and 75 percent of TNCs have no alliance with other TNCs in Ireland – even including the low-end contracting activities. The more advanced technological and business relationships pursued by the TNCs with other companies were mostly outside of Ireland and were presumably entered into as part of the parent corporation's business relationships. However, the figures do indicate the success of some Irish branches of TNCs in integrating into the business networks and strategic operations of the parent corporation's operations. The restricted character of the linkages to local firms is consistent with the limitations placed on TNC subsidiaries by their relative lack of autonomy and the constraints posed by the parent's corporate strategy.

Table 6.1. Local and International Alliances among Companies, 1997

	No		Yes, with Irish Companies		Yes, with Multi-nationals Based in Ireland		Yes, with Companies Outside of Ireland	
	IR	TNC	IR	TNC	IR	TNC	IR	TNC
Technology								
Codevelopment of new technology	59	66	17	4*	5	4	28	34
Sharing existing technology	62	57	17	5*	4	7	23	39*
Creation of technical standards	86	91	7	0*	2	0	7	5
Business								
Comarketing	50	71*	21	2*	4	5	29	21
Joint Ventures	66	73	18	2*	5	0	18	25
Labor-Contracting								
Contracting labor from partner	70	61	18	21	2	2	15	18
Contracting labor to partner	61	82	25	5*	6	5	19	9
Contracting for Services								
Contracting for design and/or multimedia services	75	84	16	7	4	2	9	13
Contracting for localization and/or translation	85	75	7	13	4	11	6	7
Contracting for assembly and logistics	94	88	4	4	1	5*	4	4
Contracting for programming/coding	64	72	24	11*	6	2	14	18
Political								
Lobbying government	92	91	7	7	1	5*	1	0

* Difference between Irish and TNC firms statistically significant at the 0.05 level.

There were significant levels of contracting of labor and programming services among indigenous firms. However, there was also cooperation in more advanced relationships such as codevelopment and sharing of technology and comarketing and joint ventures. This dimension of local networking distinguishes the Irish firms from the TNCs. Even so, for Irish firms, international networks were more common than local alliances in these "advanced" business and technical areas (especially in developing technology and comarketing), whereas – as Table 6.2 shows – local networks were more important for labor- and services-contracting.

Table 6.2. Percentage of Companies Having either Technology/Business or Contracting Alliances with either Irish or International Firms, 1997

| | Percentage of Firms Having an Alliance in This Category | |
	Irish Companies	TNC Companies
Technology/Business Alliances with Irish Firms	39	13
Technology/Business Alliances with International Firms	47	59
Contracting Alliances with Irish Firms	51	34
Contracting Alliances with International Firms	35	36

Alliances with Irish and international firms were largely exclusive; among Irish firms, only 10 to 15 percent of those with an alliance with an Irish or international firm in a particular area (e.g., comarketing, contracting labor to partner) had alliances with both Irish and international firms in that area. The trend was even more pronounced among TNC firms. The most pronounced area of overlap was between technology and business alliances with international firms and contracting alliances with Irish firms; 34 percent of Irish firms and 33 percent of TNCs involved in an alliance in one of those areas were involved in an alliance in both. This only serves to underline the predominance among TNCs of alliances with Irish firms for labor- and services-contracting and with international firms for technology and business alliances. These results support the conclusion that indigenous and foreign firms occupy quite different positions in TDCCs (Gereffi, 1994).

Although these data cannot provide definitive evidence whether the emergence of international partnering "crowds out" local linkages in the business and technology areas, it does show that local and international alliances in marketing and technology were usually relatively separate. Of those firms with Irish alliances in technology or marketing, 40 percent had international alliances in those areas, compared to 52 percent of those firms with no Irish alliances; 29 percent of firms with international alliances in technology or marketing had Irish alliances in those areas, compared to 45 percent of those with no international alliances. The international alliances were usually complemented by contracting with Irish firms for labor and programming services, but a diversified set of alliances with Irish and international firms in the technology and business area was more rare: 29.2 percent of Irish firms had no alliances in this area, 31.8 percent had only international alliances, 23.4 percent had only Irish alliances, and 15.6 percent had both Irish and international alliances.

Whether those firms with international but no Irish alliances once had Irish alliances that were subsequently crowded out is impossible to say. However, some interviewees did suggest that their ties with other local firms were stronger when they were younger and less established. This may, of course, make perfect sense for the firm. Nonetheless, it does suggest that the most successful export-oriented firms may become less dependent on the industry around them for their core activities and capabilities. However, the negative relationship between Irish and international alliances is not statistically significant (chi-square) and the evidence is suggestive at best.

INSTITUTIONS AND GLOBAL NETWORKS

What might explain the variation between firms in the types of alliances they pursue and in the spatial reach of those networks? Table 6.3 presents a series of regression analyses of factors shaping the number of areas in which firms have alliances with Irish firms, international firms outside Ireland, or multinational subsidiaries. This is not a count of all the networks of any particular firm but rather a measure of the range of areas (e.g., comarketing, contracting labor) in which a firm has at least one alliance with another firm; it is a measure of the "breadth" of areas in which firms have alliances, rather than a measure of network density or structure. Nonetheless, it gives us important information regarding the particular types of networks that are important to firms.

Table 6.3. *Explaining the Pattern of Interfirm Networking for Irish Firms*

	Breadth of Irish Technology/ Business Networks	Breadth of Irish Contracting Networks	Breadth of International Technology/ Business Networks	Breadth of International Contracting Networks	Breadth of Networks with Multinational Subsidiaries in Ireland
Age of Firm	−0.003	−0.01	−0.01	−0.01	−0.03*
Permanent Employees 1997	0.0009	0.0008	−0.005	0.002	0.007*
Grant Aid 1980–1996 (in 10,000s)	−0.0002	0.0001	0.008*	0.002	−0.001
Product Orientation	0.003	−0.0007	0.0007	−0.003	−0.002
Export Orientation	−0.002	−0.0008	0.01*	0.008*	0.001
Constant	0.68*	0.98*	0.52*	0.43*	0.52*
Adj. R^2	−0.02	−0.03	0.15	0.08	0.07
N	132	132	132	132	132

* $p < 0.01$
** $p < 0.05$
*** $p < 0.10$

Firms tended to have broader networks with Irish firms than with international firms or TNC subsidiaries. However, the models explain none of the variation in the breadth of those networks; local networks may emerge more "organically" from interpersonal relations and business contacts than networks with international firms. Larger firms appeared to have more links with TNC subsidiaries, probably because a number of them were "bodyshops" that keep several contract programmers on their payroll.

The most interesting results, however, relate to participation in international networks. It is clear that Irish firms' involvement in international markets was closely associated with their involvement in international interfirm networks, because export orientation increased the likelihood of participating in a wider range of both business and technology alliances and contracting alliances. The level of grant aid received by a firm also had a significant impact on participation in business and technology alliances with international firms but a much weaker relation to contracting alliances. State aid was, therefore, associated with a more "desirable" pattern of integration into global networks and, indeed, was more "selective" in that regard than the level of a firm's integration into export markets. This is consistent with the patterns discussed in the last chapter in which the state aggressively promotes integration into the global economy but sponsors particular forms of integration into global networks and divisions of labor. Ultimately, this process shifts a growing proportion of the industry from a position as a subsidiary of TNCs to more rewarding international networks in areas such as codevelopment of technology and standards, as well as comarketing and joint ventures.

Irish firms also increased their own levels of foreign investment and the gap between inward and outward investment narrowed sharply through the 1990s. Much of this activity is concentrated among the leading banks, construction, and food companies, but technology companies were also increasingly involved in investing outside Ireland. Investments by high-technology companies are likely to occur early in the company's existence and to be quite small (CFM Capital, 2001). Even though 11 percent of indigenous firms' workforce in 1995 was overseas (NSD, 1995), the core corporate and development functions of most indigenous firms remain in Ireland. Cryan (1999) suggests that this early foreign investment is linked to the need to network with major partners, customers, financiers, and technology communities in the United States and is primarily related to market access rather than production cost or other "vertical" considerations (Barry, Gorg, and McDowell, 2001). Table 6.4 demonstrates that it was older, larger, and more export-oriented firms that employed the highest proportion of their workforce overseas. Such expansion was also related to involvement in labor-contracting.

EMBEDDING THE REGION: THE ASSOCIATIONAL STATE

If the state has shaped the form of internationalization of leading indigenous firms, it has also sponsored a process of association-building in the industry,

Table 6.4. Factors Affecting Overseas Employment among Indigenous
Software Firms

	% of Worldwide Employees Who Are Not Employed in Ireland
Age of Firm	0.004***
Permanent Employees 1997	0.002*
Grant Aid 1980–1996 (in 10,000s)	−0.00007
Product Orientation	0.0004
Export Orientation	0.001*
Irish Tech Networks	−0.03*
Irish Contracting Networks	0.03**
International Tech Networks	0.0001
International Contracting Networks	0.01
Networks with Multinationals in Ireland	−0.02
Constant	−0.07*
Adj. R^2	0.36
N	132

which embeds firms in the region by building institutionalized "relational assets" (Storper, 1997). A set of networks, centers, forums, and groups provides an associational infrastructure for information-sharing, cooperation, and innovation in Irish software. Although these bodies are often outside the state or semiautonomous from it, in most cases they have been founded through state initiatives and underwritten by state guarantees and funding. Nonetheless, they form a distinct layer of institutional spaces and social networks between the state agencies and the companies in the industry. A software developer's comments reveal the way that informal associational networks can have an important impact even when not explicitly recognized by the actors involved:

"Those industry groups are really just talking shops, they don't have any real impact. But in fairness, I suppose I'm being a bit bilious toward them. I do meet a lot of people there. The informal human networks are more important than the formal industry or professional association stuff. Then I'll ring up Michael and say, 'What was that tool you were talking about to debug program X? And where would I get it?' So it's good that way. There's a lot that goes on among the people that go there." (developer/manager, U.S. TNC doing development in Ireland)

The first wave of such institution-building was in the early 1980s. The National Microelectronics Research Center (NMRC) was founded in Cork in 1980. Its focus was on research into microelectronic technology and, although it has been successful and works closely with some of the more prominent electronics TNCs, it has had relatively little impact on the software sector. A second smaller institution, the National Microelectronics Application Center (MAC), was also founded at that time and was charged with bringing electronics to Irish industry. Based at the

University of Limerick (UL), it provides technical advice and houses up-to-date equipment for industry use. It succeeded relatively early in building connections to innovative local firms, although in its early years, those connections were apparently closer to the larger TNC operations (Sklair,1988). In 1996, MAC was fully self-funding, employed sixteen staff, and had a turnover of 1 million IEP. MAC is reported by interviewees to have had close relations with many software firms and it has actually worked more than the NMRC with smaller companies – although NMRC is more significant for the high-tech sector as a whole. A senior MAC executive argued:

"Our core skill is the development cycle rather than any particular technical area. We spend a lot of time talking with entrepreneurs – 90 percent may decide that their idea is not on, usually because the idea is out there already or they are too soon or too late vis-a-vis the technology curve. We get a lot of business from the remaining 10 percent. Typically, the people we are dealing with, it's their first time through the cycle, they get upset at any shocks."

There is an educational return to the industry here in terms of the 90 percent who do not pursue a doomed project – even though MAC does not receive any payment from these companies. Indeed, the primary role of the MAC is a more specialized educational contribution than the development agencies can provide:

"We can lay out the potential of smart products for the entrepreneurs. We've helped in that regard, we have an education role, we can guide entrepreneurs, we push them on first-class global standards, let them know what is expected."

Another institution set up in 1980 was the Innovation Center in Plassey Technological Park near UL. This center provides similar "educational" services, as well as laboratory space and other facilities and services, for a modest fee (Sklair,1988). Many of the companies set up within the Plassey Park and availing of the Innovation Center have been software companies such as Piercom and Software Architects International.

A more direct effort was made to upgrade the business capabilities and technological sophistication of software companies when the National Software Center (NSC) was founded in Dublin in 1984. Ultimately ill-fated (see Chapter 9), the NSC provided a range of business and technical services to software companies. Beginning in 1984 with objectives of identifying promising markets, defining product requirements for those markets, and acting as a spearhead for joint ventures in product development, the NSC moved toward an increased focus on marketing assistance, product quality assurance, technical assistance, software production methods, and liaising between industry associations and the industrial-development agencies by the time it closed in 1988. Although opinions regarding its effectiveness are mixed, industry journal reports of the time are mostly favorable (*Irish Computer*, June 1985, March 1986, May 1986, July 1987).

After a wave of activity in 1980, it was not until the late 1980s that the technology sector saw further institutional innovation. Most of the innovations took place under the banner of the Programs in Advanced Technologies (PATs), funded by EU Structural Funds under the Operational Program for Industry, 1989–93. Eolas, the agency dealing with science and technology, had made a series of proposals regarding programs to support leading and potentially strategic technologies – among them software. However, whereas Eolas set up the other PATs, the software PAT was

"set up by the then Department of Industry and Commerce under the auspices of the newly established NSD toward the end of 1991." (Clarke,1995, p. 48)

The NSD was established under another EU-funded initiative: the Software Support Measure, which was part of the Irish Industry Program. Together, the NSD and the three centers established under the software PAT provided a new basis for the industry infrastructure in the late 1980s and early 1990s.

The software PAT initially consisted of three centers. The Center for Software Engineering (CSE) had the greatest impact on the software industry, promoting quality in software production and the ISO9000 quality standard (Clarke, 1995, Chapter 7). CSE was helped by its good relationship with Dublin City University (DCU), where it had been founded in 1989 before being brought into the software PAT in 1990. Furthermore, CSE maintains close relationships with industry because the board spans academia, industry, and state agencies. The other two PAT centers – Multimedia Technologies Ireland (MTI) and the National Institute for Management Technology – ran into difficulties. Both were more focused on smaller constituencies: the small multimedia industry and executives in business outside of high-tech, respectively – and this made their relationship to the software PAT somewhat problematic. Within these constituencies, however, they were reasonably well evaluated (Clarke, 1995, Chapters 8 and 9). Indeed, most of the PAT schemes across a variety of sectors have received favorable evaluations.

However, both centers were closed or sold in a reorganization of the PAT scheme in 1997. PAT was reorganized and aimed at encouraging academic research in specific areas of advanced software technology. Ten research groups in all seven universities were linked together in research networks around three areas of technology: network, intelligent, and high-performance computing. Thus, the refocusing of the PATs took them back toward an original mandate to develop and diffuse advanced technologies, whereas the more purely promotional activities were left to the CSE. This was possible in part because of a range of other bodies that had emerged to carry out broadly promotional activities under schemes that were not part of the PAT, but which were nonetheless relevant to the software industry. The PAT programs make a similar, often hidden educational contribution to that of the MAC; as a director of one PAT program said:

"We play a largely unobserved role. People come in to see us with a very specific tiny question but that always leads out to broader questions about how the company is organized and so on."

These important waves of institution-building in 1980, the late 1980s, and the late 1990s have been supplemented by the steady emergence of a network of other institutions. The Localization Resource Center (LRC), established at UCD and now at UL, promotes quality and resource-sharing in the localization sector of the software industry and has been instrumental in setting up a successful industry forum, the Software Localization Interest Group (SLIG). This is not the only industry association set up by a state agency – MTI helped start the Irish Interactive Multimedia Association, which persists after the demise of MTI – and the NSD had a close relationship with the Irish Software Association (although that body has been in existence since the 1970s).

A network of institutions, therefore, provided technical and business information of various kinds and degrees of specialization to different sectors within the software industry. These institutions are a way in which the state can provide an everyday impetus toward world-class technical, business, and quality standards without being directly involved, in regulating the firms – a measure that would be politically difficult. The staff of these centers become the everyday teachers and advisors of the industry. However, they also gather a great deal of up-to-the-minute information from the industry and can be a valuable source of information for the central state agencies when they need to make rapid shifts or adjustments in policy. They are staffed primarily by people with a background in industry who sometimes maintain that involvement on a part-time basis. As we will see in Chapter 8, this makes these centers politically acceptable to the industry.

Supplementing the technical institutes and associations is the NSD, which was originally funded by the EU and established within the IDA; however, it became part of Forbairt when the agencies were reorganized in 1994. Its role, although somewhat unclear at first (Clarke, 1995, Chapter 5), has evolved to become a central focal point within the state agencies for dealings with software. Although the everyday work of grant assessment is carried out by the International Services Program within Forbairt, the NSD is represented on grant-giving committees. It also fulfills many of the "educational" and "networking" roles discussed previously relative to the state agencies. However, the NSD was primarily a strategic link between the industry and the state development agencies. It was founded in response to the Software Industry Working Group (1989) – a working group with representatives from industry, the civil service, and the state agencies. It also plays a role within the state agencies, where it represents the interests of the software sector on various internal committees. As such, the software industry has a unique institutional presence within the state agencies, reflecting the priority given to the sector by the state. Furthermore, the NSD constantly monitors and reviews the key issues for the software industry and the operation of the institutions and infrastructure supporting the industry. It was a prime mover in refocusing the activities of the PATs and in the debates over a growing pressure on skills and the issue of access to capital. The success of the NSD led to its transformation to the National Informatics Directorate in 2000, with responsibility for a broader range of sectors.

The final set of institutions that is an important part of this infrastructure also has close ties to the state: the universities. In addition to their direct contribution in educating the labor force and conducting research, the universities have played a central role in developing the associational infrastructure of the industry. University computer-science department lecturers and professors have been involved in many of the leading industry-wide initiatives that led, among other things, to the founding of the NSD (Ryan, 1997). Several academics, including Michael Ryan at DCU and Kevin Ryan at UL, became involved in many of the industry debates over the years, particularly those relating to skills supply and research capability. The computer-science departments have liaised closely with industry over curriculum content and with the state over skills supply requirements (Ryan,1997). They have also been home to most of the innovation institutions mentioned previously and, in some cases, have maintained close connections to those centers. The universities are deeply embedded in this network of institutions and, in most cases, see themselves as active participants in the national economic development project – of course, in many cases this may coincide with extra funding for university activities.

The universities are also at the heart of a new state emphasis on funding for scientific research. In 2000, the established institutions were dwarfed by the establishment of Science Foundation Ireland (SFI), which channeled more money than ever before into university research, university–industry joint research, and institution-building. It is striking, however, that – similar to private-capital investment – it was only *after* industry growth and development were established that this major commitment was made. Hobday (1995) makes a similar point regarding industrial upgrading in the Asian Tigers: it appears that institutions that can give an initial boost to industry learning and innovation are economically and politically crucial in the process of development. Nonetheless, by 2001, many in Ireland were asking not whether enough science and engineering research funding was available but rather whether industry had the organizational capacity to absorb the research that was being conducted. Furthermore, the 'top-down' approach of SFI seems at odds with the existing network of institutions, many of which have been threatened by spending cuts in 2002 and 2003.

Through these various bodies, a layer of associational governance (Cohen and Rogers, 1992; O'Donnell, 2000) has been established that both mediates and complements the state–industry relationship discussed previously and facilitates effective formulation and implementation of policy. Whereas no one institution can be said to have had a decisive impact, the value of a network of such institutions lies in sustaining social relationships and diffusing new ideas and perspectives on technological and organizational issues.

The software-industry survey in 1997 provided some insight into how those local relationships and institutions intersected with local and global business networks to sustain innovation during the industry's growth. The survey asked about the importance of various external connections to the firm's ability to innovate. The most prominent sources of innovation are, not surprisingly, those most closely linked to the critical business processes of the firm: internal training, direct business relationships, and information that is available relatively inexpensively. Less important than those sources but still playing a critical role is the industry infrastructure of innovation: social networks among entrepreneurs and employees and institutions and programs providing access to new technologies (Malerba and Torrisi, 1996; Ó Riain, 1997; Price Waterhouse, 1997). These processes help spread information and innovations throughout the industry as a whole; they are the factors that promote a learning industry, whereas the factors considered in this chapter promote a learning firm.

Moreover, the local and international orientation of firms shapes the relative importance of these external sources. A series of regression analyses (not reported herein) suggest some interesting patterns. The analyses investigated the relative effect of export orientation, product orientation, grant aid, types of interfirm networks, firm age, and firm employment on the importance placed on each of the sources of innovation. The more export-oriented a firm is or the broader its networks are in any area (except with subsidiaries), the more likely it is to place importance on contacts with partners. The Internet is more important for firms involved in technology–business networks, whether Irish or international; employee contacts and turnover are more important for firms involved in contracting networks.

However, export-oriented firms and those with international "high-end" alliances have a distinct profile: they are more likely than other firms to rely on licensing, learning from competitors, and links to universities. None of the other factors have any effect on those sources. Although grant aid has no effect, links to universities – a critical part of the associational infrastructure – are important for precisely those export-oriented firms with international technology networks at which policy is directed. Indeed, these are the characteristics of firms that are promoted by state grant-aid.

State grant aid and industry associational structure combine to promote a particular model of "glocalization" of the industry. Again, a consistent picture emerges of an internationalizing industry with multiple global–local connections but that is also undergoing a more selective, state-mediated process of integrating leading firms into higher-end networks, and supporting them through the universities in pursuing the product-exporting growth strategies promoted through the grant-aid mechanism.

HIERARCHIES, MARKETS, AND GLOBAL CORPORATE GOVERNANCE

Internationalization of firms not only restructures alliances with other firms but often results in significant changes in ownership and control of the firm. Increasing integration into network forms of organization has made neither hierarchies nor markets irrelevant as forms of corporate governance – indeed, in many ways, the three broad types of governance are symbiotic. We have seen the importance of networks for Irish software firms. Until recent years, selling one's company (i.e., incorporation into a hierarchy) was the primary way that Irish software entrepreneurs cashed in their assets once they had built up their company. However, Irish firms have begun to acquire other firms and to trade their stock on the NASDAQ and other stock exchanges, entering the market for corporate governance in Anglo-American capitalism with often problematic consequences.

Acquisition has historically been a common destination for indigenous companies. However, there are significant differences between the various acquisitions that have taken place within the industry. Although an acquisition may provide valuable additional investment and access to technology or marketing resources, research in the United Kingdom indicates that acquisition has – at best – a neutral and – at worst – a detrimental effect on company performance (Dickerson et al.,1997). This may be due to the acquisition of the company for "asset-stripping" purposes or to a lack of "fit" between the corporate structures and strategies of the acquired and acquiring companies. In the case of an international acquisition of a local firm, the danger for the local industry is that the local firm's operations will be moved out of the area or may be curtailed as the company is pushed into a subsidiary status within the corporation.

Journalist John Sterne's analysis of eighteen takeovers (domestic and international) in the Irish IT industry between 1986 and 1989 concluded:

"IT acquisitions in this country, with just a couple of exceptions, have meant job losses rather than gains and reductions, not increases, in the functions and responsibilities of organizations here. Every so often, though, an agreement is struck which builds on what has gone before, strengthening instead of weakening the country's technology base." (*Irish Computer*, March1992, p. 44)

Promising companies such as Glockenspiel and Workhorse are no more, bought by Computer Associates and Aldus, respectively, in the early 1990s to obtain the skills of a couple of key personnel with little interest in maintaining the firm as a going concern.

However, these intellectual asset-stripping acquisitions diminished in frequency and acquisitions in the 1990s were increasingly based on strategic reasons. The acquisitions of Insight (by Hoskyns in 1988, now owned by Cap Gemini), Kindle (by ACT in 1992, owned by Misys since 1995), Credo (by Misys in 1994), and Quay Financial Software (by CSK Software in 1993) have resulted in the passing of a significant part of the banking and financial software sector into foreign ownership. The companies have continued to grow and remain major competitors in their niche markets while expanding their range of products and geographical markets. When key staff stay at the company and the company continues to operate relatively autonomously with improved access to the new parent's resources, the company seems to prosper. In these cases, the company retains its independent indigenous character but gains access to new resources. The difficulties appear to arise when the acquisition is aimed at simply gaining access to particular personnel (i.e., the asset-stripping strategy) or when the new parent attempts to fold the Irish operation tightly into the parent's structure (i.e., the subsidiary strategy).

Although the acquisition of large numbers of Irish firms by international companies could be of potential concern, it has not so far undermined the growth of the Irish industry. Spin-offs and start-ups continue to emerge, sometimes started by people who left existing companies after their acquisition. When Quay Financial Software was sold to CSK, its technical director was involved in developing the U.S. market for one of the company's key products. However, he left soon afterwards with other key personnel to found his own company, Macalla, to work on related technology. Although large firms may be able to control the direction of innovation to some extent through acquisition, they cannot control the flow of people and information in industries such as in Ireland where interfirm boundaries are relatively porous.

Furthermore, Irish high-technology companies began to undertake significant acquisitions of other companies. IT and telecommunications companies accounted for 9 percent of the value of all acquisitions by Irish companies in 1999, spending 369,915,000 IEP on forty-four acquisitions. In 2000, they spent 1,928,681,000 IEP on sixty acquisitions and accounted for 23 percent of the value of all acquisitions. After domestic acquisitions, the next most popular location is the United States, followed by the United Kingdom and then Europe. Nonetheless, this acquisition activity was still outweighed by sales of Irish IT and telecommunications companies to foreign interests (CFM Capital, 2001).

In the late 1990s increasing numbers of software companies looked to float their shares on the stock exchange. The technology-oriented NASDAQ exchange in the United States has attracted the most attention and undoubtedly provides the greatest financial returns. By 2001, only seven Irish software companies had gone public on NASDAQ, many fewer than Israeli and Indian software companies. Some of those companies ran the acquisition gauntlet before finally going public. CBT Systems (now Smartforce) was sold to Hoskyns from the United Kingdom in 1987 and bought back in 1991 before going public in 1995. Iona Technologies was part-owned by Sun Microsystems and had some negotiations with it regarding further equity investment before going public in 1997. Other prominent candidates for flotation on NASDAQ, such as Aldiscon and Expert Edge, were acquired by international firms. In the boom of the late 1990s, firms emerged in Ireland with an explicit focus on NASDAQ.

With such limited experience, it is difficult to say what the exact implications of going public internationally are for local industrial development. It is clear that U.S. investors like to see a significant company presence within the United States. The company is likely then to make U.S. markets a priority; however, because this is the fastest expanding export market for Irish software, it is hardly a problem for Irish firms. However, investors also want to see management and development presence in the United States. There are differences between Iona Technologies and Smartforce/CBT Systems that may be suggestive. Iona has remained heavily embedded in the Irish software industry. Its CEO, Chris Horn, plays a prominent role in industry affairs and chaired the government-sponsored Commission on Future Skills. Iona has retained its headquarters in Dublin despite an extensive presence in the United States, and has listed its stock on the London and Dublin exchanges, as well as the NASDAQ exchange. In contrast, Smartforce/CBT relocated its headquarters to Silicon Valley and hired Jim Buckley, a prominent former Apple executive and Silicon Valley insider, to be its chairman. Furthermore, the founders of CBT/Smartforce have been involved in new start-ups such as Riverdeep and Knowledge Well, which are based in the United States – although they may set up development centers in Ireland. Iona, however, seems to have made a self-conscious effort to remain tied to the Irish industry.

There are certainly powerful pressures, therefore, to locate significant functions in the United States, which is reinforced by the involvement of venture capitalists who tend to want their companies close by (in Silicon Valley, in particular) – where they can make the most of the venture capitalist's company's ties but where they can also be closely monitored. Nonetheless, firms that go public are likely to maintain significant development functions in Ireland because disengaging from their development base could be risky. Further software-development operations are likely to grow more quickly in the company's non-Irish locations.

Of course, this NASDAQ fever was dampened by the 2001 collapse in the stock market. Each of the "Big Seven" endured catastrophic falls in stock price. Riverdeep and Datalex delisted from NASDAQ, and Parthus and Smartforce merged with overseas firms. Although Trintech and Iona remain independent public companies, they have endured sustained losses and low stock prices, leaving them vulnerable to acquisition. Whereas the indigenous-software industry grew slightly in 2002 and EI continued to support numerous start-ups, the "Big Seven" laid off large numbers of employees – cutting employment by half or more in many cases. In some respects, it proved easier for privately held companies to ride out the ups and downs of the boom because publicly held companies were vulnerable to acquisition and under severe pressure to manage their quarterly results, according to U.S. investment markets' definition of "good performance" – typically including significant layoffs. The bad times for Irish software were nowhere near as catastrophic as previous downturns, however. A regional dynamic of growth persisted and, indeed, became more important as foreign investment slowed and large indigenous firms ran into trouble. Even those firms that were acquired continued as going concerns and were major industry employers. Nonetheless, as discussed in Chapter 11, the current difficulties in the Irish and international high-tech industries are clear reminders that "development" is not linear and irreversible but is, in fact, a politically contested process that generates continuous, albeit different, challenges as it unfolds. The firms which integrated most deeply into the Anglo-American financialized system of corporate governance, through acquisition and stock flotation, were the firms which found it hardest to ride out the industry downturn.

CONCLUSION

Developmental statism relies heavily on indirect state influence, the shaping of organizational culture and practices, and the embedding of those firms in the local industry. However, the very success of developmental states points up the limits of their own power; the "glocalization" of firms raises the broader issues of the accountability of Irish firms and the democratizing of development. Going public on NASDAQ creates a powerful discipline on a quarterly basis for adhering to the business norms favored by U.S. investors – the "shareholder conception of control" that has made the maximizing of share price and "shareholder value" the dominant concern of U.S. managers since the 1970s (Fligstein, 2001). The inflow of capital into the industry promised to move the leading Irish indigenous firms from strong technical innovators to the position of being a strategic player within their markets with the R&D and marketing muscle to sustain that position. However, in taking up that position in international markets, indigenous firms subjected themselves to the vagaries of markets for global governance and their employees to the norms of neoliberal Anglo-American capitalism. DNSs, unlike the East Asian DBSs, do not provide "patient capital" on a scale that encourages firms to avoid markets for governance. The accountability of firms, even where locally embedded, remains a central issue: Can firms be made as accountable to society as they are to markets for corporate governance? The next chapter considers this issue, exploring how the new workplaces of the software industry are embedded in international labor flows and class formation, patterns of workplace politics, and the national labor politics of social partnership.

7

THE CLASS POLITICS OF THE
GLOBAL REGION

The "glocalization" of the software industry has created not only a new industry and new firms but also a new labor force and class relations. A rising technical–professional class has been a significant element of the shift toward a post-industrial occupational structure in Ireland, one characterized at the same time by upskilling and polarization. This technical–professional labor force is increasingly globalized – both in terms of the national origin of employees and, more significant, with regard to the extensive migration experience of many of those workers. Glocal capital meets glocal professional labor in a match made by the glocal state (Brenner, 1998, 1999). With flat organizational structures and high employee turnover, the class compromise in the software workplace is transformed. The ramifications of this compromise are felt not only among professional workers but also in the national polity as national social-partnership agreements fragment under pressure from the spiraling wages of the nonunion sector, creating a new politics of inequality in the DNS.

THE GLOBALIZATION OF SOFTWARE LABOR

Technical labor in Ireland has been internationalized almost from its inception – working in TNCs or emigration were the most likely career destinations. However, similar to the globalization of Irish software firms, one form of globalization characterized by branch-plant employment and brain drain has been at least partially transformed and upgraded into transnational technical communities linked by migration circuits and globalized workplaces.

Software and engineering emigration

Table 7.1 shows the emigration rates of computer-science graduates compared to those of engineers and all graduates in Ireland from 1984–85 to 1995–96. The figures refer to the percentage of graduates who had emigrated one year after

Table 7.1. Emigration Rates of Degree-Level Graduates, 1984–1996

| | Computer Science | | Electrical/Electronic Engineering | | All Subjects |
	Female	Male	Female	Male	All
1984–85	25.7	23.5	—	30.4	11.5*
1985–86	36.5	22.3	—	44.9	13.2*
1986–87	36.6	29.6	—	34.8	19.5
1987–88	26.5	24.6	33.3	44.7	25.6
1988–89	28.8	23.5	31.4	34.0	26.0
1989–90	17.0	24.6	31.1	41.3	24.8
1990–91	21.0	19.3	31.4	23.8	19.0
1991–92	10.3	7.9	28.2	21.8	15.4
1992–93	17.5	15.6	10.5	15.1	13.3
1993–94	12.3	12.9	14.3	15.6	14.7
1994–95	17.1	20.0	19.6	19.5	17.8
1995–96	14.4	15.0	23.3	18.1	15.8

Note: The total number of female graduates was fewer than fifty in computer science until 1987 and in every year in engineering. It was fewer than thirty until 1986–87 in engineering.
Source: Higher Education Authority Annual Reports.

graduating. Significantly more graduates emigrated in a second wave in subsequent years such that for some computer-science classes, and certainly for some engineers, the total emigration was well over 50 percent of the class.

The decision to expand technical education, although beneficial in the long run, appeared to many in the 1980s to have merely led to a brain drain of dramatic proportions. With almost half of electronic engineers and more than a quarter of computer scientists emigrating within a year of graduating in the mid-1980s, it seemed that the Irish educational system was merely a training ground for the high-technology industries of the United Kingdom, the United States, and Germany (McLaughlin, 1994). In the 1990s, however, emigration decreased significantly – at first, mostly due to declining international conditions, as is clear from the rise in the unemployment rate in Ireland to between 5 and 10 percent for those graduates from only 2 to 4 percent in the 1980s. However, as the 1990s continued, both emigration and unemployment declined, reflecting the improving conditions in the Irish economy.

For many engineers and computing professionals, unemployment was not the only alternative to emigration. In fact, emigration persisted in the 1990s even as companies complained lustily about skills shortages and there were significant flows of return migration. This is partly due to the overeducation of engineers that led to significant numbers choosing emigration rather than work on relatively mundane tasks in production-oriented subsidiaries of TNCs (Wickham, 1989). Dissatisfaction with the levels of personal taxation were the cause of many engineers' decision to emigrate. However, the search for "more interesting work" or "better experience" were also critically important reasons for both engineers

(Wickham, 1989) and accountants (Hanlon, 1994). The semiperipheral Irish economy produced mass migration toward the core regions (Corcoran, 1993; Hanlon, 1994; McLaughlin, 1994):

"These young engineers consider themselves in an international labor market and therefore believe that Ireland has little to offer them . . . . For them, technically challenging work is almost identical with high-technology work: access to such work is not only intrinsically rewarding, it also ensures that their qualifications and knowledge remain up to date – and, hence, that they can continue to be in demands on the international job market." (Wickham, 1989)

Hanlon (1994) found that Irish accountants similarly valued international experience highly and that international experience could contribute to advancement within the Irish industry, thereby prompting Irish professionals to go abroad for a while to get experience.

Emigrant and transnational communities

Given that many of these emigrants left Ireland with at least half an eye to returning, it is not surprising that many maintained relatively close links to other Irish emigrants abroad and to Ireland itself. Historically, Irish emigrants have formed close communities in their destinations but have had low rates of return migration (Miller, 1985). Furthermore, Irish emigration before the 1980s was predominantly semiskilled in nature. However, Barrett and Trace (1998) provide evidence that young people with third-level degrees were much more likely to emigrate in the 1980s and 1990s than those with only second-level qualifications. Table 7.2 shows the changing distribution of Irish immigrants to the United States between 1970 and 1990, a trend toward professionalism that seems to have increased in the 1990s.

More significant than the percentage changes is the expansion in absolute numbers. This influx of professional and managerial workers did not simply integrate into existing immigrant communities but also began to develop its own

Table 7.2. Managerial and Professional Occupations Among Irish-Born Residents of the United States (Percentages equal total number of immigrants.)

Years of Entry to United States	Managerial		Professional	
	Female	Male	Female	Male
1985–89	1,032 (2.2%)	3,419 (7.3%)	2,874 (6.2%)	5,708 (12.3%)
1980–84	448 (2.8%)	1,587 (10.0%)	855 (5.4%)	2,109 (13.3%)
1975–79	111 (1.5%)	470 (6.4%)	346 (4.7%)	941 (12.8%)
1970–74	121 (1.7%)	426 (5.9%)	477 (6.6%)	1,037 (14.4%)

Note: 1980s immigrants' occupations from 1990 census; 1970s immigrants' occupations from 1980 census.
Source: U.S. Census.

class-specific institutions. A variety of alumni associations from Irish universities emerged in major U.S. cities and "Irish Networks" aimed specifically at graduates and business professionals were founded in the United States, United Kingdom, and Tokyo. Established emigrant communities were changed by these new immigrants. For example, new bars emerged that appeal particularly to the new professionals whereas others continue to operate as the traditional centers for socializing and job-hunting among construction workers (Corcoran, 1993). The Irish Bank pub in the heart of San Francisco draws a group of legal and business professionals and three or four new bars in Silicon Valley draw more technical professionals.

Most important are the informal social networks that are maintained both locally with friends from college, one's hometown, or people working at the same company. This is reinforced by ethnic networks passing information about job opportunities and by a certain amount of chain migration within the IT industry. Transnational links have also been facilitated by the emergence of the Internet. Irish newspapers such as the *Irish Times* and the *Sunday Business Post*, popular among professionals, had their publications on the worldwide web, including job advertisements from the mid-1990s. Furthermore, many emigrant professionals now subscribe to the *Irish Emigrant* weekly email news bulletin from Ireland. In 1997, the *Irish Emigrant* claimed,

"We have reached something of a milestone with this, the five hundredth edition. For five hundred successive weeks, the *Irish Emigrant* has been distributed around the world from the first edition in February 1987, which went to some fifteen to twenty people, to the current edition, which will reach seventy-nine countries and we estimate will be read by more than fifty thousand in its electronic and hardcopy forms."

Cheaper telecommunications and travel make it easier for emigrants to maintain their "Irishness" (Corcoran, 1992). As one software developer who had worked in a small Irish company in Dublin in the 1980s told this author:

"There are transnational contacts among the developers from that time, we send each other email all around the world."

The IDA and EI use their local offices in Silicon Valley to organize social and business dinners where Irish people working in the Valley are encouraged to return home as entrepreneurs, to partner with Irish companies, or to recommend business contacts for Irish companies. Indeed, in 1998, funding was made available through the Millennium Fund to support returning emigrants wishing to start a business in Ireland.

Professional emigrants became an economically and politically significant group in their own right. They developed various connections to one another – in Ireland, within their destination industries and regions, and transnationally. These connections may be part of the reason why there have been such high rates of return migration in recent years: those who left in the hard years of the 1980s maintained their social and professional connections to Ireland so they could return relatively easily when the economy picked up in the 1990s.

Immigration and the Irish software labor force

Immigration to Ireland completes the migration circuit. The software industry globally has relatively high rates of labor migration between countries and particularly to the leading U.S. universities and major centers such as Silicon Valley (Office of Technology Policy [OTP], 1997; Saxenian, 1997). The Irish software labor force in 1997 was only slightly more international than the population of the country as a whole (Ó Riain, 1997), although immigrants have become increasingly important in the software labor force in recent years. The Quarterly National Household Survey shows that non-Irish nationals were proportionally more likely to be in the business-services sector, which includes software. Whereas 8.3 percent of Irish nationals in full-time employment worked in business services, 15.1 percent of British nationals, 21.3 percent of EU nationals, 18.2 percent of U.S. nationals, and 17.0 percent of other nationalities worked in the sector. The majority (91 percent) of the sector's employees were Irish nationals, however.

Among indigenous software companies, the use of non-Irish labor in 1997 was more likely among product-oriented firms and firms involved in international labor-contracting networks. We might speculate that two somewhat different streams of professional immigration existed at this point: one focused on attracting labor for specific product-development needs and skills and the other focused on contract-labor relationships. However, little is known about the careers and experiences of non-Irish workers in Ireland, including their experience of an increasingly virulent racism.

However, by far, the largest source of employees for the software industry is Irish nationals, many of whom have been part of the largest migration flow into Ireland: the return migration of Irish immigrants. Unfortunately, it is difficult to gather data on the return migration of specific groups and no data is available on software professionals specifically. However, we can put together a useful picture of overall return migration patterns and where software professionals might fit into those patterns.

Even in the 1980s, when more than 350,000, or one-tenth, of the population emigrated, fully 150,000 previous emigrants returned (NESC, 1991, p. 58). In the 1990s, return migration increased as emigration decreased, so that net migration – resulting in the loss of fourteen thousand people per year between 1981 and 1986 and twenty-seven thousand per year between 1986 and 1991 – resulted in the growth of the population by two thousand per year between 1991 and 1996 (CSO, 1997a, p. 10). Even this understates the rapidly increasing rates of return migration in this crucial period, as Table 7.3 indicates.

These trends refer to the entire population. However, return migrants are disproportionately professionals. Interviewees in the software industry regularly reiterated the importance of return migrants to the growth of the industry:

"Return migrants were crucial, the industry could grow using those resources. Other countries wouldn't have had the people,"

Table 7.3. Inward Migration Rates by Country and Year of Return for Usual
Residents of the Republic of Ireland, 1996

Country of Previous Residence	United Kingdom	Other EU Countries	United States	Other Countries
Total percentage of population who ever lived there for one year or more	7.8%	0.7%	1.0%	1.3%
Returned 1981–90	64,100	6,700	8,900	13,000
Returned 1991–96	83,800	14,900	14,200	20,900
Per Annum Rate of Return 1981–90	7,100	700	1,000	1,400
Per Annum Rate of Return 1991–96	16,800	3,000	2,800	4,200
Rate of Return 1995–96	20,700	7,400	5,100	7,300

Note: The figures for emigrants who returned between 1981 and 1990 and between 1991
and 1996 are based on those people enumerated in the Irish census of 1996. There is a bias
to underestimate those numbers because some returnees may have died and others may
have emigrated again.
Sources: CSO, 1997a; Tables M and N.

argued one indigenous entrepreneur. Of those who returned to Ireland between
1983 and 1988, 28.3 percent were in professional or technical occupations, by
far the largest occupational category among return migrants (NESC, 1991, p. 91).
Furthermore, those workers had an unemployment rate of 12.0 percent, compared
to rates of 35 percent for all return migrants and more than 70 percent for unskilled
laborers. Although return migrants as a whole faced significant problems when
returning to Irish society (Hannan and Ó Riain, 1993, p. 161; NESC, 1991, p. 93),
professionals were clearly better able to move between positions in the international
and domestic economies.

This professional bias within return migration continued in the 1990s. Specific
CSO tabulations indicate that from 1994 to 1996, 30.4 percent of those who returned were professional or technical workers.[1] Barrett and Trace (1998) found
that in the mid-1990s, return migrants and non–Irish-born immigrants both had
higher average levels of education than the Irish population as a whole.

It is clear, then, that return migration has been a consistent feature of postwar
Irish migration but has increased rapidly since the early 1990s. These return migration flows are heavily professional in composition, and professionals are the
most successful return migrants. We might expect these trends to be amplified for
software professionals who work in an industry with relatively standard global

1　Based on Labour Force Survey data provided by the CSO. Analysis carried out in joint project with
　Breda McCabe, ESRI/University of Toronto.

technologies and whose industry has been expanding domestically and internationally for the past twenty years.

It is critical, however, that this return migration is not the end of a "one-time" migration fostered by the difficult times of the 1980s. Certainly, many of those who left under duress in the 1980s are now returning, often with families (CSO, 1997a). However, it appears that professional migration is now a durable migration circuit for at least a certain proportion of professionals. Although there has always been a certain degree of professional emigration and immigration, both flows were amplified during the 1980s and 1990s. Graduate emigration continued in the 1990s even as opportunities expanded at home. Furthermore, in the population as a whole, the 15 to 24 age group continued to show net migration of more than twenty thousand a year in the early 1990s (CSO, 1997a, p. 20). Emigration seems to be an established option for Irish young people; what distinguished the 1980s were the sheer numbers involved and the extent to which practically every age group showed net emigration. Nonetheless, the critical point is that a circuit of migration and intersection with the global economy has been established for young Irish professionals – a circuit that seems likely to persist into the future, although the *levels* of emigration and return migration will continue to be shaped by economic conditions at home and abroad. The fact that this is a migration circuit rather than a brain drain of one-way emigration has enormous implications for the Irish software industry. Even as internationalization threatens to undermine the skill base of the industry through overqualification in the local labor market, it also renews and deepens that skill base through the return migration of employees with valuable international experience – a process that contributes to the training of a quarter to a half of the professional workforce.

GOVERNING THE GLOBAL WORKPLACE: THE LIMITS OF THE DEVELOPMENTAL NETWORK STATE

The state, therefore, has played a critical role in shaping the emergence of new firms and a new labor force – both of which are integrated into the global economy in more rewarding ways than in an earlier era. Firms are increasingly likely to be involved in global business and technology networks as partners rather than subsidiaries. Technical–professional workers are closely tied to transnational technical communities but have a much greater range of opportunities for technically interesting work in Ireland than in an earlier era of "branch plants and brain drain." The promotion of those globally integrated technology-product firms and technical communities has been a central part of the DNS's strategy in Ireland.

However, extensive state intervention in education and training did not transform how established structures of social inequality shaped labor supply. Ireland has low rates of social mobility between classes (with very low relative mobility rates) that persisted through the boom of the 1990s (Breen and Whelan, 1996; Erikson and Goldthorpe, 1992; Hout, 1989; Hout and Jackson, 1986; Whelan, Breen, and Whelan, 1992). Third-level education is the primary and dominant route into professional and technical positions in the high-technology industries such as software. The educational system is deeply inegalitarian as research supports the thesis of "maximally maintained inequality" up until the 1970s (Raftery and Hout, 1993) and into the 1990s (Whelan and Hannan, 1999):

"The effects of social origin [on educational attainment] do not change except when the demand for a given level of education is saturated for the upper classes." (Whelan and Hannan, 1999)

Despite the rapid educational expansion in Ireland during the past thirty years, class inequality has not decreased and the advances of the less privileged social classes have occurred largely due to the absolute expansion of educational and economic opportunities. The reliance of the leading industries of the 1990s (e.g., software) on educational qualifications means that they do little to improve access to economic rewards for those left behind in the process. Economic and educational development has been undertaken under the rubric of a populist national ideology and not aimed at goals of tackling social exclusion.

There are also significant gender inequalities within the software labor force (Ó Riain, 1999, Chapter 2). This inequality exists within the educational system and, indeed, intensifies moving farther through the system. In 1995, 41.3 percent of third-level computer-science diploma/certificate graduates were women – below the 44.8 percent of all diploma/certificate graduates in that year (HEA, 1996). Although more women than men went directly into employment from the diploma/certificate level, it was not necessarily of benefit to them in the long term because diploma and certificate holders are more likely to be hired into test and support roles than into software development (Ó Riain, 1999). A much greater percentage of men (63.6 percent) than women (44.1 percent) go on to further studies and eventually get a degree (HEA, 1996).

The situation is worse at the degree level. Only 29.8 percent of computer-science–degree graduates in 1998 were women, and a smaller proportion of women are likely to pursue postgraduate education. Nonetheless, the gender inequalities in third-level computer science are marked and increase as one moves through the system. Furthermore, after an improvement in the percentage of women computer-science graduates between the mid-1980s and the early 1990s, the percentage decreased once again.

Although the state supported the restructuring of work and employment practices in software, extensive state intervention shifted in only the most minimal way the existing structures of class and gender inequality. Society was mobilized by the state in a way that was compatible with the needs of international capital and that maintained inequalities within Ireland itself. Social transformation and integration into the global economy do not undermine the structures that reproduce inequality of opportunity or outcome; in this respect, industrial development in Ireland has been too locally embedded.

Furthermore, the DNS had little influence in shaping the class and gender compromises between those transnational firms and workers in the workplace and the labor market. The outcome of "network development" has been the creation of a significant number of "global workplaces" in the Irish economy – workplaces where networked firms and technical professionals have forged new patterns of workplace politics, quite separate from the industrial-relations regimes already in place in Ireland (Roche, 1998). The nonunion workplaces remain relatively autonomous from the neocorporatist "social-partnership" institutions in place in Ireland since 1987. Nor do professional bodies for technical workers in IT have much influence over work and labor-market conditions, other than a limited role in credentialing. Firms are increasingly answerable to their "network partners" and to external investors or capital markets. The politics of the global workplace is forged under those conditions and shapes an unstable relationship between firms and professional employees.

Goldthorpe (1982) argues that whereas less-skilled employees are bound to the firm by their labor contract, managers and experts are bound to the firm by a "service relationship" in which they are promised not only the immediate benefits of salary and so on but also the prospective benefits of a career. Erikson and Goldthorpe argue that

"A service relationship can thus be understood as the means through which an employing organization seeks to create and sustain such commitment; or, that is, as a functional alternative to direct control in regard to those employees whom the organization must to some significant extent trust to make decisions and to carry them through in ways that are consistent with organizational values and goals." (1993, p. 42)

Among the workers likely to be involved in a service relationship are those with specialized knowledge and expertise (Erikson and Goldthorpe, 1993; Goldthorpe, 1982); engineers and other technical professionals have historically fitted this picture of the "trusted workers" relatively easily (Kunda, 1993; Whalley, 1986).

However, in industries such as software, less hierarchical and more decentralized organizational structures, with flatter internal hierarchies, weaker internal labor markets and the reduction in the absolute number of management positions has challenged the traditional service relationship. Whereas in the economy as a whole in 1997 the ratio of managers to professionals and associate professionals was approximately 1:2.5, in software it was about 1:11, which indicates the relatively flat organizational structures in software and similar industries (Tansey, 1998, p. 41; Ó Riain, 1999). The prevalence of job-hopping as a career strategy and the importance of local labor markets are reflected in the fact that a quarter of the firms in the software-industry survey had employee turnover of 25 percent or more in 1996–97 (Ó Riain, 1999). Furthermore, the local labor market was almost as important a route into senior technical and management positions as internal labor markets in 1997 (Ó Riain, 1999). But this more turbulent relationship has taken on a relatively clear institutional form: work organization based around project teams working to a deadline and careers increasingly relying on "job-hopping" within and between firms. The traditional career structure leading from expert into managerial positions, therefore, has become more problematic and the link between the engineer and the employer more ambiguous.

Furthermore, informationalization of the economy has created many occupations in which work identity is defined not necessarily by workers' relationship to the employer but rather to the craft (Piore and Sabel, 1984), the "technical community" (Ó Riain, 2002; Saxenian, 1994), or the "occupational community" (Van Maanen and Barley, 1984; Whalley and Barley, 1997). These trends mean that the corporate effort to secure expert employee commitment through building career and cultural attachment to the corporation have been heavily undermined with such "corporate culture" models of commitment in the minority in areas such as Silicon Valley (Baron, Burton, and Hannan, 1996). These tenuous commitments to the employer – and of the employer to the employee – are also present within the Irish industry (Ó Riain, 2000b).

The institutional ground on which the class interests of knowledge workers are reconciled within the workplace, therefore, has shifted, making it necessary for firms to try to devise a new set of relationships that can bind the underlying class interests of the professionals and experts to those of the company. This is achieved through the restructuring of the workplace around the autonomous project team. The mechanism for controlling the design project team is the project deadline. Because the final requirements are usually somewhat vague and the actual work done by the team cannot be directly supervised by management, the deadline becomes the focus of management and team efforts. "Do what needs to be done to get this specification working by the deadline" is the broad task of the team. The deadline is the mechanism by which management brings the intensification of time into the heart of the team (Ó Riain, 2000b). It is also an attractive mechanism of control because direct authority over the work process is undermined by the expertise of the employees and the need for rapid communication and cooperation. In contrast, time can be regulated through the use of the deadline with only a limited local managerial presence and with relatively little ongoing exercise of managerial authority. Once the project is completed, however, the controlling power of the deadline becomes less effective. The demand for expert workers becomes more salient as they pursue a career strategy based on their location as an independent agent in the market. Companies attempt to capture those workers back into the orbit of the company by offering stock options or increased pay that can later be turned into investments. Experts are asked to choose between the vagaries of life as independent small businesses (with themselves as the "business") and the commitments of becoming "captured capitalists" within the firm, tied in by "golden handcuffs" such as stock options. Approximately 20 percent of software-development firms offered stock options to managers and staff in the late 1990s (CSR, 1996, 2000) – most of which were worthless by 2002–03.

In an ethnographic study of a software-development team in a U.S. company in Ireland in 1997, this author found that a new ground is emerging upon which the struggles of the global information economy will be waged (Ó Riain, 2000b). This new "contested terrain" of the global workplace is a system of "time–space intensification," in which workers in the global workplace experience not the "end of time and space" but rather their rising to a new level of intensity. Space is intensified by the necessity of local cooperation and the increased use of project teams in the face of the challenges posed by the global economy. Time becomes an evermore pressing reality in the deadline-driven workplace. This time–space intensification shapes the structure of both work and careers in the global workplace. Careers are built using mobility between firms to bargain for improved wages and access to technical learning; those mobile careers only increase the importance of close interactions and strong local cooperation while working on any particular project. Out of these underlying structures emerges a set of dynamics, organized around the project deadline, that not only give the global workplace its dynamism but also generate certain costs and dilemmas for the participants in it. Conflicts over the dilemmas of time–space intensification constitute the new politics of the globalization of knowledge work.

What then will be the central controversies on this new contested terrain? Two phases of time–space intensification – before and after the deadline – create characteristic advantages and dilemmas for knowledge workers such as the software developers discussed in this chapter, for software firms, and for the (largely invisible) social actors beyond the industry with an interest in its social organization. Although these dynamics and dilemmas have been recognized for some time in the global informational industries, globalization intensifies them (see Kidder, 1981, for a classic account of a computer-design team).

Certain characteristic organizational problems are likely to emerge. The intensification of time and the pressures imposed by the deadline create the conditions that lead to employee burnout. In my study of a software development team, this was manifested in the exhaustion of the team members up to and after the deadline and also in the decision made by the senior manager of the project (five months after I left the team) to resign due to overwork. The pressure and introverted character of the predeadline phase, and the resulting insulation of such workers and the organization of work from any kind of broader social accountability, make it more difficult to reconcile the team structure and culture with broader social concerns. This is most obvious in the work–family nexus, where work demands come to dominate family life, leaving little space for workers to negotiate alternative work and family-time arrangements.

The postdeadline phase of high mobility creates significant volatility and insecurity in the labor market so that employees lack strong employment guarantees. Even in the tight labor market of the late 1990s, "employment security" gave way to "employability security." However, when career gains are based on the threat of mobility, this seems to inevitably lead to increased labor-market inequality because the threat to leave is only effective when replacing the employee is difficult. Because it is inherently based on scarcity, the limits of mobility as a universal career strategy are clear. The new workplace institutions have created pressures for longer hours and more individualized bargaining over pay and other financial benefits, which contribute to the dominant social problems that have emerged in Ireland of rising inequality and increased pressure on the social reproduction of labor (e.g., childcare, housing, transportation). Tackling these problems is more difficult for the state given the lack of a mechanism for shaping the character of the class compromise with the leading high-tech sectors, even as employers and unions in other sectors were increasingly integrated into national policy networks through social-partnership institutions.

THE POLITICS OF INEQUALITY

Although national corporatist institutions have played a key role in the recovery of the Irish economy, they have only a tenuous relationship to the most dynamic globalized sectors such as software. Efforts to extend the institutions of national social partnership "upward" to the global level through unionization of TNCs have been weak and mostly unsuccessful. The negotiations that take place within the social-partnership institutions regarding pressing problems of childcare, work hours, inequality, and urban congestion can only draw on a partial set of mechanisms for addressing the causes of those problems – the institutional and political mechanisms for incorporating the high-tech sectors into solving them are weak and at times nonexistent. The DNS, in promoting the union of transnational capital and transnational technical communities, has created workplaces that, so far, sit largely outside any effective form of public governance or social accountability. Ultimately, the politics of the state runs up against its "final frontier": the politics of production (Burawoy, 1985).

The tensions in the relationship between the social-partnership and high-tech development models came to the fore in the late 1990s. Wage inequality increased drastically in Ireland through the 1990s, even though it was already one of the most unequal OECD nations (Atkinson, et al., 1995). The major component of the increase in inequality has been a growing gap between the middle and the top of the income distribution. Whereas the average income of the top 10 percent was 195 percent of the median income in 1987, by 1994 that percentage had grown to 224 percent (Barrett, Callan, and Nolan, 1999). The level and increase in wage inequality was greater than even in the United States. Barrett et al. reported that most of the increase in wage inequality was accounted for by an increase in the supply of skilled labor and by rapidly increasing returns to education – made possible by the institutional changes at work and in the labor market.

Neocorporatism in other countries has been associated with a lessening of wage inequality (Hicks and Kenworthy, 1998). The Irish case clearly represents an exception, which is explained by precisely the multiple and fragmented structure that is the flip side of the DNS. Neocorporatist wage bargaining in Ireland, particularly in the later agreements, contained provisions for special local bargains that would exceed the terms of the national agreements (Taylor, 1996). Furthermore, there was widespread departure from the terms of the agreement in later years, particularly in industries such as software that had difficulty holding onto employees who had various local and global opportunities. Geary (1998) presented evidence for 1991–97 that showed that in that period, 51 percent of respondents said that pay awards at their workplace adhered to the terms of the national agreement, 44 percent said that awards exceeded the agreement, and 5 percent said that awards were less than the terms of the agreement. Barrett, Callan, and Nolan provided further details of the results:

"Looking at union versus nonunion workplaces, 70 percent of union firms said their awards did not differ from the national agreement while 25 percent said they exceeded them. For nonunion firms, however – which would include significant numbers of multinational firms – fully 63 percent said that their awards exceeded those nationally agreed. In addition, 39 percent of firms stated that one reason for exceeding the terms of the national agreement was to retain staff who were in short supply." (1999, p. 95)

Neither did changes in tax and social welfare mitigate those inequalities in the 1990s. Callan, Nolan, and Walsh (1998) showed that tax and welfare changes from 1995 to 1998 resulted in the poorest 30 percent of the population making 2 percent less than if their income had increased at the same rate as the average increase in income for the population. During the same period, the top 10 percent of earners benefited from tax changes to the extent that they made 4 percent more than would have been the case if they had simply followed the average income increase. Therefore, there is a significant element of policy choice in these political tensions.

The inequality is more relevant given the trend toward dual-earner families, with 32 percent of couples as dual-earners in 1996, up from 16 percent in 1986 (O'Connor, 1998, p. 110). 75 percent of households in the top income decile, 65 percent of the second decile, and 52 percent of the third decile have two or more persons at work. The software industry also relies heavily on the hidden subsidies provided by spouses (almost always women) who are not in paid employment and on the parents of the often young software-developer workforce (a number of whom are likely to still be living at home). There is also likely to be a link between the expansion of professional and low-wage service occupations because these services emerge in part to solve the work–family dilemmas of the expanding professional classes. In 1994–95, 27.8 percent of household spending in the state on "services and other expenses" was by the top income decile and another 18.6 percent was accounted for by the next decile – up from 27.0 percent and 17.9 percent, respectively, in 1987. The top two deciles accounted for 55 percent of spending on nonresident domestic service, 72 percent of spending on resident domestic service, and 60 percent of spending on child care (including babysitting).[2] As dual-earner professional couples grow as a proportion of the workforce – a process driven in part by industries such as software – they are likely to stimulate simultaneously the growth of personal-service occupations.

Although high wages in software and even income inequality do not necessarily pose a problem for economic growth (although they may), they do pose a political dilemma for autocentric development. The dilemma becomes more pressing if the expansion of high-wage occupations is a driving force in generating what have

2 Proportions calculated on the basis of data in CSO, 1997, pp. 46–7, and CSO, 1988, pp. 44–5.

historically been low-wage service occupations. Each pay agreement has been passed by a slimmer margin than the previous, and it is possible that the 18 month long agreement signed in 2002 may be the last. Unionized workers who lived under wage restraint since 1987, seeing others outstrip them at an increasingly rapid rate, became less willing to sacrifice their wages to keep inflation low for those accumulating high profits and high wages elsewhere in the economy.

At the heart of the contemporary politics of inequality is the clash of two middle classes. The Irish occupational structure has been transformed in recent decades, with rapid growth in professional employment and slightly less rapid growth in services employment. Technical–professional growth is driven primarily by business services, high-tech manufacturing and finance, commerce, and insurance. Significant numbers of professional jobs also have been created in social services, creating an important political split between technical and social-service professionals. Whereas technical professionals are typically male, nonunion, and work in the private sector, social-service professionals tend to be female, unionized, and work in the public sector. Underneath the façade of a seamless shift toward a postindustrial, professionalized labor force lies a seething politics – a noisy clash of two middle classes, each growing ever more distant from the low-paid service workers who rarely take their place on the political stage. Buffered from the worst of the malaise of the 1980s by their job security, although still suffering considerably, social-service workers found themselves outstripped by the second middle class – a newly emergent class of technical professionals – and increasingly chafed at the rising cost of living, particularly in Dublin. Both middle classes are heavily supported and subsidized by the state, as has been discussed. Their politics are in large part directed at the state – albeit often at different apparatuses within the state – and they generate significant problems of coordination and conflict-management for the state system.

In the process of economic development, the majority of Irish society has also acquiesced to the increasing gap between themselves and the rising professional and business classes. The intense battles waged over public-sector pay were evidence that those workers in a position to do so are increasingly willing to take action to redress the inequality. What seems doubtful is whether those at the lowest rung of Irish society, caught between a burgeoning service sector of casual employment and a weakening welfare effort, can mobilize the resources to at least keep up with the rest of Irish society. The Irish formula of "solidarity without equality," which held together autocentric development under Global Post-Fordism, began to unravel. Social inclusion and cohesion require evermore political effort in the face of the fragmentation of national solidarity by glocalization and postindustrialism – although inequality is not inevitable, the political project of social solidarity and inclusion has become more difficult to pursue successfully. Although the DNS has promoted socioeconomic development in significant ways, it has only further exposed the raw wounds of the politics of inequality.

PART III

THE POLITICS OF THE DEVELOPMENTAL NETWORK STATE

8

INSTITUTIONS OF THE DEVELOPMENTAL NETWORK STATE

Riven as it is by the politics of inequality, the Irish state has been nonetheless successful in many important respects – under challenging conditions of dependency, unequal exchange, and national indebtedness, a turnaround in the economy was fashioned in a process that was extensively sponsored by a variety of state agencies. But how, most observers ask, did this state know what to do? How could it be so rational? Most analysts assume, with Chalmers Johnson, that a successful state is one whose "plan rationality" is superior to the "market rationality" of decentralized exchange (Johnson, 1982). The plan-rational state must in turn be some version of the "high-modernist" state that James Scott lambasts for its inability to be sensitive to local context and circumstance (Scott, 1998). Bourdieu (1999) actually defined the state as the "bureaucratic field" – simultaneously ignoring the many other bureaucracies outside the state and the many varieties of state organizational form.

Typically, analysts also assume that the rational state is a national state. Ferguson and Gupta (2001) shed significant light on how state rationalities become nationalized. They argue that states are spatialized according to particular properties that they characterize as "vertical encompassment":

"Verticality refers to the central and pervasive idea of the state as an institution somehow 'above' civil society, community, and family .... The second image is that of encompassment: here the state (conceptually fused with the nation) is located within an ever-widening series of circles that begins with family and local community and ends with the system of nation–states. This is a profoundly consequential understanding of scale, one in which the locality is encompassed by the region, the region by the nation–state, and the nation–state by 'the international community'." (2001, pp. 2–3)

These features of states come to be seen as "commonsensical" as they become embedded in a host of routine practices within the organizations of the state;

thus, states produce the spatial and scalar hierarchies – they do not simply exist within them. State organizational forms, spatialities, and rationalities are mutually constitutive.

This state project of the production of vertical encompassment is important for states because it allows state agencies to identify themselves with a particular and widely legitimated level of authority (i.e.,"the national") and to claim an elevated status as the legitimate authority over all those existing "below" it. Globalization, then, poses a threat to the stability of the arrangements of economic, social, and political scale. The verticality and encompassment of the state are undermined by its lack of "boundary control" and the ability of mobile actors to "exit" the national system of constraints and incentives (Scharpf, 1999). The state can be "hollowed out" as dominant actors move up to operate at higher international and global levels.

However, if states can produce verticality and encompassment, they may also produce other organizational forms and spatial scales. Debates regarding the impact of globalization on the state have taken the state-created imagery of vertical encompassment too seriously and have conceptualized the relationship among the local, national, and global in a zero-sum fashion, where gains at one level must necessarily mean a loss of power and capabilities at another. We have seen throughout this book how state actions stretch across spatial scales and interlocking social structures. We need, therefore, to replace the hierarchical imagery of vertical encompassment with a view of social structures as *heterarchical*, with different levels integrating in different ways in a structured but uneven manner (Kontopoulos, 1993). The heterarchical view of social structure supports a view of globalization as a reconfiguration of relationships among local, national, global, and so on. Different spatial scales are entangled in different ways within particular economies, and national economies may consist of a variety of such different local–national–global combinations (Brenner, 1999). National political economies will be built not *between* the local and global but rather *out of* them.

Scott argues that state bureaucracy implies a universalizing and decontextualizing of state practices. The Irish state is certainly standardizing and bureaucratic but its agencies can also be sensitive to multiple sets of circumstances and actors. Johnson argues that states are effective by being more plan-rational, devising plans in a centralized core of expertise and implementing them through bureaucratic structures. However, effective and rational states can be as adaptive as they are strategic and can combine detailed plans with flexibility in implementation. The DNS is characterized by multiple embedded autonomies of the state, which are held accountable as much through external as internal means of accountability and which are integrated together in a loosely coupled state structure. Neither the proponents nor the critics of state rationality have developed the language that can make sense of such a state. This chapter attempts to fill that void, providing an account of the institutional conditions under which such a state might be maintained and act effectively. The next chapter provides an account of the political conditions for the emergence of such a DNS.

THE NATIONAL RATIONAL STATE IN IRELAND

For Evans (1995), effective states sustain deep ties to society while maintaining an autonomy from that society, ensuring an ability to develop and pursue a course of action that can rise above purely sectional interests. The problem of "overembeddedness" of state agencies in private social groups is mitigated by the bureaucratization of state organizations. The "Weberian" characteristics of bureaucracy – orderly long-term careers, meritocratic recruitment and promotion, rational organization, high status of officialdom, and so on – provide a measure of autonomy to state organizations by insulating them from becoming tied too closely to external actors. "In general, individual maximization must take place via conformity to bureaucratic rules rather than via exploitation of individual opportunities presented by the invisible hand." (Evans, 1995, p. 49). Informal internal networks, such as ties among school classmates, can also be crucial to the coherence of state bureaucracies, as Evans argues in relation to Japan. However,

"the fact that formal competence, rather than clientelistic ties or traditional loyalties, is the prime requirement for entry into the network makes it much more likely that effective performance will be a valued attribute among loyal members of the various *batsu* [groups based on attendance at a particular university]." (Evans, 1995, p. 49)

The Irish civil service is highly centralized and bureaucratized. Civil-service careers are orderly and based largely on internal competition. Most civil servants enter the bureaucracy directly from secondary school (or, more recently, university) rather than from college and are socialized into civil-service norms at an early stage of their careers (Breen et al., 1990). This author's assessment is that the Irish civil service (and the industrial development agencies) would score highly on the Evans and Rauch scale of state "Weberianness":

- many new economic policies originate within state agencies;
- more than 90 percent of higher officials enter the civil service via a formal examination system;
- a typical higher-level official spends between twenty years and their whole career in those agencies;
- in at least a few cases, someone who enters the agencies early in his or her career through a higher civil-service examination could expect to move up several levels within the civil service and then move up to the top of the agency on the basis of political appointments;
- it is unusual (although increasingly more frequent in the industrial-development agencies) for higher officials to spend substantial proportions of their careers in the private sector;
- higher officials' salaries have been approximately 80 to 90 percent of those of private-sector managers with roughly comparable training and responsibilities;
- bribes are a negligible portion of civil servants' incomes;

- between 1970 and 1990, salaries in industrial development agencies kept pace with those in the private sector;
- civil-service exams are an important component of entry to the bureaucracy;
- and, among graduates of the country's most elite universities, a public-sector career has been considered the best option for those who are risk-averse.[1]

My assessment gives Ireland a score of 12.5 on the 14-point scale, which compares favorably to the highest-scoring countries in the Evans and Rauch study, such as Singapore (13.5), South Korea (13), and Taiwan (12). Such a level of bureaucratization has long existed within the Irish state; as early as 1962, a leading civil servant referred to the widespread reputation for difficulty and competitiveness of the examinations through which graduates entered the civil service (Whitaker, 1962, p. 266).

Furthermore, the Irish state has a highly developed set of mechanisms at its disposal for "governing" the society. These mechanisms are linked in large part to two major historical projects of social control of the Irish population. The first is British colonial rule, in which many of the early mechanisms of state governance over society were tested between 1650 and 1900 before being implemented in Britain. Ireland was, in fact, a crucial staging ground for innovations in government that certain elites wished to implement in Britain (Carroll Burke, 2001). Many contemporary agencies – such as the Ordnance Survey, the Geological Survey, and the Office of Public Works – date back to this historical period. The greatest influence was within the civil service itself, which remained remarkably stable after independence in 1922 so that – similar to the Japanese influence in Korea and Taiwan – colonialism left a coherent, rationalist bureaucracy in place – even if in the Irish case it also left an economy racked by dependence and unequal exchange. The bureaucratic administration of Irish society was further deepened by the growing power of the Catholic Church in the second half of the nineteenth century. A religious purpose was pursued through an intense institutionalization of Church influence and a routinization of that influence through religious orders' central role in education (including third level) and health care. As Fahey puts it, the Catholic Church's

"grasp of mass schooling in Ireland placed at its disposal one of the principal instruments of modern social engineering . . . . No doubt the appeal to tradition was an important basis for the Church's authority. But the Church of the nineteenth century was a new species of organization, fertilized in part by tradition but endowed also with much of the newly evolved social and cultural equipment of the modern world growing up alongside it." (1992, p. 263)

The means of bureaucratic administration and government, therefore, were widespread within Irish society but were not deployed in the pursuit of economic development and shaping private enterprise until much later in Irish history. Writing before the turnaround of the 1990s had become apparent, Breen et al. argue that

1   The language here reflects the questions posed by Evans and Rauch to their panel of experts in each country in their sample. Ireland was not included in the study, which focused on thirty-five "developing" countries.

"In Ireland, state expansion was registered primarily in the state's growing role of paymaster. Control of key areas affecting the class structure, in education for example, remained in the hands of other institutions, such as the churches." (1990, p. 17)

However, the central state has gradually wrested some of this control back toward itself, due to the declining legitimacy of the Church's position in those sectors and to the Church's declining ability to sustain itself organizationally, as vocations have dropped rapidly. The Irish state's role in governing economic action is widely legitimated within the political culture: opinion polls found that, through the 1980s and the 1990s, a majority of the population saw the primary responsibility for providing employment as falling on government rather than private business (Fitzgerald and Girvin, 2000). Indeed, opinion polls in 2002 showed much higher levels of public trust in the Irish and EU bureaucracies than in either political parties or the Catholic Church. The particular form of bureaucratic government varies, however, from agency to agency, as evidenced by the governance of third-level education, the IDA, and the indigenous development agencies.

The ability of the state system to govern the population is well illustrated in the critical case of the Irish state's ability to manipulate the supply of graduate labor. The Irish system of third-level education emphasizes direct recruitment into specific college courses from the national standardized state examination, the Senior Certificate. Most professional and vocational degrees are entered in one's first year of third-level education, unlike countries such as the United States in which the bachelor's degree is often only a prelude to more specialized graduate studies. Irish school-leavers are tracked early on into their specialized fields of study. Furthermore, there is a finite number of places in any particular course, a number decided within the universities but also negotiated between the universities and the government, which controls the majority of university funding. When students leave secondary school, they apply to a centralized agency that handles applications to almost all college courses. The students rank their course choices from 1 to 10 and are then assigned the top place for which they qualify based on the points they have accumulated from their state examinations. In this way, the students' options are heavily constrained by government and college decisions about the funding of specific numbers of places in specific courses. The government and the universities used this system to greatly expand technical and vocational education through the 1980s and 1990s, regardless of student preferences. Although demand for those courses has been strong in Ireland, there is no doubt that this system gives the Irish state a much greater capacity to mold the labor market for specific economic sectors than in other countries.

The establishment of the Regional Technical Colleges (RTCs) in the 1960s and the NIHE in 1980 was explicitly designed to refocus the educational system toward the labor-market needs of the economy. Furthermore, these institutions were much more directly controlled by the state than the existing universities, increasing the state's ability to influence the future development of the educational system, particularly the nature and level of technical-labor supply (Clancy, 1989).

The state bureaucracies responsible for industrial development have also been strengthened. The IDA and other development agencies have more freedom in recruitment than the civil service, but the broad characteristics of a Weberian bureaucracy still apply to those organizations. Despite consistent allegations of corruption against politicians, the state development agencies have been mostly above reproach – even in some of the most dubious circumstances, the development agencies have maintained their developmental focus (O'Toole, 1996; chapters 5, 10, and 14).

Although its board membership changes, the IDA's executive leadership has been stable, with only three chief executives between 1969 and 1999. The IDA developed a strong corporate identity of its own, as the complaints of one IDA project officer in 1998 make clear:

"There's a lot of guys in Wilton Place [IDA headquarters], I call them the NCOs [non-commissioned officers] of the IDA, they are busting their asses getting companies into Ireland .... They do an enormous amount of work and they are only getting thirty thousand. The system isn't set up so that they can be rewarded... those guys could do a lot better outside the IDA, but they stay and do it because they want to do it for the country."

With strong internal-promotion patterns and little mobility out of the IDA, it forms a cohesive unit within the Irish state with a strong focus on its given objectives of attracting FDI. It has also been able to internally build up significant skills in terms of knowledge of international markets and the politics and economics of industrial location.

The IDA's power within the state is unusual for an agency that attracts foreign investment, with the exception of the agency in Singapore. As one IDA project officer said,

"We have more clout within Ireland than the Dutch and Scots do in their countries."

This power gives the IDA the ability to provide a "one-stop shop" for TNCs locating in Ireland because the IDA can deal with government departments and other state agencies to provide for the TNCs' needs, whereas the TNCs need only have a relationship with the IDA. The IDA, therefore, has a strong corporate identity, highly developed internal-promotion patterns, and significant internal skills. Its place outside the conventional civil service gives it a flexibility in internal organization and a freedom to maneuver that is unusual for state agencies. It also has a position within the state that gives it some latitude in its operations while allowing it to maintain some clout within the state apparatus as a whole.

This is in marked contrast to the range of state agencies and bodies that indigenous companies deal with, although this side of the system has been rationalized with the foundation and growth of Forbairt and its successor, Enterprise Ireland. Each agency had developed its own cultures and skills over the years, and the complexity of the organizational task facing Enterprise Ireland is illustrated in the variety of pension plans listed in the Enterprise Ireland 2000 Annual Report: it covers employees recruited by the IDA, Eolas, National Board for Science and Technology (NBST), Irish Goods Council, and An Bord Tráchtála (ABT). Many of those agencies had developed their own organizational cultures. Ex-NBST employees speak of the cohesive organizational identity within the NBST, built in part of its isolation from the dominant industrial-policy agencies and its relatively participatory organizational structures. However, they had merged in 1988 with the Institute for Industrial Research and Standards – an industrial testing organization with little relationship to the science-policy community at NBST – to form Eolas, an umbrella science and technology body. The system of agencies on the indigenous side is much less centralized and cohesive, although still effective.

Bureaucracy, then, is a critical component of the effectiveness of the Irish state, but the particular form that this bureaucracy takes also shapes in important ways the abilities of state agencies to promote certain activities and relationships and their weakness in promoting others. If global–local connections are forged through organizational strategies and those strategies are embedded in organizational practices and structures, then the organizational issues become the terrain on which much of the politics of globalization is fought out. Understanding this terrain in greater detail and depth helps us understand the politics of globalization in a more subtle and ultimately effective way. We can draw on "neo-Weberian" theories of organizations that emphasize the multiplicity of environments within which organizations are embedded, the variety of forms of accountability and information flow within organizations, the different extent to which organizational structures are loosely or tightly coupled, and – finally – the contingent and contextual character of rational action and rationalities within organizations (Perrow, 1986). The remainder of this chapter discusses each dimension of organizational structure and explores the character of the industrial-development agencies of the Irish state under each. Classic Weberian bureaucratic characteristics are not enough to explain the particular form of the effectiveness of the industrial-development agencies.

MULTIPLY EMBEDDED

Even within the area of industrial policy and development, Irish state agencies are embedded in multiple external constituencies. Enterprise Ireland (and previously its various constituent agencies) is embedded primarily in the indigenous high-technology entrepreneurial class but also in a broader coalition of business and academic interests around science and technology. At times, this alliance has extended to parts of the EU and OECD. IDA Ireland has close ties to the managers of TNC subsidiaries in Ireland but also works to maintain ties with management around the world in firms that are current or potential investors.

Table 8.1 is an overview of how particular state agencies and commissions are formally embedded in other parts of the state and various segments of civil society. The table indicates the backgrounds of board members of various organizations and commissions. It begins with the National Economic and Social Council (NESC), which is the primary public institution related to the social-partnership

Table 8.1. The Embeddedness of State Agencies and Commissions

	State							Business						
	Civil Service	Forfás	IDA	EI/Forbairt/ABT/FÁS	HEA	Other government[a]	Academic	Private Business - Irish	Private Business - TNCs	Industry Associations	Agricultural Organizations	Professional Associations[b]	Community Groups	Unions
NESC 2001	*						*			*	*		*	*
NESC 1996	*						*	*		*	*		*	*
Forfás Board 1994	*	*	*	*			*	*						*
Forfás Board 2001	*	*	*	*			*	*	*					*
IDA 1997	*		*			*	*	*	*					*
IDA 1999	*		*			*	*	*	*	*				

	IDA 1990	Enterprise Ireland 2000	ICSTI 2000	STIAC 1995	Competitiveness Council 2001	Industrial Policy Review Group 1990	Telecomms Task Force 1993	Information Society Commission 2001

Table of representation (asterisks denote representatives).

[a] Includes Marine Institute, former civil servants, and agency executives, Plato Ireland (a local economic-development partnership), Telecom Eireann, Teltec Ireland, Bioresearch Ireland, and ESB.

[b] Includes Irish Science Teachers Associations, Irish Research Scientists Association, and Institute of Engineers of Ireland.

Each asterisk in the table stands for one representative from that particular group.

neocorporatist institutions.[2] NESC is followed by Forfás, the state agency that acts as an "umbrella" industrial-policy agency, conducting research, developing policy strategy, and reviewing the performance and policies of IDA Ireland and EI. The boards of IDA and EI follow. Several more specific forums and bodies follow:

- the Irish Council for Science, Technology, and Innovation (ICSTI);
- its precursor, the Science, Technology, and Innovation Advisory Council (STIAC);
- the Competitiveness Council, which operates under the aegis of Forfás;
- the Industrial Policy Review Group, a one-time body established to produce the "Culliton Report" on industrial policy in 1991;
- the Telecommunications Task Force, concerned specifically with telecommunications industry issues; and
- the Information Society Commission, a body charged with promoting the Information Society and linked to the Department of An Taoiseach.[3]

NESC is in many ways a classic neocorporatist institution, with representation from the peak associations of industry, agriculture, and unions. Community-group representatives were typically appointed by the government of the day, but their representation has been increasingly institutionalized. There is some academic representation and the state representatives are all high-ranking officials from within the civil service. There are significant differences in the pattern of embeddedness between the social-partnership institutions and the other bodies, suggesting that under this encompassing national social partnership lies a more complex and unequal pattern of social representation and state embeddedness. Community groups and agriculture are not represented anywhere else in Table 8.1 but in NESC and union representation is greatly decreased. Although this picture would obviously be different if bodies dealing with agriculture, social services, and the workplace were included, it is nonetheless striking that these social partners are mostly unrepresented in issues of industrial policy and science and technology.

Usually in the form of a representative from the Irish Congress of Trade Unions, unions are represented on the Forfás Board, the Competitiveness Council, the Industrial Policy Review Group, and the Information Society Commission (whose membership was extended after an initial dispute in 1997 about the technology and business bias of its membership). Unions have input, therefore, into general industrial-policy strategy, although in a minority compared to business representatives. The Telecommunications Task Force came to its conclusions based on a board composed entirely of private business people and state officials, despite the fact that many telecommunications workers are unionized.

Outside NESC, business representation is almost entirely through individual business people, not industry peak associations (the primary association is the Irish Business and Employers Confederation [IBEC]). Private business is well

2   The National Economic and Social Forum (NESF) is a partner institution for the NESC, which encompasses most of the other organized social groups that are excluded from the NESC (e.g., Irish National Organization of the Unemployed, the Small Firms' Association, and so on).

3   Department of the Prime Minister.

represented on all bodies, especially those dealing with industrial policy and science and technology. TNC executives are particularly well represented in the more "encompassing" Competitiveness and Information Society bodies, whereas indigenous industry is better represented within the state agency boards. It would be a mistake to read too much into these differences, however, given the selective nature of the data. However, indigenous industry does have a significant presence within the state agency boards (in the case of IDA Ireland, these are often banks) and, therefore, has some input into policy, given the overall historical thrust of policy toward attracting foreign investment. This is all the more consequential because the agency boards can intervene directly in agency affairs, shaping the thrust of agency practices, as well as reviewing major grant and other financial decisions. However, in the case of EI and particularly IDA Ireland, it is clear that the dominant influence is the demand of what the agencies call their "client" companies.

Academics play a role in policy formulation, although in two different ways. In the case of NESC and economic- and industrial-policy institutions, the academics are usually economists and are included in an advisory role – not as representatives of actors who ultimately will be affected by those decisions. In the science and technology bodies, the academics are more heavily represented, are usually natural scientists, and combine an advisory role with a role representing the universities and academics as actors who will play a central role in implementing the policy decisions. Professional associations representing science teachers, research scientists, and engineers are also represented on those bodies. So too is the HEA, the state body that governs the university sector. Perhaps the relatively weak purchase of neoliberalism within state agency practices is related to the dominance of business executives and state officials (both planning-oriented occupations) rather than economists within the industrial development regime – in sharp contrast to countries such as Mexico where economists promoted an aggressively neoliberal agenda (Babb, 2002).

Finally, the various agencies of the state are embedded in one another in interesting ways. The civil service is the exclusive source of state representatives in NESC but only has a single representative on the Forfás, EI, and IDA boards. Forfás has representatives from the other state agencies; otherwise, there is relatively little interconnection between the agency boards. However, it must be remembered that, in addition to direct reporting relationships to Forfás (and of Forfás to the Department of Enterprise, Trade, and Employment), the senior executives of Forfás, IDA, and EI are in constant contact with one another and, in many cases, located in the same building in Wilton Place, Dublin.

Overall, then, the encompassing nature of the social partnership institutions, such as NESC, is only weakly reflected in the memberships of the boards and commissions dealing with industrial and science and technology policy and practice. Private business is more strongly represented across the board, including indigenous industry. Academics play a less important role in shaping science, technology, and innovation policy. Unions have some representation but only at the level of general strategy. Although the civil service dominates the social-partnership institutions, it retains a relatively light representation on the other boards. Each of the state agencies, task forces, commissions, councils, and review groups described herein has a high degree of autonomy, at least to the extent that it can be measured by formal memberships. In short, the industrial and innovation policy regimes are characterized by multiple embedded autonomies, with business in a clear position of privilege even within this particular "policy space."

The multiple embeddednesses of the Irish state are also seen in the more informal connections that develop around each of the industrial-development agencies. Understanding the position of the IDA requires us to turn Evans's concept of embedded autonomy around somewhat because it is precisely the autonomy of the IDA within the Irish economic-development regime and its embeddedness in an international community of potentially mobile firms that has made it such an effective agency in attracting foreign investment. The IDA is a quasi-independent state agency, although it receives its funding from and must report to the Department of Enterprise, Employment, and Trade and to the cabinet minister in that department. In 1969, the IDA became an agency outside of the civil-service structure and it has become increasingly independent, until recent years, of the rest of the state economic-development regime. Most of the initiatives in industrial policy until the early 1990s were developed through the IDA.

The IDA has deep ties to the TNCs, abroad and in Ireland, which are first formed through the IDA's international offices. The project officers in these four European, six U.S., and five Asian–Pacific offices (as of 1999) establish an early relationship with many companies in their area and ultimately hand off the companies to their counterparts in Ireland. Generally, the IDA is available to handle any problems that the TNCs might have: as one long-time TNC manager said,

"We're a little cut off out here but we have a good relationship with the IDA officers. I can always ring Kieran [McGowan, CEO of IDA Ireland] anyway."

Often the local and international ties are combined to good effect. For example, ties to a TNC head office might be useful in developing a closer relationship between an Irish supplier firm and the parent firm in the United States. As one IDA officer told this author:

"Sometimes we have to use our contact with the United States to get around the local TNC manager who's trying to get all the credit for himself and won't tell head office about this supplier in Ireland."

The ties to TNCs are also manifested in the political arena – and occasionally even reach the public ear. In 1997, a measure was before the Irish parliament limiting the work week to 48 hours per week (averaged over a six-month period). This legislation was in compliance with an EU directive on working hours, although the business community wanted to adopt a less restrictive version. The legislation was being passed relatively quietly until it emerged that Kieran McGowan, CEO of the IDA, had sent a letter to the relevant cabinet minister arguing that this would not be acceptable to TNCs locating in Ireland – a letter that was later withdrawn in the face of the controversy. Nonetheless, the IDA was clearly seen and expected to represent the interests of TNCs within the Irish economy. Indeed, TNCs in Ireland have not organized into any significant trade association. They may be active in the Irish Business and Employers Confederation and the U.S. Chamber of Commerce will sometimes take a role in policy discussions, but it is usually the IDA that speaks most clearly for the interests of the TNCs.

The IDA also will call on the TNCs occasionally to use their political clout to support IDA efforts within the political realm. The IDA, among others, had been pressing the government in 1996 and 1997 to provide further funding for education and training of staff for the software industry and the IT sector more generally. Seeing a small announcement in the Sunday paper of a forum on "The Future of the Software Industry," I attended a business breakfast in one of the major universities in June 1997. Among the attendance of some fifty people were several officials from state economic-development agencies, the Department of Education, the Department of Enterprise and Employment, industry associations, and the university in question. Most of the attendees, however, were general managers and other senior managers of software TNCs. The program consisted of talks by an academic and by Kieran McGowan of the IDA regarding the software-skills shortage and its dimensions. McGowan encouraged the software managers to let the politicians know the extent of the skills shortage and how it was affecting them. A discussion ensued, ending with more exhortations to the software managers to make their political pressure felt. The IDA, therefore, undertook to create and facilitate a coalition consisting of TNCs, the two relevant expansionist government departments (i.e., Education and Enterprise/Employment), and the IDA to support the political goal of expanding the labor supply. The IDA became not only a representative of the interests of the TNCs but also a political organizer of the TNCs. As one senior IDA executive commented:

"We would have been very astute politically within Ireland. Instead of visiting the minister on our own, we would bring two or three heads of TNCs with us. Then you get them saying 'If you do this, then we'll do that' and that kind of thing. We would blatantly use the multinationals to influence government . . . . It was a good thing for Ireland . . . . We would bring the minister out to Silicon Valley and so on once or twice a year. They would know what it's like, they would see it isn't just us talking."

Indeed, the Minister for Enterprise, Trade, and Employment of the day attended an Enterprise Ireland sponsored event in Silicon Valley that I also attended. The minister was part of a trade mission along with fifteen managing directors of Irish high-tech firms and was 1 of about 150 people, mainly Irish emigrants well placed in Silicon Valley companies, attending the function. This elite among emigrants had easy access to the minister in an informal setting, while being exhorted to return or invest in Ireland.

Clearly, on an everyday "service" level and on the level of national politics, the IDA was deeply embedded in the TNC sector. This combination of its embedded-ness in the most powerful faction of capital in the Irish economy and its position of "autonomy with influence" within the Irish state made the IDA a potent force within the Irish industrial-policy regime and an effective competitor in the market for mobile investment.

The state agencies that promote indigenous firms are embedded in a different set of social actors. The indigenous development-policy regime emerged slowly and in a piecemeal fashion from the 1970s forward and is characterized by the embedded autonomy of a set of state agencies in the learning communities of the indigenous industry.

"We have relatively close contact with the companies, a lot of face-to-face. A very fertile planning area is you take a group of companies on a trade mission to Japan and in the bar the world is changed; I'm exaggerating but there's some truth to it,"

as one senior EI official put it. Nonetheless, the smaller size and greater number of Irish firms creates a different dynamic for EI than for the IDA. As an IDA executive said:

"Enterprise Ireland doesn't have something the IDA has – IDA was far closer to its companies. Enterprise Ireland is trying to influence government, talking about policy and strategy and not needs of specific companies; it's not as effective. The views of TNCs have more political clout than of an Irish firm. Enterprise Ireland has a lot of interaction with companies but seen from the outside, they are not seen as representing the companies. Government wants to see agencies being close to companies, rather than being independent."

Although the character of the embeddedness of indigenous development agencies may not help their political position, it does assist them in shaping the industry. Although the close face-to-face ties developed through the grant-aid process and the associational infrastructure of industry are important, those agencies do not rely on them as the sole basis of information and influence. Huge amounts of data on individual companies are held by state agencies in the form of survey data and data from the grant-aid process. In addition, officials within the agencies monitor "their" companies more closely. A director of one of the PAT Centers claimed:

"There is a constant gathering of information. Companies approach the PATs. Then there are specific firms, records of firms on databases. We also every now and then do sectional trawls, we look through all the firms and identify the ones which have some potential, the really strong ones, the no-hopers. Then we approach the ones that have some promise, try and get them to make the most of what they've got, develop their technology."

Although most of this data is not available at the level of the individual company to most state officials, the level of detailed information on small subsectors of industry available within the agencies facilitates highly contextualized interventions in the industrial-development process.

We can gain a greater understanding of the role played by social networks in embedding state agencies by tracing the various social networks that overlap state and industry within the software-policy community since the 1970s. It began with the NBST in the late 1970s, moved on to the NSC from 1984 to 1988, and was most recently institutionalized within the NSD and the various centers of the PAT in software.

Two of the leading figures on the IT side within the NBST were Robert Cochran for software/data processing/microelectronics and Jim Mountjoy for telecommunications. Cochran had come from another state agency and also had experience in an IT-user organization. He later went on to work on software quality and development tools for the NSC, while also managing his own software company, Generics (a technically sophisticated operation that went out of business in 1990). In the 1990s he was director of the Center for Software Engineering (CSE) and ran another software-development-tools company. He has also periodically been on the executive committee of the Irish Software Association (ISA). Clearly, then, his career has straddled state, semistate, private sector, and industry-association organizations.

Mountjoy has also had overlapping affiliations. With a Ph.D. in telecommunications engineering and extensive experience in the Department of Posts and Telegraphs, he worked at the NBST where he wrote a report in 1980 regarding the options for economic development based on the upgrading of the telecommunications infrastructure (NBST, 1980). Later, in the 1980s, he left to move into private industry with Baltimore Technologies and subsequently his own firm, Euristix. From this vantage point in the private sector, he continued his involvement in economic-development issues, writing a report in 1991 for the Industrial Policy Review Group on "Communications and Economic Development" (Euristix, 1991).

The NSC and NSD have provided similar stories. Many of those involved in the NSC have gone back into private industry while remaining in touch with the policy community. The first NSD director, Barry Murphy, had been the managing director of Insight Software, an Irish company sold to Hoskyns from the United Kingdom in 1988. NSD director until 1996, he moved on to work with the Cullinane Group Ireland (CGI), an organization founded by U.S. software-industry veteran, John Cullinane, to invest in Irish software companies. CGI also conducts research on the software industry and related topics, including a report entitled "Israel: A High-Tech Model for Ireland?" (CGI, 1997). Murphy was also involved in writing the strategy document published by the Irish Software Association in March 1998 before returning to the private sector. The second NSD director, Jennifer Condon, came from the industry to work on the marketing side of the NSC in the mid-1980s. She was then managing director of ICL's IT Center in Dublin from 1988 until 1996, when she joined the NSD. When Condon joined NSD, the staff consisted of the director and three other staff members: two from within the state-development agencies and a third with a background in the industry. This ensured a combination of embeddedness in the industry and a certain autonomy of focus and objectives. A further group of prominent software managers was involved in policy initiatives within the industry, either through the ISA or as participants in groups such as the Software Industry Working Group in 1989 or the Software Consultative Committee in the 1990s. Furthermore, there is significant overlap with the educational sector as prominent computer-science professors have liaised closely with industry and the state in various forums (Ryan, 1997).

These social networks are certainly a critical dimension of the embedded autonomy of the state in the indigenous software-development sector. The ability of individuals to move among private, public, and semipublic organizations or to interact freely across those organizational boundaries gives the state the embeddedness necessary to make and implement effective policy. They have been augmented, however, by a layer of decentralized associational institutions, such as the PAT centers, which, along with other similar institutions, have built a close link between the state and industry – blurring the boundary between public and private sectors – while maintaining a developmental focus. Typically, these centers (described in detail in Chapter 6) are located in universities, with governing boards drawn from the university, industry, and state agencies. For example, each PAT has a director within EI, a manager in each university center, an academic director from the university, and connections to the EI "development advisors" who deal directly with companies in that subsector. More formal arrangements also exist for state-sponsored consultation between industry and the universities, such as the industry–higher education consultative committee sponsored by the NSD through the 1990s.

The indigenous development agencies are also embedded internationally. Unlike the IDA Ireland connections to TNC headquarters, those agencies have built connections to EU agencies and, in recent years, to emigrant communities. By 2000, EI had widely dispersed twenty-nine market offices outside of Ireland: three in the United Kingdom, fifteen elsewhere in Europe, three in the United States, six in Asia, and two elsewhere in the world. The primary focus of the market office is assisting Irish-owned firms in breaking into international markets, but they can also play a role in connecting emigrant communities to the Irish technology industry.

Furthermore, each agency has a distinctive internal organizational culture, developed in part through an interaction with the different constituencies. Agencies develop procedures, practices, and ways of conceiving of problems and strategies that reflect in large part the constituencies within which they are embedded. The state takes on a "class character" (Offe, 1974) but it can be shaped by multiple classes. We can see in the organizational cultures of the state agencies the "class characters" of the state. The IDA's lens for conceiving of industrial development is the lens of foreign-investment attraction and the perspective of the TNCs, whereas EI increasingly provides an institutional space within which the world view of indigenous entrepreneurs dominates. Because these agencies practice industrial development on the ground, it is the class-based notions of development that dominate industrial-development practice. Concerns for the interests of workers are held at a distance not only by relations within and among firms but also by the character of the state. In the same way, industrial development in Ireland is highly gendered – agency officials see issues of gender or class inequality as almost completely outside their scope. Despite the fact that such issues may be discussed within the social-partnership institutions and even occasionally in Forfás, they rarely surface within the everyday practice of the agencies in their relationships with firms and universities.

Through its various agencies, the Irish state is deeply embedded in a variety of social actors, through both formal and informal networks. The very multiplicity of those connections suggests that we must be careful in talking about "the" state because the multiple agencies of the state are often embedded in different social, political, and institutional contexts (Carroll Burke, 2001).

Mixing information-gathering by informal networks, formal administrative means, and expert-driven surveys, the agencies are able to work with a clear and highly contextualized picture of the Irish economy. In fact, given a more "network" state structure, Scott's argument (1998) is turned on its head. By rendering society more "legible" to the state, strategies of governance more adapted to the particular circumstance are made possible; universalization and standardization are not inevitable. This is not to deny, of course, that such governance may be all the more effective in enhancing state power precisely because it is more contextualized; however, it is a more complex question than that implied by Scott's analysis of the "high-modernist" state doomed to fail due to its standardizing gaze.

EXTERNALLY ACCOUNTABLE

Given the close ties between state agencies and social groups, why don't these ties collapse into an antidevelopmental form of clientelism and rent-seeking? This question is particularly pertinent given the long history of clientelism in Irish politics and the continuing revelations of scandals involving bribery and corruption in beef, property, and banking, among other sectors. In the industrial-development regime, these problems have mostly been avoided through relatively highly developed – although distinctive – structures of accountability.

The state agencies in Ireland are characterized by many of the classic features of Weberian bureaucracies. However, as we have seen, they are also in an unusually autonomous position outside the formal civil service and operate through a wide range of decentralized institutions (see Chapter 6). How can such a network of decentralized institutions be compatible with the bureaucratic structures that have been discussed? In fact, the Irish state system combines a logic of internal accountability through bureaucratic organization with a logic of external accountability based on performance requirements and monitoring of the various constituent parts of the state system – each part is characterized by "accountable autonomy" (Fung, 2001). Fung and Wright (2001) suggest that there is an organizational alternative to command and control by experts, aggregative voting, and strategic negotiation – all of which are present in the political process in Ireland through centralized planning, elections and catch-all politics, and neocorporatist bargaining. They argue for a model of decision-making that they call "empowered democratic deliberation." This approach devolves power to the local units of the system, promoting bottom-up participation and encouraging a focus on deliberation around practical problems.

However, there are also

"linkages of accountability and communication that connect local units to superordinate bodies." (Fung and Wright, 2001, p. 22)

This is a form of coordinated decentralization in which local units are autonomous but receive resources from the center and are accountable to it for their performance. Such systems, therefore, are state-centered rather than voluntaristic. Fung and Wright conceive of this institutional alternative as one that empowers ordinary citizens; however, in the case of Irish industrial and technology policy, it operates within elites. The rough equality of power that Fung and Wright conceive of as a background condition only operates within the technology regime, not between this regime and the rest of society. Nonetheless, within the regime – and particularly on the indigenous side – there are significant elements of a class- specific accountable autonomy.

We have seen that a dense network of institutions exists, which are largely centrally funded but which operate with some degree of autonomy. A number of mechanisms exists in the Irish case to make them accountable. The first is the multiplicity of actors involved in the bodies that generates a certain degree of transparency – particularly when actors with potentially conflicting interests are included (e.g., academic and industry participants in research forums). This is true of both the formal board memberships analyzed in Table 8.1 and the informal networks discussed previously. Word travels fast within the Irish technology- and industrial-policy community if something is awry.

However, such networks are always subject to particularism and corruption, and require additional institutional forms of accountability. Bureaucratic reporting on decentralized decisions would stifle the very flexibility that the various agencies and centers enjoy. Alternatively, making the centers accountable through market discipline and pushing them to become commercially viable have had disastrous consequences. Perhaps the primary reason for the collapse of the NSC in the 1980s was the conflict generated by the demands put on it to undertake a mission of upgrading the industry while at the same time requiring it to be commercially viable. Caught between devolving into a development-services organization or competing with the major firms in the industry, the NSC lost industry support and was ultimately closed (for more detail see Chapter 9). The PAT centers have also suffered under pressures to be self-funding. As a director in one of the innovation-promoting institutions told this author:

"Our promotional role ended when the money ran out . . . . We made the same mistake with the PATs. If people want missionary work, then they have to pay for it."

Accountable autonomy in the Irish technology regime is, therefore, based primarily on the use of external evaluations. Autonomy from their business constituency is maintained by the performance requirements placed on the various agencies, centers, and programs. These requirements are given a cutting edge by the regular evaluation of programs, often mandated by the EU, and publication of those evaluations. In the case of software, a detailed evaluation of the Software Support Program was published in 1995 (Clarke, 1995). Forfás published a long series of evaluations of various centers and programs,[4] usually drawing on external

---

4   These include reviews of the technology center program, the basic research-grants scheme, R&D
    policy and interventions, the various EU research and industrial-development programs, Teltec

evaluators. International panels of experts and external reviewers have become the standard institutional model for grant-giving and program-evaluation within the realm of science and technology. This does not mean that there is complete transparency in the system; rather, a powerful impetus for performance is created by the public or semipublic availability of such evaluations. The increased ability of the public to gain access to such information through the provisions of the Freedom of Information Act (1997) reinforces those pressures – although this ability has been curtailed somewhat since 2002.

Furthermore, poor evaluations can result in closure, sale, or reorganization of such programs. For example, as part of this process of constant shifting and experimentation with state and semistate agencies, in the 1990s the National Institute of Management Technology was sold, the Multimedia Technology Institute restructured, and the CSE given new responsibilities. Due to requirements of the EU funders, such centers are subject to significant and detailed external evaluation. They are also ultimately subject to the control of the state and, therefore, will also reflect broad policy concerns. For example, the CSE set targets for the uptake of quality procedures within the industry as a whole. In 1997, the CSE, at the request of the NSD, instigated programs aimed at diffusing quality procedures into small software firms, based on its prior success at diffusing such procedures among larger firms. As one senior industrial-policy official stated:

"Organizations tend to get complacent and set in their ways, especially with jobs for life and precedents like in the civil service; that's no reflection on the individuals involved, it's more of an organizational consequence. Therefore, it's well worthwhile almost to make changes for the sake of making changes every now and then, although not in an arbitrary way. In the early 1990s, the old IDA had been there for over twenty years – it wasn't a bad idea to stir it up a bit, even if people there are not that happy about it. You still need to get them to buy in, though."

However, the various organizations also retain a clear and distinct identity, with the accountability and social ties of bodies such as the NSC and the NSD to the broader state apparatus, maintaining their "developmental" focus rather than being completely captured by the industry's short-term objectives. In the case of software, the industry has appealed for such state intervention. Industry representatives argued for a NSD in the late 1980s, claiming that there was a need for a body that

"should act as a focal point for new firms, liaise with state agencies and government, seek linkage opportunities for Irish companies, and monitor the implementation of the National Plan which the industry intends to develop in partnership with government." (ICSA, 1988)

These dense formal and informal networks and internal and external structures of accountability maintain and reproduce the structure of multiple embedded autonomies within the Irish state technology- and industrial-policy regime.

Ireland, AMT Ireland, the Applied Research Program, BioResearch Ireland, the mentor program, and more.

LOOSELY COUPLED

The organizational structure of the Irish state, therefore, consists of a range of embedded autonomies of the state, linking specific agencies with particular organizational cultures and capacities to particular social groups. IDA Ireland is the agency with the closest ties to foreign capital, EI has a diverse set of connections to indigenous networks of innovation, and general issues of policy and coordination are handled by an umbrella body, Forfás. The Departments of Enterprise, Trade, and Employment and of An Taoiseach have close ties to national employer and labor organizations. The agencies have significant internal flexibility in their dealings with their constituencies.

The state structure is also characterized by a high degree of flexibility in the relationship between the units of the state apparatus, diffusing the significant conflict that remains. Furthermore, each agency is connected in different ways to different parts of the EU political apparatus. Rather than a cohesive and relatively insulated national state apparatus, the Irish state consists of an apparatus that is deeply embedded in a "network polity," forging sociopolitical alliances out of constantly shifting local, national, and global components. In transforming itself to operate within a locally and globally networked economy and polity, state governance itself is "rescaled" as the prior privileged role of the national level gives way to a glocal form of state (Brenner, 1998, 1999).

As we have seen, the various agencies of the state have distinct organizational cultures. These multiple centers of policy and practice often take on different emphases in promoting capitalist development. Social-partnership institutions are dominated by a modified European Social Democratic view of development, at least from the union side. The Department of Enterprise, Trade, and Employment is more likely to articulate a neoliberal view of development, through both the minister and the senior civil servants. This conflict has come increasingly into the open as a debate over whether Ireland should pursue European or U.S. models of capitalism. The industrial-development agencies rarely debate the utility of market mechanisms in promoting development but rather concentrate on the intensive promotional activities discussed in this book, with Forfás focusing on science and technology, IDA on foreign investment, and EI on indigenous capabilities. There is surprisingly little overlap on an operational basis, therefore, between the various organizations – although they do conflict and take on a shifting balance of power (reflected in the following chapter discussing changes in industrial-policy regimes).

Nonetheless, this is not a set of isolated organizations. There are many bridging mechanisms that connect these loosely coupled organizations. A multitude of informal relationships makes extensive communication across organizational boundaries within the state a fact of life. The agencies are connected to a certain degree through memberships on each other's boards. Reflecting the historical dominance of the IDA, many of the leading figures in the various agencies have worked together within the IDA. Both John Travers, first chief executive of Forfás, and Sean Dorgan, chief executive of the IDA, were civil servants in what is now the Department of Enterprise, Trade, and Employment.

Furthermore, this loose coupling is facilitated by a strong center within the state and particularly by the unquestioned hegemony of a view of industrial development as the promotion of competitiveness within international markets using all the agencies and resources of the state. Regardless of the complexion of government, industrial policy has been remarkably insulated from party politics, and the emphasis on foreign investment has rarely been questioned publicly. This overarching acceptance of the terms of global capitalism enables the variety of ways in which it becomes translated into industrial development practice. However, this internal flexibility comes at the cost of effectively excluding consideration of alternatives to global competitiveness as the guiding principle of economic life.

STILL RATIONAL AND NATIONAL AFTER ALL THESE YEARS?

The image of the DNS is bound up with the notion that a cohesive state can provide a more rational strategy than market rationality for national development – through its greater coordination, more long-term focus, more intense use of expertise, and greater focus on the goal of national development. How rational and national, then, is the DNS with its multiple agencies and constituencies, loosely coupled and externally accountable?

Ireland is clearly not Japan – and the Irish state officials know it. As one senior official put it:

"In Japan, you had MITI [the industrial development ministry] doing planning but in Ireland you had agencies that did things and translated experience into policy. The trade board worked with companies doing export marketing; IDA worked with TNCs, saw the constraints and tackled them; Forbairt worked with indigenous companies. A great example which made a big contribution was in the early 1990s, we could see the big bar to software growth was lack of venture capital. We felt the companies were selling too early and losing control – therefore, we had to think about how to grow them bigger earlier. We started venture capital funds which paid spectacular dividends for us. Enterprise Ireland got 25 million from equity last year and 50 million this year. The reason we got that was we responded to what was seen as a block at the time.... We are nonideological regarding state intervention. In Ireland it's a 'pragmatic school,' not the 'Chicago School'."

Rationality may be responsive and adaptive as well as strategic and agenda setting.

"Was it strategy or adaptation/rolling? Rolling is more dominant than strategy overall, but that's good. We have good fundamentals, and then we roll. Now and again, there is strategic change but rolling evolution is the dominant thing,"

says another senior official. Senior officials from a wide range of agencies give similar answers in considering whether the agencies have been pragmatic or strategic in their actions. Some reject the terms of the question, arguing that rational strategies should be as responsive to circumstances as they are driven by expert analysis and long-term planning:

"It is still important to keep in mind the overall objective of industry policy. There is no grand design or grand plan, but there was a consistency to industry policy over the years. Measures and policies have shifted but there has been a consistent thread – it's a question of identifying it. I see a logical relationship there from the 1920s, though all the policy changes. It is based on the ultimate objectives – employment and higher living standards arising out of market-led activities. That's the core and then there is a whole series of strategies to get there. Some things work, others don't, you hold onto the things that work. There is a continual process of experimentation going on, rediscovery going on, evaluation of where we are on a constant basis. That's ingrained into the system almost at this stage, new people take it on – the constant experimentation and adaptation . . . I wouldn't see that so much as pragmatic – in fact, it's the opposite, it's keeping your eye on the higher principle; pragmatism suggests a focus on the means, this is about keeping your eyes on the ends."

The agencies' approach to broad industrial policy is similar to their approach to shaping firms. The broad outlines of what are the desirable features of a dynamic economy or firm are widely shared, but the means through which they are implemented vary a great deal and are much more negotiable. Built on a legacy of planning within government departments and the IDA, the shift to a discourse of enterprise and the promotion of enterprise (Carr, 1998) has taken not a neoliberal form but rather a peculiarly statist form. State agencies intervene intensively in the "cultural production of enterprise" (Carr, 1998) and, ironically, are unwilling to rely on the entrepreneurial spirit to produce concrete enterprising activities. Often, those working in the system seem somewhat at a loss to explain their own model of organization and action:

"Ireland is a funny economy. We have a fairly statist economy, I'm amazed sometimes, you'd think we were communists the way we go on! The state has a strong but healthy hold on things. Quite a lot of central thinking goes on. There is a close relationship between the state and business. It might be out of sync but it is almost Russian or Chinese in its way of doing things. The closest would be the French, the way they manage things, but without the French bureaucracy. A problem gets translated into a solution quickly here – for example, the E-Commerce Bill moved very quickly, it was passed before some countries would have ever identified the problem."

This official, the same official quoted previously in distinguishing Ireland from Japan, now likens Ireland to a communist state but one with less bureaucracy and closer ties to business. Clearly, the officials of the Irish state agencies do not have the vocabulary to describe their own rationalities and practices. This void is often filled with talk of "enterprise" (Carr, 1998) and neoliberalism. However, the concrete practices of these organizations reflect a different perspective on state governance of economic life.

Rationality lives in the DNS but as a much more diverse, contextualized set of rationalities within an overarching framework that defines certain underlying principles of competitiveness, growth, and national development. Each agency pursues its own rational strategies for implementing those broad principles by connecting them to other icons of capitalist modernity: science and technology, trade, entrepreneurship, rational bargaining, and so on.

Fitzgerald and Girvin (2000) point out that nationalism and a strong pride in national identity have remained a core element of Irish political culture, even as other core values such as farming, religion, and – to a lesser extent – the family have waned. If anything, national pride has increased as integration into global flows has intensified. However, nationalism is a more elastic ideology than is often thought. Economic nationalism in Ireland has been associated with national self-sufficiency, the nation as a world-class location for investment ("a place among the locations"?), national social partnership, and the fostering of a national culture of enterprise. Each cultural construction mobilizes the nation in a different set of discourses and practices, each providing not just a symbolic currency but also a binding force that enables particular political-economic projects (O'Donnell, 2000).

State officials are proud of their role in developing the Irish economy, and even those skeptical of their own impact frame their criticisms in terms that they were not allowed to do more. One official, unsolicited, said:

"I've been at the IDA since the 1970s. I like it, it's an interesting place to be part of doing something, you know, something nationally."

Another, recently arrived from the private sector, remarked,

"There is a very high sense of commitment to a public service ethos in here; I would have been skeptical about that, but it's real. It's not quite 'we're doing it for Ireland' but there is a sense that it's a good thing."

Such openly nationalist sentiments are more common among IDA officials and TNC subsidiary managers as they see themselves as strategizing to win more of the global pie "for Ireland." One official commented:

"The strong culture of the IDA? That has been a feature of the organization in all of my time there. It's semipatriotic. We always felt we were in an important job, it was prestigious, had status attached to it. Staff felt that they were doing something that was good for the country and felt that they were effective. The staff know if they're achieving something, they are the ones who know. I remember when we got the first IBM investment in 1982, in the teeth of the recession, we knew it was a big breakthrough at the time, we were very excited, even people not directly involved within the organization."

The ideology of managers in indigenous high-tech firms is less openly nationalist – partly because there is a presumed correspondence between the growth of those firms and the growth of the Irish economy. This presumption has been at the heart of the critiques of foreign investment over the years and is shared almost universally across the state agencies and departments.

CONCLUSION

The Irish state is not quite the state that Chalmers Johnson had in mind when he argued for the potential superiority of the plan rationality of the state over market rationality. Nonetheless, this is a state that remains both rational and national, albeit in multiple and rapidly changing ways. Multiple organizational rationalities are shaped by multiple local and global constituencies, are held accountable through external evaluations, and complement and conflict with one another within a loosely coupled state structure.

The national state may be characterized by an increasingly "flexible citizenship" for those lucky enough to be able to lay claim to citizenship itself (Ong, 1999). However, this does not spell the end of the national state nor of its developmental aspirations and capabilities – instead, they are transformed as are the character of the nation and membership within it. The embeddedness of different agencies of the state in multiple local and global constituencies and institutions means that the nation to be imagined is now a much more eclectic project, to be produced from many locals and globals, rather than the more bounded national entities that were constructed under embedded liberalism.

Nonetheless, the state remains bound to the national territory and to its population. The state is perhaps the only entity within the nation that has resources but that cannot emigrate – and, in the 1980s, the promise of job security and decent wages within the state helped retain significant numbers of the Irish population and elites within the territory. Whereas capital and labor fled the country, the state was pushed into experimentation and action by a legitimation crisis of huge proportions. The next chapter discusses how a series of such crises and their political and institutional resolutions have shaped the character of the DNS in Ireland.

9

POLITICS AND CHANGE IN DEVELOPMENT REGIMES

POLITICS, INSTITUTIONS, AND REGIME CHANGE

Under what conditions does a DNS emerge? The analysis in this book has emphasized the link between the development strategies of the state and the organizational practices and structures through which they are developed, negotiated, and implemented. Any explanation of the emergence of the DNS, therefore, requires an explanation of both the content of its development strategies and its institutional forms. Linking these two is a critical part of the DNS story because it proves to be the case that the organizational politics of the state exerts a critical influence on its strategies.

This raises the complicated issue of the origins of organizational strategies and structures. A brief review of this thorny set of issues is necessary before turning to the empirical analysis of the Irish case. Perhaps the most widespread answer to this question, and the heart of economic theories of organizations, is that organizational strategies and structures emerge to solve problems in the most efficient manner. The dilemma for such explanations is why we find such a variety of organizational forms – even, as we have seen, in types of developmental states. Williamson (1975, 1985) emphasizes the conditions under which different organizational forms minimize transaction costs – with hierarchical forms emerging primarily when specific assets exist that tie actors to more long-term relationships. If a level of trust exists that can sustain relationships over the long term without internalization through hierarchy, then we see the emergence of the network forms of organization (Jarillo, 1988).

Is trust among participants enough to explain the network character of the DNS? There are several problems with such a view. Firstly, it overstates the distinctions among markets, hierarchies, and networks – in the Irish case, all three organizational forms, and others as well, are intertwined to create a complex institutional form. Secondly, each form relies to a certain degree on trust but also on bargaining and admilystration. The trusting relationships built between the NSD and the software industry are based on a background of hard bargaining in the 1980s; occasionally, these relational assets must be protected through further bargaining with external challengers. In essence, although the form of transactions (i.e., social relationships) is critical to explaining the rise of particular organizational forms, it only poses the question as to why transactions (i.e., relations) take the form that they do rather than some other form.

Perhaps particular social relationships are more effective in certain technological contexts than others, so that organizational forms are contingent on conformity to the technological environment (Burns and Stalker, 1961; Lawrence and Lorsch, 1967; Perrow, 1986, pp. 140–6). Is the DBS better suited to a world of more predictable routine production and the DNS better able to respond to more uncertain and dynamic environments? Again, there is an element of truth here – Chapter 2 suggested that network statism, network industrial structures, and "open-systems" information technology appear to be linked to one another. It is problematic, however, to view technology as an independent force, isolated from organizational strategies and creating external pressures on organizations. In fact, organizations play a critical role in shaping whether work tasks are routine or nonroutine or, indeed, whether innovation is a central component of organizational strategy (Perrow, 1986). Analysis of the developmental role of the state in the Irish software industry suggests that a key goal of state action is to promote firm innovation strategies over routine coding and software production – all within the same technological environment. Organizations must be able to undertake certain tasks successfully, but how organizations are constructed shapes the kinds of tasks they seek to undertake and the technologies they use and create, as much as technology and tasks shape the organization.

Others question whether organizations are formed by concerns for efficiency or technical performance at all and argue that organizational structures are shaped primarily by conformity to prevalent institutional norms. These norms can be long-established "social logics of organizing" in national societies (Biggart and Guillen, 1999) or the dominant "rational myths" of modernization (Meyer and Rowan, 1977). However, there are many logics of organizing at work in the Irish economy across the period we have studied, and no overarching cultural logic explains the particular mix of dominant institutional norms at any particular time. Indeed, in the previous chapter we saw how flexible even such a core value as nationalism can be as it is institutionalized in various ways within multiple apparatuses within the state.

Furthermore, the distinction between technology and culture is overdrawn. In fact, they are interdependent: culture exists not as disembodied ideas, beliefs, or logics but rather as concrete practices or technologies that order relations among categories of social actors. Technologies are ways of doing things, which depend crucially on shared understandings of the "tools" being used and the "objects" being shaped or created by the technologies; indeed, technologies are "material cultures" (Carroll Burke, 2002a, 2002b). These "cultural technologies" take on concrete and enduring institutional forms but are also subject to creative forms of recombination and mobilization under specific circumstances. Technology and culture are critical components of any organizational structure or developmental strategy but must be mobilized by particular coalitions of actors and through various modes of collective action.

In this chapter, I propose a political–organizational approach to understanding the emergence of network developmentalism. The organizations of network developmentalism emerge as outcomes of historically contingent political struggles within capitalism – much as Dore (1973, 1983) argues for the Japanese system of "relational contracting" and Jacoby (1988) argues for the large corporation in the United States. Organizations do solve problems in the world and must attempt to be at least effective. Political coalitions, therefore, build organizations that are at once effective and politically advantageous, to undertake tasks that this coalition has defined as strategic. As Tilly (2000) points out, these tasks typically involve exploitation by one social category or another and/or the hoarding of resources by particular actors. Gradually, as organizational forms are put in place for these purposes, other organizations emulate the forms or adapt to them in order to try and secure some of the gains of the new institutionalized regime (Tilly, 2000, Chapter 6). The shape of state institutions is particularly critical here:

"The shape of initial regulatory institutions has a profound effect on subsequent capitalist development. They define the current state of rules and what is permissible. They also provide guidelines for how states can be subsequently organized to intervene in economies as new issues arise." (Fligstein, 2001, p. 40)

Political coalitions mobilize, restructure, and even create organizations to institutionalize their political programs. These regimes, once institutionalized, are relatively stable due to their ability to structure patterns of incentives and shape the pattern of recurring social relations (Block, 1994) and order actors' cultural understandings of the social field in ways that sustain the advantage of the dominant actors (Fligstein, 2001). In short, they become hegemonic by providing both concrete concessions to those included (and even those exploited) and a "concrete phantasy" that orders actors' understanding of their circumstances (Gramsci, 1971, p. 126).

Powerful though organizational arrangements are, they also change. There are two primary sources of change: internal and external. Given the origins of most organizations in exploitation and resource-hoarding, simmering internal conflicts exist within even highly institutionalized regimes because those who are exploited or excluded are clearly susceptible to mobilization in support of a different organizational project. Part of the reason this happens relatively rarely is because of the power of existing regimes to impose heavy costs on resistance to the dominant order. External challenges to the existing regime stem from the existence of other regimes that offer alternative models of organizing. These models will sometimes compete directly – as in the case of U.S.–Japanese competition in electronics. Or alternative regimes may provide "models" that can be used to pressure the regime and challenge its "concrete phantasies." Finally, internal challengers may draw on alliances forged directly with actors within other regimes in order to gather resources for struggles within their own regimes. Globalization has increased the availability of opportunities for such ties (Ansell, 2000) – as seen, for example, in the importance of EU policy to indigenous-technology advocates in Ireland.

Typically, opportunities for challengers to generate change arise when political or economic crises occur that destabilize existing regimes (Fligstein, 2001, p. 36). What makes the state unique as an organization is a claim to legitimacy that is based on an unusual degree of universalism and a responsibility to the whole political community within which it is located. The state may not actually pursue the collective interest in a universalist manner but it is deeply influenced by its claim to do so – casting it time and again into "legitimation crises" (Habermas, 1976; Offe, 1984). However, crises must be defined as such to become a basis for mobilization in and of themselves. It is those who are hegemonic within the regime that have the greatest power to define the character of crises – although crises do tend to open up the possibilities for new alliances and new rules (Fligstein, 2001, p. 36). Crises open spaces for new political projects: alliances can attach their project to a crisis, even if at first glance it is not directly relevant (in a process akin to Cohen, March, and Olsen's (1972) "garbage-can" theory).

This chapter examines two major historical periods of turbulence and change in the Irish industrial policy regime from this political–organizational perspective. The first is the emergence of the FDI industrial-policy regime from the social and economic crisis of the 1950s. The second is the emergence of the DNS amid the crisis of the 1980s. Chapter 11 considers the alternative pathways within a third possible period of change: the contemporary era, characterized by the intensification of the politics of inequality within a global economy. In each case, I begin by examining how an emergent crisis in the political economy opens up a space for alternative industrial-development projects. I then examine the political forces, domestically and internationally, that are mobilized to pursue particular regime-building projects and explain the reasons why particular projects won out over time. A critical component in this process is the institutional politics of regime change, where for each period I examine how institutional spaces opened up for new organizational forms and how those forms and structures in turn became institutionalized. My explanation of organizational and regime change, therefore, combines an analysis of crises, political mobilization, and institutional change – all located within an understanding of the new social forces created by each period of capitalist development. The rational state is a product of politics, not planning. The DNS is a product of political compromise, not network cultures or technologies.

This chapter undertakes the task of specifying more clearly the process through which embedded autonomies are created, maintained, and weakened. I argue that a similar set of conditions was in place in the case of each of the embedded autonomies analyzed in the previous two chapters. A crisis of the existing regime destabilized the institutions governing economic and industrial policy – in the 1950s, this led to the dismantling of protectionism and, in the 1980s, to a search for complementary strategies to attract foreign investment. The weakening of the previous regime does not determine which sets of policies and institutions will take its place, if any, and in both the 1950s and the 1980s there were several potential alternatives. However, in each case, the regime that emerged was based on an alliance between a new socioeconomic actor (i.e., foreign capital in the 1950s and technical professionals in the 1980s) and agencies within the state that were relatively marginal to the existing regime but had sufficient resources to sustain the early stages of institution-building (i.e., the IDA in the 1950s and the network of state technology agencies and centers in the 1980s). In short, the development path that could become institutionalized in a particular embedded autonomy was the path that prevailed. In each case, the new socioeconomic actor required the mediation and support of agencies within the state to negotiate a place within the national political economy. The agency required a certain level of resources that could sustain it until its development strategy was legitimated by industrial successes.

Finally, once the embedded autonomy of a particular mode of globalization has been established, a process of institutionalization typically takes place whereby both the state agency (or agencies) and the social actors undergo a process of learning. Embeddedness and autonomy shape one another through the institutionalization of particular ways of viewing and handling problems of development. Those meanings and practices then become the foundation of the organizational culture of the state agencies. This process of learning and institutionalization is supported by the shared interests of the agency and its allies in society. The routines and practices create a repertoire of problem definitions and meanings given to issues in the development process, generating shared sets of commonsense responses to such dilemmas. The regime becomes normalized and potentially hegemonic.

THE RISE AND INSTITUTIONALIZATION OF THE FOREIGN INVESTMENT REGIME

The economy of the Republic of Ireland underwent a rapid transformation after the mid-1950s from one of the most protected economies in the world to one that placed the greatest emphasis on free trade and attracting foreign investment. The conventional account argues that an economic crisis of the 1950s prompted a small cadre of leading civil servants to develop new strategies for economic development, turning the economy outward toward foreign trade and investment (Breen et al., 1990). Certainly, the state was crucial in this process, but the reasons for the remarkable dedication to the pursuit of foreign investment in the Irish political economy are more complex than this picture of a "rational state" can convey.

Crisis: the dilemmas of national self-sufficiency

Over the eighteen years it spent in government from 1932 to 1948, Fianna Fáil (a populist catch-all party) pursued a policy of national self-sufficiency and protectionism motivated by an ideological emphasis on the centrality of the farm family to the moral and economic well-being of the nation. This rural fundamentalism was challenged in the 1950s by a severe economic crisis, which decimated rural areas through mass unemployment and emigration. Breen et al. (1990) argued that protectionism and import-substitution industrialization exhausted itself in the 1950s after the "easy" market opportunities had been taken advantage of, producing an economic crisis in the 1950s to which the state elite responded with a shift to an export-led model. Others have argued that the crisis was not necessarily a crisis of protectionism but rather the result of a collapse in agricultural exports and a set of deflationary economic policies pursued by the Department of Finance in the early 1950s (Girvin, 1989; O'Hearn, 1990).

Regardless of the causes, a space was opened up for the consideration of alternatives to protection, and with Marshall Plan funds flowing into Europe, the resources were potentially available to support at least the early stages of such a shift in policy. The document that is often seen to both herald the severity of the crisis and the beginning of a way out is *Economic Development*, a report authored by T. K. Whitaker, the secretary of the Department of Finance. The report urged a shift in state investment from social spending to "productive" investment and focused on the agricultural sector. It opened the door ideologically – particularly given that it emerged from the historically fiscally conservative Department of Finance – to a degree of state developmentalism hitherto unheard of in the Irish economy. However, the gap between the strategy envisaged in the report – promoting state investment in agriculture while sustaining high levels of protection – and the actual changes in the Irish economy – heavy foreign investment in manufacturing in a context of rapidly decreasing tariffs – is substantial. Class and institutional politics combined to produce this unanticipated and striking outcome.

Politics: diverting pressures for development

Mjoset (1992) argued that, in contrast to other small Northern European economies, Ireland notably failed to create an autocentric national economy in which sociopolitical mobilization and economic performance combine to generate pressures for a widespread Fordist system of production and consumption. As outlined in Chapter 3, a weak national system of innovation generates social marginalization and mass emigration, which in turn weakens sociopolitical pressures to improve the system of innovation. This relationship was reinforced by economic reliance at first on live cattle exports to Britain and later on U.S. foreign investment, neither of which offered much opportunity for building a national version of Fordist development. Sociopolitical factors also reinforced the basic vicious circle with the Catholic Church exerting a heavy conservative influence on institutions such as the family and the educational system and maintaining a political focus on the needs of small owner–occupier farmers. The catch-all nature of the main political parties, specifically the cross-class hegemony of Fianna Fáil, also led to a populism that weakened the ability of the marginalized classes to build a strong left-leaning political party (Mair, 1992). Emigration and, therefore, industrial and economic transformation never made it seriously onto the political agenda. The sociopolitical pressures that might have forced a more sustained program of national development were diffused by the idiosyncratic factors in the Irish case (Mjoset, 1992).

If social mobilization could not generate the necessary pressures to promote developmentalism in the European style, then perhaps the state could mobilize indigenous capitalists to promote development after the East Asian fashion; a version of the DBS was a possibility. Although the state had largely viewed itself as complementing the market in the 1930s and the 1940s, the then-minister for Industry and Commerce (and later Taoiseach), Seán Lemass, became increasingly concerned with the inefficiency of protected indigenous industry. Lemass's vision was of a self-sufficient but efficient economy. To that end, he made various attempts to introduce measures to support state intervention in Irish firms with a view to improving their efficiency. His efforts to form an Industrial Efficiency Bureau in 1947 failed in the face of resistance from a united domestic capitalist class and a deflationary coalition within the state headed by the Department of Finance. By the time the crisis of the 1950s was playing out, the political attempt to mobilize indigenous industry had already been repulsed (O'Hearn, 1990). Part of the difficulty in creating an alliance between the state and domestic capital appears to have been each group's different religious background. Ireland had become increasingly Catholic in the wake of independence; members of the Church of Ireland accounted for only 4.9 percent of the general population in 1936. The civil service also had become increasingly Catholic, with only 8.6 percent of civil servants being members of the Church of Ireland in 1936. However, elements of the Protestant Ascendancy remained well after independence with a continuing high proportion of Protestants among major farmers, professionals, and – crucially – employers and business executives (20 to 25 percent of whom were Protestant in 1936) (Foster, 1988, p. 534). Whether or not this was a crucial factor, state efforts to mobilize indigenous capitalists failed.

By the 1950s, a vacuum existed in economic policy. Domestic capitalists were strong enough to resist efficiency measures but too weak, as it turned out, to block the free trade that would ultimately decimate them. The land reforms of the second half of the nineteenth century had created a large class of small farmers who proved ready supporters of Fianna Fáil's rural nationalism. On the other hand, the absence of a significant class of large landowners strong enough to control the state (on the Latin American model) meant that one significant obstacle to the transformation of the economy was not an issue in Ireland.

In this vacuum, external forces were more likely to be able to shape Irish development. O'Hearn (1990) argued convincingly that the process of change was heavily influenced by international forces. Combining his account with that of Girvin (1989), we can compile a comprehensive picture of the reasons for the strength of the FDI regime from the early 1960s forward. Ireland became eligible for Marshall Aid in the late 1940s, and the expansionist coalition within the Irish state was anxious to use the funds to develop its agenda. However, there were numerous conditions attached to Marshall Aid, the primary condition being a steady and significant move toward free trade. International agencies such as the IMF, dominated by the U.S. government, pushed free-trade measures through the 1950s until the restrictions on foreign investment and the tariffs and quotas around Irish industry began to weaken. As O'Hearn argued, it was foreign capital that pushed the free-trade agenda; the export-led industrialization regime that followed was as much the consolidation of the power of foreign capital as it was the actions of a state elite (O'Hearn, 1990).

Institutions: the IDA as the center of industrial policy

However, involvement with the Marshall Plan cannot explain the unusual degree to which the pursuit of foreign investment became a dominant feature of the Irish political economy. Ireland, although more involved in the Marshall Plan than had been thought (Whelan, 2000), was less heavily incorporated into it and related European integration projects than many of the countries that Mjoset (1992) lists as more successful in developing autocentric national economies. There is little in the Irish experience of the Marshall Plan that explains the policy focus on foreign investment, rather than simply the possibility of that focus. In posing the power of international capital against the power of the state, O'Hearn is led to ignore the specific ways in which the Irish state was transformed by this new policy regime and the character of the alliance with international capital. Focusing instead on the embedded autonomy of the IDA in foreign capital allows us to fully investigate the institutional compromise underpinning the new regime.

The IDA was founded as an agency within the Department of Industry and Commerce. It was initially envisaged to have two broad sets of objectives: firstly, the provision of incentives to industry (mainly Irish) to start new businesses; and secondly, a set of powers to call witnesses and investigate firms relative to inefficiencies within the firm. As such, it bore the stamp of Lemass's project of generating efficient indigenous industry. Once again, in the face of capitalist and Department of Finance resistance, its investigatory powers were removed from the IDA before it even began its duties. Although the IDA was founded as an agency primarily to support indigenous industry, the "indigenous efficiency" industrial-policy option had been largely defeated by the early 1950s and was off the agenda for the remainder of the period (O'Hearn, 1990).

Whitaker's *Economic Development* report did mark a shift in Department of Finance thinking toward a more expansionist agenda and a legitimation of economic planning. In this sense, the Department of Finance had become more favorable to the expansionary, interventionist strategy expounded by Lemass and the Department of Industry and Commerce for many years – although with little emphasis on attracting foreign investment in manufacturing. However, crucial differences remained and how they were reconciled through the 1950s had a critical impact on the institutionalization of the FDI policy regime right up until the 1980s.

Lemass and his Department of Industry and Commerce never wanted free trade but were forced to accept it as a condition of Marshall Aid. Lemass was originally critical of the IDA, which was introduced while he was in opposition:

"He rightly concluded that the division between the IDA and Industry and Commerce would weaken policy coherence .... The ambiguous nature of the institutional arrangements between the IDA and Industry and Commerce also weakened the integrity of the civil service. This was a major consideration for Lemass; after all, he remained a statist, one who believed that the state should be utilized for development." (Girvin, 1989, p. 178)

However, in the early 1950s, he made a compromise with the IDA that was institutionalized in the late 1950s. Lemass agreed that the IDA should continue to play a role but that it should consist almost entirely of promoting new industry. The IDA was excluded from a developmental role toward existing industry at this point and was effectively oriented toward new and less protected sectors. The ability of domestic capital to mobilize against attacks on protection shaped the early evolution of the policy regime:

"Although . . . grants were not formally limited to export-orientated industries, this was certainly the intention and that is how it worked out for many years. Indeed, it would have been politically difficult to operate a grant scheme in any other way at that time because of the objections which would have arisen from competing domestic industries, whereas new production for exports could not reasonably be opposed as threatening the market of existing firms." (Kennedy, Giblin, and McHugh, 1988, p. 63)

During the 1950s, the IDA built up significant status within the state apparatus (Girvin, 1989). The possibility of focusing on FDI was becoming a reality and in 1957 Lemass agreed – still attempting to protect Irish industry with hopes of increasing its efficiency – that foreign industry could locate in Ireland as long as it exported most of its products. Economic nationalists envisaged that this would lead to a lessened dependence on the old colonial power Britain and increased contacts with the rest of Europe and the United States (Brown, 1982; Wickham, 1980). The economic and institutional basis for a "dual economy" was laid during this period because the IDA was left to focus on new international investment for export, whereas on the indigenous side, agricultural exports continued to dominate (motivating the decision to join the EEC in 1973) and Irish industry's efforts at efficiency continued to flounder. Only in 1966 was the function of assisting Irish industrialists transferred from the Department of Industry and Commerce to the IDA (Fitzgerald, 1968, p. 240). Ironically, the basis for this division and the subsequent neglect of indigenous development, was Lemass's persistent determination to tackle the problems of indigenous industry directly.

Relationships to both domestic and international forces continued to shape those institutions. In 1973, Ireland joined the EEC with Britain and Denmark, providing it with a huge advantage in attracting foreign investment because it could now combine the advantages of a low-cost, low-tax Export Processing Zone (EPZ) with access to the European market. There were tensions within this relationship, however. The European Commission (i.e., the bureaucratic arm of the EEC) objected to Ireland's bias in favor of exports and forced a change in the corporate tax codes. Ireland was allowed to offer such low tax rates in part because of its official status as a peripheral region within the EEC. As Ireland grew rapidly in the 1990s, tensions over those special provisions for Ireland grew correspondingly and complaints were voiced, by Germany in particular, regarding the desirability of facilitating the low tax base for foreign investment within the EU. However, the Irish were able to maintain the balancing act and in 1997 announced a new corporate tax rate of 12.5 percent guaranteed until 2015. Nonetheless, significant tensions remain over French- and German-led initiatives to harmonize corporate tax rates in the EU. The Irish government also pursued friendly relations with the U.S. government, drawing on the growing political power of Irish Americans and extensive historical links to the United States. Those relations focused mainly on negotiations around the conflict in Northern Ireland but also had substantial economic components, including special visa allocations for Irish immigrants between 1991 and 1994 (Corcoran, 1993; O'Hanlon, 1998) and a variety of schemes for promoting business links between Ireland and the United States. The Irish government, therefore, was able to position the Irish EPZ as a supply region located at the crucial geographical, political, and economic intersection between the United States and Europe (see O'Hearn, 2001, for a long historical view of Ireland's place in this "Atlantic Economy").

Although the FDI regime was driven by the alliance of foreign capital and the IDA, it could not succeed without mobilizing domestic support – if not directly for FDI, then at least for the broader socioeconomic order built around it. The 1960s saw another period of Fianna Fáil electoral dominance between 1959 and 1973, driven by a particularly effective form of catch-all politics and resulting in the remarkable ability of Fianna Fáil to draw votes from across the class structure (Whelan, 1994). The quality of social citizenship in Ireland expanded markedly during the 1960s and 1970s as health and educational services were improved and coverage of income maintenance expanded (for details, see Ó Riain and O'Connell, 2000). The Irish experience of welfare-state expansion stands in stark contrast to the Scandinavian pattern, in which the expansion of social citizenship took place along two dimensions: (1) universalistic entitlements created solidarity among and between social classes; and (2) a commitment to reduction of inequalities pervaded all areas of policy, thus reinforcing the solidaristic quality of the welfare state (Myles, 1989). In Ireland, the principal commitment has been to achieving solidarity, through the expansion of the coverage of the social insurance system and through the provision of basic levels of service, but the commitment to reducing inequalities has been slight. The Irish welfare state can thus be characterized as a "pay-related" welfare state that provides a basic minimal level of security and service on near-universal grounds to all resident citizens, but one that mixes public and private components in a manner that allows those with advantages generated in the market to supplement their citizenship rights with their own resources (O'Connell and Rottman, 1992). The class-based character of the Irish welfare state is reflected in the pensions system in which retired middle-class employees, former public servants, and middle- and high-income self-employed enjoy considerably enhanced incomes compared to retirees from other social classes (O'Connell and Rottman, 1992; Ó Riain and O'Connell, 2000). The Irish state built widespread populist support around its weak national system of innovation through a measure of welfare-state universalism while holding back the flight of the middle classes to the private sector by providing them with significant benefits through the welfare state. Unlike in Scandinavia, where middle-class benefits from the welfare state are used to maintain loyalty to a system that reduces inequalities, class inequalities are often exacerbated in the Irish welfare state. Nonetheless, a powerful broad popular support for the role of the state in the economy has been sustained through this interaction of industrial and welfare policy.

This has also been achieved across the rural–urban divide despite the rapid decline in agricultural employment that historically sustained rural areas. In a revealing analysis, Hannan and Commins (1992) documented the persistence of a small-scale landholding sector of the population and its unusual success in adapting to changes in the Irish economy, particularly when compared to the urban lower working class who often share similar incomes. Hannan and Commins analyzed farm-household survival strategies and educational and social-mobility strategies, providing a picture of an active and vibrant rural population pursuing a place in the new class structure, even as the basis of the farm-family system declined around them. Their analysis suggests that many of the anthropological accounts of the pathologies of rural Ireland may have told only one side of the story. They also document, however, how this social mobilization was supported by particular state policies that favored farm households. The favoritism toward the small-farm sector took the form of state redistribution of land holdings after independence through the Land Commission (a state agency), a dedicated program of rural industrialization (focused on male employment) administered by the IDA in the 1970s, and the channeling of EC price-support policies toward smallholders (Hannan and Commins, 1992, pp. 97–100). It was rooted in the power of the rural bourgeoisie within the political system.

The outcome of the institutional compromise surrounding the emergence of the FDI policy regime was to depoliticize and institutionalize the FDI regime, surrounding it with welfare state, agricultural, and regional policies that built broad populist support. Meanwhile, indigenous development was hyperpoliticized in the form of widespread clientelism. The FDI regime dominated the traded sector of the economy, whereas nontraded sectors contained primarily domestic firms and were dominated by clientelism. These were the less-than-promising conditions in the 1960s and 1970s for the emergence of the indigenous development-policy regime. Before turning to this issue, and the rise of the DNS, let us examine the IDA's institutional position in greater detail.

Case study: explaining the IDA's semi-autonomy

The unusual power of the IDA within the Irish state helps to explain the weakness of the institutions supporting indigenous industry until the late 1980s. Both the

IDA's success in attracting investment to Ireland and its difficulties in generating indigenous development are based on this institutional compromise.

The dual-economy institutional structure, split between foreign and indigenous sectors, was solidified in a number of ways through the 1960s and 1970s. The early success of the IDA in attracting foreign investment in the 1960s established its legitimacy. During the 1960s, however, the Department of Industry and Commerce retained a significant role in economic planning, producing a series of economic plans for 1958–62, 1963–68, and 1965–72. However, the Department was soon caught up in assessing and managing the dismantling of protection, a process that persisted into the 1970s. In 1969, the IDA took on direct grant-giving powers; that same year, it was restructured as a semistate body outside the civil service but reporting to the Department of Industry and Commerce. This administrative independence and its exclusive focus on "new" industry (mainly foreign) gave the IDA a specific corporate culture organized around a clear set of goals.

How did the IDA manage to gain this position of semi-autonomy? The intellectual work of conceptualizing future paths of economic development had been carried out by Whitaker and a small group of civil servants in the Department of Finance in the 1950s. However, throughout the 1960s, the IDA dominated industrial promotion. IDA executives in the 1960s formulated their view of policy mostly by responding to their experiences in the market for mobile investment. In moving outside the Department of Industry and Commerce, they sought the freedom to adapt, not to strategize. Lemass, then Taoiseach, had long championed semistate agencies as "drivers" of economic development. In a 1961 address, he argued forcefully for the usefulness of semistate bodies, partly because of doubts regarding civil-service departmental abilities to carry out such functions. He pointed to the ability of such agencies to hire specialized staff or staff with commercial experience, the greater autonomy in decision-making possible within such agencies, and the belief that people would cooperate more readily with such agencies. Furthermore, he argued against closer legislative oversight and accountability of such bodies (Lemass, 1961). Again, Lemass's ideological push for state-led indigenous development laid the groundwork for IDA institutional success.

Even given this relatively permissive political situation, IDA executives mobilized for autonomy using a mechanism that was to become commonplace in the Irish political economy and which, ironically, would rebound on the IDA: the use of an external review of the agency. Invited by the IDA, the international consulting firm of Arthur D. Little wrote a report entitled "Review of the Structure of the Industrial Development Authority" in 1967. The review recommended that staff recruitment, retention, and compensation be placed in the hands of the IDA by withdrawal from the civil service; that the IDA's decision-making power be enhanced by the transfer to it of the functions performed by some other agencies and the strengthening of its board and top executive structure; and that the resources available to the IDA be significantly increased (Little, Arthur D., 1967, p. 6). Throughout the report, the emphasis is almost entirely on the role of the IDA in attracting foreign investment rather than promoting indigenous industry.

The IDA gained its semi-autonomy in 1969 and gradually became the center of policymaking as the Department of Industry and Commerce became more marginalized:

"Our impression is that the Department's practice has tended more toward intervention in operational matters while devoting little attention to the strategic plans formulated by the agencies. We are not in a position to substantiate this impression, but to the extent that it may be true, it represents an inappropriate means of control." (O'Malley, Kennedy, and O'Donnell, 1992, p. 132).

The debate over regional employment in the late 1960s and early 1970s provided the IDA with a platform upon which it could build its policy-development role. It developed a series of regional development plans that focused on the even dispersal of employment through rural areas and small- and medium-sized towns – despite an initial consultants' report in 1968 that had recommended the creation of a small number of concentrated "growth poles." This proved politically unworkable and the IDA was able to cement its political position by solving a political problem for the government and civil service.

The success of the IDA in wresting control of policy away from the civil service is reflected in the clear expectation in public discussions of industrial policy during the 1970s and early 1980s that the IDA is the body that must address those issues, with little mention of the Department of Industry and Commerce (SSISI, 1976, 1982). This national developmental mission was not lifted from its shoulders or wrenched from its grasp, depending on point of view, until the 1980s. Nonetheless, the IDA remains a powerful force. When the state industrial-development agencies were reorganized in 1994, the leading executives of the strategy body, Forfás, came from the IDA, not from the indigenous development agencies.

THE RISE OF NETWORK DEVELOPMENTALISM

Lemass's efforts to use the state to improve the capabilities of Irish business were defeated in the late 1940s and early 1950s. Between then and the mid-1980s, the relationship between indigenous industry and the state consisted of two main strands. In the protected sectors, extensive battles ensued in an attempt to prolong protection, although those sectors ultimately had to face international competition, usually to their disadvantage (Jacobson, 1989). Those sectors began to suffer in the mid-1960s, were faced with serious problems upon entry to the EEC in 1973, and were decimated by the recession of the early 1980s (O'Malley, 1980, 1989, 1992). Before the industrial revival of recent years, Irish industry had a weak presence in the traded sectors of the economy; in some respects, it could be said that no coherent policy regime existed to support potential firms that might emerge in those traded sectors.

Many other sectors of the economy enjoyed a clientelist relationship with the state. Construction and property development made disastrous aesthetic contributions to Irish society while seemingly unable to escape various dubious relationships between developers and politicians (MacDonald, 1985). Meanwhile, in sections of agriculture – most famously, the beef trade – corruption was rampant and ties between politicians and beef barons became the focus of a major public inquiry in the late 1980s (O'Toole, 1995). The 1990s brought a series of public inquiries into similar scandals in property, telecommunications liberalization, radio, banking, and other sectors. The ability of the state to secure markets for those industries – either through planning measures in the case of property or through state intercession in the EU, or with potential customers in developing countries in the case of agriculture – created a different dynamic than that which ultimately emerged to support the indigenous software industry. Those sectors were heavily involved with specific politicians and particularly with Fianna Fáil as a party. The state agencies were not insulated from political interference in the same way that they were in the high-technology sectors, where the presence of TNCs, the peculiar position of the IDA partly outside the state, and the limited personal ties of politicians to the sector made clientelist relations less viable. Politicians did attempt to influence the location of factories, but this had relatively little effect on the development of the industry and was consistent with the regional focus of IDA policy through the 1960s and the 1970s. In contrast, clientelism was the byword of state–business relations in sectors such as beef and property – much as it was in the polity at large (Chubb, 1982; Higgins, 1982) – and agencies such as the IDA found it almost impossible to insulate themselves from political interference. In one notorious case, for example, the IDA was committed to a strategic plan supporting a leading beef-processing company, Goodman International. However, there were suspicions that Goodman's commitment to implementing the plan was less than enthusiastic, and the IDA was reluctant to contribute the huge amounts of money demanded by the company. As later emerged in an official inquiry, however, the IDA came under enormous pressure from senior government ministers to provide the cash and the plan was ultimately approved (O'Toole, 1995, pp. 116–33).

Any serious effort to build a developmental role and capacity for the state in the indigenous sector had to negotiate its way between three broad alternatives or threats to that model: first, an exclusive focus on foreign investment as the catalyst of indigenous industry (the strength of the export platform model); second, a political inability to impose efficiency and effectiveness on the indigenous firms (the weakness of a DBS model); and, third, the danger of clientelist relations of patronage emerging between the new indigenous firms and the state, much as they had across most other sectors.

However, factions within the Irish state were, in fact, able to build a policy agenda around indigenous high-technology development, most successfully in the software industry. The elements within the state were able to do so for three main reasons: a crisis of the existing development regime, expressed both socially and institutionally; the emergence of a new constituency that supported indigenous development for global markets, consisting of a new middle class of entrepreneurs and technical workers; and, finally, new institutional spaces that emerged within and on the margins of the state were funded in important ways by EU Structural Funds and allowed the institutionalization of the indigenous development regime. The remainder of this section reviews each of the three factors, which have not yet been extensively analyzed in the Irish context. Finally, I will analyze the transition from the NSC of the 1980s to the NSD and the Software Support Program of 1989 to 1993 as a case study of how the three sets of factors operated together to institutionalize a new industrial-development regime.

The explanation of the transition between regimes is consistent with the theoretical perspective advanced at the beginning of this chapter. The crisis of the FDI regime opens up the possibility for multiple embedded autonomies of the Irish state. However, the actual alternatives that emerge are not the creation of a visionary state elite nor of structural tendencies in the economy but rather are promoted by a state–society alliance and the embeddedness of the state in specific social classes – in this case, technical professionals. Finally, the new institutional spaces are the arenas in which the new embedded autonomy of the state matures, where the organizational capacities, routines, and cultures necessary for effective state action can develop. Embeddedness and autonomy develop historically and together shape the institutions that come to underpin the new policy regime.

Crisis: dilemmas of the FDI regime

We have seen that in the early 1980s, the Irish economy faced apparent collapse. This structural crisis in the Irish economy and society highlighted the weaknesses of the FDI model as one of national economic development.

These concerns came to a head with the publication of a report by the Telesis Consultancy Group in 1982, which was heavily critical of the prevailing model of development. Telesis was contracted by NESC, representing the "social partners," to conduct a study of the existing policies regarding industrial development. Telesis severely criticized the sole reliance on foreign-owned firms, arguing that

"Foreign-owned industrial operations in Ireland with few exceptions do not embody the key competitive activities of the businesses in which they participate, do not employ significant numbers of skilled workers, and are not significantly integrated into traded and skilled subsupply industries in Ireland." (Telesis Consultancy Group, 1982; quoted in O'Malley, 1989, p. 167)

The report was widely quoted in the media at the time and, although a national debate could hardly be said to have ensued, it did cause a stir within the policy community (see SSISI, 1982, for example). The IDA defended itself robustly (*IDA News*, 1982, No. 2), but as we have seen, the general tenor of policy did shift through the 1980s to consider some of the recommendations of the Telesis Report. The IDA felt it necessary to reorganize internally in 1988 to create two divisions that would look after foreign-owned and indigenous industry.

Politics: the rise of the technical professional class

A space had opened up, therefore, in which new models of economic develop-ment could be advanced as candidates for institutionalization. Two major new policy regimes emerged from the dark times of the 1980s: a social-partnership regime based initially on national tripartite wage bargains but extending over time to include other social and business groups and partnerships at the local level (O'Donnell, 2000), and a set of institutions supporting the development of indige-nous firms and innovation.

The state, through its heavy investment in education, had meanwhile created a new class basis for an indigenous technology-promotion and business-expansion agenda. The state had effectively pushed the population away from the historically popular professions, using its unusual capacity to shape labor supply to dispro-portionately expand the number of vacancies in engineering, computer science, and other technical fields through the 1980s and 1990s. Despite the massive brain drain of the 1980s (Wickham, 1989; NESC, 1991), several of those who stayed started their own companies. They combined with a trickle of people from the foreign-owned sector and from user organizations to form a constituency that could support the new agenda. The Irish Computer Services Association (ICSA) (later the Information and Computer Services Association and then the Irish Software Association) actively attempted from the early 1980s forward to shape government policy regarding the software industry, particularly from the point of view of the indigenous firms.

The culture of the Irish industry also played a role in creating a motivation for developing the industry as a whole over and above the financial rewards involved. In educating a technical labor force, the Irish state created a group of employees and potential entrepreneurs who were not part of the existing roads to accumulating wealth: agriculture, property, low technology, domestically traded products, and established professions such as medicine and law. In many cases, the employees set themselves consciously against the established way of getting ahead in Irish so-ciety. They were also critical of the opportunities available within the transnational corporations, in many cases choosing emigration over the less challenging jobs available in the production-oriented transnational companies (Wickham, 1989). This, then, was a ready constituency for a development project aimed at devel-oping a technologically sophisticated indigenous industry. The managers in the industry resented the dominance of property, agriculture, the professions, and the transnationals. The developers saw themselves as a technical elite who were as good at their jobs as anyone in the world and who rejected the restriction of their opportunities by the Irish economic situation. Many of the emigrants who left in the 1980s were extremely bitter, although others stayed because, in the words of one senior engineer within the industry,

"There was a point when some people just said 'Fuck it, I'm not going to the United States, I'm going to try and make something work here. I want to work in Ireland'."

Managers and developers were part of a technology- and market-oriented "counterculture" within the Irish economy that could be the carrier of a capitalist development project (see Carroll Burke, 2002a, for a discussion of a comparable "engine culture" among the early innovators of the Industrial Revolution). Some of the priorities of the development project were shaped by the composition of this counterculture, particularly its middle-class and male character.

This cohesive local community oriented to global technologies and markets proved to be a supportive constituency for efforts to develop indigenous industry for global technical markets. The changes in state policy throughout the 1980s found a constituency that, even if not thrilled to have to deal with the state, could see the value of the measures being promoted and were in broad sympathy with the more developmental orientation of the state and its efforts to upgrade indigenous industry. Software entrepreneurs and workers were largely oriented toward export markets, particularly those in firms with a product focus. Despite some controversies within the industry over the tendency of the Irish state to contract with overseas software houses for their needs, the state could never be a major factor in finding markets for those firms. Developmentalism, rather than clientelism, became the dominant model of state–business relationships.

New institutional spaces

We have seen how the IDA's position relative to the rest of the Irish state both isolated and institutionalized the FDI industrial-policy regime. Such institutionalization would appear to be a crucial element of the effectiveness over the medium to long term of any policy regime because it allows the accumulation of resources, skills, and political legitimacy and alliances. An existing regime is, therefore, likely to "crowd out" other regimes unless they can create such "safe" institutional spaces in which they can avoid attack from the existing regime.

There had always been elements within the Irish state that were concerned with indigenous development, which was reflected in part in how the Telesis report came to be written; in the process it helped define the malaise of the 1980s as bound up with problems of industrial policy. This was far from inevitable because neoliberal orthodoxy, both in the early 1980s and since then, has paid relatively little attention to industrial structure and policy but has emphasized fiscal contraction and macroeconomic stabilization (McAleese, 1999).

The strand of rational state planning that had persisted within the Irish state through Lemass's era reemerged in the Fianna Fáil government of 1977–81 as the Department of Economic Planning and Management, with Martin O'Donoghue as Minister. O'Donoghue and the Department are best remembered in Ireland for their ill-fated attempts to jumpstart the economy in Keynesian fashion through increased public spending, failing to anticipate the flight of capital out of the country through fiscal and trade flows. The Department, however, had hoped to build a capacity for promoting indigenous industry and began the process of hiring the Telesis consultants. After the abolition of the Department of Economic Planning and Management, some of the senior civil servants moved to the Departments of the Taoiseach, Finance, and NESC, where the Telesis review of industrial policy resurfaced. Despite resistance from the Department of Industry and Commerce, the review was commissioned and the planners within the state apparatus were able to use Telesis as the basis for a white paper on industrial development in 1984, which incorporated many of Telesis's suggestions. The semi-autonomy of the IDA proved crucial because it rendered it open to review from elsewhere in the polity where full autonomy would have undermined those mechanisms for generating change in industrial-policy institutions.

A similar process led to the so-called Culliton Report of January 1992. Worried by potentially damaging U.S. reforms of taxation of international revenues and struck by the continuing weakness of indigenous industry, some civil servants and the social partners combined to place a further review of industrial policy on the agenda – signaling this in the social-partnership agreement of January 1991 and resulting in the Culliton Report, which was compiled in the second half of 1991. Ultimately, the Culliton Report led to the reorganization of the industrial-development agencies between 1994 and 1998. As one longtime IDA executive said:

"Telesis? It is regarded as a bad chapter for us inside. We felt they didn't understand our business as well as they should have – it was a tough time for us. Culliton was another tough time – they recommended the split. We have now started an internal process of looking ahead. It's an effort to strategically take hold of it, avoid external reports and pressure. We were caught napping by Telesis and Culliton. We should have started thinking about issues like that internally. Culliton is a very good report, it made broader issues part of the competitiveness agenda, that would have been great. Operationally, we would have preferred to have had divisions within the IDA, not separate agencies."

Forced by external reviews and pressure to develop greater internal-review processes, the IDA executives are left to regret their weakened position.

The hegemony of the FDI model and the IDA within the national policy regime was, therefore, somewhat shaken by the events of the early and mid-1980s. The FDI model now became one part, if still the dominant part, of industrial policy. This policy now included two critical new elements: a greater emphasis on a developmental approach to indigenous industry arising out of the Telesis controversy, and a broader macroeconomic management by the social partners dating from 1987 and emphasized in a second review of industrial policy in the Culliton Report (1992). However, suggesting a new industrial-development strategy was one thing; developing the institutions and capabilities to put it in place was quite another.

In this respect, a series of other state bodies, discussed earlier, concerned primarily with the "science, technology, and innovation" agenda and oriented toward indigenous industry proved important – although their success in raising R&D spending levels and promoting innovation was limited until the late 1980s (O'Malley, 1980, pp. 62–3). An increasingly sustainable and autonomous institutional space became available within which the indigenous development and national system of innovation agendas could be pursued.

An ex-employee of the NBST, still working within the development agencies, argues that

"There was a kind of 'skunkworks' within the civil service to find ways of putting science and technology on the agenda. The National Science Council was the big breakthrough . . . . The next trick pulled by those civil servants was a Review of the Science Council . . . . The OECD will do reviews, to a very standard formula, if invited by the government. You'll find a whole series of those reports by the OECD on different countries. That led to the NBST. The early years of NBST were very exciting – we were advocating involvement in international programs, in university–industry cooperation."

The NBST, originally set up as a relatively strong body influencing science and technology policy, quickly ran into a series of political problems. Those agencies were necessary to provide legitimacy for Ireland with the OECD and, more importantly, with high-tech firms. However, they were also dangerous because agencies such as the National Science Council produced embarrassing reviews of the poor state of science and technology in Ireland. As one observer put it:

"The IDA didn't need them, they interacted with them but at the end of the day it was 'so what'."

Neither was there much support within government departments for allowing the emergent technical communities, an unknown quantity at best, to shape policy; as one ex-NBST employee said:

"The government didn't want these 'hairy lads in sandals' involved in making policy and so on, having an influence."

Neither were the science-policy communities well versed in working the political system – in the words of one senior civil servant,

"The science and technology lobby have done themselves no favors over the years, I saw this from elsewhere in the system. They argued for higher percentage of GDP 'in order to get up to international standards, we must be a crowd of gobshites, we need to get up to international averages.' That never works with government, you have to make your argument in a way that makes sense to government, which is organized on a functional or sectoral basis (education, health, agriculture, industry, and so on). A minister has a set of instruments – it's to the extent that you can show that your instruments, if they get resources, will realize the objectives, then you will be successful. They needed to do that for S and T; looking for money for S and T as an end in itself was never going to work, percentage of GNP indicator is an outcome of that, not a cause . . . . The universities didn't want to argue for themselves. They hate being asked to justify themselves, they should be independent but also they have to deal with reality and be accountable."

Indeed, as the alliance among technical entrepreneurs, universities, and state agencies has developed, the universities have experienced this as a double-edged sword, procuring increased resources but under conditions of greater commercial pressures and external accountability.

In addition to these areas of direct competition with the IDA and government departments for decision-making authority, other conflicts emerged. The NBST regularly produced policy statements in areas that affected other powerful bodies – clashing on one occasion with the Electricity Supply Board over its recommendations for increased support for wind power. It was also under pressure in the harsh economic times of the 1980s to be self-funding, which can create significant problems (as discussed in Chapter 7). Gradually, the support of even its most reliable allies – the universities – began to soften:

"The NBST was an idea before its time. We were fighting against the idea that technology can be bought, that Ireland is too small to have an indigenous technological capability. Universities were traditionally starved of cash, until the late 1990s. There was no research money, only European funding – that's how they kept research alive in the universities. The university perspective on NBST was that it was a way to give money to the universities for research, they supported that aspect of NBST. They didn't support it for policy, coordination, and so on, they didn't see it all as part of the same package. Under the budget constraints of the 1980s, we lost the support of the universities as money being channeled to them lessened. It was very difficult for NBST to show results because of the culture at the time of 'there's no need for indigenous capability in science and technology' or 'the IDA is looking after it anyway'."

In the face of those political difficulties, the agencies turned repeatedly to external sources of support, from elsewhere in the world polity where science and technology are increasingly institutionalized values (Boli and Thomas, 1998). The National Science Council was founded as the outcome of a joint OECD–Irish government review of "Science and Irish Economic Development" undertaken in 1963 as part of Lemass's push for industrial modernization while responsibility for indigenous industry still lay within the Department of Industry and Commerce (*Science and Irish Economic Development*, 1963). A 1974 OECD review of national science policy explicitly supported the National Science Council's recommendations for its successor's structure and even named the new entity – the soon to be formed NBST (OECD, 1974). A further review in 1978 was critical of the overemphasis on foreign investment (OECD, 1978). Being able to draw on institutionalized international agencies was a powerful legitimation tool for this emerging "skunkworks" within the civil service.

The science and technology agencies also turned regularly to Europe.

"NBST did get recognition for international connections – Europe, etc. – Ireland did well in Europe, we had a good effect there. It was one of the few niches left to us in Irish policy, no one else looking at international issues, at the funding of research – that was our big contribution. European money kept research in universities alive." (ex-NBST employee)

Peterson and Sharp (1998) documented the many ways in which science, technology, and innovation policy in the EU have been bound up with improving the EU science and technology base and labor force in the interest of competitiveness, but also with the goals of promoting collaboration across member states and promoting economic and social cohesion. The Irish indigenous innovation coalition was able to take advantage of not only the increasingly institutionalized world-polity institutions dealing with science and technology but also with a very elaborate set of specific programs being operated within the EU.

The new state institutions relied heavily on EU funds for their activities. Many of the programs undertaken in the science and technology arena were funded primarily by European Structural Funds. These funds were designated for Ireland as part of an effort to develop the peripheral regions of the EU in the face of the upcoming Single European Market in 1992. Many have commented on the impact of the influx of this capital from the EU, attributing Ireland's growth to those funds. However, the Irish state had compiled significant amounts of capital before without being able to develop the economy around them. What was significant about the Structural Funds was that they were the means by which a variety of new, sometimes experimental, measures could be taken without having to fight the rest of the state agencies for funding (see O'Donnell, 2000, for a broader discussion of the impact of the EU on "experimentalism" in Ireland). The new development regime could develop alongside the old and did not have to challenge the old development model directly for funds and priority, except in rare cases. Furthermore, the EU funds came with significant requirements in terms of performance and outcome evaluation and accounting. Although sometimes creating administrative nightmares, this also helped to foster a climate in which regular evaluation of policies became the norm and where clientelism was mitigated. It was not only the financial impact of the EU funds that was crucial, therefore, but also the institutional space it facilitated for new initiatives. In this case, international funds were used to promote an indigenous-development agenda.

Case study: from NSC to NSD

The transition from the NSC to the NSD as the leading state agencies dealing with the software industry illustrates some of these processes. From 1984 to 1988, the NSC provided a range of technical and marketing services to the Irish software industry. By the early 1990s, the NSD had taken over its policy and informational role, ABT had taken over its marketing services, and the PATs were providing most technical services to the industry. In the story of these institutions and the transition from one to the other, we can learn much about relations between the various parts of the state and the software industry as the industry has grown.

In 1983, it emerged that two proposals were being developed for a NSC. The NBST had created a committee with representatives from a variety of state agencies, the higher-education sector, and the indigenous software industry to propose a center that would provide a range of services to the industry on a nonprofit basis. Meanwhile, the IDA had developed its own proposal, which emphasized a significant degree of employment within the center itself and envisaged the involvement of major multinationals (*Irish Computer*, February 1983, p. 11). The IDA's failure to appreciate the subtle arts of embedded autonomy in the indigenous sector was shown by the industry's consternation at its failure to consult with it (*Irish Computer*, June 1986). By late that year, the IDA's power at the time was reflected in the fact that its proposal was adopted even though it had little support from the indigenous industry. At the time, the ICSA was dominated by the indigenous firms, especially the larger Irish software companies. Their attitude was summed up in their column in *Irish Computer*:

"The Association's attitude is quite simple. If the interests of the indigenous computer-services companies are safeguarded and promoted, and if there is a proper structure within which they can influence the new body in the interest of their members, then it will have the association's support. If these conditions are not met, in the words of a member of the ICSA executive committee, it will be 'total opposition'." (*Irish Computer*, December 1983, p. 31)

These pressures did help shift the NSC toward a greater emphasis on services for indigenous companies, although indigenous firms still worried about an emphasis on the TNCs. Their anxieties were only added when the industry representatives on the first board of the NSC came primarily from the TNC sector (*Irish Computer*, July 1987). The center was also required to be self-funding and some computer-services companies, especially the consultants, were worried about competition in product development and technical services from a state-owned agency. The director of the NSC, Brian Dugan (an American), emphasized the concerns of indigenous companies from the start – defusing some of the tensions (interview in *Irish Computer*, October 1984). The activities of the NSC in providing marketing information, quality-assurance services, and supporting local small firms found favorable mention on numerous occasions throughout 1985 and 1986. The concerns over a focus on multinationals proved unfounded and the NSC cooperated closely with the ICSA in 1986 and 1987 to build a closer relationship. When the second board of the NSC was announced in February 1988, the chairman, the chief executive of the center, and a third board member all had backgrounds in the indigenous industry, whereas the other members came from various state development agencies (*Irish Computer*, February 1988). It seemed that the NSC had become an early institutional space for the indigenous development model, and its shift toward the indigenous sector reflected the increasing concern for indigenous development in the period after the Telesis Report of 1982.

However, in June 1988, the NSC was closed with practically no prior warning. As part of the previous year's review of the development agencies, which resulted in the founding of Eolas and the reorganization of the IDA, the NSC had come under the scrutiny of officials in the Department of Industry and Commerce. Despite ongoing discussions with the ICSA and the resolution of some long-running problems, the Department ultimately decided to close the NSC. The relative isolation of the Department from the industry meant that they were unlikely to have had the working relationship with the ICSA and other firms in the industry that would enable them to assess the value of the NSC. There is some suggestion that there was an ideological bent within the Department against such interventionist approaches. One Department official told me ten years later that

"Industry came to us and said that they didn't believe in the NSC. All the NSC did was to get together a pool of skilled people applying for EU contracts and competing with industry."

The NSC might have survived if the IDA had been a strong supporter. However, the IDA relation to the NSC was ambiguous from the beginning and the NSC was passed from executive to executive within the IDA during its existence (*Irish Computer*, June 1988). Without the support of the Department or the IDA, the NSC was politically vulnerable.

Finally, there was the thorny issue of self-funding, which weakened support from the ICSA and the indigenous industry. In a report on the industry in 1988, consultants hired by the ICSA argued:

"The most contentious issue with regard to the IDA relates to the NSC .... The NSC was required to be self-supporting in the long run. There was from the outset a potential conflict between the 'public good' element of the NSC and its need to generate revenue. This conflict is at the root of the industry's perception of the NSC and its need to generate revenue. This conflict the NSC originated within the industry. The objectives sought by industry were those listed above [i.e., those of the NSC], but its view was that the NSC's board should be representative of the industry although funded by the state. In practice, it is difficult to see how a state board can be made representative of an industry. Ultimately, government appoints board members, and there is no necessary communality between different interests in the industry. However, the principal difficulty with the NSC as seen by the industry related to its need to make money. In effect, the industry felt that the body charged with the development of the industry was competing with the people it was intended to encourage. It is claimed that as a consequence of this concern with making money, the NSC never focused sufficiently on the development of the industry, and was thus irrelevant to large segments of the industry." (ICSA, 1988, pp. 19–21)

The issue of competition was overstated because the four or five NSC staff working on consulting could hardly have been a major threat to the industry. However, the consultancy firms had a prominent position in the ICSA at this time and were less than supportive of the NSC. But the more fundamental issue was that the need to make money forced the NSC to focus its attention away from the firms that most needed its help. As one prominent NSC staff member told this author ten years later:

"The fundamental flaw of the NSC was a contradiction between the need to help the industry and the need to be self-funding. These were incompatible to some extent. We never had more than twelve people, five on the marketing side and five on the engineering side, and two managing. The larger companies had forty or fifty people working for them at the time, they had a lot more resources than the NSC had. They could pay for the NSC's services but they didn't see a need for them, they could do it themselves. We could help the smaller companies a lot, even to talk with them for an hour about marketing and so on. But they didn't have the money to pay for an hour, let alone a full feasibility study."

We can see then that the NSC, after managing to extricate itself from the IDA agenda, fell victim to tensions between indigenous industry and the state regarding the appropriate role of the state, with the state anxious to gain some revenue while industry argued for state-funded husbandry of the industry. The state pushed a neoliberal vision of statism, while industry pushed for state developmentalism. These tensions became too difficult to reconcile and the NSC project failed despite making what appears to have been some significant contributions to the industry during a critical period in the 1980s. However, even as the NSC was being closed, two other policy exercises were underway that would lead to new software industry institutions. A subboard within Eolas was examining proposals to raise the technical level of the software industry. This resulted ultimately in proposals for the software PAT (Eolas, 1989b, 15–17). Meanwhile, the ICSA study mentioned previously was putting forward proposals for a new National Software Director, with two support staff, who would

"Realize the following objectives: (i) to seek linkage opportunities for Irish companies . . . ; (ii) to act as a catalyst to younger companies, providing advice, expertise, and encouragement; (iii) to act as an interface between the industry and state agencies . . . ; (iv) to liaise with government regarding public sector work (tendering); (v) to monitor the implementation of the National Plan which the industry intends to develop in partnership with government."
(ICSA, 1988, p. 53)

A working group was formed to report to the Minister for Industry and Commerce in late 1988. The working group consisted of a chairman from the Department, three representatives of indigenous software (including the final chairman of the NSC board), and three representatives from the state agencies. In their report of February 1989, they echoed almost word for word the ICSA proposal for a NSD (Software Industry Working Group, 1989, p. 11, Appendix D). They also supported the efforts of An Coras Tráchtála in marketing and Eolas in raising quality standards in the industry (Software Industry Working Group, 1989, pp. 15, 18).

This flurry of proposals and activity shows the extent to which a network of organizations had emerged within the software industry that could provide a safety net in the event of the collapse of a critical part of the industry infrastructure such as the NSC. The fall of the NSC did not create a complete vacuum and within a year, new arrangements were being made to undertake the crucial tasks it had performed. Embeddedness proved its worth even after helping to bring down the NSC.

In November 1989, the Minister for Science and Technology (within the Department of Industry and Commerce) announced that he had obtained EC funding for a support program for software. The program combined the ICSA/Software Industry Working Group proposals for a National Software Director with the Eolas proposals for technical assistance and quality assurance. Ultimately, of the services provided by the NSC between 1984 and 1988, the strategy and information services were performed by the NSD, the marketing services were consolidated in An Coras Tráchtála, and the technical services were taken over by the software PAT and especially the CSE. The NSD was established within the IDA in 1991 under the directorship of Barry Murphy, a longtime manager in the indigenous software sector and ex-member of the executive committee of the ICSA. It was moved into Forbairt in the reorganization of 1994, consolidating its focus on indigenous companies.

These institutions were discussed in detail in Chapter 6. A number of features distinguished them from the circumstances of the NSC and made them viable institutions. An exhaustive process of consultation led to their foundation, unlike the IDA proposal for the NSC. They were firmly located within the indigenous sector of the industry and although the PATs and the NSD have some responsibilities for TNCs, they are secondary to promotion of indigenous industry. Policy formulation was given a greater institutional focus by its location in a separate agency within the development agencies. Policy and strategy capabilities within the industry were thereby strengthened, as reflected in the NSD Strategic Review of 1993 (NSD, 1993). This review was used as a model by the Indian software-industry trade association in its first major strategic review (NASSCOM, 1996). The self-funding issues were never fully resolved formally, but in practice the CSE has not been put under severe pressure to become totally self-funding. A review of the software-support measure argued that although the CSE could never be fully self-funding, it served a valuable purpose and should continue to be publicly funded (Clarke, 1995). The pain of the funding issue for the state, of course, was softened by extensive EU funding of the NSD and the PATs. This also allowed the schemes to be developed without significant opposition from other areas, which might have had to give up some of their funding if the NSD and PATs had been funded completely from within Irish state funds.

The embedded autonomy of the state in the indigenous sector deepened during the 1980s, and the indigenous-development model was able to carve out its own institutional space during the 1980s. This space emerged from the weakening legitimacy of the IDA relative to indigenous industry during the 1980s, the increasing strength of the constituency supporting indigenous development (primarily through the ICSA), the consolidation of the state agencies dedicated to indigenous development, and the availability of European funds to ease the political opposition to new programs and weaken industry resistance to the state raising funds from the services it provided.

The software-sector agencies reflect the dynamics of transition within the political economy as a whole. A crisis undermined the policy regime – in this case, the FDI regime – that had previously "crowded out" alternative or additional regimes. The embeddedness of state institutions in segments of society, particularly a newly confident technical–professional class, determined which new regimes would win out and the parameters within which agencies would operate effectively. Finally, resources from outside the system (in this case, EU funds) provided the opportunity to create new spaces in which new organizational capabilities and cultures could be developed within the state to create effective state action through bodies such as the NSD. The embeddedness of those agencies and their own relatively autonomous structure and culture (derived from within the state apparatus) shaped one another and, ultimately, the organizational culture of the state agencies that would support industry development.

CONCLUSION

If institution-building is a critical component of development, it is also a difficult and unpredictable task. Ireland has seen two major shifts in state development policy, a dramatic shift toward foreign-investment–based industrial policy and free trade in the 1950s and a less well understood shift toward network developmentalism in the 1980s. Each regime shift required a combination of a crisis of existing power structures, the rise of a new sociopolitical constituency, and the organizational space for the institutionalization of the new regime within the agencies of the state. Developmentalist institutions emerged in an often tense relationship to the clientelist, neoliberal, and universalist political relations that surround them. These institutions, and the strength of the political constituency that underpins them, are threatened by the neoliberal thrust of government macroeconomic and fiscal policies. In Chapter 11, we consider what potential futures might be in store for the "Irish model" and the prospects for protecting and extending autocentric development; but first, we turn in Chapter 10 to a comparative consideration of DBSs and DNSs in the global economy.

10

DEVELOPMENTAL BUREAUCRATIC AND NETWORK STATES IN COMPARATIVE PERSPECTIVE

The DNS in Ireland is distinctly different from the classic cases of the DBSs in Japan and South Korea. This conceptual distinction also casts light on important differences between cases of state developmentalism that have typically been homogenized under the category of "*the* developmental state" (Woo-Cumings, 1999). If the developmental state is posed against strategies relying on foreign investment, how can we make sense of Singapore, which combines a heavy reliance on foreign investment with extensive state control of the economy? If state developmentalism rests on close relationships between the state and the indigenous business class, how do we interpret the Taiwanese developmental state, promoting an indigenous capitalist class with which it had distant and often tense relations? What do we make of the Israeli case, where state developmentalism reemerged in the 1990s after liberalization, although in a profoundly different form than in the 1960s?

Although the great variation among the Asian Tigers is widely recognized, the dominant theoretical debates still center on categories that cannot make systematic sense of this variation. Debates regarding state, market, culture, world-system position, and related concepts have failed to disentangle the critical similarities and differences among the Tiger economies. Analysts who emphasize the variation within the Asian Tigers have tended to focus on significant differences in business organization and turn primarily to cultural explanations based on family structure and inheritance patterns (Biggart and Guillen, 1999; Biggart, Hamilton, and Orrú, 1997; Guillen, 2001; Hamilton, Feenstra, and Lim, 2000). Meanwhile, those who provide state-centered explanations of industrial development have either tended to theorize "*the* developmental state" or noted the significant differences between the cases without providing a theoretical or conceptual analysis of them. Wade's (1990) excellent analysis of the Taiwanese case notes a range of major differences between the Korean and Taiwanese cases, but provides no explanation of them in an account that emphasizes their shared "developmental state-ness." For Wade, "The difference with Korea is one of degree rather than kind." (1990, p. 324).

This chapter uses the concepts of the DNS and DBS to explore how economic and political differences between South Korea, Taiwan, and Singapore have been institutionalized in particular patterns of state–society relations. South Korea is perhaps the paradigmatic case of the DBS. Singapore combines the institutions of the DBS with a focus on foreign investment that resonates more clearly with the economic model of the DNS. Taiwan, although attracting foreign investment, is a DNS that has focused primarily on building indigenous firms linked to international networks. The Israeli political economy is another, surprising, case of a DNS. Israel has built a strong indigenous high-technology sector linked to global networks out of the ashes of a close state–business alliance that collapsed in the 1980s. The fact that we can find non-Asian cases with similar developmental dynamics to leading Asian Tiger economies – Singapore and Ireland, Taiwan and Israel – suggests that unqualified culturalist explanations of Asian success are misguided. In making sense of the variation among a classic DBS (South Korea), two DNSs (Taiwan and Israel), and two economies based on foreign investment (Singapore as DBS and Ireland as DNS), this chapter demonstrates the utility of the concepts of DBS and DNS in explaining the variation in capitalist state developmentalism and the multiple political logics of capitalism.

The first part of this chapter explores the variety of industrial-development strategies employed by the developmental states in the computer industry. The second section explores the institutional foundation of those various strategies, emphasizing that different institutional forms do not necessarily determine strategic choices but rather make certain state structures more effective than others in carrying out particular kinds of strategies. The third section shows that institutions are not designed as organizational tools to pursue particular strategies but rather emerge as the legacies of historically overlaid political struggles. The particular regimes that emerge in those countries cannot simply be "read off" from an external logic of capital accumulation, a historical cultural patterning of social logics of organization, or even the "founding" political coalitions and regimes of the early period of industrial development. Nonetheless, those institutions formed of political conflict significantly shaped economic outcomes. Finally, the last section of the chapter outlines how each country's form of state developmentalism articulates with the Global Post-Fordism of the international computer industry.

STRATEGY: EXPORT FIRMS AND GLOBAL REGIONS

South Korea is the paradigmatic DBS – a more hierarchical regime and more truly a "latecomer" to industrialization than Japan, the closest comparable case. From the 1960s, a close alliance between business and the state has been at the heart of the highly successful Korean development model – with business exchanging export performance for strategic protection, subsidies, and plentiful finance on the part of the state. This alliance is organized through tight personal networks among state and corporate elites that preside over highly centralized organizational structures. Although labor is excluded and repressed, economic growth has been relatively egalitarian.

As Wade summarized the Korean development strategy, the government

"undertook a fundamental reshaping of the investment structure through land reform and a publicly owned banking system; created an enclave of relative stability for long-term investment decisions through its control of key parameters (foreign exchange rates, interest rates, and aggregate demand); modulated the economy's exposure to international competitive pressures in the domestic market; restricted the activities of foreign companies in Korea so as to keep control in Korean hands; aggressively pushed exports; and exercised leadership in selected industries." (1990, p. 307)

State strategies emerged historically in a series of stages so that by the late 1980s, a range of policy instruments were in use to different degrees in different sectors. Bae (2000), drawing on Amsden (1989), describes three main periods: (1) the export promotion of light industries using unskilled labor through government policy instruments, such as preferential credit allocation and trade protection; (2) industrial upgrading through sectoral policies, such as subsidized credit, tax policies, and direct government control over firm entry and decision-making in "heavy industries" (although including electronics); and (3) the push into technology- and skill-intensive sectors in a liberalized global economy, using government R&D activities and support, policies to improve the supply of skilled labor, and liberalized trade and financial policies (Bae, 2000, pp. 124–5). Banks were critical in the Korean developmental strategy because state control over banking and, therefore, finance was critical to governmental bargaining power with capital. Protection was extensive but administered in a more selective way than in Latin America – it is this selectivity that renders it a tool of industrial policy, providing both shelter and support for firms but also enabling the state to help shape firm preferences. The Korean state was more likely to aggressively and directly intervene in firms' decisions than the Taiwanese state – although using this power to strengthen those very firms.

Electronics was targeted as a critical sector from the early 1970s and the state provided loans, created cooperative information-sharing institutions, provided a market through procurement, took on some design work, and built an information infrastructure that was used to boost industry production as well as provide infrastructure. Although low labor costs were important, more significant was what Amsden (1989) calls "industrialization by learning": the hard slog through which Korean firms (and firms in the other Asian Tiger economies) "caught up" in parts of the electronics industry by a steady process of learning through a variety of production arrangements, critically as Original Equipment Manufacturers (OEMs) for firms in "core" countries. This steady, unglamorous learning – not "leapfrogging" to higher generations of technology development – was the basis of East Asian industrialization (Hobday, 1994, 1995).

State interventions have changed as the demands of electronic firms have changed:

"During the 1960s, government assistance followed the entry of foreign companies to make electronics products in Korea. Then, for an extended period during the 1970s and 1980s, the Korean government led rather than followed the entry of Korean firms into semiconductors,

Table 10.1. Strategies of State Developmentalism in Comparative Perspective

	South Korea	Taiwan	Israel	Singapore	Ireland
Accumulation Strategy	National Champion Export Firms	Global Region Based on Indigenous Firms	Global Region Based on Indigenous Firms	Global Region Based on Foreign Firms	Global Region Based on Foreign Firms
Selectivity of State Support of Firms	High	Low	Low	High*	Low
Reliance on FDI	Low	Medium	Low	High	High
Integration of Indigenous Firms into Global Networks	Low	High	High	Medium	High

* Many firms are majority-owned by the state.

telecommunications, and computers. It took major initiatives in the area of products and technologies, put sizable amounts of resources behind those initiatives, and got different results than had firms received no such guidance. During the 1980s, however, the government has been moving toward more of a followership mode, but now following the major Korean companies as they show themselves to be capable of casting global shadows. It has been concentrating more on basic R&D, leaving commercialization and marketing to the firms and setting its R&D agenda in consultation with them." (Wade, 1990, p. 319)

Bae (2000) found that, although sectoral targeting has decreased overall, the computer industry has remained a major priority for the Korean state with significant supports such as protection, procurement, finance, R&D support, and liberalization in pursuit of increased access to international technology and markets. Evans argues that in Korean IT, creating an entrepreneurial industry required an entrepreneurial state that designed a variety of institutions, "all of them aimed at pushing the local information-technology sector forward just a bit faster than it would have gone on its own" (Evans, 1995, p. 141). The cumulative effect of these myriad interventions was substantial.

However, as Table 10.1 illustrates, the other developmental states in this analysis pursued various strategies that differ significantly from the South Korean model. The South Korean model relies on selective support of indigenous firms whose primary relationship to the global economy is as exporters (at least initially). However, the other developmental states are more likely to build global regions by supporting a range of often-competing firms that are integrated into global networks. In Taiwan and Israel, this strategy is built around early ties to the diaspora and to transnational technical communities. Ireland and Singapore (and Taiwan, to a much lesser extent) built their global-region strategy on an initial reliance on foreign investment. However, each has built on that often-limited approach in different ways – whereas Ireland built elements of an indigenous high-tech bourgeoisie around FDI, Singapore historically channeled funds from the FDI strategy into supporting state and semistate commercial ventures. Let us examine each case in more detail.

Singapore's governmental institutions are even more centralized and hierarchical than those of Korea. However, contrary to the Korean model, in Singapore the DBS has pursued an industrial-development strategy based almost entirely on attracting FDI. This combination of bureaucratic institutions and foreign investment is a surprising one, given that "strong states" are often prized by many precisely for their ability to avoid dependence on foreign capital. FDI has been central to the industrial development of the Singapore city–state since independence in 1965, although there have been significant shifts from a reliance on low-cost labor to upgrading operations in Singapore and sending low-skill work offshore, and more recently to attempts to improve local productivity and innovation.

At the heart of Singapore's industrial development were foreign electronics firms.

"The electronics industry quickly became, in terms of both job creation and output, the mainstay of this MNE [multinational enterprise] presence and of Singapore's manufacturing industry. In 1975, wholly- and majority-owned foreign firms already dominated the manufacturing sector and in 1992 accounted for nearly three quarters of manufacturing output and 85 percent of direct exports. . . . The reliance on foreigners, together with Singapore's lack of an indigenous technological contribution to manufacturing, marks the Republic as not being a developed country. . . . Although after 1981, as MNEs poured into Singapore to make computer components and peripherals, manufacturing took on an increasingly high-tech look, the Republic's chief attraction remained reliable and adaptable unskilled, especially female, labor." (Huff 1995a, pp. 741–2)

Surrounding the foreign firms, however, was a huge range of state enterprises involved in a wide range of sectors, especially iron, steel, and shipbuilding and later in traded services such as trading, banking, and air transport. These enterprises were mostly started afresh and were efficient and profitable (Huff, 1995a, b). In the mid-1980s, government owned or partly owned 490 companies that often blended infrastructure provision and commercial ventures. This was accompanied by significant direct investment in infrastructure, financed primarily through public-sector saving (three fifths of national savings in 1984), and by private-sector saving, which was largely stimulated by the government-controlled Central Provident Fund.

"The rapid gains in real wages and home ownership for Singaporeans induced acceptance of government wage control, which completed a 'virtuous circle' of macroeconomic policy: low inflation, with consequent real exchange rate competitiveness, helped to ensure continued foreign capital inflows giving access to MNE technology and marketing which made real wage gains possible. Furthermore, these gains were largely guaranteed, since Singapore citizens were almost assured of a job." (Huff, 1995b)

Huff (1995a) showed how those features combine to form Singapore's distinctive model of economic development. The key feature was government control over wages and labor, which enabled the attraction of FDI and the ending of unemployment. This in turn enabled the state to force a high level of domestic savings, which were mobilized – primarily through state-run contributory funds – to finance the building of a superb infrastructure – both for business and the social reproduction of the population (e.g., through housing provision). Low wages and excellent infrastructure maintained the flow of FDI, whereas the heavy state subsidies of housing and other costs of social reproduction combined with labor repression and incorporation to sustain popular support for the regime. Intense labor control by the state ensured low inflation in a context of tight labor supply.

Korea and Singapore are polar cases of DBSs, therefore – whereas Korea has closely guarded access to channels of participation in the global economy to build local business groups, Singapore's bureaucratic state has avidly pursued foreign investment and trade links while subsidizing business and public infrastructure but struggling to create a local bourgeoisie.

Taiwan and Israel represent quite different cases of developmentalism. Each was remarkably successful in the IT industry in the 1990s, fostering a strong local system of innovation from within a myriad of global ties. Foreign investment figures prominently in the economy, especially in Taiwan, but transnational technical communities and migration ties were just as important. Each country developed a network of state agencies and associations that supported, guided, and promoted local networks of innovation. In contrast to the Irish case, however, they built a system of innovation dominated by local rather than foreign firms. How they have done so is a fascinating story, especially given their origins in different developmental coalitions in the 1960s.

Taiwan presents a puzzle for students of states and development. Although clearly successful in terms of capitalist development and characterized by a "strong" state, the link between state and development in Taiwan is particularly unclear. State policy is said to be more "arm's-length" than in Korea (Wade, 1990), whereas state–society linkages are "poorly understood" (Evans, 1995). Castells neatly poses the central contradiction of "the rise of flexible capitalism under the guidance of an inflexible state" (1992, p. 41) but never resolves it. The image of cohesive developmental bureaucraticism obscured the particular character of Taiwan as a DNS.

The Taiwanese model has undergone significant changes over time; nevertheless, we can identify certain critical features of the Taiwanese development strategy and institutions. The Taiwanese state in the 1950s was certainly less "hands-on" than the Korean state in directly influencing firm decisions. However, it is going too far to say that the state only set the context or was "more market-oriented" than South Korea. Although the state did not "pick winners" among firms, as the Korean state did, it still shaped the activities of firms: "Even after most import and foreign exchange controls were lifted, the government exercised its will through the myriad licenses necessary for a firm to operate; the requirement of prior approval for foreign loans and technology agreements; public ownership of the banking system, which held interest rates much higher than in most Third World countries;

vagueness in tax laws such that politically uncooperative firms could be threatened with audits; and so on" (Amsden, 1985, p. 98).

The state-owned enterprises in key upstream sectors played a direct developmental role and provided critical infrastructure that the indigenous networks of small firms could not create (Evans, 1995; Wade, 1990). Most banks were owned by the state, which proved to be a critical instrument for channeling increasingly high Taiwanese savings into the economy (Wade, 1990) – an institutional factor often neglected by those who focus on Taiwan's high savings rates. The associationalism of the Taiwanese state was reflected from the beginning in the central role played by sectoral associations, collecting monies for a "cooperative fund" and providing mutual subsidies by paying "export bonuses." Although such associations were autonomous, they received state support, and the exact details of their agreements had to be approved by the state (Lin, 1973, p. 108); the KMT party thoroughly penetrated all societal associations on the island (Gold, 2000).

Although there was a broad shift from protection toward exporting in the 1960s, protection was used strategically throughout both to support nascent exporters and to encourage them to move into particular sectors (Lin, 1973, pp. 87–97). As Gold said:

"It is important to emphasize that export-oriented industrialization did not mean the end of ISI [import substitution industrialization], but the evolution of a close relationship whereby local capital now produced largely for export the parts, components, and finished goods that were previously produced for domestic consumption. The state took the lead in opening new foreign markets, soliciting DIF, linking domestic and foreign capital, and fine-tuning the investment climate. The result was a complex linkage between foreign and local investors, with nearly all of the domestic bourgeoisie 'internationalized' to a greater or lesser degree." (1988, p. 185)

Taiwan's industrial structure certainly reflects historical and cultural influences (Biggart and Guillen, 1999; Orrú et al., 1997); however, the specific institutional forms those influences took were profoundly shaped by state policy. Taiwanese policy was directed at supporting a general shift of firms into particular sectors and activities rather than at shaping the decisions of individual firms to pursue particular goods or markets, as in Korea. As has been widely noted, Taiwanese business groups – allthough significant – are much smaller and less centralized than Korean business groups (Hamilton, Feenstra, and Lim, 2000). Chung (2001) argued that the critical factors shaping the emergence of those business groups from the network of small family firms in the Taiwanese economy were state policy and the institutional environment. The critical moment in the formation of those business groups is the formation of the second firm – signaling a shift away from the standalone firm. Chung found that the critical factor in business-group formation was state tax policy, which is reflected in the formation of the crucial second firm within more than half the business groups in the 1964–68 period. Chung argued that this period is significant because it falls right after the combination of the 1960 Statute on Investment (which favored the formation of new firms over the expansion of existing capacity) and the deregulation of numerous industries between 1960 and 1964, which enabled firms to take advantage of the provisions. Right at the beginning of the push for export-led development, therefore, state actions profoundly shaped the characteristic decentralized and densely networked "flexible" Taiwanese industrial structure.

After rapid growth in the 1960s, export-led industrialization (ELI) ran into problems of scarce labor, protectionism in foreign markets, and outdated infrastructure, which led the state to turn to vertical ISI to support deepening (which was quite effective) and to efforts to promote vertical integration (which were not) (Gold, 1988). EPZs were established after 1965 and FDI pursued in electronics as the basis of attempts to move beyond these problems. FDI was concentrated in electronics, chemicals, and textiles for export; overall levels of FDI were similar to Brazil in 1971 (Amsden, 1985, p. 93). The electronics industry in 1977 accounted for 16 percent of exports and was 85 percent foreign-owned (Gold, 1988). Taiwan was no more exempt from the limitations of FDI than any other nation – the bulk of this investment contributed little more than low-skill assembly of high-tech products. However, over time, the Taiwanese economy became much less dependent on foreign investment as Taiwanese firms were able to upgrade their positions within international production networks – moving toward OEM, Original Design Manufacturing (ODM), and even innovation (Saxenian, 2001; Hobday, 1995).

This upgrading was attained through an increasingly complex and interlocking set of international and local networks. Taiwan, like the other Asian Tigers, was able to take advantage of the transborder expansion of the multilayered Japanese system of subcontracting throughout the region (Arrighi, Ikeda, and Irwan, 1993, p. 61). Taiwan, however, was less closely tied to Japanese production than Korea. It also became increasingly integrated into the "China Circle" because in the 1980s,

"various actors in the People's Republic of China (PRC), Taiwan, and Hong Kong have pursued economic integration as a strategy of upward mobility in the world economy. This economic integration seems to be mutually beneficial and has greatly enhanced the competitiveness of the PRC, Taiwan, and Hong Kong in the world economy. On the one hand, the PRC has helped to solve the developmental problems of Taiwan and Hong Kong by providing them with cheap labor, resources, and investment opportunities. On the other hand, Taiwan and Hong Kong have contributed to the development of the PRC through providing employment opportunities, market stimulus to local enterprises, and the vital information and contacts to reenter the world market." (Hsiao and So, 1993, p. 146; So and Chiu, 1995)

Perhaps most significant, however, is the growing efforts of the state to woo overseas Chinese to return to Taiwan or to form technology or business linkages with Taiwanese firms and institutions. Many of the overseas Chinese had received a university education in the United States and had long experience and close social ties to centers of technological innovation such as Silicon Valley (Saxenian, 2001). The very multiplicity and complexity of the international connections created an environment for Taiwanese firms that offers a rich variety of social and material resources and opportunities.

However, the international connections were grounded locally by a growing institutional thickness within the Taiwanese political economy, particularly around IT. A range of powerful institutions was developed to support high-technology entrepreneurship and innovation – including the centers for technological research such as Electronics Research & Service Organization (ERSO), the Hsinschu Science-Based Industrial Park (HSIP), industry–university linkages, and industry and professional associations (Hsu, 1997). Hsu (1997) argued that ERSO shifted from domination of the private sector in the 1970s through public–private competition in the 1980s to collaboration and consultation in the 1990s. Its technology role shifted correspondingly – in the 1970s, ERSO obtained foreign technology and transferred it to local firms, but it lost this leading role in the 1980s as local firms became more powerful (Meaney, 1994). In the 1990s, ERSO acted as a provider of collective goods; promoted consortia, associations, and information sharing; used its connections with almost all the integrated-circuit firms; and provided external R&D support to smaller enterprises (Hsu, 1997). ERSO's changing roles reflected the growing importance of these semi-autonomous institutions as mediating forces, creating networks within the political economy rather than as creators and diffusers of policy. The majority of Taiwan's leading IT companies are located in the HSIP, which has fostered agglomeration and shifted from a mere location to a vibrant industrial district (Hsu, 1997; Meaney, 1994). The HSIP was founded in 1980 and, by 1983, local capital held 70 percent of the investments (Gold, 1986). Also significant within these institutions are various industry and professional associations and the increasingly important role of universities as research partners (Hsu, 1997; Meaney, 1994, p. 179).

The Taiwanese political economy is characterized, therefore, by the growing importance of flexible state-sponsored institutions as a critical supporting and guiding force, connecting the relatively small Taiwanese firms with their myriad international networks. Managing this multiplicity while facilitating and fostering entrepreneurship and innovation has been critical to the significant industrial upgrading in Taiwan over the past twenty years.

Whereas Taiwan's DNS emerged in a context of continuing state developmentalism, the DNS in Israel emerged from tumultuous changes in the political economy. Between World War II and the oil crisis of 1973, Israel's political economy was driven by a successful developmental state – financed by capital inflows and military aid and managed by an autonomous state bureaucracy in negotiation with big business and the Histadrut labor federation (i.e., a large-scale business organization in its own right). The 1970s and 1980s brought a wave of economic liberalization that combined with electoral populism to produce a rapid decline in economic fortunes. It also resulted in a profound restructuring of economic institutions and, in particular, an attack on the Histadrut and any other nonmarket institutions. The 1990s, however, brought a surprising industrial resurgence in high-tech and the emergence of a globalized business elite that was increasingly vocal in its support of the peace process.

The Israeli developmental state before the oil crisis was based on a close alliance between big business, labor, and the state. The 1952 New Economic Policy was based on ISI (with little export orientation) but with significant state-investment support financed heavily by external sources:

"Capital transfers were Israel's major source of investment capital and revenue enhancer throughout the 1950s and represented roughly 20 percent of all resources" (Barnett, 1996, p. 122)

Levi-Faur (1998) argued that the Israeli state was just as developmental as the Korean or Taiwanese state during this period. Providing extensive protection for firms, the state also played a critical role in the bank-dominated financial system by channeling much of national savings through the state by restricting banks' savings schemes. This, along with reparations and international aid, helped finance the public loans that accounted for 29 percent of gross investment between 1956 and 1972 (Levi-Faur, 1998, p. 73). The state also intervened in industrial development – most importantly in textiles, which was also a significant sector in early industrial development in Taiwan and Korea. Critical to this growth was the 1957 Textile Industry Development Plan, which allocated investment, set targets, and regionalized production investments so that more than ten integrated textile mills were established, underwritten by loans and grants that could total up to 80 percent of any overall investment. Between 1958 and 1968, textile and clothing exports grew sixfold, becoming Israel's most important manufactured export commodity by the 1970s (Levi-Faur, 1998, p. 77). Large sections of the economy were either fully within the public sector or dominated by the Histadrut, the labor federation organization that was a major goods producer and provider of social services.

Between 1950 and 1973, these institutions generated growth rates of approximately 9 percent, export growth of 15 to 20 percent, and domestic investment in the 1960s at levels comparable to Taiwan and even Korea (Levi-Faur, 1998). Indeed, there were many similarities to Taiwan and Korea – each had experienced colonial modernization, limited connections to TNCs, received significant U.S. aid and/or reparations that were channeled through their state bureaucracies, significant international diasporas (in Taiwan and Israel), and faced military threats and problematic international status. However, Israeli GNP per capita was much better in 1950 and,

"although less impressive than those of either South Korea or Taiwan, the Israeli trade performances were exceptionally high and certainly fit into the category of excellent export performances." (Levi-Faur, 1998, p. 76)

In the 1970s, however, the Israeli political economy underwent a dramatic liberalization and a decline into what has been called "the lost years." Silver (1990) argued that Israeli state-led success ran foul of its own contradictions because mobilization in civil society and the workplace raised wages even as competition throughout the semiperiphery became more intense. Levi-Faur suggested that the explanation of the poor performance from 1974 to 1989 lies in a "domestic political crisis reducing state autonomy on the one hand and change in the government economic strategies toward more 'liberal' policies on the other." (1998, p. 66).

However, the same pressures pushed Israel toward a strategy of attempting to move into "core activities" (Silver, 1990) through industrial upgrading. Despite the rhetoric of liberalization, the state remained a strategic pivot (Shalev, 1998).

Hyperinflation in the 1970s threatened the legitimacy of the state, and in 1985 a stabilization plan was introduced that was unorthodox in its own (successful) measures and proved to be the beginning of a renewed round of liberalization (Barkey, 1994; Shalev, 1998). Since then, the state's role has been transformed from the broker of a national corporatist development strategy toward a DNS strategy:

"The state has reduced or eliminated its control of the capital and foreign-exchange markets, yet its role in wooing big multinational corporations, marketing Israeli-made weapons technology, and subsidizing high-tech start-ups has, if anything, increased." (Shalev, 1998, 2000)

The government remains central to the economy even in an era of liberalization. Aggregate social spending has not fallen, although there has been a weakening of entitlements, a shift back toward education spending, and

"while automatic and indirect capital subsidies have been dramatically cut, targeted incentives are more generous than ever . . . especially assistance to start-up companies in high-technology fields which was three times higher in real terms in 1992–1994 than in 1985–1987." (Shalev, 2000. p. 136)

Despite free-trade deals and nominal financial liberalization, the government dominated capital markets until very recently. Kleiman (1997) found that

"repeated statements as to the liberalization of this [capital] market notwithstanding, no single foreign financial institution, be it a commercial bank, an insurance company, or a stock exchange broker, had commenced operations in Israel by the end of 1996."

Industrial-development strategy is based on a transformed pattern of state support of Israeli business.

High-tech industry, although coming into its own in the 1990s, had its roots early in Israel's history (Autler, 1999). As early as the 1940s and 1950s, science and academic research were highly advanced in Israel, often through links to the military. In the 1960s, the connections of the Jewish diaspora, particularly in the United States, to Israel combined with heavy defense investment to produce large defense-oriented technology firms. The 1967 French embargo on arms sales after the Six Day War pushed the Israeli government to develop its own R&D capacity. Nonetheless, this R&D capacity remained firmly within the universities and the defense contractors until the 1980s. In the 1980s, there was significant FDI by high-tech firms, although for the most part the indigenous start-ups of the 1980s and 1990s did not have close links to those TNCs. More important were the ever-deepening ties between Israeli high-tech and the Jewish and Israeli professional diaspora. These transnational technical communities, supported by a wide range of government institutions, became the basis of a vibrant system of indigenous innovation that emerged (as in Taiwan) in the midst of extensive international ties (Autler, 1999).

Much is also made of the unusual significance of the military in the Israeli political economy. However, relatively little commercial-industry development has resulted from the commercialization of military technology, direct military procurement, or even the relatively low number of spin-offs from the military. More important has been the opportunity the state has had through military service to channel people into technical fields and the role of military service in fostering training and networks through technical units (Autler, 1999). Return migration from the United States and military-service networks helped build technical communities; the military served as a "public space" for technologists (Breznitz, 2002b). The structure of networks varies across sectors: whereas the semiconductor industry is linked to U.S. FDI and academia, the networking sector is linked to the military (Autler, 1999).

State support is extensive for all levels of business development in high-tech, and takes the form of matchmaking, investment, and consultative support (Autler, 1999; Sokolov and Verdoner, 1997). The Ministry of Science and Technology, which includes the Office of the Chief Scientist (OCS) (set up in 1984), is very active. The Israeli Export Institute provides sales and marketing support (Sokolov and Verdoner, 1997). An incubator program, initiated in 1991 through the OCS, supports the early start-up phase with physical facilities, business support, and guidance into networking and investment. The state holds onto equity from this process and profits are typically reinvested in the incubator scheme.

R&D support is extensive and coordinated by the OCS (Autler, 1999). As early as the 1960s, the Israeli government provided capital grants and fostered science parks to build the civilian economy. It was among the earliest states (if not the first) to give R&D grants to individual firms (Roper and Frenkel, 1998). The OCS runs a scheme to connect theoretical research in universities and applied research in firms, and also runs the magnet scheme, which targets precompetitive R&D and encourages R&D cooperation (Autler, 1999; Sokolov and Verdoner, 1997). Matimop, the public center for R&D, carries out contract research and joint ventures. A major factor in boosting Israeli innovation has been the Bi-National Industrial R&D (BIRD) scheme, which shares the costs of a joint R&D project 50/50 with each U.S. and Israeli partner (Autler, 1999). Grants average between $100 thousand and $500 thousand; the state retains repayment rights but not equity or intellectual property rights. By 1994, two hundred of the projects led directly to sales of about $1.7 billion (Sokolov and Verdoner, 1997). R&D grants have remained at 50 percent of project cost since the 1960s, and overall government support for R&D is high: in 1994, government supported 26 percent of business non-defence R&D in Israel, compared to only 10 percent in Ireland (Roper and Frenkel, 1998).

The state also has been central to the provision of venture capital, beginning its efforts in 1985. However, success came only with the Yozma scheme, operating since 1993, which shares the risk of loss with firms and provides favorable terms to successful firms for buying back the Yozma shares (Autler, 1999; Sokolov and Verdoner, 1997). Links to the United States are extensive in all areas of high-tech industry, and policy ties through interfirm alliances and transnational technical communities are more critical to Israeli high-tech than foreign investment (Autler, 1999).

The science and technology agencies of the Israeli state have been central to managing the relationship between multiple global ties – FDI, aid, migration, and diaspora – and local networks and institutions based around highly agglomerated technical communities within Israel (Autler, 1999). This has been highly effective as high-tech has expanded rapidly:

"From 1968–83, for example, high-tech industry in Israel increased its share of output from 6 to 24 percent and its share of exports from 5 to 28 percent." (Roper and Frenkel, 1998, p. 8, quoting Teubal)

Ultimately, then, the Israeli state no longer picks industrial "winners" or directly influences their decisions, but rather has constructed a range of institutions that effectively foster innovation and learning, support business development, and channel firms toward specific types of activities (e.g., R&D) that contribute to more durable economic success.

INSTITUTIONS OF STATE DEVELOPMENTALISMS

A necessary (although not sufficient) condition of effective development strategies is an economically and politically sustainable set of supporting institutions. Each developmental strategy discussed herein is deeply embedded in different forms of developmental state institutions. Although all of these cases are bureaucratized states embedded in socioeconomic actors, the form of this "embedded autonomy" varies from case to case (Table 10.2).

Table 10.2 outlines the primary sets of actors in which each developmental state is embedded. Whereas the Korean state is most narrowly embedded in local capital, the Irish state is multiply embedded in local capital, transnational technical communities, and foreign capital, which continues to have a major influence on the industrial-policy regime. Multiplicity is a particular feature of the Irish case, which is only emphasized when we consider the importance of social-partnership institutions at the macroeconomic level and membership in the EU, the most formally institutionalized network polity in the world. Nonetheless, both Taiwan and Israel are also multiply embedded and rely heavily on network institutions to shape industrial development. There is no easy correspondence between state structure and developmental strategy – we cannot "read off" strategy options from an analysis of state structure, nor do state structures simply emerge to pursue particular strategies. However, certain organizational structures facilitate different relations of conflict, solidarity, and influence. Some types of states will be better at bringing to fruition certain kinds of policies than others.

Table 10.2. Comparative Developmental State Institutions

	South Korea	Taiwan	Israel	Singapore	Ireland
Embeddedness in Local Capital	High	High	High	Low*	High
Embeddedness in Foreign Capital	Low	Low/Medium	Low	High	High
Embeddedness in Transnational Technical Communities	Low	High	High	Low	High
Organizational Form of State Industrial Development Regime	Bureaucratic	Network	Network	Bureaucratic	Network

*However, the state is part or whole owner of many local firms.

As has been widely remarked, a tight policy network between big business and the state in Korea makes it easier for the state to guide large firms' decisions and makes the growth of increasingly large firms less threatening to the state. This, in turn, has strengthened the hand of the industrial-development agencies within the state – comparing Taiwan's and Korea's state bureaucracies, Wade argued that

"both bureaucracies are highly centralized, but the Korean one more so because the Ministry of Trade and Industry [in Korea] is able to exercise more leverage over other ministries than Taiwan's Ministry of Economic Affairs." (1990, p. 323)

The state bureaucracies are highly selective and operate on largely meritocratic principles, with a correspondingly strong "corporate culture" (Evans, 1995, p. 51). This was, however, bypassed by the predatory regime of Syngman Rhee until its overthrow in 1961 by Park Chung Hee – these military reformers had a strong solidarity based on shared military service and military-academy experiences, which provided a "nonbureaucratic" base for the bureaucratic structure of the state. Therefore, even the most bureaucratic of systems ultimately rests on specific political foundations.

Evans (1995) argued that Korea involved powerful state and private actors earlier and on a more sustained basis throughout development projects and provided closer public–private cooperation than other aspiring developmental states, such as Brazil or India. Nonetheless,

"embeddedness under Park was a much more "top-down" affair than the Japanese prototype, lacking the well-developed intermediary associations and focused on a small number of very large firms. The size and diversification of the largest chaebol did give them interests that were relatively encompassing... in sectoral terms so that the small number of firms did not limit the sectoral scope of industrial growth. Still, the Korean state could not claim the same generalized institutional relation with the private sector that the MITI system provided..." (1995, p. 53)

Korea then pursued a development strategy based on a close alliance between the state and a small number of large business groups, the *chaebol*. Both the state and the chaebol were organized hierarchically so that the development regime in Korea consisted of closely connected state and business elites, which were embedded in other constituencies and institutions in a highly top-down manner.

If South Korea has been the paradigmatic developmental state, the statist character of Singaporean development was slow to be recognized, given its extreme reliance on foreign investment and openness to trade (Huff, 1995a,b; Lim, 1983). Ties between the English-educated political elite and the Chinese local entrepreneurs were almost nonexistent, and foreign capital and the state became the central actors in economic development. The types of links that the Korean state developed with the elites of the chaebol were never likely to emerge with the managers of the transnational corporations that located in Singapore. However, business elites were drawn into the state through the wide range of state enterprises that provided a type of fusion of state and business interests outside the FDI sector.

Labor was heavily repressed and controlled in Singapore because the imperatives of export-oriented industrialization required securing low labor costs and industrial peace. Goals of national development became hegemonic and legitimized the political exclusion of labor (Deyo, 1989). Between 1967 and 1977, the government took over the labor market, weakened unions, eliminated strikes, and forced wages down compared to competitors. This repression was combined with incorporation; in 1970, the state set up a tripartite body to set wage guidelines and also pressured TNCs not to bid up wages (Huff, 1995a, p. 740). The National Wages Council, drawing labor representatives from the government-controlled trade-union confederation, did preside over substantial wage increases but, for example, in the mid-1980s it recommended an effective 20 percent pay cut with little or no unrest. "Market discipline" played a small role as a direct mode of labor control in Singapore, unlike in Ireland (Suarez, 2000).

For Coe and Yeung (1999), Singapore is a city–state in which the global and national scales are juxtaposed, with the state playing a central role in the process of meshing them together. The state institutions that have undertaken this task are highly centralized – based primarily around three ministries and a range of tightly interlocking directorships (Huff, 1995a, p. 744). Huff (1995b), quoting Silcock, says that about fifty people "made the difference" for Singapore. There was a high level of economic expertise in the technocracy although it was not dominated by economists. Furthermore, this bureaucratic organization extended through the state as a whole:

"Leadership achieved effective implementation of plans and policies through the lower levels of bureaucracy by a willingness to pay government officials as much or more than the private sector and an emphasis on individual accountability." (Evans and Rauch, 1999; Huff, 1995a, p. 749)

The Singaporean state is perhaps the closest example of a state that was able to pursue a "plan rationality" of its own – along the lines suggested by Johnson

(1982). However, this plan rationality was always tempered by a close attention to developments in the international economy.

"Singapore planners ..., helped by intelligence from the Economic Development Board [EDB] overseas offices, closely monitored the world market.... For example, the potential of electronics was spotted on a 1966 ministerial visit to Taiwan." (Huff, 1995a, p. 748)

The EDB, much like the IDA in Ireland, tried to identify the "best" (i.e., higher value added and skill) sectors for Singapore and constantly revised the lists. Overall, however, industrial-development aims were general, and industrial policy was much less targeted toward firms than in South Korea or Japan.

Neither was the plan rationality of the Singaporean state set in stone; rather, these were plans that operated in response to international trade and investment conditions.

"Perhaps the most important reason why government interventionism succeeded in Singapore was because of a pragmatism – the test of what works – rather than rigid ideological commitment to a free market or to state direction. There was a clear understanding of the limitations of smallness and extreme openness for an economy such as Singapore's in departing from free trade to govern the market." (Huff, 1995a, p. 1435)

Whereas state embeddedness in foreign capital and control of society enabled a highly successful development strategy based on foreign investment, the interaction of strategy and institutions reinforced the subordinate position of local capital. It was only in the late 1990s that local capital became a more important political presence, as discussed in the next section.

In contrast to the DBS institutions of South Korea and Sinagpore, a DNS has developed as a gradual "filling in" of the social, political, and organizational space between state and local bourgeoisie in Taiwan. In the 1950s and 1960s, the newly arrived Kuomintang state from the Chinese mainland was largely disconnected from the Taiwanese small business-owning bourgeoisie. The 1970s saw the emergence of a new developmental coalition in electronics and related industries. These industries relied more heavily on FDI and the overseas Chinese diaspora, and built a set of institutions to support the new social and political ties. Nonetheless, this regime built on the existing industrial base rather than replacing it – for example, many of the returning immigrant high-tech entrepreneurs were the sons (and some daughters) of the earlier generation of business owners (Gold, 1986). The institutions supporting this strategy of high-tech upgrading became progressively "thicker" through the 1980s, with happy results as electronics firms shifted from low-cost assembly to OEM production and even innovation in the 1990s (Saxenian, 2001). Taiwanization, internationalization, and democratization of the state have reshaped development strategy and institutions in Taiwan, but the state remains central to economic development – shaping, articulating, and mediating new patterns of economic interests and coalition-formation.

As we have seen, the institutions of development in Taiwan highlight the folly of false oppositions between centralization and decentralization – in fact, each can be dependent on the other. In Taiwan, a strong central state facilitates the autonomy of a variety of mediating institutions that can act "flexibly" because they are rarely constrained by worries at the center regarding political competition. Wade argued that, compared to Korea,

"the Taiwanese government . . . is less centralized with power over industrial policy issues dispersed amongst more ministries and agencies. Officials have a narrower scope for the exercise of their authority and use it more circumspectly in their dealings with private firms. At the top of the government, coherence may be achieved by the same person occupying top positions in several different organizations, wielding influence that attaches more to his person than to the positions themselves." (1990, p. 324)

The institutional thickness so central to Taiwan's political economy has its roots relatively early in its history of industrial development. The Kuomintang (KMT) state created a number of relatively autonomous economic agencies in the 1940s to handle the chaotic economic situation and to deal with U.S. agencies (Haggard and Pang, 1994, p. 61). These agencies operated "between" the large state-owned sector and the central political structure. The apparent complexity of their organizational structure and their constant changes were offset by a system similar to interlocking directorates. Furthermore, the agencies had an unusual level of organizational independence, due to their financing through U.S. aid; they were exempted from civil-service regulations and, therefore, were able to pay much higher salaries:

"This enabled the agencies to recruit and train highly competent staff, to attract talent, and to maintain an organizational esprit de corps." (Haggard and Pang, 1994, p. 63)

Similarly, Taiwanese science- and technology-policy agencies are both centralized and autonomous, according to Hong (1997). An institutional capacity was developed within the state by the foundation of the Industrial Technology Research Institute (ITRI), which had a high degree of autonomy, and the formation within ITRI of ERSO, a research organization that focused on the integrated-circuit industry. Originally funded entirely by the state, by 1988 ERSO received 20 to 25 percent of its funding from the state, whereas ITRI received 55 percent (Meaney, 1994).

In addition to building up this local institutional network, the state became highly internationalized from at least the 1960s forward (specifically in the IT sector). The key individual in the development of IT policy, Y.S. Sun, had been trained at the Tennessee Valley Authority in the United States. He prompted the Chinese Institute of Engineers to organize biannual seminars in the 1970s to facilitate communication between Taiwanese and overseas Chinese engineers (Meaney, 1994, p. 174). Links to Silicon Valley were developed as early as the 1960s (Saxenian, 2001) and a Technical Advisory Committee was set up in the United States in the 1970s that proved to be a key source of information on technical development in the United States integrated-circuit industry (Meaney, 1994).

Local firms, state institutions, and international networks became so closely fused that it was difficult to tell where one institution began and the other ended.

The first director general of Hsinschu Science-Based Industrial Park (HSIP) had been research director at Honeywell in Minneapolis (Meaney, 1994, p. 178). In 1979, the Science and Technology Advisory Group (STAG) was set up under the cabinet to operate as a check on the particular interests of those in ERSO and other state agencies. STAG consisted (usually entirely) of U.S. advisors and was "constantly challenging" ERSO (Meaney, 1994, p. 180). In 1984–85, it expanded its organizational capacity with Technical Review Boards, consisting primarily of overseas Chinese. Meaney argued that the interests of the Americans in STAG were rooted in either anticommunism or trying to help promote competition with Japan. In this, their interests converged with key Taiwanese officials, and this convergence was deepened through the institutional ties:

"This convergence was not simply a matter of a momentary coincidence of interests between actors in the core and semiperiphery as a dependent development model might suggest, but was a product of a complex of personal and professional relationships among Taiwan officials and technical personnel and overseas Chinese engineers and executives." (Meaney, 1994)

This was the concrete organizational form taken by Taiwan's favorable geopolitical relationship to the United States (Cumings, 1987).

Institutionally, then, as much as economically, Taiwan is characterized by a state-managed fusion of global, local, and national, achieved primarily through a network of institutions that form a multilayered, networked system of institutional supports. Castells' (1992) "inflexible state" proved to be surrounded by a network of more flexible institutions and associations.

Although the overall structure of Israel's polity is dominated by central bureaucracies and the security state, the state agencies concerned with science, technology, and industrial development are organized through dense institutional networks. Nonetheless, those networks rest on state bureaucracy. Although Israel only scores moderately on international comparisons of the bureaucratic character of the state (Evans and Rauch, 1999), a variety of authors have argued that the state technocracy was characterized by bureaucratic autonomy, at least prior to the 1970s (Barnett, 1996; Levi-Faur, 1998). In terms of securing state autonomy, it was

"critical that foreign aid and unilateral transfers were channeled through state apparatus with relatively few strings." (Barnett, 1996, p. 123)

Barnett argues that its nationalist ideological commitments and external security pressures forced the state to avoid the worst of predatory state behavior.

Nonetheless, the state has also been embedded in critical social actors – although this embeddedness has shifted from the Histadrut before liberalization to high-tech business in more recent years. Overall, though,

"The structure of policy networks in Israel, as a consequence of the dominance of state organizations in political economic spheres, resembles the pattern illustrated by the Netherlands and Germany more so than that of the Anglo-American nations. Namely, policy forums, though established by state organizations, are connected through elite persons representing nonstate corporations and interest groups." (Maman, 1997, p. 280)

During 1974–81 and 1986–88, Israel's polity was characterized by overlapping "networks of networks," with many interlocking memberships in policy forums among finance and labor, transportation, and agriculture. Maman argued that the importance of these policy forums is not their formal power but rather the informal networks to which they give rise. During the stabilization crisis, from 1982–85 the financial policy network became more autonomous, with only one case of an interlocking membership (in this case, with the industry-policy forum) and the number of nonstate actors involved decreased (Maman, 1997). Stabilization and liberalization were projects of an autonomous state par excellence, although there was a rapid return to overlapping policy networks. The 1990s saw increasing ties to international technical communities, often through the Jewish diaspora, which had been central to developing important policy and market ties to the United States. Through institutions such as the BIRD program, close ties developed among high-tech capitalists and technology policymakers in the United States and Israel – influenced decisively, of course, by the continuing U.S. support for Israeli territorial and security policy and Israel's growing isolation from European nations under Sharon.

Johnson's model of a "national, rational" state drawing on a central "plan rationality" (1982, see Chapter 8) is ultimately misleading. Developmental-state rationalities are much more contingent and localized than Johnson suggested and are deeply embedded in the particular forms of embedded autonomy of each state. These embedded autonomies are in many cases as glocal as they are national. Clearly, these are still institutions of developmental states but they take myriad forms, producing significant differences in capacities and socioeconomic consequences.

THE POLITICAL HISTORY OF DEVELOPMENTAL BUREAUCRATIC AND NETWORK STATES

The previous discussion was couched in terms of "effectiveness," as if countries could simply "choose" their development strategy and institutions. However, throughout this book, I have stressed the political shaping of both strategy and institutions. The overarching demands of world-system dynamics, position in the international division of labor, cultural traditions, and other factors certainly shape the construction of developmental coalitions. However, I have argued that significant space remains for politics that can make a difference in critical ways. Furthermore, this politic is often to be found in the mundane conflicts over organization-building in economy, polity, and society. To paraphrase Von Clausewitz, organization-building is:

"continuation of policy by other means. It is not merely a political act, but a real political instrument, a continuation of political intercourse, a conduct of political intercourse by other means."

Sociologists have pointed to the power of processes of institutionalization in shaping economic and social outcomes – control over the trajectory of institutionalization is perhaps one of the least theorized forms of power but one of the most recognized in the practice of politics.

Table 10.3 summarizes the critical moments of institution-building in each of the five cases discussed in this book. Following McMichael (1996) and selecting artificially clear-cut dates of transition, I classify each economy's historical development of the particular combination of development strategies and institutions outlined in Tables 10.1 and 10.2 under three periods corresponding to recent transformations in the broader global political economy. McMichael argued that recent decades have seen a shift from a "development project," based on subordinating markets to public goals of building and stabilizing national economies, which was hegemonic through the 1950s and 1960s; through a period of "liberalization" and attack by capital on the constraints posed on it in the developmentalist period, operating through the collapse of Bretton Woods in the early 1970s and the debt crisis of the 1980s; to a "globalization project" based on global networks of capital that attempts to dominate national states and societies. These world-system transformations do not determine the outcome of development politics but rather profoundly shape the terrain on which that development politics can be undertaken.

Each of the three Asian developmental states starts from a different set of state-society alliances in the 1950s and 1960s. Whereas Korea is characterized by close ties between state and local bourgeoisie, Taiwan's state and domestic bourgeoisie are deeply split by ethnic and political divisions – and Singapore has a weak domestic bourgeoisie. Nonetheless, each of the different developmental alliances weathers the period of liberalization by holding international financial capital and institutions at bay while simultaneously suppressing popular mobilization. Having avoided the fiscal crises of the state-racking core countries at the time, each Asian Tiger promoted industrial upgrading, albeit in different ways. In Taiwan especially, democratization and internationalization promoted significant institutional change because this gentler form of liberalization allowed the state to build new network institutions supporting a new high-tech development strategy. This was also possible in Taiwan where a political "space" existed between state and society that was not present in Korea, with its dense ties between state and business elites.

Liberalization came late to Korea as the globalization project took hold globally, but it did so with disastrous effects, resulting in the financial crisis of 1997–98 as financial liberalization split the chaebol apart from the national coalition that underpinned its organizational models. Paradoxically, the earlier and more thorough internationalization of Taiwanese business made it easier for the Taiwanese political economy and the state to manage processes of liberalization. Meanwhile, Singapore is struggling to build network institutions in an effort to promote its own domestic bourgeoisie alongside the TNCs.

The cases of Ireland and Israel are different from the Asian Tigers. The dismal failure to mobilize the domestic bourgeoisie in the interests of development left Ireland seeking FDI, which quickly became institutionalized as the hegemonic

Table 10.3. Comparative Historical Development of Developmental Bureaucratic and Network States

Era	South Korea	Taiwan	Israel	Singapore	Ireland
The Development Project (1950–73)	*Chaebol* links to Japan; state-sponsored industrial system	State developmentalism at arm's length from bourgeoisie; ethnic and political divisions	Rapid growth through close state–business–union ties	FDI; keep wage costs low through repression and subsidies for social reproduction	FDI; tax incentives the central instrument
Liberalization (1973–90)	Upgrading through learning; increased power of chaebol	Upgrading through "institutional thickness"	Liberalization and crisis; political space for new state agenda	Upgrading by autonomous state	Liberalization and crisis; political space alongside the FDI agenda
The Globalization Project (1990–)	Liberalization and crisis	Network institutions around transnational technical communities and FDI	Network institutions around transnational technical communities	Attempts to build "institutional thickness" around FDI	Network institutions around FDI

policy in the 1960s. Meanwhile, Israel was characterized by a unique form of national coalition that supported successful state developmentalism through the 1960s. The two cases differed from the Asian cases, however, in two critical respects, each linked to their greater integration into Anglo-American democratic capitalist institutions. Each faced popular mobilization that generated inflation and fiscal problems for the state, while at the same time each was heavily influenced by the rise of neoliberal economic thought within the United States and the United Kingdom. Nonetheless, the state did not disappear from the stage as neoliberals might have wished. Neoliberal attacks on the existing institutions combined with economic crises to open up political space for new developmental projects within the political economy. In Ireland, this took the form of coexisting institutions supporting foreign investment, local innovation, and even neocorporatist "social partnership." In Israel, continuities with the earlier regime were also clear: the high-tech sector emerged from the academic and defense establishments but under the guidance of newly minted state institutions. In each case, under the neoliberal attack, the state is the innovator, seeking out new constituencies and promoting new development projects.

This section can only touch on the factors that shaped the rise of different developmental state regimes, but we begin by considering the particular historical conditions of the DBS in South Korea. Some authors emphasize a continuity with the past – either political (Kohli, 1994) or cultural (Orrú et al., 1997). Others focus on a break in Korean history around the early 1960s and the rise of the Park regime, in which an autonomous state was able to impose an export-oriented development strategy on the chaebol, while at the same time demanding and obtaining relatively exacting performance standards. Chibber (1999) offered a middle road: the state did play a critical role, but the possibility of building an export-oriented strategy with the support of big business was made significantly easier by the existing connections between the Korean *chaebol* and Japanese firms. The state gained significant power from its control over finance, but this did not necessarily mean that it could simply impose its will on the chaebol, against its own preferences or interests:

"The key to the origins of ELI in Korea would thus seem to lie in the means by which state managers were able to elicit a switch to the new strategy by the business class without triggering a downturn in the investment climate." (Chibber, 1999, p. 322)

Chibber points to the importance of the balance of class forces that enables and constrains the strategies that the state is able to undertake. His emphasis on the importance of Korean firms' class alliance with Japanese firms is in many ways the mirror image of analyses that stress the power of the landed aristocracy in Latin America to block statist developmentalism. Chibber argues that ELI was critical to the rise of the developmental state, not the other way around – or perhaps, less controversially, each evolved in a manner in which institutional change and economic development were interdependent. Korean firms were willing to support the ELI development regime because they already had connections with Japanese firms that shaped the definition of their own interests in ways that were compatible with the state model.

Once the state is able to put a regime in place, this in turn can significantly reshape those class forces. The *chaebol's* place at the center of the economy was consolidated by state policy.

"The overwhelming presence of the business groups in the Korean economy has its roots in the importance of political connections to obtain such resources as permits to enter new industries, government contracts, subsidized loans, export incentives, import licenses to acquire equipment and raw materials, and permissions to hire workers. The state policy-making apparatus created by General Park in the 1960s preferred to deal with a handful of entrepreneurs for obvious control reasons and persuaded the favored ones to enter risky undertakings by expanding their licenses in already established and profitable industries, protecting them from foreign imports, and lending them money at subsidized rates." (Guillen, 2001, p. 76)

The chaebol grew to the point that it again began to resist the state's developmental efforts in the late 1980s, pushed for liberalization, and became heavily internationally indebted with disastrous results in the financial crisis of 1997–98. But, as Chibber emphasizes, simply having a balance of class forces in place that makes possible a particular developmental strategy does not guarantee that strategy will be forthcoming nor that it will be successful. And, we might add, a particular balance of class forces may be compatible with a wide variety of developmental strategies – which strategy, or strategies, that emerge victorious can depend heavily on conjunctural political struggles. Chibber's research showed that although we must reject any notion of a state simply being able to impose a developmental strategy on an unwilling economy, the contribution of the state to upgrading within the ELI political coalition remains crucial.

Singapore also illustrates the importance of political coalitions, although as the opposite case in which a powerful state resisted connection to local capital and made alliance with foreign capital that would not undermine its local dominance. With independence in 1959, Singapore faced a crisis, with unemployment around 9 percent and the prospect of losing British bases that accounted for 10 to 15 percent of national income. In 1959, it joined with Malaya to form Malaysia, and from 1960 to 1966 it pursued a strategy of Import Substitution Industrialisation (ISI) behind protection, with heavy government investment in infrastructure generating growth of 5.7, percent PA. The split with Malaysia in 1965 created a moment of great political uncertainty in which Lee Kuan Yew emerged as a dominant leader, splitting with the leftist wing of the People's Action Party (PAP) and creating an autonomous state apparatus under his control. Both local entrepreneurs and labor were excluded. A split between English-educated political elites and the Chinese business class and trade unions excluded local entrepreneurs from the development project. The older Chinese trade unions also were excluded and new trade unions formed by the now dominant PAP, "which did not have roots in the older Chinese radicalism" (Huff, 1995b, p. 1431).

This process had begun even before the shift to ELI. A wave of communist labor organizing after World War II led to communists and moderate English-educated middle-class nationalists combining to form PAP in 1954, united by their anticolonialism. Yew gradually gained control of the PAP for the more moderate middle-class nationalists. Between 1959 and 1965, the state repressed labor by deregistering unions, encouraging employers to fire union leaders, arresting leaders, and freezing union assets, as part of its efforts to eliminate political opposition (Suarez, 2000). The fact that pressures to provide low-cost labor for ELI existed does not, however, explain the specific form that labor-control strategies took, which were often also shaped by preexisting political logics (Suarez, 2000).

After taking advantage of this political moment in 1965 to sideline other political groups, Yew was then under enormous pressure to generate growth and benefits to legitimize the new government. In this context, the turn to FDI was as much a political as an economic consideration, offering the prospect of economic growth without the dilemmas of political compromise. The hegemony of the regime was facilitated by rising living standards as manufactured exports took off and, from the late 1970s forward, were supplemented by financial and business services. Between 1960 and 1993, GDP increased thirteenfold – although in 1992, 32.8 percent of national income accrued to nonresidents or noncitizens (Huff, 1995a).

This was further reinforced by the strength and expansion of state institutions. At independence, Singapore had inherited economic strength and an administration that worked and went on to build a variety of strong institutions on that foundation. In 1959, the Economic Development Board (EDB) was set up to spearhead industrialization by direct participation in industry (Huff, 1995a, p. 737) and soon came to focus on FDI. Similarly to Ireland, the institutionalization of a focus on attracting FDI in a powerful semi-autonomous agency combined with the initial success in attracting that investment to cement the regime's emphasis on FDI. Further institutional developments in the 1960s were offshoots of the EDB – including the government-owned Development Bank of Singapore and the Jurong Town Corporation, based on a new industrial estate, and the Monetary Authority of Singapore, a kind of quasicentral bank, in 1971. Throughout the 1970s and 1980s, broader social control was consolidated through the heavy use of mass media and social discipline, facilitated by a legal system that is only partly independent of the executive. Whereas South Korea's state had been pushed toward building exporting firms by a domestic capitalist class with export ties, the Singaporean state, less subject to those political constraints, found it much more difficult to build an indigenous industrial capacity.

These problems drew the attention of Singapore's policymakers, with a major policy push in Singapore to increase Total Factor Productivity (TFP), at least partly after the controversy over Krugman's contested critique in 1994 of the Asian Tigers as relatively unimpressive in terms of productivity growth. The Singaporean state even set a target of 2 percent annual TFP growth and set up a government agency to promote it (Ermisch and Huff, 1999). Although this target bears the hallmark of developmental bureaucraticism, the state is simultaneously attempting to build institutions reminiscent of "network states." A major element in Singapore's recent efforts in IT, aimed at becoming a global hub for IT operations, has been a growing emphasis on consultation and associational networks.

"The key dynamic here is the corporatization of National Computer Board (NCB) functions that lend themselves to private sector adoption through public–private partnerships and strategic alliances. This shift in emphasis means that the NCB will no longer be the sole source of expertise for developing IT policy, and reflects the accumulated size and maturity of Singapore's contemporary IT industry. As a result, the NCB's promotional efforts for IT in Singapore will increasingly be focused on specific industry clusters." (Coe and Yeung, 1999, p. 9)

Coe and Yeung argued that the Electronic Commerce (EC) master plan developed in 1998 drew on significant interagency collaboration, with some degree of success.

"We suggest that Singapore illustrates the kind of progressive 'institutional thickness' that is necessary to mobilize such initiatives. While the NCB has played a crucial coordinating role, the success of EC policy formation in Singapore arguably rests on the large number of parties that have been consulted, covering a broad range of ministries, statutory boards, foreign multinationals, local businesses, and educational establishments. This pluralistic approach, although undeniably strongly marshalled by state institutions, has speedily produced a coherent policy framework well in advance of other countries in the region." (1999, p. 13)

By the 1990s, plan-review procedures were

"being used as a means of publicity to mobilize support for government economic strategy." (Huff, 1995a, p. 1434)

Nonetheless, the network state in Singapore remains much less developed than in Taiwan or Israel. Taiwan and Israel represent different paths toward network institutions, with Taiwan "filling in" the social space between state and society over the past thirty years, whereas the tight relationship between state and capital in Israel in the 1960s was ruptured by liberalization, with network institutions emerging in the new political space.

The small firms characteristic of Taiwanese industry already existed in the 1950s, but their importance was reinforced by the Kuomintang desire to avoid challenges from large firms, such as the chaebol in Korea. Political considerations shaped many critical features of the Taiwanese political economy: the destruction of the landlords by the Japanese colonists and the KMT, the drive for development based on the KMT military regime's need to legitimate itself in a new country, and state support for small firms based (at least partly) on a desire to avoid building an alternative power bloc to the state. Japanese colonialism had some developmental consequences in Taiwan, first in pursuit of making it an agricultural appendage and then later focusing on industry. Although World War II took away many of the gains, a relatively high level of literacy and the economic structure implanted by the Japanese remained, with their attack on the large landlords particularly significant because it removed one of the major class obstacles to developmental coalition formation (Amsden, 1985, pp. 79–82). The KMT regime, under political pressure to move away from the corruption that had characterized it on the mainland, ended landlordism and created a class of smallholders in the early 1950s. Part of the reason they were able to do this was that they were totally separated from the Taiwanese elite, unlike on the mainland where they had failed to implement such a program in the 1930s because the landlords were their nationalist base (Amsden, 1985). For their part, family firms were drawn into dealing with the state through the state's control over key resources. They became increasingly incorporated into the state as they sought out the resources the state had to offer and, in the process, became more visible to it politically (Winckler, 1988: p. 169).

We have already seen how those political concerns were translated into the emergence of "flexible capitalism under the guidance of an inflexible state." However, the 1970s and 1980s brought significant changes. Winckler (1988) argued that the incorporation of the new bourgeoisie into the state was significant in the 1970s. Neither were all of the small-firm "guerilla capitalists" incorporated equally:

"By the late 1980s and early 1990s, the guerilla capitalists were undergoing a fundamental differentiation. Some were successfully upgrading into high-tech industries, which often brought them into cooperative linkages with state laboratories; others moved their production offshore (ironically in many cases to the People's Republic of China), thus severing their ties to the state in all but the most indirect manner." (Clark and Lam, 1998, p. 130)

The incorporation of the high-tech bourgeoisie, in particular, changed the state as it became progressively more Taiwanized, internationalized, and democratized. The Taiwanization of the state began in the late 1970s, well before the ending of martial law in 1987. Natives and Taiwanese children of mainlanders, many of whom were educated abroad and had to be attracted back with political liberalization, were given political appointments (Gold, 1986, p. 114). Key portfolios remained a mainlander reserve and the military remained strong with significant repression of protests. However, they did face increasing challenges to their legitimacy (Gold, 1986). The influence of foreign capitalists, U.S. technical advisors, and overseas Chinese grew as did the power of return migrants. Gold wrote in 1986 that

"Taiwan's future rests in the hands of an elite, many of whose members hold green cards" (1986, p. 106)

and this trend has, if anything, become more significant (Saxenian, 2001). This held true also among economic elites because many of the new bourgeoisie in the technology sectors in the 1970s and 1980s were foreign-trained sons of successful Taiwanese businessmen (Gold, 1988, p. 189).

Taken together, then, in the late 1970s and early 1980s, a new coalition emerged to challenge the traditionalists:

"Younger social and natural scientists holding doctoral degrees from American and European universities, some developmental technocrats, a large group of regional and local politicians from Taiwan, and a number of young members of the central parliamentary bodies who had emerged from by-elections, combined into a reformist coalition." (Domes, 2000, p. 120)

By the early 1990s, they were successful in gaining prominence for their agenda within the KMT so that, in addition to democratization within the political system as a whole, government offices outside of the center were increasingly independent and competition within the party increased. Commentators differ on whether this implies the waning of KMT power (Gold, 2000) or a more complex relationship between the KMT and the polity with increased internal competition within the KMT (Domes, 2000).

Industrial upgrading, institutional thickening, and social and political change have resulted in a different polity from the arm's-length state–society relationship of the 1950s. Brodsgaard and Young argue that

"both Taiwan and the PRC are finding that as they develop they have less need for a state that simply imposes policy, and more need for a state that provides the institutional arena for the articulation and mediation of interests and information. Taiwan appears to be well on the way to developing such a state." (2000, p. 9).

Taiwan's state bureaucracy lacks the close ties with domestic business that characterized the Korean developmental state. However, this space between state and society has been filled with institutions that created a DNS in Taiwan and underpinned its ongoing success in the IT industry.

The Israeli developmental state was distinguished from the Asian Tigers in the 1960s by its relationships with labor and the interconnectedness of the state and the Histadrut, which functioned as a quasistate in a number of areas. This changed in the 1970s with liberalization, which was driven in large part by a shift in the upper reaches of the bureaucracy in which socialists were replaced by economists. The economists were strategically placed in the defense and finance ministries and were able to shape interpretations of "the crisis" such that

"the pure liberal ideology in Israel has not been represented by any political party but only by the academic economists in the country." (Barnett, 1996, p. 127, quoting Yair Aharoni; Levi-Faur, 2000, p. 169)

The very autonomy of the state enabled this shift to occur relatively rapidly, particularly in the face of a sense of looming crisis (Barkey, 1994; Barnett, 1996). Indeed, if liberalization neutralized the role of the state in some areas, it was in many cases a welcome relief for state elites. The 1985 stabilization plan and the creation of a national unity government created the conditions for the first time for a state autonomous from the Histadrut:

"This autonomy provided the capacity to reduce the state budget and subsidies, to neutralize the power of groups that in the past penetrated state apparatuses, and to open up the Israeli economy to global financial markets and forces." (Grinberg and Shafir, 2000, p. 126)

This in turn created the institutional and political space for a re-embedding of the state in the emergent high-tech bourgeoisie. Shalev argued that the state shed resources, and the power deriving from that, in return for increased autonomy that was gained by using 'market discipline' to control other actors and that

"the shift in industrial policy from blanket subsidies to 'picking winners' in high-tech fields is testimony to the renewed (albeit 'market-conforming') steering capacities of the state." (2000, p. 149)

But the market-conforming state institutions discussed in the previous section profoundly transformed Israeli participation in global markets and, with that, the structure of social and political interests.

The unusual Israeli form of corporatism has its roots in the early socialist foundation established by Zionists in the 1930s and 1940s. There was no capitalist class in Palestine, which was not attractive to metropolitan capital, with too few resources and people and too much conflict. This was a blessing in disguise – it created the pressure for innovative solutions to the dilemmas of economic development and meant that the space existed in which to pursue them (Barnett, 1996, p. 119). The institutions of the Kibbutzim and the Histadrut – initially designed to be labor's representative – came to hold significant investment resources. Indeed, Barnett (1996) argued that the influence of domestic capital never equaled the power of the Histadrut. The Histadrut was a stand-in for many state functions, emerging from the pre-1948 lack of governmental machinery among the semi-autonomous Jewish community in the mandate territory (Kleiman, 1997). Shalev argued that

"In the Israeli context during the late 1950s, the commitment of the state to containing unemployment was not a 'compensation' or a 'guarantee' won by the trade union movement in return for good behavior in the industrial relations arena, as corporatist theory would anticipate. Instead, a transition to full employment was made desirable by considerations of state-building and domestic politics, and possible by a unique combination of factors favoring economic expansion." (1992, p. 223)

Shalev (1998) argued that between 1948 and 1966, a synergy of foreign capital and immigration – and a state positioned strategically distributing foreign capital, directing immigration and settlement, and allocating housing – generated rapid growth. The unusual conditions in Israel meant that

"the state's choice between sustaining or retreating from its commitment to full employment was softened for a whole decade by a variety of buffers which . . . rested on the inflow of gift capital, a ready supply of 'marginal' labor, and the advent of generalized political exchange between the Histadrut and the state." (Shalev, 1992, p. 225)

However, after a decade of rapid growth,

"The shift to full employment upset power relations by reducing the dependence of ordinary workers on the state and the ruling parties." (Shalev, 1998; Silver, 1990)

the state used the recession in an attempt to impose a "market discipline" on the various actors. This worked for labor, which toned down its demands, but not for capital, which still resisted exporting until devaluation and a variety of positive incentives – in fact, it may have weakened the Labor Party's mass political support and laid the groundwork for their loss in 1977 (Shalev, 1992, p. 223). Shalev argues that a political crisis of the Mapai (i.e., Labor Party) in the 1970s was based on the undermining of the four pillars of its support: its successful formation of support among less advantaged voters provided those voters with resources and, therefore, choices other than the Mapai, its reliance on the Histadrut as a mobilizing force was undermined by internal fragmentation within the Histadrut, including the growing independence of managers; the autonomy granted the state by inflows of foreign gift capital was weakened by the changing character of those inflows, particularly the tying of U.S. aid to arms purchases; and,

"Due in no small part to the cumulative effects of the state's own benevolence, big business grew and solidified and the state's capacity to control the economy according to political criteria was correspondingly impaired." (Shalev, 1992, p. 286)

Continuing subsidies of business combined with a populist new government in 1977 to create a fiscal crisis of the state. The electoral troubles for labor, losing power in 1977 for the first time, prompted the shift to the private-sector, promarket forces within the coalition, with other ministries competing with defense (Barnett, 1996). Whereas Barnett (1996) argued that Israel shifted from an Asian developmental state to a Latin American clientelist state in the 1980s, Barkey pointed out the resilience of the autonomous state in pushing through the stabilization plan of 1985. Compared to Argentina,

"The Israeli state did not have to confront entrenched interests ready to veto reform attempts through unconstitutional means if necessary." (Barkey, 1994, p. 55)

Into the space created by this disembedding of the state from the Histadrut, and to some extent from big business, stepped a series of new institutions (described in the previous section) supporting the new high-tech–led industrial development regime. In many respects, however, the new policy regime is

"not necessarily replacing or directly attacking old features and norms but is struggling to take its place alongside them." (Levi-Faur, 2000, p. 170)

The structure of elite interests has been transformed, however:

"If the second generation of the LSM [Labor Settlement Movement] elite . . . made their careers in the various public bureaucracies, the third generation, those who have come of age after 1967, were drawn to the private sector. At the same time, increased economic opportunities opened up new avenues of mobility for individuals from social strata outside the LSM. In this new environment, business executives, even of government- or Histadrut-owned corporations, could make themselves autonomous by raising equity through the newly opened private venues. They have been the principal champions of economic liberalization and of the integration of Israel's economy with the world market through the reduction of tariff and administrative barriers." (Shafir and Peled, 2000, p. 9)

The analysis of developmental-state regime changes demonstrates the power of the global economy. Transformations in the world system exert powerful pressures on each political economy, and those economies most reliant on foreign investment find themselves significantly constrained by that dependence. Each case considered in this chapter benefited from a favorable geopolitical relationship to the

United States and, in many cases, received extensive financial aid. Crucially, however, this aid was channeled through the state, reinforcing its position in the domestic polity. However, this power of the global economy is not determining – the analysis shows too that there is significant room for politics. Transformations of the global economy are shaped by local and national strategies and there is also significant variation in the developmental outcomes within a particular world-historical period. Each case country built a different set of connections and each remains shaped by those connections. The most "successful" cases of high-tech development at the end of the 1990s – Taiwan and Israel – were not the least connected. They were the economies that avoided dependence on TNCs – unlike Ireland and Singapore – and the worst of financial liberalization – unlike Korea. They built institutions that have enabled them to connect more profitably to the global economy and to continue to promote industrial development within those connections. Internationalization is a multifaceted process, incorporating a multitude of forms of participation in and connectedness to the global economy, which creates both constraints and opportunities for developmental projects.

Finally, the analysis suggests that a necessary (but not sufficient) condition for the emergence of network-state institutions is the presence of a political and institutional space within the polity that is neither crowded out by existing networks nor fragmented by clientelism or antistatism. This is most likely to occur during a crisis in a system with well-established state institutions, creating spaces within a relatively cohesive institutional framework. In Israel, liberalization undermined the existing coalition. In Taiwan, this space existed due to the disjuncture between state and society from early in its contemporary economic development. Although this space allows network institutions to emerge, it does not mean that it will occur at any particular historical juncture. This depends on the emergence of a new alliance between state and society that is able to institutionalize itself sufficiently rapidly to avoid attack from existing institutional actors. Often, the emerging alliances will turn to international ties to buttress their early development, avoiding the need to compete with local and national actors. The development of the international IT industry made it a likely source of such international resources and offered possibilities for new alliances with the emergence of new sectors and new classes. In Taiwan, Israel, and Ireland, transnational technical communities emerged as the basis of the new regime, although incorporated into each political economy in a somewhat different way.

Labor exclusion and subordination has been a central feature of most of the developmental states. DNSs in the 1990s often reincorporated labor but primarily through technical communities of transnational professionals, rather than as the national representatives of the labor force as a whole. Once again, dilemmas of inequality become central to the contemporary politics of the DNS. Although the Taiwanese and Israeli cases are clearer success stories, the Irish case represents a particularly intriguing case for other political economies around the world. Under those conditions, it suggests that network institutions can emerge and promote development even in an unpromising context such as that in Ireland in the 1980s – high national debt, dependence on FDI, and rampant clientelism and corruption. Those are the unpromising conditions facing many political economies attempting to build developmental coalitions to deal with the exclusions and exploitations of the globalization project. But even if such states emerge and can promote forms of network development, they are increasingly integrated into an international system of Global Post-Fordism. What are the dynamics of this system and what implications do they hold for different forms of state developmentalism? Those are the questions of the final section of this chapter.

STATE DEVELOPMENTALISMS AND THE CONTEMPORARY WORLD SYSTEM

Developmental states are caught up in the world economy in complex and sometimes contradictory ways. They face challenges of dependency and late industrialization, while at the same time navigating complex geopolitical waters as successful capitalist development disturbs existing domestic and international patterns of conflict and compromise. Ultimately, state developmentalisms are constrained by the world system and are also a critical element in its historical transformations. The Asian Tigers illustrate the point. Facing enormous challenges of late industrialization and dependency, the Asian Tigers benefited from a geopolitical position of importance to the United States in its struggles with China and the USSR (Cumings, 1987) and from the dominant "development project" discourse (McMichael, 1996). Both security and development politics in the 1950s and 1960s facilitated a role for the state and, whereas domestic institutional and political conditions were also in place, the stage was set for rapid development of the Asian Miracle.

It is a mistake, however, to read this history as the emergence of state developmentalisms within the constraints of world-system dynamics. As we have seen, the international and domestic politics of capitalism shapes patterns of state developmentalism profoundly, but the regimes that emerge contain important "recombinant" institutional and political innovations that cannot be simply read off from their founding conditions. Furthermore, the accumulation of such innovations can transform the world system. The rise of East Asian firms in global capitalism and the intensification of global competition have been crucial features of contemporary global capitalism.[1] In particular, the decline of manufacturing employment in the core was driven not only, or even primarily, by foreign investment and capital flight but also by the rise of East Asian competition in those sectors. The influence of the Asian Tigers went further, promoting a new model of the social organization of work and business, based on teams and "relational contracting" and promoted desperately around the world in a process of "Japanization" of business organization.

---

1   It is a mistake, however, to see market competition as the driving force of contemporary capitalism, neglecting its interaction with broader social structural patterns of regulation and accumulation (see e.g. Brenner, 2002)

The East Asian competitive challenge also drew a policy response from the embattled U.S. economic policy regime. Caught between more intense global competition and the increasing effectiveness of labor unions to make wage gains at home, the U.S. state faced a crisis of profitability and legitimacy (Arrighi and Silver, 2001; Krippner, 2003). This crisis was intensified by declining U.S. hegemony in the world system, the very hegemony that facilitated the rise of the Asian Tigers (Arrighi and Silver, 2001). The tax cuts of the Reagan years produced massive deficits and the U.S. state began to actively promote a distinctive path through the fiscal crisis – the financialization of the economy and the attraction of foreign capital to enable the U.S. to postpone the difficult political choices it faced (Krippner, 2003). Drawing on an already established managerial concept of the firm as a collection of financial assets (Fligstein, 1990), a financial boom was engineered to avoid the difficulties caused by U.S. weaknesses in production and social reproduction.

States, networks, and the "Glocal" IT industry

It is the interaction between global production systems and an increasingly liberalized Anglo-American financial system that is the context for DNS strategies. Unable to harness financial capital as South Korea and Japan had done, they have instead attempted to build durable regional economies that can better sustain the shocks of the financial bubbles in this system, while capitalizing on boom periods such as the late 1990s. The financialization of the economy has been further intensified in IT because financial bubbles are historically characteristic of the period of emergence of new techno-economic paradigms (Perez, 2002). This is a profoundly unstable system because the promotion of financialization and markets through the globalization project (McMichael, 1996) threatens to cannibalize the very foundations of the IT economy. DNSs are caught in a highly contradictory relationship to this global regime – while promoting integration into global financial and product markets, they also seek to embed those markets in local and national contexts that can sustain production and innovation, protecting them from the corrosive effect of marketization and financialization (Lundvall et al., 2002; Polanyi, 1944). DBSs and DNSs continue to play a central role in sustaining the global IT industry, even as they are faced with new dilemmas due to their participation in this glocal regime.

The basis of U.S. industrial leadership in the 1980s was increasingly shaky because the most basic requirements of the industry – a steady supply of educated labor and a "world-class" production capacity – were in danger of not being met within the United States. The number of graduates with computing degrees fell steadily from the mid-1980s and U.S. production quality had fallen dramatically behind the East Asian economies in the 1980s. Nonetheless, in the 1990s, the United States was reinstated at the center of a global social structure of accumulation in the IT industry, building on the very successes of East Asia that challenged U.S. commercial hegemony in the 1980s. U.S. industry has been able to avail of extensive government investments in technical education around the world through the migration of skilled labor and degree-level students, and global production networks in East Asia have enabled the U.S. industry to piggyback on the state-sponsored advances in production capabilities within that region.

Saxenian (1999, p. 10) pointed out that in 1965, only forty-seven scientists and engineers immigrated to the United States from Taiwan, but in 1967 – two years after the Immigration Act liberalizing immigration from non-European countries – 1,321 did so. This was further boosted by a 1990 act that almost tripled the annual quota of visas based on occupational skills. Of the Silicon Valley labor force, 24 percent was foreign-born in 1990, rising to 29 percent in high-tech industries and 32 percent of engineers. Two thirds of the foreign-born are Asian, with the majority from India or China, especially Taiwan. There was a huge increase in the number of Chinese students receiving doctorates in the United States in the 1990s, whereas the numbers from India, Taiwan, and South Korea remained relatively stable. The United States benefited greatly, therefore, from direct migration of educated labor, as well as from the subsidy by foreign governments of the earlier education of a high proportion of doctoral students in science and engineering. Of course, if those students return to their home countries, they also provide a certain subsidy to their home economy because their higher education has been underpinned in part by the U.S. state and higher-education sector. Regardless of the financial calculus, however, non–U.S. labor has been critical to U.S. high-tech growth and immigration has solved an enormous problem of labor supply to which the decentralized and inegalitarian structure and politics of U.S. education was ill placed to respond.

The contribution of the Asian states goes beyond labor supply, however. In the 1980s, the American strategy of focusing on cost reduction through offshore production rather than on technological leadership engendered harsh criticism as the consumer segment of the U.S. electronics industry went into steep decline. Believing that U.S. firms were locked into this "low-road" system of production, many commentators argued that the U.S. electronics industry was in a terminal condition as it lost its position in one segment after another (Borrus, 1997). By the 1990s, however, it became clear that the U.S. electronics industry was undergoing a revival that was only in part due to the difficulties of Japanese firms. Japanese firms had built hierarchical international production networks – reflecting their successful domestic production strategies. American firms, by contrast, entered into alliances with increasingly sophisticated suppliers, often through the kinds of local strategies for upgrading described previously. In addition to generating local industrial upgrading in the newly industrializing economies that could successfully forge such alliances, this had the surprising consequence of revitalizing American industry in a number of product areas, and – in the process – intensifying the competitive pressures on Japanese firms (Borrus, 1997). The U.S. firms came to rely heavily on the production capabilities and technological sophistication of suppliers in the China Circle, Singapore, and South Korea – enabling American firms to lower costs, improve turnaround times, and escape dependence on Japanese suppliers who were also their competitors. However, the new suppliers are also potential competitors, suggesting a new axis of global competition with a geographical shift from Japan to the China Circle and an organizational shift from competing hierarchies to competing global networks (Arrighi and Silver, 2001; Borrus, 1997). This is all the more critical given that "first-tier suppliers" or "turnkey contract manufacturers," operating relatively autonomously, have come to occupy a critical position in global production networks (Sturgeon, 1999). Sturgeon also suggested that these production networks are increasingly taking on a "merchant" character such that the networks can be broken and reassembled relatively easily and quickly because the lead U.S. firms have reasserted control over the key technology and marketing functions. The long-term "relational contracting" of Japanese firms (Dore, 1983) is less central to those networks than to the Japanese networks that had been the basis of its industrial success. The U.S. high-tech industry has increasingly and effectively integrated East Asian production networks into its own global operations. Indeed, this contribution of Asian economies in production has, in some cases, extended to the realm of innovation where U.S. and Asian high-tech firms and regions are increasingly linked through both interfirm alliances and "transnational technical communities" (Saxenian, 1999).

The U.S. system of innovation, therefore, has been supported by its own state's political protection and the investment of other states in developing skilled labor and strong institutionalized production networks. This is the flip side of the vaunted U.S. system of innovation in which high rates of entry and exit, along with quick movement into and out of new technological fields, can generate high rates of entrepreneurship, sustained in large part through active capital markets (Storper, 1997). The entrepreneurship and private associationalism of the U.S. system are increasingly integrated with and dependent on transnational connections.

High-tech entrepreneurship has been internationalized. Saxenian reported that in 1998, 24 percent of Silicon Valley firms had an Indian or Chinese CEO, suggesting a very high (and probably underestimated) rate of entrepreneurship among those groups (1999, p. 23). This percentage has increased over time, with 13 percent of the firms started between 1980 and 1984 compared to 29 percent of those started between 1995 and 1998 having Indian or Chinese CEOs (1999, p. 24). This is likely stimulated in part by the glass-ceiling effect suggested by the slow progress of nonwhites from professional to managerial occupations. Although Indian and Chinese immigrants in Silicon Valley are highly educated, with more than 70 percent having a bachelor's degree or (usually) more, they are more heavily concentrated in professional than in managerial occupations. Among whites, the ratio between professional and managerial occupations is 1:1; for Indians, it is 1:3 and for Chinese it is 1:2.5 (Saxenian, 1999, p. 18). The incentive for a significant amount of the entrepreneurship in Silicon Valley can be traced in part not to the "openness" of the U.S. system, therefore, but to its partial closure. Immigrant entrepreneurs rely heavily on a wide variety of ethnic professional associations in Silicon Valley that provide valuable mentoring, information, and networks to people with extensive resources, including significant venture capital (Saxenian, 1999). Chinese and Indian high-tech professionals operate across a complex set of overlapping local and transnational networks, within and across ethnic boundaries. In the process, they add a valuable dimension to the vibrant regional economies of places such as Silicon Valley – as the once-closed military–industrial complex becomes inextricably linked to transnational capital and labor.

Mowery (2001) argued that there has been a gradual shift from U.S. technological hegemony in 1950 to a global multipolar system of innovation, extending first to Europe, then Japan, and now even to a select number of newly industrializing countries. The major change in this system in the late 1980s and early 1990s was the rise of levels of foreign investment in the United States to the levels that existed in Europe for quite some time. Foreign investment in R&D has remained almost constant as a share of total U.S. R&D spending and the early stages of innovation are the least internationalized, so that overseas operations tend to be focused on exploiting existing technologies. On the other hand, foreign firms now engage with U.S. firms through a wider variety of channels of internationalization of innovation (i.e., patenting, licensing, alliances). Taken together, these developments have seen a new relationship between TNCs and certain regions:

"Specific sites become centers for specific technological competences and attract considerable investments by multinational firms in R&D and often production" because of "the growing returns to specialization in specific technological activities or competences, some apparent decline in 'scope economies' among specific competences . . . and the increased international dispersion of these competences." (Mowery, 2001, p. 151)

Challenged by the Asian Tigers since the 1970s, the success of U.S. regions such as Silicon Valley rests only partly on regional dynamics of innovation and growth. It is the intersection of those regional dynamics with financialization of the economy through the attraction of foreign capital, the struggle for control over global production networks, and the international promotion of institutional environments favorable to the United States that explains the boom – and, indeed, the bust – of the IT industry in the past ten years.

Dilemmas of development in a glocal economy

These characteristics of the global IT industry have created dilemmas for developmental states, as DBSs have seen their national coalitions fractured and DNSs have been subject to massive increases in inequality. The highly concentrated industrial structure and capacity to mobilize large investments – which had been strengths of the Korean industrial system in markets such as memory-chip production – were now liabilities in rapidly changing markets such as PCs and software, in which network connections were often as critical as large in-firm investments (Dedrick and Kraemer, 1998). Anchordoguy's (2000) analysis of Japan's difficulties in software can be extended to Korea. She argued that Japan's reliance on state targeting, centralized business groups, bank-centered financing, weak intellectual property, and production engineering – so crucial to its success in mechanical engineering, steel, semiconductors, and computer hardware – were liabilities in the networked world of software design (we might add personal computers, data communications, and information services). Furthermore, its successes in IT had brought Korea to the edge of technology development in only a few areas – in most cases, the success of Korean firms remained based on OEM rather than on their own design, marketing, or branding (Evans, 1995; Hobday, 1995)

"In short, the Korean industry, despite its well-deserved world renown, was not immune from the self-doubts and second thoughts that were the rule in Brazil and India. On the one hand, Korea was not sure that it had really constructed the kind of industry that it needed for long-run development. . . . On the other hand, not even commercial success could be taken for granted" (Evans, 1995, p. 178)

All this was brought to a head in the late 1990s by the Asian financial crisis. The Korean state underwrote a system of business financing that enabled huge investments through massive debt-to-equity ratios, sometimes as high as 7:1 (i.e., for Samsung). Whereas in the 1980s, those were guaranteed government loans, in the 1990s, similar debt-to-equity ratios were based on international loans. This disembedding of the *chaebol* from the financial institutions of the developmental regime created disastrous results in the financial crisis of 1997–98 (Wade and Veneroso, 1998). The high-debt model of the Korean firms was undermined by the inflow of much less patient foreign capital (Biggart, 1998). More broadly, this also reflected the declining power of the state to influence increasingly powerful and internationalized firms that had turned more often to international financial speculation and accumulation as they had become disembedded from the national developmental coalition – using the same financial resources built up by that regime to disembed themselves (Chibber, 2002; Wade and Veneroso, 1998; also see Gao, 2001, on similar dynamics within the Japanese political economy).

A balance of class and state forces had enabled the paradigmatic DBS to emerge in the 1960s in Korea and had sustained the rapid growth in the following three decades under the hierarchical guidance of a closely connected set of state and chaebol elites. It was now being undermined by the clash between its own institutions and the opportunities for disembedding offered to large corporations by the increasingly globalized and speculative world economy. Korea remained one of the fastest-growing economies in the world at the end of the 1990s, even after the disasters of 1997–98, but a deep ambiguity shrouded the developmental bureaucraticism that had once presented a sure façade to the world economy and those who study it.

Singapore, too, has shifted its strategies to attempt to build an alliance with local technical communities that can serve as the basis of a local system of innovation. There is little indication of political or economic liberalization in Singapore, unlike in Korea and Taiwan, but the promotion of an indigenous technical–professional class is likely to spur on such processes (Huff, 1999; Rahim, 1998). Huff (1999) pointed out that, because it relies on FDI, Singapore still lacks a strong local middle class that elsewhere provides the basis of increasing opposition to the state and promotes democratization. Middle-class timidity is also strongly fostered by the Singapore state's emphasis on autonomy and reputation at the expense of genuine political participation and individual initiative. This has made Singapore remarkably disciplined and efficient but, more importantly, through discouraging creativity and risk-taking, it has seriously weakened within Singaporean society the mainspring of productivity growth. From a somewhat different perspective, the ultimately successful developmental state depends on a balance between autonomy and embeddedness. With insufficient quantity of the latter, "projects that engage the energy and intelligence of business cannot be constructed" (Huff, 1999, p. 239). The question for the DBS of Singapore is whether the measures to promote participation within the essentially state-dominated society and economy will be sufficient to elicit the participation of the nascent technical class. If not, efforts to improve total productivity and promote innovation are likely to founder. But if the state opens up an institutional and political space for the new middle class, it may undermine its own distinctive combination of FDI and statist development, reconciled through tight state control of savings and investment.

Taiwan has had perhaps the greatest success of the cases considered here in handling the contradictions of the contemporary global economy. The Taiwanese model is based on dense networks of firms that are often highly flexible but have problems of internal underinvestment and external bargaining power. The Taiwanese state has attempted to build large trading companies since the late 1970s as a response to those dilemmas – but these attempts have failed (Fields, 1995). Faced with competition from the state-owned enterprises and the business groups and with government fear of upsetting a delicate political balance, the efforts to increase scale in Taiwanese firms proved relatively weak and almost completely unsuccessful. However, the small scale of Taiwanese firms has not been a major issue within the economy, given their deep embeddedness in a variety of business and institutional networks that provide the resources that cannot be maintained within the firm. It is these institutional networks that enable the Taiwanese firms to avoid collapsing into fragmentation and the traps of low-skill subcontracting. The managed multiplicity of its international connections has prepared Taiwan well for the contemporary era of globalization and has enabled it to sidestep some although not all of the worst features of dependency. The state has also guarded its own position – particularly in relation to financial liberalization. Weiss (1999) argued that whereas in Korea, financial reform was seen as a way of cutting the knot between the state and the chaebol in a process of liberalization, in Taiwan persistent geopolitical pressures have kept state developmentalism alive. Isolation from international institutions only intensifies this situation. Taiwan saw a steadying "opening" of the financial system but always monitored by the state – in the stock market the state promoted local participation before foreign investors were allowed in so that the influx of foreign capital would not destabilize the market (Weiss, 1999). This stands in clear contrast to the difficulties created by the liberalization of capital flows in Korea.

The greatest dilemmas facing the DNS of Taiwan are inequality and geopolitics, both of them linked to the incorporation of the society and economy into a variety of global networks. The commitment to egalitarianism in the Taiwanese model will be more difficult to maintain when economic fortunes are determined through participation in local–global connections, with a new technological elite increasingly threatening to "pull away" from the rest of Taiwanese society. In addition, its close ties to the United States and China are a source of both strength for Taiwan and vulnerability as relations between the United States and China fluctuate, in ways that are largely beyond Taiwan's control. Although the DNS in Taiwan forged a highly successful economic-development trajectory in the 1990s, it remains to be seen whether its social and political consequences can be managed as effectively.

Israel and Ireland have both faced rapidly rising inequality, at least partly as a consequence of the DNS development strategy; this challenge was discussed extensively in the Irish case in Chapters 3 and 7. Israel also faces great difficulties in incorporating a dynamic high-tech sector into the national economy through what remains of its centralized corporatist institutions. In the Israeli case, a further factor is the interaction of economic globalization and the faltering peace process. Shafir (1999) argued that the growing autonomy of the business community after 1985 in Israel created a new actor, which pushed for progress in the peace process in the interests of smooth participation in the global economy. Peacemaking and liberalization were deeply interconnected as recasting the conflict in terms of an obstacle to globalization opened up room for a non–zero-sum view of the conflict that was impossible as long as it was conceived only in national terms (Shafir and Peled, 2000). Throughout the 1990s, Israel experienced a tenuous virtuous circle of industrial resurgence, economic growth, and a deepening peace process. However, the assassination of Rabin and a series of electoral defeats for the Labor Party has combined with the recent U.S. "War on Terrorism" to legitimate a backlash against the agenda of "economic globalization and peace" as the strong security state was able to reassert itself, undermining the peace process. It remains to be seen whether the elites that support the Israeli DNS are willing to promote peace in the interests of globalization as avidly as they have promoted globalization in the interests of peace.

This study has shown that DNSs are emerging as states scramble to derive new strategies and institutions in the face of globalization, postindustrialism, and financialization. Even as DBSs struggle in the face of Post-Fordist production and the internationalization of capital, the DNS builds its strategy around the fostering and reconciliation of the local Post-Fordist networks with global capital. The developmental state reconstitutes its own territoriality to mediate between local and global, promoting the emergence of a glocal state (Brenner, 1998, 1999).

However, DNSs have shifted away from the challenge posed by the DBS to existing models of capitalism. They focus on ways of integrating indigenous innovation institutions with the dominant international innovation and financing systems. Most critically, this involves integrating national and regional systems with the system of innovation in the leading regions of the United States and the markets for capital in Silicon Valley and Wall Street. The success of Japan and Korea caused panic in the United States and those economies are currently being disciplined by the "Wall Street-Treasury-IMF Complex" for their cheekiness. The new DNSs of Ireland, Israel, and Taiwan complement their indigenous strengths in innovation with a deeper integration into globalized capital and labor flows, which allows them to avoid such confrontations. They do not challenge the U.S. economy but rather seek to cooperate in extending it transnationally. Even though the role of the state is different than in the United States, at the firm level every effort is made to ensure organizational isomorphism and compatibility with the leading U.S. firms and financial institutions. The emergence of these new Asian Tigers is at the same time the consolidation of the internationalization of the U.S. model of capitalism. In that process of consolidation, however, a social embedding of the economy is constantly at work, creating new social relations and institutions that are the basis of future unpredictable and contested transformations. The final chapter considers what transformations might emerge from the contradictions and dilemmas of contemporary state developmentalism.

11

FUTURES OF THE NETWORK STATE

POLITICS AND THE MAKING OF THE GLOBAL INFORMATION ECONOMY

Market fundamentalists have argued their case loudest just as its shaky foundations have been most clearly exposed. Rising inequality, exploitation, and exclusion have shown the claim of global markets to provide widespread prosperity to be hollow. In the United States, bastion of the market, financial speculation and corporate crime accompanied by ballooning executive compensation have shown up the failure of markets for corporate control to provide genuine accountability.

The "dot.com" boom, and the ICT sector more generally, was the shining jewel in the crown of the market fundamentalists. Driven on by entrepreneurial innovation, financial markets, and telecommunications liberalization, the ICT sector was said to be the leading sector of the "new economy," leading growth and driving organizational change. But as the ICT boom has faded to widespread layoffs and industry consolidation, a tension has been exposed within the new economy between the social structures that sustain innovation and the financialization that cannibalizes those social foundations (Lundvall et al., 2002). This current crisis does not spell the end of the "information age," which is surely only in its early infancy (Freeman and Louca, 2002). It does expose some of the contradictions at the core of the market fundamentalist vision of the information economy, a vision made real in the 1990s by the Washington Consensus.

But underneath this mythology of the market, the making of the global information economy rests on very different underpinnings. The ICT sector was forged out of a series of historical class compromises between capital and technical communities, embedded within a variety of state developmentalisms. After World War II, the computer industry was created through a U.S.–led military developmentalism in which the state served as both the primary investor in R & D and the major market for high-tech goods. Embedded within national Keynesian economies, those forms of state developmentalism created global firms and a new ICT industry.

Those global firms were challenged in the 1970s and 1980s by firms supported by the DBSs of East Asia, protecting and financing their business groups while pushing them toward improved export performance. Network developmentalism was built on the foundations of the global production system and fostered by the interaction of global firms and emergent economies. DNSs created a network of global regions by shaping firm culture and practices, supporting innovation, and creating local associational infrastructure. The global information economy existed not in a disembedded global market but rather was deeply embedded in a variety of historically and politically constructed social structures of innovation and accumulation.

CONTRADICTION AND CHOICE IN THE CELTIC TIGER

The Celtic Tiger economy was built from within the global production networks, with state and social forces combining to build a global region within the transnational flows of capital, labor, and technology. Ireland had long pursued a policy of foreign investment and free trade, but it was only when a new development regime emerged that emphasized local structures of innovation that the conditions for indigenous upgrading and employment growth were put in place. In the spaces between a persistent political clientelism and continuing reliance on foreign investment, a state–society alliance fostered an improved local basis for innovation and local and national social-partnership institutions provided a dense layer of new deliberative public institutions.

Market theorists see the state as setting the environment for firms, warning of dire consequences of rent-seeking and clientelism if state agencies go beyond this market-creating role. However, the state in Ireland has been more deeply involved: mobilizing resources, shaping firm culture and practices, defining the industry, "making winners," shaping forms of global integration, and creating associational infrastructure. State agencies are an ever-present part of the daily life of high-technology industry in Ireland and have carved out a policy regime from within a hostile environment of national state reliance on foreign investment and international monitoring of state aid. The Irish case is not a development model to be swallowed whole, but rather offers provocative insights into how state and society continue to be crucial to economic life, even in an era and a sector in which the "globalization project" of the market fundamentalists held full sway. The experience of development in Ireland poses the Polanyian dilemma of the tension between market society and the always embedded economy in stark terms – but it is out of this contradiction between market and society that political choices emerge.

The Irish story is most often read as a case of foreign-investment–led growth and it would be ludicrous to argue that FDI is not central to the economy. However, this is not the critical point to be taken from the story of the Celtic Tiger. To the extent that the FDI boom is part of the story, it is in many important respects impossible to replicate across more than a small number of economies. Furthermore, the FDI boom of the late 1990s is just as likely to have been driven by upgraded local capacities as local upgrading is to have emerged from linkages to foreign firms. The lessons of the Irish case relate to the emergence of a global region from within a policy regime focused on FDI – the more significant industrial upgrading and innovation in Israel and Taiwan show what more can be achieved once innovation networks are emphasized, rather than attracting FDI.

The Irish software industry emerged first and foremost from a dynamic of growth sustained by state and social embedding of global market connections. It was only after this developmental dynamic was in place in the late 1990s that global finance entered the industry. However, the Irish system lacks an account of its own success that recognizes this state and social embedding, rendering it politically vulnerable to the populist neoliberalism of the current government. Weakening the tax base and cutting spending, party politics threatens to undermine the institutions that have sustained indigenous innovation and growth – just as continued investment could solidify those institutional foundations. The orthodox reading of the current decline in growth rates in Ireland is that economic growth has created wage pressures that have fueled the highest rate of inflation in the EU, damaging "competitiveness" and slashing growth rates. This has come at the same time as a downturn in the international and particularly the U.S. economy, which has reduced foreign investment (although inflows have still been substantial). The orthodox answer is to maintain (or restore) wage restraint and sustain cost competitiveness.

But the diagnosis and the cure are mistaken. The current economic difficulties in Ireland fundamentally reflect the dilemmas of managing a development transition from a low-wage to a high-wage economy – industrial upgrading has become not just a motor of development, however incomplete, but also now a necessity. The difficulties of the Irish economy are less a matter of "competitiveness" than of the failure to build a deeper and more inclusive form of autocentric development around the DNS. As noted in Chapter 3, wage competitiveness is of uneven importance in the Irish economy. The most dynamic high-tech sectors either rely more heavily on tax breaks than low wages or have never had the benefit of wage restraint and have seen rapidly rising wages outside the partnership agreements throughout the 1990s. On the other hand, wages have remained too low in many services sectors and it is perverse to call for further restraint. Where wage restraint has been most important is in the least sophisticated sectors of Irish industry and in managing the public-sector pay bill to assist in reducing public debt. Simply calling for "wage restraint" cannot address the complexities of the variety of upgrading strategies required in different sectors and the politics of balancing those sectoral differences within the national political economy.

Focused on a narrow concept of cost competitiveness, the neoliberal strategy will undermine this necessary upgrading. Figure 11.1 shows a potentially vicious circle of declining investment, rising inequality, and – ultimately – the weakening of co-ordination capacities and the social basis of the knowledge economy (i.e., the social reproduction of labor and of relations of learning). Nonetheless, this is the strategy that the current government has pursued: cutting back on public spending (already

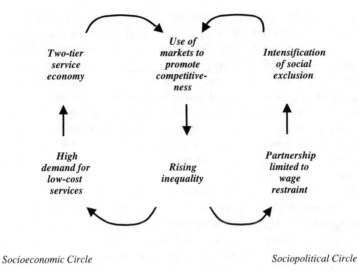

Figure 11.1. The Vicious Circle of Neoliberal Cost Competitiveness

at a remarkable low proportion of GDP) and, in the process, undermining the very institutions that have had important developmental impacts in the Celtic Tiger.

The reduction in the numbers of young people in the population has been taken as an opportunity for cost-cutting in education rather than a chance to implement smaller class sizes and other forms of educational development. Reduction in funding for research undermined the stability of the network of innovation institutions just as a new set of institutions was being established. Commercialization and cutbacks have, for example, combined to threaten the CSE. With reduced public funding in recent years, the cutbacks in funding to DCU have left the CSE in deep financial trouble and facing closure or management buyout. Despite wide university and industry recognition of the important role played by the CSE in developing the software industry, a critical part of the institutional infrastructure of the software industry is undermined by the priority put on cost-containment over collective investment. More broadly, students in primary and secondary schools walked out of their classes in 2003 to protest the increasingly poor physical condition of their school buildings.

The "competition state" is certainly a part of the Irish political economy, but such strategies undermine rather than promote "competitiveness." The combination of neoliberalism and populism of the current Fianna Fáil/Progressive Democrat government is ultimately at odds with the interests of the new developmental coalitions that have emerged around the indigenous innovation institutions. It is unclear, however, to what extent this nascent developmental coalition has a coherent sense of its own foundations or how significant a political force it is likely to become in defending those foundations.

This mirrors the tensions within the global information economy where financialization in the industry core in the United States has undermined social spending and threatened the reproduction of labor and organizational capabilities in the industry. The globalization project has been not so much about the spread of free markets in and of themselves but more about the securing of those assets through financial markets, foreign investment, and selective migration policies. Even as the U.S. state sucked huge amounts of capital out of the rest of the world economy in the 1990s (Silver and Arrighi, 2002), it also increasingly came to depend on the investments of other states in their labor and organizational development. The debates in Ireland regarding the policies and institutions that might sustain development through the knowledge-based economy are just one element of a larger politics of the social conditions and state strategies that can create a sustainable global information economy with an ever-broadening base of users and producers. The global information economy will continue to be critically shaped by the changing forms of capital, states, and technical communities and the sociopolitical compromise that emerges glocally among them.

Although financialization threatens the social embedding of the economy, successful development strategies can be undertaken that limit the effects and that emphasize the interdependence of society and economy (Lundvall et al., 2002). Figure 11.2 outlines the potential virtuous circle of the socially embedded economy in the Irish case.

The thrust of the model outlined in Figure 11.2 is toward the deepening of social partnership and the reversal of the trend toward greater inequality. Central to this is the system of innovation, which, broadly conceived (Lundvall, et al. 2002), is a critical institutional mechanism for influencing the overall structure of occupations, characteristics of jobs, and labor markets. Autocentric development under National Fordism rested on a relatively egalitarian occupational and wage distribution – conditions that have recently been eroded. However, the occupational and employment differences were historically created, not technologically determined. The system of innovation can be a crucial mechanism for shaping employment conditions and egalitarian access to education and employment while simultaneously providing for learning organizations and increased labor supply.

There is no reason to accept that the information economy is inherently unequal – the rising inequality of the past decades has been driven by a variety of political trends and has been avoided in other successful informational economies such as Finland (Castells and Himanen, 2003). In the informational sectors, it has been increased by the individualist organization of informational careers and labor markets, the devaluing of the collective character of informational work and narrowing what counts as knowledge, and the restriction of the role of users of technology in technical design (Ó Riain, 2002). Informational work is, in fact, deeply collective and the most successful high-tech "global regions" operate through broad and overlapping communities of producers and users and extensive collective investment in knowledge and knowledge workers. These conditions are common to the most dynamic sectors of the Celtic Tiger, the regional system of Silicon Valley and its global networks, and the Scandinavian information societies – even if realized in different ways. Establishing an innovation system that was built around those premises, and resisting the U.S. temptation to simply commercialize knowledge, would be a critical step in promoting a more egalitarian and democratic form of autocentric development. As Figure 11.2 shows, it could be the basis of reducing inequality and deepening democratic participation.

THREE FUTURES OF THE DEVELOPMENTAL NETWORK STATE

The developmental state – whichever form it takes – is not a "solution" to those dilemmas of capitalist globalization, now or in previous similar historical periods. Capitalist development is a dynamic process, constantly throwing out new and different dilemmas. But neither is state developmentalism just chasing capitalism, condemned to simply become a "competition state." Developmental statism is best seen as a vital terrain of the politics of capitalism – if it promotes capitalist social relations, it also contains many of the state and social institutions that continue to embed market processes. By promoting capitalist development, developmental states render themselves vulnerable to the very neoliberal policies that undermine them. On the other hand, by embedding those same processes in social institutions, developmental states make real the possibility of embedding market relations within expanded social rights. The political battle between neoliberalism and social democracy is cast more clearly, then, in the successful developmental state.

This is a necessary but risky politics for progressives, always risking the ascendancy of neoliberalism even while strengthening the social and institutional basis of the economy (which is typically hollowed out by underdevelopment). DNSs have often promoted inequality, making the case for building social rights around developmentalism more urgent. But it is a particularly difficult task in the contemporary era. Social-democratic regimes of the postwar "Golden Age" were able to use the dynamics of relatively coherent national societies and economies to support their goals of social solidarity and national Keynesian economic growth (Mjoset, 1992). But in an era of Global Post-Fordism, the DNS has no such advantage – those solidarities and growth feedbacks must be politically constructed and maintained across multiple spatial scales and interlocking sociopolitical regimes. Politics becomes more crucial rather than less, but also more difficult.

Table 11.1 outlines three potential futures that might be built around the institutions of the network state. The three futures correspond in some respects to Esping-Andersen's (1990) "three worlds of welfare capitalism" with a neoliberal model based on high levels of commodification and social reproduction through the market; a conservative model based on state support of an elite of workers in a two-tier system and social reproduction through the family; and a social-democratic model with high levels of universalism and state-supported social reproduction (Esping-Andersen, 1990, 1999).

Each case is compatible with network development. The neoliberal model is the most obvious: many have analyzed the rise of the entrepreneurial state and

Table 11.1. Three Futures of the Network State

	Neoliberal Network State	Conservative Network State	Social Democratic Network State
Work and Inequality	High rewards to private investment in "human capital"	High rewards to unequal public investment	Socializing knowledge and technical communities
Risk and Security	Individualized portfolio of benefits	Two-tier welfare state	Flexibility within universalism
Governance	Free markets, strong states	Solidarity without equality; uneven extent of social partnership	Decentralized institutions within encompassing social partnership
: National	Prison-informational complex	Accountable autonomy of state institutions	Democratic deliberation in a participatory society
: International	Securing the rights of capital; permanent war to secure political legitimacy in face of social costs of neoliberalism	Negotiating within the world polity	Accountable multi level global governance

declining welfare spending as an inherently "neoliberal" model (Jessop, 2002). In an era of increasing mobility and inequality, the neoliberal solution is to individualize social benefits, making them portable and reducing "drag" on the market. In practice, however, social exclusion accompanies neoliberalism on a massive scale. In the United States, this has resulted in what many call the "prison-industrial complex" but what might be better called the "prison-informational complex" with a growing divide between the successful "information-based" sectors of the economy and the growing numbers of prisoners and others who have been oppressed and excluded by the liberal model. On a global scale, this punitive model extends to any populations that react violently to their exclusion from or oppression within the globalization project, as evidenced in contemporary U.S. foreign policy. Imprisonment at home and permanent war internationally serve important political functions – securing popular support even in the face of economic decline for neoliberal and neoconservative regimes such as that of Bush's White House in 2002–03. The neoliberal tendencies of the current Irish government have been reflected in its support of the war on Iraq, despite massive public opposition.

The "conservative" model relies more heavily on state support of sections of the population and their participation in the system of network development. Subsidized by state education, health, and other social spending, an elite of workers is able to combine the benefits of state and market, pulling away from the rest of the society that is supported (but at a lower level) by the state. The extreme exclusion found in the neoliberal model is less likely – what we find instead are institutional

forms of social partnership organized in a hierarchy that favors elite access to institutions of the state. Although notoriously difficult to categorize, the Irish case
conforms in many respects to such a model (Ó Riain and O'Connell, 2000).

Social-democratic models rely on a more democratic set of "partnership" institutions and on the socialization of technical communities. These are symbiotic with
the embedding of the high-mobility, network economy within a framework of universal benefits and rights. The benefits and rights are neither individually portable
and stratified as in neoliberalism, nor based on state elitism as in the conservative
model – they provide flexibility within universalist institutions. The Scandinavian
economies, with their high levels of universal provision of health care and child
care, secure employment and unemployment benefits, and centralized social partnership, have fostered their own highly successful technical communities. Having
begun by building "information societies" through extensive public provision of
technology and skills, those economies are now highly competitive in the "information economy." (Castells and Himanen, 2003). Social democracies are also
caught up in the tensions between markets and social embedding – in particular,
the attempt to reconstitute social democracy at the EU level is constantly in tension
with the market-building aspects of the EU project (Scharpf, 1999).

TOWARD SOCIAL RIGHTS IN THE DEVELOPMENTAL NETWORK STATE

Let us return briefly to the Celtic Tiger, then, to discuss in more detail the prospects
for building a social-rights state on the institutions of the DNS, as outlined in
Figure 11.2. What limitations and possibilities on future political strategies have

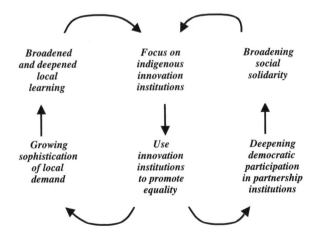

Socioeconomic Circle   *Sociopolitical Circle*

Figure 11.2. The Virtuous Circle of the Socially Embedded Economy

been created by the DNS in Ireland? Although the Celtic Tiger clearly promoted marketization, it simultaneously developed a dense network of deliberative institutions, linked across local, national, and global scales. Building the Schumpeterian export capacities of the economy does not in itself make social democracy unlikely – the Scandinavian social democracies were Schumpeterian exporting economies par excellence. The transition from developmental to social-democratic network state requires protecting social institutions from the market processes that they underpin, and transforming those institutions so that they become vehicles of universalism and inclusion and something more than carriers of capitalist development and industrial upgrading. Successful state developmentalism is a necessary but not a sufficient condition for such an expansion of social rights – it provides both the economic basis for the provision of universalist social rights and the institutional infrastructure that may be used to implement it. Developmental states can become the basis for reinvented social-rights regimes at local, national, and global scales – but whether they are thus transformed or simply become vehicles for mobilizing populations to be "competitive" depends on the strength and creativity of forces outside the state mobilizing for social rights through using, pressuring, and transforming the institutions of the developmental state. It is this politics that ultimately determines the future of the DNS. The following final sections, broken down along our dimensions of state developmentalism (see Chapters 2 and 9), briefly outline directions for the politics of a more egalitarian and democratic model of development "beyond the Celtic Tiger."

Strategies: socializing knowledge, building inclusionary systems of innovation

The DNS has promoted industrial upgrading in Ireland, although it can hardly be claimed that Ireland has yet escaped the perils of dependency. Nonetheless, a significant set of institutional capacities for supporting knowledge industries and technical communities has been established. These institutions have not, however, been used to tackle problems of inequality and exclusion in the information economy – whether along class, gender, racial, or other lines.

This is not inevitable. The relative institutional richness puts Irish society in a better position to tackle inequality than in the 1980s. Furthermore, there are compelling economic reasons to include previously excluded social groups within the information economy "project." Negotiating labor supply and skills shortages with industry provides state agencies with a golden opportunity – as yet ignored – to provide much stronger channels of inclusion into the economy. This will also involve transforming working conditions to address problems of long hours and insecurity while retaining the flexibility and autonomy of technical communities – simultaneously lessening some of the burdens of social reproduction that accumulated so rapidly in Ireland in the late 1990s (Ó Riain, 2002).

A more inclusionary system of innovation would not simply expand access to the existing system but would also be more open to varieties of knowledge. The Irish innovation system is cast narrowly around communities drawing almost entirely on highly technical knowledge. This creates a set of dominant understandings of the relation between technology and society that sees the logic of technology as dominating social relations. In building an information society, the hegemony of this technicist vision must be replaced with a view of technology as a social product, shaped by and dependent on social relations. Technical communities must be connected to other communities of discourse, breaking down the hierarchical relationship between "producers" and "users" of technology. Again, there are compelling economic justifications – any high-technology industry that can provide a new model of user involvement with technology will position itself at the front of the international technology industry and contribute to broader processes of autocentric development.

Institutions: democratizing embeddedness

The institutions of the DNS are more open to external influence than those of the DBS. Multiply embedded and externally accountable, institutional mechanisms exist for extensive external influence on the state institutions. However, these agencies – although public in many respects – are selectively embedded and accountable. External accountability in the DNS is real but unequal and elitist. Nonetheless, the institutions of innovation are supplemented by more broadly embedded and democratically deliberative institutions of local and national partnership (O'Donnell, 2000). These institutions only confirm a growing interest in emerging "networked" forms of public governance in the United States and elsewhere, incorporating new forms of accountability: in local government (Fung, 2001), welfare (Handler, 1996), and regional labor markets (Benner, 2002). Varley and Curtin (2001) show that local partnerships in Ireland – potential arenas for co-optation and clientelism – are also potential vehicles for legitimate claim-making by local communities. In many cases, these communities are cut off from the political and economic system and their only previous contact with the state was through being administered by its social-service agencies.

It is surprising, therefore, that there is little political mobilization around the institutions of partnership in Ireland – even though the social-partnership model has become the standard organizational model for public-policy deliberation in Ireland, partnerships have rarely been the focus of proposals or mobilizations regarding how they might be further democratized or reformed. Such a politics could build on yet another valuable set of institutional capacities that exist in Ireland today but had no counterpart in the 1980s before the Celtic Tiger phenomenon.

Autocentric development: flexibility and universalism

Finally, the strategies of inclusion and democratization must be firmly embedded within a well-resourced and universalist social-rights state (Block, 1994). Many observers have presented policies to promote inclusion and participation as substitutes for universalist social-rights provision. I have emphasized deeper forms of inclusion and democratization, and even those more developed social forms must be supported by a significant commitment to universalist social provision. Institutional mechanisms exist in Ireland to address the widespread experience of individualized labor-market insecurity by distributing the risks of flexibility collectively – drawing on existing elements of active labor-market policy, universalist components of the welfare state, and union representation. Ultimately, the progressive forces within the national state will have to assert themselves at the transnational level if they are to secure the future of local and national accountability of capital. At a minimum, "prudential regulations on capital mobility" (Wade, 1998) at the international level will be required. Here, the future development of the EU, uncertain as it is, will be crucial to reversing financialization and securing social rights.

The cooperative relations within technical communities in global regions ultimately must be supported by collective institutions if they are to persist. Collective institutions were crucial to the formation of those communities as governments, universities, and large firms played critical roles. The mobility of workers and learning across networks are, in fact, facilitated by regulation and social provision that provide security and mechanisms for collective decision-making regarding common problems. If such collective institutions assuring security of income and long-term learning can be strengthened, technical communities may emerge as an important alternative model of economic organization to increasing corporate dominance. Technical communities surrounded by state and union guarantees of security and located within egalitarian "information societies" are likely to prove more sustainable in the long term than the isolated elites tied to unstable capital markets in the United States. They would certainly be members of a better society.

Of course, much of what happens will depend on politics, which cannot wait for the perfect vision of hindsight. Developmental states expose more clearly the political choice between neoliberalism and social democracy. In a time when neoliberalism promises financial speculation, impoverishment, corporate criminality, and permanent war, the choice is clear between "social democracy and barbarism." The roads to social democracy will be uncertain and are likely to be surprising in a world of transformed technology, organization, and territory. Even as they promote capitalist globalization, DNSs offer both political choices and institutions with which those choices might be made. In the face of growing exploitation and militarization in an uncertain global order, a politics of equality and democracy is more necessary than ever.

Appendix A

METHODOLOGY OF THE STUDY

The research in this book is based on a series of research efforts, in the course of which various types of data were collected. This appendix briefly outlines the methodological approach of the study, describes the various research efforts that together constitute the book, and describes the specific data employed in the analysis.

METHODOLOGICAL APPROACH

This is a multimethod research project. However, the central methodological approach of the study is the use of a detailed ethnohistorical case study of the software industry as an entry point for investigating the space for local economic development and political shaping of development in the face of economic globalization. In essence, the research employed an "extended case method" (Burawoy, 1998): the growth of the software industry in Ireland was taken as an anomalous case for theories of globalization, which could not explain the emergence of such a dense local agglomeration under the guidance of the state. The task of explaining this anomaly became the basis for reformulating existing theories of globalization (as discussed in Chapter 2).

Although the case-study approach was the foundation of the study, I drew on various research methods and logics at different stages. I employed a "logic of variation" at times in the analysis, particularly with regard to establishing the salience of state intervention in shaping software firms (see especially Chapters 5 and 6). This was combined throughout with ethnographic data from documents and interviews that shed light on the precise character of this "state effect." In Chapter 10, a comparative approach is employed that seeks to explain diversity across cases that are analyzed as holistically as possible (Ragin, 1994). The case is the building block of this study. However, in addition to the case study of software and the Irish development regime, I employed a logic of variation to explain elements of the case and a comparative logic that extends and reformulates the theoretical framework across a broader range of cases. The research throughout proved to be a dialogue between the detailed exploration of cases and the reformulation of theory.

RESEARCH STRATEGIES

Research for the book was conducted in three main overlapping phases. Although each theme outlined in the following sections was pursued throughout, the emphasis of the project evolved as it progressed.

Software industry analysis, primary data gathered from 1995–1997

The central focus of this period of research was the intersection of local and global networks of production. Beginning in late 1995 in Silicon Valley, and through eleven months of research in Ireland in 1996 and 1997, I gathered various types of data on these topics.

A series of wide-ranging interviews was conducted with the following groups:

- managers and executives in indigenous companies (twenty-five interviews)
- managers and executives in multinational companies (twenty-seven interviews, ten of which were in Silicon Valley)
- software-development engineers at various stages of their careers (eight in Dublin, six in Silicon Valley; twenty interviews also conducted in Dublin for USTech case study described as follows).

I undertook an ethnographic case study in early 1997 of USTech (a false name used to protect the company's anonymity). The study lasted three months and was conducted with the permission and assistance of company management and the full knowledge of company employees (for a more detailed discussion, see Ó Riain, 2000b). The case study consisted of the following research methods:

- twelve weeks spent working as a technical writer on a software development team
- twenty interviews conducted with engineers and developers working in the company
- fifteen interviews with company managers
- attendance at fifteen team, department, and management meetings (not including meetings of the team on which the author worked)

Furthermore, I undertook a survey of the software industry that is described in detail at the end of this appendix.

Analysis of the development regime, primary data gathered
from 1997–2000

As it became clear that local networks had become central to Irish success, I pursued the question of the policy and institutional conditions that underpinned their emergence. This led me to the question of the state, which has been treated extensively in this book.

I interviewed individuals working in state agencies, universities, technology and innovation centers, industry associations, and related industry participants and observers (i.e., eighteen interviews in 1997 and twenty in the summer of 2000).

I have also gathered extensive documentary data, including most of the official reports issued regarding industrial development, science policy and the IT, and related industries over the past four decades. It includes the annual reports, policy statements, and other publications of relevant state and industry associations. I comprehensively reviewed the complete back issues of the industry magazine *Irish Computer* until the early 1990s. Since that period, I have subscribed to the online industry magazine *IT's Monday*. Both publications lean heavily in those periods on the expertise of a long-time and deeply knowledgeable industry journalist, John Sterne. He is the indirect key informant for much of this study.

Finally, Forfás kindly provided me in 2001 with data on grant aid from 1980 to 1999. These data were provided for the software firms that responded to the software-industry survey I conducted in 1997. These data were provided on a confidential basis and were essential to the statistical analysis of the effect of state aid, which is outlined in Chapters 5 and 6.

Comparative analysis of developmental states and IT, secondary analysis carried out 2000–2002

The final stage of research was the comparative analysis of developmental states and the attempt to understand the evolution of the international IT industry and the diversity within, in terms of the evolution and interaction of bureaucratic and flexible developmental strategies and institutions. This analysis is based entirely on secondary sources. However, it also benefited enormously from the close interaction I had with a group of colleagues, then at the Department of City and Regional Planning, University of California–Berkeley. We have been meeting as the "Comparative High-Tech Regions" group since 1998 and have worked on issues of high-tech regional development in Israel, India, Taiwan, the United States, and Ireland (Autler, 1999; Egan, 1997; Parthasarathy, 2000; Saxenian, 2001; Zook, 2001).

SURVEY OF THE SOFTWARE INDUSTRY

A survey of software companies was conducted in Ireland in July 1997 to gather information on primary markets, product and export orientation, occupational and other characteristics of company workforce, qualifications required for certain positions, recruitment into senior positions, sources of information for innovation, and alliances with other companies.

The population of firms in the software industry was defined by the criteria used by the NSD, which provided a list of firms in the industry. The list was based on the NSD survey of the industry conducted in 1995, but a substantial number of new firms have been added to the list since then. Some of the firms on the list had subsequently gone out of business and, therefore, were not part of the survey population.

A pilot survey was sent to thirty-four companies in May 1997 to which twelve companies responded. Based on those responses, a slightly amended survey was sent out to the entire population (including the firms that had not responded to the pilot survey). The survey was administered by the Survey Unit of the ESRI in Dublin.

Of the 466 firms that received a survey, 254 responded – resulting in a response rate of 54.5 percent, which is above average for such surveys. The responses of the firms were weighted according to data provided by the NSD about whether a company was Irish-owned or a subsidiary of a multinational corporation, as well as to which size bracket it fell into in 1995 (i.e., 0–10 employees, 11–50, 51–200, 201+, unknown). The weighting was carried out so that the overall number of cases used for statistical tabulations remains at 254. The largest change induced by the weighting procedure was to dampen down the impact of Irish companies with between ten and fifty employees on the overall statistics because the response rate had been particularly high among this group. Furthermore, it is likely that new firms are underrepresented in the population and in the sample used in this survey because the NSD list had not been fully updated to consider all the firms formed since 1995. Finally, six companies were removed from the analysis because they stated that they received more than 60 percent of their revenues from hardware.

Two other sources of data were used in the survey research. Forfás provided data in 2001 on state grant aid from 1980 to 1999. These data were provided for the software firms that responded to the software-industry survey I conducted in 1997. The data were drawn from the centralized Business Information System held by Forfás, which consolidates a wide range of state-agency data regarding firms. Several searches of the system by Forfás resulted in a comprehensive list of grant payments, broken down by year and category of payment. Every effort was made to match each firm with grant-payment data (including checking under previous names). Although there may be administrative errors in recording or processing the data, it is likely that they are fewer than any errors in recall that would have occurred had the respondents been asked about grant payments on the survey. Finally, the NSD software-industry directory of 1993 lists company employment by a number of raw categories (e.g., 1–10, 11–30). These data were used as the basis of a longitudinal analysis of state grant aid and change in employment between 1993 and 1997, in a subset of companies for which all relevant data were available (see Chapter 5).

BIBLIOGRAPHY

Amsden, A. 1985. "The State and Taiwan's Economic Development," pp. 78–106 in P. Evans et al. (eds.), *Bringing the State Back In*. Cambridge: Cambridge University Press.

Amsden, A. 1989. *Asia's Next Giant: South Korea and Late Industrialization*. Oxford: Oxford University Press.

Amsden, A. 2001. *The Rise of "The Rest": Challenges to the West from Late-Industrializing Economies*. Oxford: Oxford University Press.

An Córas Tráchtála. 1987. *The Irish Software Industry*. Dublin: An Córas Tráchtála.

Anchordoguy, M. 2000. "Japan's Software Industry: A Failure of Institutions?" *Research Policy* 29: 391–408.

Ansell, C. 2000. "The Networked Polity: Regional Development in Western Europe." *Governance* 13, 3: 303–33.

Arrighi, G. 1999. "Globalization, State Sovereignty and the 'Endless' Accumulation of Capital," pp. 53–72 in D. Smith, D. Solinger, and S. Topik. *States and Sovereignty in the Global Economy*. London and New York: Routledge.

Arrighi, G., S. Ikeda, and A. Irwan. 1993. "The Rise of East Asia: One Miracle or Many?," pp. 41–66 in R. Palat (ed.), *Pacific-Asia and the Future of the World System*. Westport, CT: Greenwood Press.

Arrighi, G., and B. Silver. 2001. *Chaos and Governance in the Modern World System*. Minneapolis: University of Minnesota Press.

Atkinson, A. B., L. Rainwater, and T. Smeeding. 1995. *Income Distribution in OECD Countries: Evidence from the Luxembourg Income Study*. Paris: OECD.

Autler, Gerald. 1999. "The Globalization of High Tech: The Silicon Valley–Israel Connection." Berkeley, CA: University of California at Berkeley, Department of City and Regional Planning, master's thesis.

Babb, S. 2002. *Managing Mexico: Economists from Nationalism to Neoliberalism*. Princeton, NJ: Princeton University Press.

Bae, Y. J. 2000. Ph.D. Dissertation. Department of Sociology, Duke University.

Barkey, H. J. 1994. "When Politics Matter: Economic Stabilization in Argentina and Israel," *Studies in Comparative International Development* 29, 4: 41–67.

Barnett, M. 1996. "Israel in the World Economy: Israel as an East Asian State?," pp. 107–41 in M. Barnett (ed.), *Israel in Comparative Perspective: Challenging the Conventional Wisdom*. Albany: SUNY Press.

Baron, J., M. D. Burton, and M. Hannan. 1996. "The Road Taken: Origins and Early

Evolution of Employment Systems in Emerging Companies," *Industrial and Corporate Change* 5, 2: 239–75.

Barrett, A., T. Callan, and B. Nolan. 1999. "Rising Wage Inequality, Returns to Education and Labor Market Institutions: Evidence from Ireland," *British Journal of Industrial Relations* 37, 1: 77–100.

Barrett, A., and F. Trace. 1998. "Who Is Coming Back? The Educational Profile of Returning Migrants in the 1990s," *Irish Banking Review,* Summer, pp. 38–51.

Barrett, Sean. 1997. "Policy Changes, Output Growth, and Investment in Irish Tourism," *Irish Banking Review*, Autumn.

Barry, F., ed. 1999. *Understanding Ireland's Economic Growth*. London: Macmillan Press.

Barry, F. 2000. "Convergence Is Not Automatic." *The World Economy.*

Barry, F., H. Gorg, and M. McDowell. 2001. "Outward FDI and the Investment Development Path of a Late-Industrializing Economy: Evidence from Ireland." Working Paper, Economics Department, University College Dublin.

Benner, C. 2002. *Work in the New Economy.* Oxford: Blackwell.

Biggart, N. 1998. "Deep Finance: The Organizational Bases of South Korea's Financial Collapse." *Journal of Management Inquiry* 7: 311–20.

Biggart, N., and M. Guillen. 1999. "Developing Difference: Social Organization and the Rise of the Auto Industries of South Korea, Taiwan, Spain, and Argentina." *American Sociological Review* 64: 722–47.

Biggart, N., G. Hamilton, and M. Orrú. 1997. *The Economic Organization of East Asian Capitalism.* Thousand Oaks, CA: Sage.

Block, F. 1987. *Revising State Theory.* Philadelphia: Temple University Press.

Block, F. 1994. "The Roles of the State in the Economy," in N. Smelser and R. Swedberg (eds.). *The Handbook of Economic Sociology.* Princeton, NJ: Princeton University Press/ Russell Sage Foundation.

Block, F. 2001. "Introduction," pp. xviii–xxxviii in K. Polanyi, *The Great Transformation.* Second edition. Boston: Beacon Press.

Block, F. 2002. "Karl Polanyi and the Writing of 'The Great Transformation'." *Theory and Society.*

Boli, J., and G. Thomas. 1998. "World Culture in the World Polity: A Century of International Nongovernmental Organization." *American Sociological Review* 62, N2:171–90.

Borrus, M. 1997. "Left for Dead: Asian Production Networks and the Revival of U.S. Electronics." BRIE Working Paper 100. Berkeley, CA: Berkeley Roundtable on the International Economy.

Bourdieu, P. 1999. "Rethinking the State," in George Steinmetz, *State/Culture.* Ithaca, NY: Cornell University Press.

Boyer, R., and J. Hollingsworth, eds. 1997. *Contemporary Capitalism: The Embeddedness of Institutions.* p. 54. Cambridge University Press, Cambridge.

Breathnach, P. 2002. "Social Polarization in the Post-Fordist Informational Economy: Ireland in International Context." *Irish Journal of Sociology* 11, 1: 3–22.

Breen, R., D. Hannan, D. Rottman, and C. Whelan. 1990. *Understanding Contemporary Ireland: State, Class, and Development in the Republic of Ireland.* Dublin: Gill and Macmillan.

Breen, R., and C. Whelan. 1996. *Social Mobility and Social Class in Ireland.* Dublin: Gill and Macmillan.

Brenner, N. 1998. "Global Cities, Glocal States: Global City Formation and State Territorial Restructuring in Contemporary Europe." *Review of International Political Economy* 5, 1: 1–37.

Brenner, N. 1999. "Beyond State-Centrism? Space, Territoriality, and Geographical Scale in Globalization Studies." *Theory and Society* 28: 39–78.

Breznitz, D. 2002a. "Conceiving New Industrial Systems: The Different Emergence Paths of the High-Technology Industry in Israel and Ireland." Samuel Neaman Institute, Working Paper 11-2002.

Breznitz, D. 2002b. "The Military as a Public Space – The Role of the IDF in the Israeli Software Innovation System." Samuel Neaman Institute, Working Paper 13–2002.

Brodsgaard, K., and S. Young. 2000. "Introduction: State Capacity in East Asia," pp. 1–16 in K. Brodsgaard and S. Young (eds.), *State Capacity in East Asia*. Oxford: Oxford University Press.

Brown, T. 1982. *Ireland: A Social and Cultural History 1922–1979*. London: Harper Collins.

Burawoy, M. 1985. *The Politics of Production*. London: Verso.

Burawoy, M. 1998. "The Extended Case Method." *Sociological Theory* 16 (1): 4–33.

Burawoy, M. 2001. "Neoclassical Sociology: From the End of Communism to the End of Classes." *American Journal of Sociology* 106 (4): 1099–1120.

Burawoy, M. 2002. "For a Sociological Marxism: The Complementary Convergence of Antonio Gramsci and Karl Polanyi." *Politics and Society*. (forthcoming)

Burawoy, M., et al. 2000. *Global Ethnography*. Berkeley: University of California Press.

Burns, T., and G. Stalker. 1961. *The Management of Innovation*. Oxford: Oxford University Press.

Callan, T., B. Nolan, and J. Walsh. 1998. "Income Tax and Social Welfare Policy," in T. Callan et al., *Budget Perspectives: Proceedings of a Conference Held on 27 October 1998*. Dublin, ESRI: Oak Tree Press.

Campbell, J., and L. N. Lindberg. 1990. "Property Rights and the Organization of Economic Activity by the State." *American Sociological Review* 55: 634–47.

Carr, P. 1995. "Riding the Juggernaut: Selectivity and Entrepreneurship in Ireland." *Irish Journal of Sociology,* Vol. 5.

Carr, P. 1998. "The Cultural Production of Enterprise: Understanding Selectivity as Cultural Policy." *Economic and Social Review* 29, 2: 133–55.

Carroll Burke, P. 2001. *Colonial Discipline: The Making of the Irish Convict System*. Dublin: Four Courts Press.

Carroll Burke, P. 2002a. "Tools, Instruments, and Engines: Getting a Handle on the Specificity of Engine Science." *Social Studies of Science*.

Carroll Burke, P. 2002b. "Material Designs: Engineering Cultures and Engineering States–Ireland, 1650–1900." *Theory and Society*. (forthcoming)

Cassiolato, J. 1992. "The User-Producer Connection in High-Tech: A Case Study of Banking Automation in Brazil," pp. 53–89 in H. Schmitz and J. Cassiolato (eds.), *High-Tech for Industrial Development: Lessons from the Brazilian Experience in Electronics and Automation*. London and New York: Routledge.

Cassiolato, J., T. Hewitt, and H. Schmitz. 1992. "Learning in Industry and Government: Achievements, Failures, and Lessons," pp. 273–315 in H. Schmitz and J. Cassiolato (eds.), *High-Tech for Industrial Development: Lessons from the Brazilian Experience in Electronics and Automation*. London and New York: Routledge.

Castells, M. 1992. "Four Asian Tigers with a Dragon Head: A Comparative Analysis of the State, Economy, and Society in the Asian Pacific Rim," pp. 33–70 in Richard Applebaum and Jeffrey Henderson (eds.), *States and Development in the Asian Pacific Rim*. London: Sage.

Castells, M. 1997. *The Information Age*. 3 vols. Oxford: Blackwell.

Castells, M., and M. Carnoy. 2002. "Globalization, the Knowledge Society, and the Network State: Poulantzas at the Millennium." *Global Networks*.

Castells, M., and P. Hall. 1994. *Technopoles of the World*. London: Routledge.

Castells, M., and P. Himanen 2003. *The Information Society and the Welfare State: The Finnish Model*. Oxford: Oxford University Press.

Central Statistics Office. 1997a. *Census 96: Principal Demographic Results*. Cork: CSO.

Central Statistics Office. 1997b. *Migration Estimates*. Cork: CSO.

Central Statistics Office. 2001a. *Total Capital Acquisitions in Industry.* Cork: CSO.

Central Statistics Office. 2001b. *Quarterly National Household Survey: Home Computing.* Cork: CSO.

Central Statistics Office. 2002. *Total Capital Acquisitions in Industry (Quarterly)*. CSO: Dublin.

Cerny, P. 1995. "Globalization and the Changing Logic of Collective Action." *International Organization* 49: 595–625.

CFM Capital. 2001. *Survey of Mergers, Acquisitions, and Disposals*. Dublin: CFM Capital.

Chang, H. J. 1999. "The Economic Theory of the Developmental State," pp. 182–99 in M. Woo-Cumings (ed.). *The Developmental State*. Ithaca, NY: Cornell University Press.

Chibber, V. 1999. "Building a Developmental State: The Korean Case Reconsidered." *Politics and Society* 27, 3: 309–46.

Chibber, V. 2002. "After the Developmental State, What? The Korean Political Economy since the Great Crisis." Paper presented at the American Sociological Association meetings, Chicago.

Chubb, B. 1982. *The Government and Politics of Ireland*. Oxford: Oxford University Press.

Chung, C. 2001. "Markets, Culture, and Institutions: The Formation of Large Business Groups in Taiwan, 1950s–1970s." *Journal of Management Studies*.

Clancy, P. 1989. "The Evolution of Policy in Third-Level Education," in D. Mulcahy and D. O'Sullivan (eds.). *Irish Educational Policy: Process and Substance*. Dublin: Institute of Public Administration.

Clark, C., and D. Lam, 1998. "Beyond the Developmental State: The Cultural Roots of 'Guerrilla Capitalism' in Taiwan." In Chan, S., C. Clark, and D. Lam (eds.), *Beyond the Developmental State: East Asia's Political Economies Reconsidered*. New York: St. Martin's Press.

Clarke, A. 1995. *Software Support Program: Final Report*. EU Structural Funds Operational Program for Industrial Development Evaluation Unit. Dublin.

Coe, N. 1997. "U.S. Transnationals and the Irish Software Industry." *European Urban and Regional Studies* 4, 3: 211–30.

Coe, N. 1999. "Emulating the Celtic Tiger? A Comparison of the Software Industries of Singapore and Ireland." *Singapore Journal of Tropical Geography* 20, 1: 36–55.

Coe, N. M., and H. Wai-chung Yeung. 1999. "Grounding Global Flows: Constructing an E-Commerce Hub in Singapore." Paper presented to the conference on "Global Networks, Innovation, and Regional Development," UCSC; November 11–13.

Cogan, D., and E. Onyenadum. 1981. "Spin-Off Companies in the Irish Electronics Industry." *IBAR – Journal of Irish Business and Administrative Research* 3, 2: 3–15.

Cohen, J., and J. Rogers. 1992. "Secondary Associations and Democratic Governance." *Politics and Society* 20: 393–472.

Cohen, M. D., J. G. March, and J. P. Olsen. 1972. "A Garbage Can Model of Organizational Choice." *Administrative Science Quarterly* 17: 1–25.

Corcoran, M. 1992. "Valuing Irishness: Identity and Ethnicity among New Irish Immigrants." Paper presented to the Economic and Social Research Institute Seminar Series, March 19.

Corcoran, M. 1993. *Irish Illegals*. Westport, CT: JAI Press.

Cryan, 1999. *The New Pioneers – Building a Winning Company in the U.S. High-Tech Market*. Dublin: Oak Tree Press.

CSR, 1996. *Technology Salary and Skills Survey*. Dublin: CSR.

CSR, 2000. *Technology Salary and Skills Survey.* Dublin: CSR.

Cullinane Group Ireland (CGI). 1997. *Israel: A High-Tech Model for Ireland?* Dublin: CGI.

Culliton Report/Industrial Policy Review Group. 1992. *A Time for Change: Industrial Policy for the 1990s.* Dublin: Stationery Office.

Cumings, B. 1987. "The Origins and Development of the Northeast Asian Political Economy," pp. 44–83 in Frederic C. Deyo (ed.). *The Political Economy of the New Asian Industrialism.* Ithaca, NY: Cornell University Press.

De la Fuente, A., and X. Vives. 1998. "The Sources of Irish Growth," pp. 112–34 in A. Gray (ed.). *International Perspectives on the Irish Economy.* Dublin: Indecon.

Dedrick, J., and K. L. Kraemer. 1998. *Asia's Computer Challenge: Threat or Opportunity for the United States and the World?* Oxford: Oxford University Press.

Department of Enterprise and Employment. 1997. *A Government Strategy for Services.* Dublin: Stationery Office.

Deyo, F. C. 1989. *Beneath the Miracle: Labor Subordination in the New Asian Industrialism.* Berkeley: University of California Press.

Dicken, P., M. Forsgren, and A. Malmberg. 1994. "The Local Embeddedness of Transnational Corporations," in A. Amin and N. Thrift (eds.), *Globalization, Institutions, and Regional Development in Europe.* Oxford: Oxford University Press.

Dickerson, A. P., H. D. Gibson, and E. Tsakalotos. 1997. "The Impact of Acquisitions on Company Performance: Evidence from a Large Panel of U.K. Firms." *Oxford Economic Papers* 49: 344–61.

Dixon, W. J., and T. Boswell. 1996a. "Dependency, Disarticulation and Denominator Effects: Another Look at Foreign Capital Penetration." *American Journal of Sociology* 102: 543–62.

Dixon, W. J., and T. Boswell. 1996b. "Differential Productivity, Negative Externalities, and Foreign Capital Dependency: Reply to Firebaugh." *American Journal of Sociology* 102: 576–581.

Domes, J. 2000. "Taiwan: State Capacity in an Asian Democracy," pp. 114–30 in K. Brodsgaard and S. Young (eds.), *State Capacity in East Asia.* Oxford: Oxford University Press.

Dore, R. 1973. *British Factory – Japanese Factory.* Allen and Unwin. London.

Dore, R. 1983. *Flexible Rigidities.* Stanford: Stanford University Press.

Drew, E. 1994. "Development of Information Technology in Ireland," Chapter 1 in E. Drew and F. G. Foster (eds.), *Information Technology in Selected Countries: Reports from Ireland, Ethiopia, Nigeria and Tanzania.* Tokyo: The United Nations University.

Egan, E. 1997. *The Spatial Dynamics of the U.S. Computer Software Industry.* Ph.D. Dissertation, Department of City and Regional Planning, Berkeley: University of California.

Enterprise Ireland, 2000. *Annual Report.* Dublin: Enterprise Ireland.

Eolas. 1989a. *Electronics Manpower Study: Trends in the Irish Electronics Manufacturing Industry up to 1995.* Dublin: Eolas.

Erikson, R., and J. H. Goldthorpe. 1992. *The Constant Flux: A Study of Class Mobility in Industrial Societies.* Oxford: Clarendon Press.

Ermisch, J. F., and W. G. Huff. 1999. "Hypergrowth in an East Asian NIC: Public Policy and Capital Accumulation in Singapore," *World Development* 27, 1: 21–38.

Ernst, D., and D. O'Connor. 1992. *Competing in the Electronics Industry: The Experience of Newly Industrializing Economies.* Paris: OECD.

Esping-Andersen, G. 1990. *The Three Worlds of Welfare Capitalism.* Princeton, NJ: Princeton University Press.

Esping-Andersen, G. 1999. *The Social Foundations of Postindustrial Economies.* Oxford: Oxford University Press.

Euristix. 1991. *The Impact of Communications on Industry and Industrial Development in Ireland.* Report to Industrial Policy Review Group, Dublin.

European Venture Capital Association, various years. *Annual Reports.*

Evans, P. B. 1995. *Embedded Autonomy*. Princeton, NJ: Princeton University Press.

Evans, P. 1996. "Government Action, Social Capital, and Development: Creating Synergy across the Public–Private Divide," Special Section, *World Development* 24, 6: 1033–1131.

Evans, P. B. 1997. "The Eclipse of the State? Reflections on Stateness in an Era of Globalization." *World Politics* 50: 62–87.

Evans, P. B., and J. Rauch. 1999. "Bureaucracy and Growth: A Cross-National Analysis of the Effects of 'Weberian' States Structures on Economic Growth." *American Sociological Review* 64: 748–65.

Evans, et al., 1985. *Bringing the State Back In*. Cambridge: Cambridge University Press.

Fahey, T. 1992. "Catholicism and Industrial Society in Ireland," pp. 241–264 in J. H. Goldthorpe and C. T. Whelan (eds.). *The Development of Industrial Society in Ireland.* Oxford: Oxford University Press.

Feenstra, R., and G. Hamilton. 2000. "Neither State nor Markets: The Role of Economic Organization in Asian Development." *International Sociology* 15 (2): 291–308.

Ferguson, J., and A. Gupta. 2001. "Spatializing the State" mimeo, Irvine: University of California.

Fields, K. 1995. *Enterprise and the State in Korea and Taiwan*. Ithaca, NY: Cornell University Press.

Firebaugh, G. 1992. "Growth Effects of Foreign and Domestic Investment." *American Journal of Sociology* 98: 105–30.

Firebaugh, G. 1996. "Does Foreign Capital Harm Poor Nations? New Estimates Based on Dixon and Boswell's Measures of Capital Penetration." *American Journal of Sociology* 102: 563–75.

Fitzgerald, G. 1968. *Planning in Ireland*. Dublin: Institute of Public Administration.

Fitzgerald, J. 2000. "The Story of Ireland's Failure – and Belated Success," pp. 27–57 in B. Nolan, P. O'Connell, and C. Whelan (eds.). *Bust to Boom? The Irish Experience of Growth and Inequality*. Dublin: Economic and Social Research Institute.

Fitzgerald, R., and B. Girvin. 2000. "Political Culture, Growth and the Conditions for Success in the Irish Economy," pp. 268–85 in B. Nolan, P. O'Connell, and C. Whelan (eds.). *Bust to Boom? The Irish Experience of Growth and Inequality*. Dublin: Economic and Social Research Institute.

Flamm, K. 1987. *Targeting the Computer: Government Support and International Competition*. Washington, DC: The Brookings Institution.

Fligstein, N. 1990. *The Transformation of Corporate Control*. Cambridge, MA: Harvard University Press.

Fligstein, N. 2001. *The Architecture of Markets*. Princeton, NJ: Princeton University Press.

Foley, A., and T. Hogan. 1998. "Start-Ups and Closures in Indigenous Manufacturing: An Analysis of the Census of Industrial Production, 1986–1995." *Irish Banking Review*, Autumn.

Forfás. 1994. *1994 Employment Survey*. Dublin: Forfás.

Forfás. 1995. *Research and Development in the Business Sector: Findings from the 1993 Census of R&D Performing Enterprises in Ireland*. Dublin: Forfás.

Forfás. 1997. *Survey of Product and Process Innovation in Irish Industry 1993–1995*. Dublin: Forfás.

Forfás. 1999. *Annual Survey of Irish Economy Expenditures: Results for 1999*. Dublin: Forfás.

Foster, R. 1988. *Modern Ireland 1600–1972*. Allen Lane: The Penguin Press.

Freeman, C. 2002. "Continental, National and Subnational Innovation Systems – Complementarity and Economic Growth." *Research Policy* 31, 2: 191–211.

Freeman, C., and F. Louca. 2002. *As Time Goes By: From the Industrial Revolutions to the Information Revolution.* Oxford: Oxford University Press.

Fung, A. 2001. "Accountable Autonomy: Toward Empowered Deliberation in Chicago Schools and Policing." *Politics and Society* 29, 1: 73–103.

Fung, A., and E. Wright. 2001. "Deepening Democracy: Innovations in Empowered Participatory Governance." *Politics and Society* 29, 1: 5–41.

Gao, B. 2001. *Japan's Economic Dilemma: The Institutional Origins of Prosperity and Stagnation.* New York: Cambridge University Press.

Geary, J. 1998. *Initial Results from the National Survey of Employee Relations and Human Resource Practice in Ireland.* Working Paper, Smurfit Business School. Dublin: University College.

Geary, J. 1999. "The New Workplace: Change at Work in Ireland." *International Journal of Human Resource Management* 10, 5: 870–90.

Gereffi, G. 1994. "The International Economy," in N. Smelser and R. Swedberg (eds.). *The Handbook of Economic Sociology.* Princeton: Princeton University Press/ Russell Sage Foundation.

Gerlach, M. 1997. *Alliance Capitalism: The Social Organization of Japanese Business.* Berkeley: University of California Press.

Gerschenkron, A. 1962. *Economic Backwardness in Historical Perspective.* Cambridge: Belknap Press of Harvard University Press.

Gilpin, R. 2003. *The Challenge of Global Capitalism.* Princeton: Princeton University Press.

Girvin, B. 1989. *Between Two Worlds: Politics and Economy in Independent Ireland.* Maryland: Barnes and Noble.

Gold, T. 1986. *State and Society in the Taiwan Miracle.* Armonk, NY: M. E. Sharpe.

Gold, T. 1988. "Entrepreneurs, Multinationals, and the State," pp. 175–205 in E. Winckler and S. Greenhalgh (eds.). *Contending Approaches to the Political Economy of Taiwan.* Armonk, NY: M. E. Sharpe.

Gold, T. 2000. "The Waning of the Kuomintang State on Taiwan," pp. 84–113 in K. Brodsgaard and S. Young (eds.). *State Capacity in East Asia.* Oxford: Oxford University Press.

Goldthorpe, J. H. 1982. "On the Service Class: Its Formation and Future," in A. Giddens and G. Mackenzie (eds.). *Social Class and the Division of Labor.* Cambridge: Cambridge University Press.

Gordon, R. 2001. "State, Milieu, Network: Systems of Innovation in Silicon Valley." Center for Global, International, and Regional Studies. Working Paper #2001–3. Santa Cruz: University of California. (Originally distributed in February 1994.)

Gordon, D., R. Edwards, and M. Reich, 1982. *Segmented Work, Divided Workers: The Historical Transformation of Labor in the United States.* Cambridge: Cambridge University Press.

Gramsci, A. 1971. *The Prison Notebooks.* Edited by Q. Hoare.

Granovetter, M. 1985. "Economic Action and Social Structure: The Problem of Embeddedness." *American Journal of Sociology* 91, 3: 481–510.

Gray, A. (ed.) 1998. *International Perspectives on the Irish Economy.* Dublin: Indecon.

Grieco, J. 1984. *Between Dependency and Autonomy: India's Experience with the International Computer Industry.* Berkeley: University of California Press.

Grinberg, L., and G. Shafir. 2000. "Economic Liberalization and the Breakup of the Histadrut's Domain," pp. 103–27 in G. Shafir and Y. Peled (eds.). *The New Israel: Peacemaking and Liberalization.* Boulder, CO: Westview Press.

Guillen, M. 2001. *The Limits of Convergence: Globalization and Organizational Change in Argentina, South Korea, and Spain.* Princeton, NJ: University Press.

Gunnigle, P. 1988. "Employee Relations in Greenfield Sites," Chapter 9 in P. Gunnigle et al. *Continuity and Change in Irish Employee Relations.* Dublin: Oak Tree Press.

Gunnigle, P., M. Morley, and T. Turner. 1997. "Challenging Collectivist Traditions:

Individualism and the Management of Industrial Relations in Greenfield Sites." *The Economic and Social Review* 28: 105–34.

Habermas, J. 1976. *Legitimation Crisis*. London: Heinemann.

Haggard, S. 1990. *Pathways from the Periphery*. Ithaca, NY: Cornell University Press.

Haggard, S., and C. K. Pang. 1994. "The Transition to Export-Led Growth in Taiwan," pp. 47–89 in J.D. Aberbach et al. (eds.). *The Role of the State in Taiwan's Development*. Armonk, NY: M. E. Sharpe.

Hall, E. 1993. *The Electronic Age: Telecommunication in Ireland*. Dublin: Oak Tree Press.

Hall, P., and D. Soskice. 2002. *Varieties of Capitalism: The Institutional Foundations of Comparative Advantage*. Oxford [England] and New York: Oxford University Press.

Hamilton, G., R. Feenstra, and E. Lim. 2000. "Neither State nor Markets: The Role of Economic Organization in Asian Development." *International Sociology* 15 (2): 291–308.

Handler, J. 1996. *Down from Bureaucracy: The Ambiguity of Privatization and Empowerment*. Princeton, NJ: Princeton University Press.

Hanlon, G. 1994. *The Commercialization of Accountancy*. London: St. Martin's Press.

Hannan, D., and P. Commins. 1992. "The Significance of Small-Scale Landholders in Ireland's Socioeconomic Transformation," pp. 79–104 in J. H. Goldthorpe and C. T. Whelan (eds.). *The Development of Industrial Society in Ireland*. Oxford: Oxford University Press.

Hannan, D. F., B. McCabe, and S. McCoy. 1998. *Trading Qualifications for Jobs: Overeducation and the Irish Youth Labor Market*. ESRI General Research Series 171. Dublin: Oak Tree Press/ESRI.

Hannan, D. F., and S. Ó Riain. 1993. *Pathways to Adulthood in Ireland: Causes and Consequences of Success and Failure in Transitions Among Irish Youth*. General Research Series No. 161, Economic and Social Research Institute. Dublin.

Harmon, C., J. Durkan, and D. Fitzgerald. 1999. "Human Capital and Growth," in F. Barry (ed.). *Understanding Ireland's Economic Growth*. London: Macmillan.

Harrison, B. 1994. *Lean and Mean*. New York: Basic Books.

HEA, various years. *First Destination of Award Recipients in Higher Education*. Dublin: Higher Education Authority.

Heeks, R. 1996. *India's Software Industry: State Policy, Liberalization, and Industrial Development*. New Delhi: Thousand Oaks; London. Sage.

Held, D., A. McGrew, D. Goldblatt, and J. Perraton. 1999. *Global Transformations: Politics, Economics, and Culture*. Stanford: Stanford University Press.

Henderson, J. 1989. *The Globalization of High Technology Production*. New York: Routledge.

Hendry, J. 1989. *Innovating for Failure: Government Policy and the Early British Computer Industry*. Cambridge, MA: MIT Press.

Herring, R. 1999. "Embedded Particularism: India's Failed Developmental State," pp. 306–33, in Woo-Cumings, M. (ed.). *The Developmental State*. Ithaca, NY: Cornell University Press.

Hicks, A., and L. Kenworthy. 1998. "Cooperation and Political Economic Performance in Affluent Democratic Capitalism." *American Journal of Sociology* 103: 1631–1672.

Higgins, M. D. 1982. "The Limits of Clientelism: Toward an Assessment of Irish Politics," in C. Clapham (ed.). *Private Patronage and Public Power*. London: Frances Pinter.

Hirschman, A. O. 1958. *The Strategy of Economic Development*. New Haven: Yale University Press.

Hobday, M. 1994. "Technological Learning in Singapore: A Test Case of Leapfrogging." *The Journal of Development Studies* 30, 3: 831–58.

Hobday, M. 1995. "East Asian Latecomer Firms: Learning the Technology of Electronics." *World Development* 23, 7: 1171–1193.

Hogan, A., and T. Foley. 1996. "The Survival and Growth of Fast-Growth Firms in Ireland." *Irish Banking Review,* Autumn.

Hong, S. 1997. *The Political Economy of Industrial Policy in East Asia: The Semiconductor Industry in Taiwan and South Korea.* Cheltenham, UK: Edward Elgar.

Honohan, P., B. Maitre, and C. Conroy. 1998. "Invisible Entrepôt Activity in Irish Manufacturing." *Irish Banking Review,* Summer 22–36.

HotOrigin, 2001. *Ireland's Emerging Software Cluster.* Dublin: HotOrigin.

Hout, M. 1989. *Following in Father's Footsteps: Social Mobility in Ireland.* Cambridge, MA: Harvard University Press.

Hout, M., and J. Jackson. 1986. "Dimensions of Occupational Mobility in the Republic of Ireland." *European Sociological Review 2:* 114–37.

Hsiao, H. H., and A. So. 1993. "Ascent through National Integration: The Chinese Triangle of Mainland–Taiwan–Hong Kong," pp. 41–66 in R. Palat (ed.). *Pacific-Asia and the Future of the World System.* Westport, CT: Greenwood Press.

Hsu, J. Y. 1997. *A Late Industrial District? Learning Networks in the Hsinchu Science-Based Industrial Park, Taiwan.* Ph.D. Dissertation, Department of Geography. Berkeley: University of California.

Huff, W. J. 1995a. "What Is the Singapore Model of Economic Development?" *Cambridge Journal of Economics* 19: 735–59.

Huff, W. J. 1995b. "The Developmental State, Government, and Singapore's Economic Development since 1960." *World Development* 23, 8: 1421–38.

Huff, W. J. 1999. "Turning the Corner in Singapore's Developmental State?" *Asian Survey* 39, 2: 214–42.

IDA. 1972. *Regional Industrial Plans 1973–77.* Dublin: IDA.

IDA. 1976. *IDA Industrial Plan 1977–80.* Dublin: IDA.

IDA. 1977. *IDA Industrial Plan 1978–82.* Dublin: IDA.

IDA Ireland. (n.d.). *The Irish Software Industry.* Dublin: IDA Ireland.

IDA Ireland. 2000. Annual Report. Dublin: IDA Ireland.

IMF. Various years. *International Financial Statistics.* IMF.

Irish Computer. Various dates. Computing Industry Magazine. Dublin.

Irish Computer Services Association (ICSA). 1988. *A Study of the Irish Software Industry.* Dublin: ICSA.

Israeli Association of Software Houses. 1995. *Israel's Software Industry 1994–1995.* Tel Aviv: Israeli Association of Software Houses.

IT's Monday. Various dates. E-Mail Industry Newsletter. Dublin.

Jacobson, D. 1989. "Theorizing Irish Industrialization: The Case of the Motor Industry." *Science and Society* 53, 2: 165–91.

Jacobson, D., and D. O'Sullivan. 1994. "Analyzing an Industry in Change: The Irish Software Manual Printing Industry." *New Technology, Work, and Employment* 9: 103–14.

Jacobson, D., and D. O'Sullivan. 1997. "The Irish Software Manual Industry: Globalization through Local Supply?" Paper presented at *Ireland, Europe & the Global Information Society: A Conference for Social Scientists.* Dublin. April 24–25.

Jacoby, S. 1988. *Employing Bureaucracy.* Berkeley: University of California Press.

Jarillo, C. 1988. "On Strategic Networks." *Strategic Management Journal* 9: 31–41.

Jessop, B. 2002. *The Future of the Capitalist State.* Cambridge: Polity Press.

Johnson, C. 1982. *MITI and the Japanese Miracle.* Stanford, CA: Stanford University Press.

Kennedy, K. 1992. "The Context of Economic Development," pp. 5–30, in J. H. Goldthorpe and C. T. Whelan (eds.). *The Development of Industrial Society in Ireland.* Oxford: Oxford University Press.

Kennedy, K., T. Giblin, and D. McHugh. 1988. *The Economic Development of Ireland in the Twentieth Century*. London: Routledge.

Kentor, J. 1998. "The Long-Term Effects of Foreign Investment Dependence on Economic Growth, 1940–1990." *American Journal of Sociology* 103, 4: 1024–1046.

Khazam, J., and D. Mowery. 1996. "Tails That Wag Dogs: The Influence of Software-Based 'Network Externalities' on the Creation of Dominant Designs in RISC Technologies," pp. 86–103 in D. Mowery (ed.). *The International Computer Software Industry*. Oxford: Oxford University Press.

Kidder, T. 1981. *The Soul of a New Machine*. New York: Avon Books.

Kim, L., and R. Nelson. 2000. *Technology, Learning, and Innovation: Experiences of Newly Industrializing Economies*. Cambridge: Cambridge University Press.

Kirby, P. 2002. *The Celtic Tiger in Distress: Growth with Inequality in Ireland*. Basingstoke: Palgrave.

Kleiman, E. 1997. "The Waning of Israeli Etatisme." *Israel Studies* 2: 2, 146–71.

Kohli, A. 1994. "Where Do High-Growth Political Economies Come From? The Japanese Lineages of Korea's 'Developmental State'." *World Development* 22, 9: 1269–93.

Kontopoulos, K. M. 1993. *The Logics of Social Structure*. Cambridge and New York: Cambridge University Press.

Korzeniewicz, R. P., and T. P. Moran. 1997. "World-Economic Trends in the Distribution of Income, 1965–1992." *American Journal of Sociology* 102: 1000–39.

Krippner, G. 2001. "The Elusive market: Embeddedness and the Paradigm of Economic Sociology." *Theory and Society 30 (6): 775–810*.

Krippner, G. 2003. *The Fictitious Economy: Finance and the Rise of Neoliberal Capitalism*. PhD Dissertation, University of Wisconsin, Madison.

Krugman, P. 1992. *Geography and Trade*. Cambridge, MA: MIT University Press.

Krugman, P. 1994. "The Myth of Asia's Miracle," *Foreign Affairs*, pp. 62–78.

Krugman, P. 1998. "Good News from Ireland: A Geographical Perspective," pp. 38–53 in A. Gray (ed.). *International Perspectives on the Irish Economy*. Dublin: Indecon.

Kunda, G. 1993. *Engineering Culture*. Philadelphia: Temple University Press.

Langlois, R., and D. Mowery. 1996. "The Federal Government Role in the Development of the U.S. Software Industry," pp. 53–85 in D. Mowery (ed.). *The International Computer Software Industry*. Oxford: Oxford University Press.

Lawrence, P., and J. Lorsch. 1967. *Organization and Environment*. Boston: Harvard University Press.

Lee, J. 1989. *Ireland 1922–1985*. Dublin: Gill and Macmillan.

Lemass, S. 1961. "The Organization Behind the Economic Program." *Administration* 9, 1: 3–10.

Levi-Faur, D. 1998. "The Developmental State: Israel, South Korea, and Taiwan Compared." *Studies in Comparative International Development* 33, 1: 65–93.

Levi-Faur, D. 2000. "Change and Continuity in the Israeli Political Economy: Multilevel Analysis of the Telecommunications and Energy Sectors," pp. 161–88, in G. Shafir and Y. Peled (eds.). *The New Israel: Peacemaking and Liberalization*. Boulder, CO: Westview Press.

Lim, L. 1983. "Singapore's Success: The Myth of the Free Market Economy." *Asian Survey* 23, 6: 752–64.

Lin, C. Y. 1973. *Industrialization in Taiwan, 1946–72*. New York: Praeger.

Little, Arthur D. 1967. *Review of the Structure of the Industrial Development Authority*. Cambridge, MA: Arthur D. Little, Inc.

Lopez, S. 2003. *Reorganizing the Rust Belt: An Inside Study of the American Labor Movement*. Berkeley: University of California Press.

Loriaux, M. 1999. "The French Developmental State as Myth and Moral Ambition," pp. 235–75 in M. Woo-Cumings (ed.). *The Developmental State*. Ithaca, NY: Cornell University Press.

Lundvall, B. A., B. Johnson, E. S. Andersen, and B. Dalum. 2002. "National Systems of Production, Innovation, and Competence-Building." *Research Policy* 31, 2: 213–31.

Luzio, E. 1996. *The Microcomputer Industry in Brazil: The Case of a Protected High-Technology Industry*. Westport, CT: Praeger.

MacDonald, F. 1985. *The Destruction of Dublin*. Dublin: Gill and Macmillan.

MacLaran, A. 1993. *Dublin: The Shaping of a Capital*. London: Belhaven Press.

Mair, P. 1992. "Explaining the Absence of Class Politics in Ireland," pp. 383–410, in J. H. Goldthorpe and C. T. Whelan (eds.). *The Development of Industrial Society in Ireland*. Oxford: Oxford University Press.

Malerba, F., and S. Torrisi. 1996. "The Dynamics of Market Structure and Innovation in the Western European Software Industry," pp. 165–96, in D. Mowery (ed.). *The International Computer Software Industry*. Oxford: Oxford University Press.

Maman, D. 1997. "The Power Lies in the Structure: Economic Policy Forum Networks in Israel." *British Journal of Sociology* 48, 2: 267–85.

Martin, R., and P. Sunley. 1996. "Paul Krugman's Geographical Economics and Its Implications for Regional Development Theory – A Critical Assessment." *Economic Geography* 72, 3: 259–92.

McAleese, D. 1999. "Twenty-Five Years A' Growing," pp. 79–110, in Rory O'Donnell (ed.). *Europe: The Irish Experience*. Dublin: Institute of European Affairs.

McAteer, J. F., and L. Donohoe. 1996. *Building Knowledge Industries: The Irish Software Industry*. SRI Consulting, Business Intelligence Program. Palo Alto, CA: SRI Consulting.

McCall, B. 1997. "Picking Winners." *Enterprise and Innovation*. July: 12–15.

McGovern, P. 1998. *HRM, Technical Workers, and the Multinational Corporation*. London: Routledge.

McIver Consulting. 1998. *Manpower, Education, and Training Study of the Software Sector*. Dublin: FAS.

McLaughlin, J. 1994. *Ireland: The Emigrant Nursery and the World Economy*. Cork: Cork University Press.

McMichael, P. 1990. "Incorporating Comparison within a World-Historical Perspective: An Alternative Comparative Method." *American Sociological Review*, 55, 3.

McMichael, P. 1996. *Development and Social Change: A Global Perspective*. Thousand Oaks, CA: Pine Forge.

McNeil, W. 1982. *The Pursuit of Power: Technology, Armed Force, and Society since A.D. 1000*. Chicago: Chicago University Press.

Meaney, C. 1994. "State Policy and the Development of Taiwan's Semiconductor Industry," pp. 170–92, in J. D. Aberbach et al. (eds.). *The Role of the State in Taiwan's Development*. Armonk, NY: M. E. Sharpe.

Meyer, J., and B. Rowan. 1977. "Institutionalized Organizations: Formal Structure as Myth and Ceremony." *American Journal of Sociology* 83: 340–63.

Miller, K. L. 1985. *Emigrants and Exiles*. New York: Oxford University Press.

Mittleman, J., ed. 1997. *Globalization: Critical Reflections*. Boulder, CO: Lynne Rienner.

Mjoset, L. 1992. *The Irish Economy in a Comparative Institutional Perspective*. National Economic and Social Council Report No. 93. Dublin: NESC.

Mowery, D. C. (ed.). 1996. *The International Computer Software Industry*. Oxford: Oxford University Press.

Mowery, D. C. 2001. "Technological Innovation in a Multipolar System: Analysis and Implications for U.S. Policy." *Technological Forecasting and Social Change* 67: 43–157.

Myles, J. 1989. *Old Age in the Welfare State: The Political Economy of Public Pensions*. Lawrence, KS: University Press of Kansas.

NASSCOM. 1996. *The Software Industry in India: A Strategic Review.* New Delhi: NASSCOM.

National Board for Science and Technology. 1980. *Telecommunications and Industrial Development.* Dublin: NBST.

National Board for Science and Technology. 1981. *Microelectronics: The Implications for Ireland.* Dublin: NBST.

National Economic and Social Council (NESC). 1991. *The Economic and Social Implications of Emigration.* Dublin: NESC.

National Economic and Social Council (NESC). 2002. *An Investment in Quality: Services, Inclusion and Enterprise.* Dublin: NESC.

National Software Directorate. 1993. *1993 Software Industry Survey Results.* Dublin: IDA Ireland.

National Software Directorate. 1995. *1995 Software Industry Survey Results.* Dublin: Forbairt.

National Software Directorate. 1997. *1997 Software Industry Survey Results.* Dublin: Forbairt.

Nelson, R. (Ed.), 1993. *National Innovation Systems: A comparative analysis.* Oxford University Press, New York.

Oakey, R. 1995. *High technology new firms: variable barriers to growth.* Paul Chapman Publishing: London.

O'Brien, R. 1986. "Technology and Industrial Development: The Irish Electronics Industry in an International Context," Ch. 6 in J. Fitzpatrick and J. Kelly (eds.). *Perspectives on Irish Industry.* Dublin: Irish Management Institute.

O'Connell, P., and D. Rottman. 1992. "The Irish Welfare State in Comparative Perspective," pp. 205–40 in J. H. Goldthorpe and C. T. Whelan (eds.). *The Development of Industrial Society in Ireland.* Oxford: Oxford University Press.

O'Connor, P. 1998. *Emerging Voices: Women in Contemporary Irish Society.* Dublin: Institute of Public Administration.

O'Donnell, M. 1981. "Engineering Manpower for Economic Development: Present and Forecast Capacity," Paper presented at *Engineering Manpower for Economic Development Conference.* Dublin.

O'Donnell, R. 2000. "The New Ireland in the New Europe," pp. 161–214, in R. O'Donnell (ed.). *Europe: The Irish Experience.* Dublin: IEA.

OECD. 1974. *Reviews of National Science Policy.* Paris: OECD.

OECD. 1978. *Policies for the Stimulation of Industrial Innovation.* Paris: OECD.

OECD. 1964. *Science and Irish Economic Development.* Paris: OECD.

OECD. 1992. *Education at a Glance: OECD Indicators.* OECD Center for Educational Research and Innovation. Paris: OECD.

OECD. 1993. *Education at a Glance: OECD Indicators.* OECD Center for Educational Research and Innovation. Paris: OECD.

OECD. 1996. (same as above).

OECD. 1997. *Information Technology Outlook 1996.* Paris: OECD.

OECD. 2000. *Ireland.* Paris: OECD.

OECD. 2002. *Information Technology Outlook 2002.* Paris: OECD.

Offe, C. 1974. "Structural Problems of the Capitalist State: Class Rule and the Political System: On the Selectiveness of Political Institutions," in K. von Beyme (ed.), *German Political Studies 1.* Sage, London.

Offe, C. 1984. *Contradictions of the Welfare State.* London: Hutchinson.

O'Gorman, C., E. O'Malley, and J. Mooney. 1997. *Clusters in Ireland: The Irish Indigenous Software Industry: An Application of Porter's Cluster Analysis.* NESC Research Series Paper No. 3.

O'Hanlon, R. 1998. *The New Irish Americans.* Boulder, CO: Roberts Rinehart.

O'Hearn, D. 1989. "The Irish Case of Dependency: An Exception to the Exceptions?" *American Sociological Review* 54: 4, 578–96.

O'Hearn, D. 1990. "The Road from Import-Substituting to Export-Led Industrialization in Ireland." *Politics and Society* 18: 1–38.

O'Hearn, D. 1998. *Inside the Celtic Tiger: The Irish Economy and the Asian Model.* London: Pluto.

O'Hearn, D. 2001. *The Atlantic Economy: Britain, the U.S., and Ireland.* Manchester: Manchester University Press.

O'Leary, J. 2000. *Growing by Knowing: How Ireland's Expansion Can Be Sustained.* Dublin: Davy Stockbrokers.

O'Malley, E. 1980. *Industrial Policy and Development: A Survey of Literature from the Early 1960s to the Present.* Dublin: NESC.

O'Malley, E. 1989. *Industry and Economic Development.* Dublin: Gill and Macmillan.

O'Malley, E. 1992. "Developments in Irish Industrial Policy since the Mid-1980s." Paper presented to Political Studies Association of Ireland Special Conference. *The State of the Irish Political System.* Cork. May 28–30.

O'Malley, E. 1998. "The Revival of Irish Indigenous Industry 1987–1997." ESRI seminar paper, 26 February. Dublin: Economic and Social Research Institute.

O'Malley, E., K. A. Kennedy, and R. O'Donnell. 1992. *Report to the Industrial Policy Review Group on the Impact of the Industrial Development Agencies.* Dublin: Stationery Office.

O'Malley, E., and Van Egeraat, C. 2000. "Industry Clusters and Irish Indigenous Manufacturing: Limits of the Porter View." *The Economic and Social Review* 31, 1: 55–79.

Ong, A. 1999. *Flexible Citizenship.* Berkeley, CA: University of California Press.

Onyenadum, E., and B. Tomlin. 1984a. "Technology Transfer Through Staff Mobility: I" *IBAR – Journal of Irish Business and Administrative Research* 6, 1: 3–11.

Onyenadum, E., and B. Tomlin. 1984b. "Technology Transfer Through Staff Mobility: II" *IBAR – Journal of Irish Business and Administrative Research* 6, 2: 15–26.

Ó Riain, S. 1997. "An Offshore Silicon Valley?" *Competition and Change* 2: 175–212.

Ó Riain, S. 1999. "Remaking the Developmental State: The Irish Software Industry in the Global Economy." Ph.D. dissertation. Department of Sociology, University of California, Berkeley.

Ó Riain, S. 2000a. "States and Markets in an Era of Globalization." *Annual Review of Sociology*, vol. 26, 187–213.

Ó Riain, S. 2000b. "Networking for a Living: Irish Software Developers in the Global Workplace," chapter in M. Burawoy et al. *Global Ethnography.* Berkeley: University of California Press.

Ó Riain, S. 2000c. "The Flexible Developmental State, Globalization, Information Technology, and the 'Celtic Tiger'." *Politics and Society* 28, 3: 3–37.

Ó Riain, S. 2002. "High-Tech Communities: Better Work or Just More Work?" *Contexts* 1, 4: 36–41.

Ó Riain, S. 2003. "State, Competition, and Industrial Change in Ireland, 1991–1999." *The Economic and Social Review*, forthcoming.

Ó Riain, S., and P. O'Connell. 2000. "The Role of the State in Growth and Welfare," pp. 310–39 in B. Nolan, P. O'Connell, and C. Whelan (eds.). *Bust to Boom? The Irish Experience of Growth and Inequality.* Dublin: Economic and Social Research Institute.

Orrú, M., N. Biggart, and G. Hamilton. 1997. *The Economic Organization of East Asian Capitalism.* Thousand Oaks, CA: Sage.

Orton, J. D., and K. E. Weick. 1990. "Loosely Coupled Systems: A Reconceptualization." *Academy of Management Review* 15: 203–23.

Osborne, R. 1996. *Higher Education in Ireland: North and South.* London: Jessica Kingsley.

O'Toole, F. 1994. *Black Hole, Green Card.* London: Vintage.

O'Toole, F. 1995. *Meanwhile Back at the Ranch: The Politics of Irish Beef*. London: Vintage.

Parthasarathy, B. 2000. *Globalization and Agglomeration in Newly Industrializing Countries: The State and the Information Technology Industry in Bangalore, India*. Ph.D. Dissertation. Department of City and Regional Planning. University of California, Berkeley.

Peillon, M. 1994. "Placing Ireland in a Comparative Perspective." *The Economic and Social Review* 25, 2: 179–195.

Perez, C. 2002. *Technological Revolutions and Financial Capital: The Dynamics of Bubbles and Golden Ages*. Cheltenham, UK: Edward Elgar.

Perez-Aleman, P. 2000. "Learning, Adjustment, and Economic Development: Transforming Firms, the State, and Associations in Chile." *World Development* 28, 1: 41–55.

Perrow, C. 1986. *Complex Organizations*. New York: Random House.

Peterson, J., and M. Sharp. 1998. *Technology Policy in the European Union*. Basingstoke: Macmillan.

Piore, M., and C. Sabel. 1984. *The Second Industrial Divide*. New York: Basic Books.

Polanyi, K. 1944 [1957]. *The Great Transformation*. Boston: Beacon.

Porter, M. 1990. *The Competitve Advantage of Nations*. New York: Free Press.

Porter, A., J. D. Roessner, N. Newman, and X. Y. Jin. 2000. *1999 Indicators of Technology-Based Competitiveness of 33 Nations: Summary Report*. Washington, DC: National Science Foundation.

Price Waterhouse. 1997. *1997 Software Business Practices Survey*. Boston: Price Waterhouse.

Raftery, A., and M. Hout. 1993. "Maximally Maintained Inequality: Expansion, Reform, and Opportunity in Irish Education, 1921–1975." *Sociology of Education* 66, 22–39.

Ragin, C. 1994. *Constructing Social Research: The Unity and Diversity of Method*. Thousand Oaks, CA: Pine Forge Press.

Rahim, L. Z. 1998. *The Singapore Dilemma*. Oxford University Press: Kuala Lumpur.

Robinson, W. I. 1998. "Beyond Nation–State Paradigms: Globalization, Sociology, and the Challenge of Transnational Studies." *Sociological Forum* 13: 561–94.

Roche, W. 1997. "Trade Union Membership in the Republic of Ireland," in T. V. Murphy and W. K. Roche (eds.). *Irish Industrial Relations in Practice*. Dublin: Oak Tree Press.

Roche, W. 1998. "Between Regime Fragmentation and Realignment: Irish Industrial Relations in the 1990s." *Industrial Relations Journal* 29, 2: 112–25.

Roche, W., and J. Geary. 2001. "'Collaborative Production' and the Irish Boom: Work Organization, Partnership, and Direct Involvement in Irish Workplaces." *Economic and Social Review*.

Rodrik, D. 1997. "TFPG Controversies, Institutions, and Economic Performance in East Asia." NBER Working Paper 5914. Cambridge, MA: National Bureau of Economic Research.

Rodrik, D. 1997. *Has Globalization Gone Too Far?* Washington, DC: Institute for International Economics.

Roper, S., and A. Frenkel. 1998. "Different Paths to Success? The Growth of the Electronics Sector in Ireland and Israel." Working Paper No. 39. Belfast: Northern Ireland Economic Research Center, Queen's University.

Ross-Schneider, B. 1999. "The Desarrollista State in Brazil and Mexico," pp. 276–305, in M. Woo-Cumings (ed.). *The Developmental State*. Ithaca, NY: Cornell University Press.

Ruane, F., and H. Gorg. 2001. "Globalization and Fragmentation: Evidence for the Electronics Industry in Ireland," pp. 144–64 in S. Arndt and H. Kierzkowski (eds.). *Fragmentation: New Production Patterns in the World Economy*. Oxford: Oxford University Press.

Ruggie, J. G. 1982. "International Regimes, Transactions, and Change: Embedded Liberalism in the Postwar Economic Order." *International Organization* 36: 379–415.

Ruggie, J. G. 1995. "At Home Abroad, Abroad at Home: International Liberalization and Domestic Stability in the New World Economy." Millenium: *Journal of International Studies* 24: 507–26.

Ryan, K. 1997. "The Irish Software Industry – Lessons Learned." *Portland International Conference on Management of Engineering and Technology*. July 1997.

Sabel, C. 1994. "Learning by Monitoring: The Institutions of Economic Development," pp. 137–65 in N. Smelser and R. Swedberg (eds.). *The Handbook of Economic Sociology*, Princeton, NJ: Princeton University Press/Russell Sage Foundation.

Sabel, C. 1996. *Ireland: Local Partnerships and Social Innovation*. Paris: OECD.

Sachs, J. D. 1998. "Ireland's Growth Strategy: Lessons for Economic Development," in Alan W. Gray (ed.) *International Perspectives on the Irish Economy* Dublin: Indecon Economic Consultants.

Sassen, S. 1990. *The Global City*. Princeton, NJ: Princeton University Press.

Sassen, S. 1997. "The State and the Global City: Notes Toward a Conception of Place-Centered Governance." *Competition and Change* 1: 31–50.

Sassen, S. 1998. "Cracked Casings: Notes Toward an Analytics for Studying Transnational Processes" mimeo. Department of Sociology, University of Chicago.

Saxenian, A. 1994. *Regional Advantage: Culture and Competition in Silicon Valley and Route 128*. Cambridge, MA: Harvard University Press.

Saxenian, A. 1997. "Immigrants and Silicon Valley." Presentation to OBIR Seminar, School of Business. University of California, Berkeley.

Saxenian, A. 1999. *Silicon Valley's New Immigrant Entrepreneurs*. San Francisco: Public Policy Institute of California.

Saxenian, A. 2001. "The Silicon Valley–Hsinchu Connection: Technical Communities and Industrial Upgrading" mimeo.

Saxenian, A. 2002. "The Silicon Valley–Hsinchu Connection: Technical Communities and Industrial Upgrading" Mimeo, Department of Urban and Regional Planning, UC Berkeley.

Scharpf, F., 1999. *Governing in Europe*. Oxford: Oxford University Press.

Schmitz, H., and T. Hewitt. 1992. "An Assessment of the Market Reserve for the Brazilian Computer Industry," pp. 21–52, in H. Schmitz and J. Cassiolato (eds.). *High-Tech for Industrial Development: Lessons from the Brazilian Experience in Electronics and Automation*. London and New York: Routledge.

Schneider, B. R. 1997. "Big Business and the Politics of Economic Reform: Confidence and Concertation in Brazil and Mexico," in S. Maxfield and B. Schneider (eds.). *Business and the State in Developing Countries*. Ithaca, NY: Cornell University Press.

Schneider, B. R. 1999. "The Desarrollista State in Brazil and Mexico," pp. 276–305, in M. Woo-Cumings (ed.). *The Developmental State*. Ithaca, NY: Cornell University Press.

Scott, A. J. 1998. *Seeing Like a State*. Berkeley: University of California Press.

Senghaas, D. 1985. *The European Experience: A Historical Critique of Development Theory*. NH: Berg.

Shafir, G. 1999. "Business in Politics: Globalization and the Search for Peace in South Africa and Israel/ Palestine." *Israel Affairs*.

Shafir, G., and Y. Peled. 2000. "Introduction: The Socioeconomic Liberalization of Israel," pp. 1–15, in G. Shafir and Y. Peled (eds.). *The New Israel: Peacemaking and Liberalization*. Boulder, CO: Westview Press.

Shalev, M. 1992. *Labor and the Political Economy in Israel*. Oxford: Oxford University Press.

Shalev, M. 1998. "Have Globalization and Liberalization 'Normalized' Israel's Political Economy?" *Israel Affairs*. December.

Shalev, M. 2000. "Liberalization and the Transformation of the Political Economy," pp. 129–59 in G. Shafir and Y. Peled (eds.). *The New Israel: Peacemaking and Liberalization.* Boulder, CO: Westview Press.

Share, B. 1992. *Shannon Departures: A Study in Regional Initiatives.* Dublin: Gill and Macmillan.

Sherman, R. 1996. "Chile's New Entrepreneurs and the 'Economic Miracle': The Invisible Hand or a Hand from the State?" *Studies in Comparative International Development* 31, 2: 83–109.

Silva, E. 1997. "Business Elites, the State and Economic Change in Chile," pp. 152–88, in S. Maxfield and B. Schneider (eds.). *Business and the State in Developing Countries.* Ithaca, NY: Cornell University Press.

Silver, B. 1990. "The Contradictions of Semiperipheral 'Success': The Case of Israel," pp. 161–82 in W. Martin (ed.). *Semiperipheral States in the World Economy.* New York: Greenwood Press.

Silver, B., and G. Arrighi. 2002. "Polanyi's 'Double Movement': The Belle Epoques of British and U.S. Hegemony Compared." Paper presented at conference on *The Next Great Transformation? Karl Polanyi and the Critique of Globalization.* Davis: University of California. April.

Silver, B. J., and G. Arrighi. "Polanyi's 'Double Movement': The Belle Epoques of U.S. and British World Hegemony Compared." *Politics and Society,* June 2003.

Sklair, L. 1988. "Foreign Investment and Irish Development: A Study of the International Division of Labor in the Midwest Region of Ireland." *Progress in Planning* 29: 147–216.

Sklair, L. 1991. *Sociology of the Global System.* Hemel Hempstead: Harvester Wheatsheaf.

Smith, V. 2001. *Crossing the Great Divide.* Ithaca, NY: Cornell University Press.

So, A., and S. Chiu. 1995. *East Asia and the World Economy.* Thousand Oaks, CA: Sage.

Software Industry Working Group. 1989. *Report.* Dublin.

Sokolov, M., and E. M. Verdoner. 1997. "The Israeli Innovation Support System – Generalities and Specifics." Working paper presented at conference on *Technology Policy and Less Developed Research and Development Systems in Europe.* Seville. October.

SSISI. 1975–6. "A Symposium on Increasing Employment in Ireland." *Journal of the Statistical and Social Inquiry Society of Ireland* 23, 3: 37–77.

SSISI. 1982. "Symposium on Industrial Policy in Ireland." *Journal of the Statistical and Social Inquiry Society of Ireland* 24, 5: 33–72.

Stallings, B. 1992. "International Influence on Economic Policy: Debt, Stabilization, and Structural Reform," in Stephan Haggard and Robert Kaufman (eds.). *The Politics of Economic Adjustment: International Constraints, Distributive Politics, and the State.* Princeton, NJ: Princeton University Press.

Steinmuller, W. E. 1996. "The U. S. Software Industry: An Analysis and Interpretive History," pp. 15–52 in D. C. Mowery (ed.), *The International Computer Software Industry* New York: Oxford University Press.

Stewart, J. 1989. "Transfer Pricing: Some Empirical Evidence from Ireland." *Journal of Economic Studies* 16, 3: 40–56.

Stewart, J. 1992. "The Business Expansion Scheme in Ireland." *IBAR – Irish Business and Administration Research* 13: 128–48.

Stewart, J. 1989. "Transfer Pricing: Some Empirical Evidence from Ireland." *Journal of Economic Studies* 16, 3: 40–56.

Stewart, J. 1992. "The Business Expansion Scheme in Ireland." *Irish Business and Administrative Research.* Vol. 13, 128–48.

Storper, M. 1992. "The Limits to Globalization: Technology Districts and International Trade." *Economic Geography* 68: 60–93.

Storper, M. 1997. *The Regional World: Territorial Development in a Global Economy.* London: Guilford.

Storper, M., and R. Walker. 1989. *The Capitalist Imperative: Territory, Technology, and Industrial Growth*. Oxford: Basil Blackwell.

Streeck, 1999. "Competitive Solidarity: Rethinking the 'European Social Model'." Working Paper 99/8. Koeln: Max Planck Institute for the Study of Societies.

Sturgeon, T. 1999. "Network-Led Development and the Rise of Turnkey Production Networks: Technological Change and the Outsourcing of Electronics Manufacturing," in G. Gereffi, F. Palpacuer, and A. Parisotto (eds.). *Global Production and Local Jobs*. Geneva: International Institute for Labor Studies.

Suarez, S. 2000. "Political and Economic Motivations for Labor Control: A Comparison of Ireland, Puerto Rico, and Singapore." Paper presented at the Annual Meetings of the American Political Science Association.

Tansey, P. 1998. *Ireland at Work: Economic Growth and the Labor Market 1987–1997*. Dublin: Oak Tree Press.

Taylor, G. 1996. "Labor-Market Rigidities, Institutional Impediments, and Managerial Constraints: Some Reflections on the Recent Experience of Macro-Political Bargaining in Ireland." *Economic and Social Review* 27, 3: 253–77.

Telesis Consultancy Group. 1982. *A Review of Industrial Policy*. NESC Report No. 64. Dublin: NESC.

Tilly, C. 2000. *Durable Inequality*. Berkeley: University of California Press.

Tuebal, M. 1993. "The Innovation System of Israel: Description Performance and Outstanding Issues," in R. R. Nelson (ed.). *National Innovation Systems: A Comparative Analysis*. Oxford: Oxford University Press.

UNCTAD. 2000. *Best Practices in Investment Promotion: Survey of Investment Promotion Agencies 2000*. UNCTAD: Geneva.

UNCTAD. 2002. *World Investment Report: Transnational Corporations and Export Competitiveness*. UNCTAD: Geneva.

Van Maanen, J., and S. Barley. 1984. "Occupational Communities: Culture and Control in Organizations," in B. Staw and L. Cummings (eds.). *Research in Organizational Behavior*. Greenwich, CT: JAI Press.

Van Rossem, R. 1997. "The World System Paradigm as General Theory of Development: A Cross-National Test." *American Sociological Review* 61, 3: 508–27.

Varley, T., and C. Curtin. 2001. "Community Empowerment Via Partnership?," pp. 127–50 in G. Taylor (ed.). *Issues in Irish Public Policy*. Dublin: Academic Press.

Vartiainen, J. 1999. "The Eocnomics of Successful State Intervention in Industrial Transformation," pp. 200–34, in M. Woo-Cumings (ed.). *The Developmental State*. Ithaca, NY: Cornell University Press.

Ventresca, M., and Rodney Lacey. 2003. "Industry Entrepreneurs: Origins and Activities in the Emergence of U.S. Electronic Database Services, 1965–1982." *Organization Science*, forthcoming.

Wade, R. 1990. *Governing the Market*. Cambridge: Cambridge University Press.

Wade, R. 1998. "The Coming Fight over Capital Flows." *Foreign Policy* 113: 41–54.

Wade, R., and F. Veneroso. 1998. "The Asian Crisis: The High-Debt Model Versus the Wall Street-Treasury-IMF Complex." *New Left Review* 228: 3–24.

Weiss, L. 1999. "Managed Openness: Beyond Neoliberal Globalism." *New Left Review* 238: 126–40.

Whalley, P. 1986. *The Social Production of Technical Work*. Albany: State University of New York Press.

Whalley, P., and S. Barley. 1997. "Technical Work in the Division of Labor: Stalking the Wily Anomaly," in S. Barley and J. Orr (eds.). *Between Craft and Science: Technical Work in U.S. Settings*. Ithaca, NY: Cornell University Press.

Whelan, C. T., R. Breen, and B. Whelan. 1992. "Industrialization, Class Formation, and Social Mobility in Ireland," pp. 105–28, in J. H. Goldthorpe and C. T. Whelan (eds.). *The Development of Industrial Society in Ireland*. Oxford: Oxford University Press.

Whelan, C. T. 1994. *Values and Social Change in Ireland*. Dublin: Gill and Macmillan.

Whelan, C. T., and D. F. Hannan. 1999. "Class Inequalities in Educational Attainment among the Adult Population in the Republic of Ireland." *Economic and Social Review* 30, 3: 285–308.

Whelan, B. *Ireland and the Marshall Plan 1947–1957*. Four Courts Press: Dublin 2000.

Whitaker, T. K. 1962. "The Graduate in State Administration." *Administration* 10, 3: 263–67.

Wickham, J. 1980. "The Politics of Dependent Capitalism: International Capital and the Nation–State," in A. Morgan and B. Purdie (eds.). *Ireland: Divided Nation, Divided Class*. London: Macmillan.

Wickham, J. 1989. "The Overeducated Engineer? The Work, Education, and Careers of Irish Electronics Engineers." *IBAR – Journal of Irish Business and Administrative Research* 10: 19–33.

Williamson, O. 1975. *Hierarchies and Markets*. New York: Free Press.

Williamson, O. 1985. *The Economic Institutions of Capitalism*. New York: Free Press.

Winckler, E. 1988. "Elite Political Struggle, 1945–1985," pp. 151–73, in E. Winckler and S. Greenhalgh (eds.). *Contending Approaches to the Political Economy of Taiwan*. Armonk, NY: M. E. Sharpe.

Woo-Cummings, M. 1990. *Race to the Swift: State and Finance in Korean Industrialization*. New York: Columbia University Press.

Woo-Cumings, M., ed. 1999. *The Developmental State*. Ithaca, NY: Cornell University Press.

Wright, E. 1997. *Class Counts*. Cambridge: Cambridge University Press.

Zook, M. A. (2001). "Old Hierarchies or New Networks of Centrality? The Global Geography of the Internet Content Market." *American Behavioral Scientist* Vol. 44. No. 10. 1679–1696.

INDEX

Index